Silas Burroughs,
the Man who Made Wellcome

Silas Burroughs,
the Man who Made Wellcome
American Ambition and Global Enterprise

Julia Sheppard

The Lutterworth Press

THE LUTTERWORTH PRESS

P.O. Box 60
Cambridge
CB1 2NT
United Kingdom

www.lutterworth.com
publishing@lutterworth.com

Hardback ISBN: 978 0 7188 9598 3
Paperback ISBN: 978 0 7188 9599 0
PDF ISBN: 978 0 7188 9600 3
ePub ISBN: 978 0 7188 9601 0

British Library Cataloguing in Publication Data
A record is available from the British Library

First published by The Lutterworth Press, 2022

I dedicate this book to my wonderful parents,
Gay Sheppard, née Howard (1920–1979),
and
David Stone (1927–2015),
whose love and support has always been with me.

Yours with best wishes
S. M. Burroughs.

Contents

List of Illustrations

Unless otherwise stated, all images are used with the kind permission of the Wellcome Collection.

Abbreviations

APhA	American Pharmaceutical Association
BMA	British Medical Association
BW&Co.	Burroughs, Wellcome & Co.
C&D	*Chemist and Druggist*
C&T	Church and Tansey, *Burroughs Wellcome & Co.*
Haggis	'The Life and Work of Sir Henry Wellcome'
HG	Henry George
HSW	Henry Solomon Wellcome
KMEC	Kepler Malt Extract Co.
LB	letter book
n.d.	not dated
OB	Olive Burroughs
PCB	press cuttings book
PCP	Philadelphia College of Pharmacy
PP/SMB	personal papers of S.M. Burroughs
RRJ	Robert Rhodes James, *Henry Wellcome*
SMB	Silas Mainville Burroughs
WA	Wellcome Archives
WF	Wellcome Foundation
WFA	Wellcome Foundation Archives

Burroughs

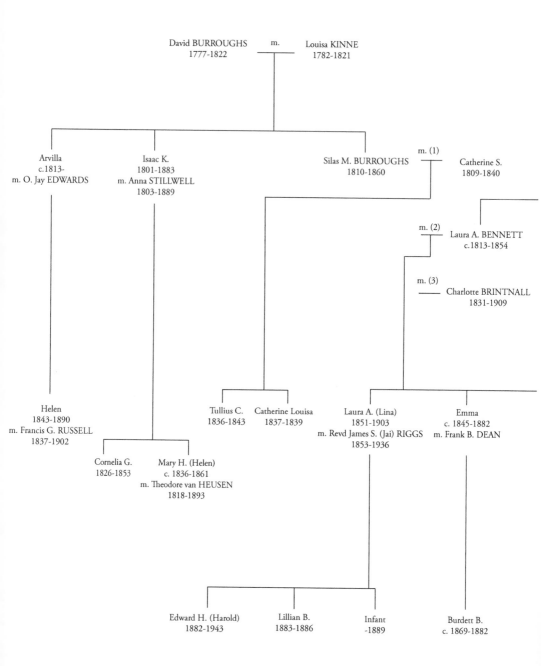

Family Tree

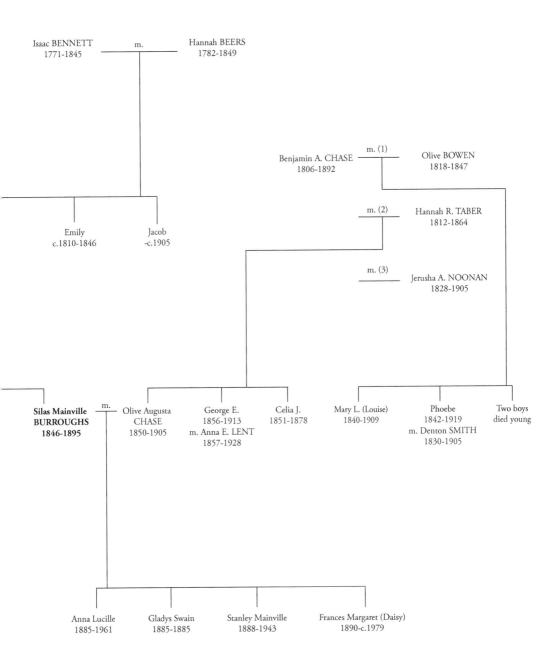

Isaac BENNETT
1771-1845

m.

Hannah BEERS
1782-1849

Benjamin A. CHASE
1806-1892

m. (1)

Olive BOWEN
1818-1847

m. (2)

Hannah R. TABER
1812-1864

m. (3)

Jerusha A. NOONAN
1828-1905

Emily
c.1810-1846

Jacob
-c.1905

Silas Mainville
BURROUGHS
1846-1895

m.

Olive Augusta
CHASE
1850-1905

George E.
1856-1913
m. Anna E. LENT
1857-1928

Celia J.
1851-1878

Mary L. (Louise)
1840-1909

Phoebe
1842-1919
m. Denton SMITH
1830-1905

Two boys
died young

Anna Lucille
1885-1961

Gladys Swain
1885-1885

Stanley Mainville
1888-1943

Frances Margaret (Daisy)
1890-c.1979

Foreword

Sir Jeremy Farrar

When I joined the Wellcome Trust in 2013 I knew all about Henry Wellcome but little about the pharmaceutical firm Burroughs, Wellcome and Co. and nothing of its original founder, Silas Burroughs.

Happily, with this engaging biography no one can now remain ignorant of Wellcome's business partner, the American Silas Burroughs: the man whose name carried clout throughout the world and whose vision was crucial in establishing the firm.

The Trust was pleased to help the author during her research for this biography. As Archivist and Head of Research and Special Collections in the Wellcome Library, Julia Sheppard was well placed to undertake this task and has used the rich archival collections of the business partners and the firm which are held by the Wellcome Collection. We had previously assisted in the publication of a biography of Henry Wellcome and a history of the firm and supported the acquisition of Burroughs's personal papers.

Burroughs was a man whose dedication to his work was born of his faith and a passion to improve the health and welfare of all and not simply to make money. He would undoubtedly have been delighted to know that from the origins of his pharmaceutical company was created the charity the Wellcome Trust, which supports medical research around the world.

Readers will enjoy discovering more about this remarkable individual. Burroughs was a man overlooked by history and virtually forgotten. He deserves to be remembered.

Sir Jeremy Farrar
Director, Wellcome Trust

Acknowledgements and Sources

Acknowledgements

Numerous people have helped me over the many years the book has been in the making. It has been an enjoyable task following Burroughs's footsteps in Victorian London, and in Europe, America and Sri Lanka, and imagining places and buildings as he would have seen them. The pandemic lockdown finally gave me no excuse but to focus on the final edit.

When I collected the Burroughs papers from the family, I was welcomed by his grandson Richard Stillwell and his wife Joan, whose stories and hospitality were a joy. Through Len Goodwin, Richard's neighbour, and Sir Roger Gibbs, then Chair of the Wellcome Trust, Burroughs's papers were acquired by the Trust. Subsequently a room in the Wellcome Building on the Euston Road was named the Burroughs Room, and the Trust greatly assisted me in my wish to write a biography. I regret that the Stillwells and several others who helped me are sadly with us no longer and cannot now see this publication.

I thank the Wellcome Trust who assisted me in many ways, in particular by giving me a sabbatical and then access to their IT department after I retired. I am grateful to Paul Beshaw (Stafford) and his former colleagues in that department for their patience and advice. Also thanks to Philomena Gibbons, who formally liaised with the Trust on my behalf and assisted them in ensuring the preservation of Burroughs's grave in Monte Carlo. Danny Truell, former chief investment officer at the Trust, and his colleague Nick Moakes discussed the finances of Burroughs Welcome & Co., which have proved hard to unravel with peculiarities and gaps and in the records.

Staff and former colleagues in the superb Wellcome Library as well as the now defunct Wellcome Trust Centre for the History of Medicine at University College London were generous with their time and help. Since most of the research material is held by the library at the Wellcome Collection, London, the archivists and librarians there have been crucial to my research, and I cannot praise them highly enough. I thank Teresa Doherty, Amanda Engineer, Toni Hardy, Phoebe Harkins, Jennifer Haynes, Isobel Hunter, Ross Macfarlane, Adrian Steel, the late John Symons and Helen Wakely.

My research has been informed by many scholars whose works are listed in the bibliography. Roy Church, Tilli Tansey, and their research assistant Declan O'Reilly kindly shared information when they were writing their history of the firm. John Davies of the Wellcome Foundation, then Glaxo Wellcome archivist, first alerted me to the existence of the Burroughs family papers. My thanks to Briony Hudson at the Royal Pharmaceutical Society of Great Britain and the British Society for the History of Pharmacy, Jonathan Liebenau and Sue Donnelly at the London School of Economics, Glenn Burchett at Glaxo Wellcome Archives, Tricia Bailey at the Livingstone Hospital, the British Library and staff at Dartford Library, HSBC Archives, the London Library and the National Archives.

All those I encountered in my research trips in America were generous with their time. In Medina, Ed Grinnell, and Catherine Cooper and staff at the Lee-Whedon Memorial Library and Richard Nellist, Todd Bensley and others at the Medina Historical Society shared their knowledge and introduced me to the town, and the Rev. Ed Bonner showed us the Presbyterian Church. Hollis Ricci-Canham and the Orleans County Historical Association and county historians of Cayuga and Auburn, New York, advised with census returns. At Broadalbin, Gordon Cornell and Kelly Yacobucci Farquhar assisted my research, and Sally Mann took me to Olive Chase's old family home and showed me where, still visible, Olive had scratched her name on an upstairs window.

From the USA I also received help and suggestions from Rima Apple, Gary Baxter, Jane Gabin, Amelie Kass, John Parascandola and staff at the American Institute of the History of Pharmacy, the American Institute of Pharmacy (Gregory J. Higby), the Buffalo & Erie County Public Library, the Beinecke Library at Yale University, the College of Physicians of Philadelphia (Ed Mormon), the Historical Society of Philadelphia, Lockport Public Library, the Library of Congress, the Masonic Library at Philadelphia, the National Library of Medicine, New York Public Library, Pennsylvania Hospital, the University of the Sciences in Philadelphia (Mignon Adams and Kim Tieger), the Swan Library in Albion (Cheryl Mowatt), and the University of Madison Memorial Library.

I owe a huge debt to my friends and colleagues for their support and encouragement over the years and apologise if I have failed to acknowledge them all. They include Sybil Spence, who showed me around Dartford and told me of the history of the town, Ruth Richardson and Kit Wilby. Help was given on the genealogy of the Burroughs family by Jonathan Bynum and Nicholas Spence. I am immensely grateful to Bronwen Manning for her shared interest and her impressive sleuth work into the family history and on Olive. She accompanied me to local archives in Broadalbin and compiled the family tree, a fuller version of which will be available at the Wellcome. Thanks also to Tony Gould, Anne Hardy, English Showalter, Margaret Willes and Stuart Anderson, who commented on parts of the draft manuscript.

I have benefited from Caroline Overy's help with the bibliography. Jennifer Haynes read the manuscript in full and made valuable suggestions. Pippa Hurd and Margaret Willes guided me with advice about publishing. Alison Rice and Jeffery Pike assisted in countless ways. Simon Jaffer and Rob Wood came to my frequent rescue with laptop and software issues and Rob performed miracles enhancing and assisting with the images. Caroline Richmond's expert copy editing, ruthless help with losing surplus words, and proof reading were essential, and I cannot thank her enough. It has been a pleasure working with Adrian Brink, Samuel Fitzgerald, and colleagues at The Lutterworth Press, and thanks also to Christine Shuttleworth for the index.

Finally my greatest thanks go to Christine Macleod and John Orbell who have effectively been my editors, giving me much of their time and the benefit of their historical expertise. The book has gained immeasurably from their input. Their faith, and that of my friends, in my completing and publishing this book has now, finally, been justified.

Sources

Wellcome Collection, Wellcome Library, London: The main collection of papers used were the personal papers of Burroughs, the personal papers of Wellcome and the archives of Burroughs Wellcome & Co., which are held across the Wellcome archive collections and the Wellcome Foundation archive. Numerous items of a personal nature relating to Burroughs will be found in the business records. The archive is incomplete and catalogue reference numbers have been amended over the years. See the Wellcome online catalogue under Wellcome Foundation for a description of the custodial history and previous numbering regimes.

Although not all the records are catalogued in detail, the majority can now be consulted online. Citation references to Wellcome items have not therefore always been given in full but should be able to be retrieved using the catalogues. For the Burroughs personal papers there is a list held by the archives.

The personal and business letter books of both partners are invaluable and are now being digitised, so will be available online. There is sometimes a duplication of letters between the partners (letters sent and copies kept). A few items are too fragile to be made available, the most serious being the personal letter book of Burroughs (1884–95), which is now largely illegible. I have extracted from it all I was able to read. Transcriptions or partial notes have been made of many of the letter books, Burroughs's travel journals and his personal letters to his wife and family. Unfortunately it appears that the letters he received from his sister and wife were not kept by him, and Stanley's letters to Burroughs were dispersed by the Burroughs family and have not been located.

The press cuttings book kept by the firm (which has been microfilmed) holds many items from Dartford newspapers, with coverage of the Phoenix Mills and letters written to the press about or by Burroughs on the firm, single tax and other issues.

Burroughs's personal papers consist of notes and travel diaries, notebooks, various draft writings by him (some of which were published), photographs, obituaries and papers of Olive Burroughs, which mainly cover her legal dispute with Wellcome after Burroughs's death.

London School of Economics: Charles Booth notebooks.
Royal Geographical Society: Burroughs–Stanley correspondence.
Royal Pharmaceutical Society: Burroughs Scholarship records.
Presbyterian Church, Medina, New York: admission records.
New York Public Library: Henry George, correspondence and diaries, microfilm.
Swan Library, Albion, New York: wills.

I have also used the following CDs and videos:

Russell, J. Waldo, *Hitching Post Days*, columns published in the *Medina Journal-Register*, 1941–60 [CDs, 3 vols].
Silas Burroughs – The Missing Story, video-documentary based on the family archives of Richard and Joan Stillwell, made for the Wellcome Trust by Oxford Brookes University Television Studio (1999). Electronic resource in Wellcome Library.

Notes

The present-day value of the financial figures given has not always been cited, as they are liable to change and there is no single 'correct' measure, but figures on the relative value of money can be checked on various websites, such as the National Archives Currency Converter or the Economic History Society's website (https://eh.net/howmuchisthat).

A fuller draft version of this biography, together with the author's accompanying research material, will be made available at the Wellcome Collection, London, in due course.

While research on this book was being undertaken, newspapers and books were constantly being digitised, which meant that there was never-ending potential information to be found. As a result I have no doubt that more can now be gleaned from press and journals. The author would be grateful to learn of any additional information and can be contacted via the publisher.

Introduction

On the afternoon of Friday 8 February 1895, a sad procession wound its way southwards from the Anglican Church in Monte Carlo, through the city streets to the cemetery at boulevard Charles III, perched on the hillside on the edge of town. The chief mourners were Olive Burroughs and Laura Riggs, wife and sister of Silas Mainville Burroughs. Many of the pharmacists and all of the English doctors of Monte Carlo followed. At the same time a special train took 200 staff from the headquarters of the pharmaceutical firm Burroughs, Wellcome & Co., in the city of London, to Dartford, Kent, home of the firm's manufacture, for a memorial service at the parish church. The church flag hung at half-mast, and tradesmen put up shutters as a mark of respect. Burroughs's many friends, leading businessmen from London, all the works staff from London and Dartford, civic officers and many inhabitants of the town attended. His sudden unexpected death, at 49, deeply shocked many people, and obituaries appeared in newspapers across the globe.

The impact of his death was all the greater because Burroughs was a hugely popular personality who inspired great friendship and loyalty through his warmth, generosity, concern for others, and ideals for creating a fairer and kinder world. The irony of his death may well have crossed the minds of some of the mourners; Burroughs was an apparently fit man who had spent his life promoting the effectiveness of pills and medicines, yet none of the products offered by his pharmaceutical firm could save him from pneumonia, a major killer in the pre-antibiotic age.

Few people today have heard of Silas Burroughs, although an older generation may recall purchasing drugs from Burroughs, Wellcome & Co., which was renamed the Wellcome Foundation Ltd in 1924, and there is a Burroughs Wellcome Foundation in America. Now even the name Wellcome no longer exists, since that firm merged with Glaxo, which subsequently merged with SmithKlineBeecham in 2000 to become

GlaxoSmithKline. Yet the name of Henry Wellcome, Burroughs's business partner, is still known today because of Wellcome's collections and the work of the Wellcome Trust, a major charity established under Henry Wellcome's will. But what of Burroughs? Who has heard of him? Why has he sunk into obscurity?

There are several reasons. Certainly his early death meant that Burroughs did not benefit from the awards and kudos that attach to successful businessmen in their later years. But there is a more important reason. By the end of Burroughs's life he and Wellcome were at daggers drawn. Their early friendship, dating from the 1870s when they were both in America, deteriorated from mistrust to hostility to dislike and, finally, to positive animosity. There were years of attempts by Burroughs to create a joint stock company and then legal battles to dissolve the firm. Amazingly Burroughs, Wellcome & Co. continued to thrive under these extraordinary circumstances. With Burroughs's death Wellcome was able to take over the firm under the conditions of their partnership agreement, although he had to fight a long hard battle with Olive, Burroughs's widow.

Understandably Wellcome subsequently had no desire to praise a man he had quarrelled with so bitterly. Neither he nor Burroughs left any autobiographical record, and Wellcome never spoke of the relationship they had once enjoyed or paid due recognition to Burroughs's role. Both the unpublished and published biographies of Henry Wellcome emphasise his importance and achievements and compare Burroughs unfavourably with him, downplaying his contribution to the success of the firm and even suggesting that he was a potential threat to its success. In 1998 this author learnt of the existence of some personal papers held by the Burroughs family, and these were transferred to the Wellcome Library. The documents, writings and photographs left by Burroughs and his family, together with records of the firm and publication of a company history, mean that it is now possible to re-examine Burroughs's life and career and the tortured relationship between the two partners.

Burroughs was not simply a brilliant hard-working salesman but a dynamic entrepreneur and manufacturer with vision and drive. He was crucial to the foundation and shaping of Burroughs, Wellcome & Co., which became internationally important for its innovative drugs in just 15 years. It emerged at a key period in the history of pharmaceutical manufacturing. We now know more about the many other aspects of Burroughs. His upbringing in upstate New York with a wealthy politician father; his world travels; his staunch Presbyterianism; his promotion of Christian socialist principles and strongly held political beliefs across a wide range of causes, including world peace; his interest in radical and liberal politics, which led to involvement in political reforms as a speaker, writer and activist who was not averse to demonstrating on the streets; his campaigning for the single tax movement and friendship with its founder Henry George; and the donation of much of his wealth to charities, both during his life and through bequests.

Silas Burroughs deserves to be remembered not just as a businessman and partner of Henry Wellcome. He was described as a 'citizen of the world' because his travels, contacts and character made an impact on people everywhere. Quite simply, without Burroughs there would have been no Burroughs, Wellcome & Co. and no Wellcome Trust. This biography will redress previous one-sided views of his achievements and justify his place in the historical record as the man who made Wellcome.

Chapter 1

Father and Son

Silas M. Burroughs was not an obscure statesman,
as he was not a common man.[1]

Silas Mainville Burroughs, the internationally successful pharmaceutical manufacturer, came from a rural community in upstate New York. Medina, his home town,[2] is a rather old-fashioned and charming backwater, between Buffalo and Rochester on the Erie Canal and close to the southern edge of Lake Ontario. It is conscious of being overlooked: when I visited it in 2002, its high-street shop sold tee-shirts displaying 'Where the hell is Medina NY?'.

His paternal grandfather, David Burroughs (1777–1822), was an early settler in the area when land hitherto occupied by Native Americans was gradually being populated.[3] By dint of hard work, financial acumen and the acquisition of well-placed property, the Burroughs family did well for themselves. Silas Mainville Burroughs snr was David Burroughs's seventh and youngest child, born in Ovid, New York, in 1810.[4]

By the time this Silas Burroughs was 30, both his first wife, Catherine, and their daughter, Catherine Louisa, aged just two, had died; their son Tullius died in 1843 when he was only seven. As a young man he worked as a merchant in nearby Selby, then joined his older brother, Isaac – a merchant, businessman, and 'influential and much respected citizen' – in his Medina store, before being admitted to the bar in Orleans County as a lawyer. At 25 Silas was village attorney and one of five Village Trustees, effectively becoming a key figure in Medina. In 1844, four years after the death of his first wife, he remarried and started a new family. Soon he was listed in the census as extremely wealthy, owning considerable land

in and around Medina. Some of
this land had been purchased
from the Holland Land Company
by his father, while some came
from his second wife's wealthy
family: Laura Adeline Bennett's
father, Isaac, was an astute
owner of property in New York
state, Pennsylvania and Virginia.
Additional money came through
farming and running a lumber
business as well as from his legal
practice earnings in Medina, but
most was through ownership of a
large amount of real estate.[5]

Burroughs's involvement in
politics started early when he
became a leading spirit in the
legislature at one of the stormiest
periods of New York state politics. He published a Democrat

1: Silas Burroughs snr, taken c. 1859
when he was the representative from
New York in the 35th Congress.

newspaper, *The Bucktail*, in 1839 and went on to produce other political
newssheets.[6] At 27 he was elected to represent Orleans County as a
Democrat member of the State Assembly (the lower house of the New York
legislature), which convened at Albany, and served four times. He was
elected in 1856 to the House of Representatives to serve as a Republican
to the 35th Congress in Washington, DC, then re-elected two years later,[7]
and was a member of a number of congressional committees, including
the Committee on Colleges, Academies and Common Schools, where
he advocated a liberal system of common school education and framed
school laws.

His son, Silas Mainville Burroughs, the subject of this biography, was
born in Medina on 24 December 1846.[8] Confusingly, he was given the
same name as his father, so throughout his life his family and old friends
called him by his second name, Mainville, and only after he settled in
England did he start using the name Silas. Emma, his elder sister, was
a year older than him, and the youngest of the family, Adeline Laura
(always known as Lina), was born on 28 October 1851.[9]

Burroughs had a privileged upbringing, since his father was wealthy
and a leading figure both locally and within the state. The family name
conferred respect. Home was an impressive mansion on the edge of the

2: The Burroughs residence, Medina. This splendid gothic
style mansion was built by Burroughs's father. It was located
where State Street Park is now.

village, constructed when he was a little boy. Located within a large grove
with a pond and fountains next to the river, it cost an estimated $10,000 to
build and was considered one of the finest residences in Medina. Victorian
gothic in style, high roofed, with tall chimneys, pinnacles, buttresses,
finials and pointed arch windows, it was unlike any other house in the
village (which abounds with federal, colonial revival, Queen Anne,
Italianate villa, empire and Greek revival styles) and was described as
'by far the most extraordinary example of the use of Gothic architecture
for residential purposes in the county'.[10] There was a large well-stocked
library, since his father was well read and had scholarly pretensions, as
well as paintings, geological specimens, and a bust of Napoleon.

When Burroughs was four his sister Lina was born. Early the following
morning his mother Laura woke up almost suffocated with smoke and
discovered a fire between her room on the second floor and the ceiling
of the floor below. She roused the servant girl nearby and managed to
leave the room with Lina. Burroughs snr was woken and, 'after finding
a secure retreat for his family, commenced a systematic attack upon the
devouring flames, with his usual promptness, coolness and execution.'
The local fire brigade assisted, but there was considerable damage.[11]
In fact this was the second time that a fire had burnt the Burroughs

property: in 1845 his father's law office and two adjoining buildings had been destroyed by fire, consuming a valuable law library worth about $4,800 which was largely uninsured. Undeterred, Burroughs snr rebuilt the mansion, although he had to withdraw his planned candidacy for the New York Assembly because the 'disastrous fire' had left him no time to canvass the county.

Tragedy struck again when Burroughs was only seven, when his mother died from pneumonia. She was only 42. Although death at this age was not uncommon, it must have been a shocking blow for all, especially for his father, for whom this was the loss of a second wife, this time leaving not one but three small children to bring up. The community was a strong one, however, and friends and family rallied round. Now more changes took place in Burroughs's life: the household expanded and, in addition to his aunt (Laura's sister, Emily Bennett), now included his other aunt (his father's sister, Arvilla Edwards), her daughter Helen, two boarders – Julia and Cornelia Beers – plus one English and two Irish servants. Laura left a considerable estate which was to pass to the children after her husband's death.[12]

Education was taken seriously in America, and by the mid-century most white children were enrolled in a primary school, although compulsory education was not introduced in the state until 1874. However, schooling was fluid before the Civil War, with children attending irregularly from the age of three or four: primary and secondary levels were not sharply defined. Broadly, schools were categorised as being 'public schools', 'common schools' or 'academies' (forerunners of the modern high school) or 'private and select schools'. Before 1850 there were few public high schools anywhere in the state, and the Medina Free Academy, founded in 1851 by Burroughs snr, led the way in the state: he 'donated' 2 acres for the building of the new school and was one of the first trustees of the village Board of Education.[13] When Burroughs attended it had over 600 pupils, of which 150 were high-school students. Pupils usually attended the academy from the age of seven (though nine was considered the proper age). At 8.30 every morning the Presbyterian church bell rang for all the village schools. Classes were held in spelling, writing, drawing, arithmetic and geometry, history and geography. In the higher classes there would be map-drawing, composition, declamation (presumably debating and public speaking), and United States history, as well as some instruction in moral and natural philosophy, French, Latin and bookkeeping. It was a traditional education and there was much learning by rote, although pupils were encouraged to question teachers and other pupils. Many years later, when Burroughs revisited the school, he remarked how much more enlightened the class teaching had become, though he did not explain in what ways. Discipline was strict and punishment severe, and it was reported that 'the biceps muscle' of Mr Devos, the assistant principal, 'must have been as well developed as a blacksmith'.[14]

When Burroughs was 16, another floor was added to the school and a large room allocated to the Burroughsian Lyceum, so named since his father had aided the venture and donated his books in his will. In addition to a library there was an extensive cabinet of geological specimens contributed by people from all over the state. The Lyceum movement flourished in the northeast of America at this time, with public programmes of lectures, debates and performances aimed at raising the social, intellectual and moral fabric of society, and Burroughs's Lyceum was considered one of the greatest literary ventures the town had ever known.

We know little about Burroughs's childhood, although a diary kept by Caroline Richards, a child living in his county at this time, gives an insight into the importance of family, religion and community, the enjoyable times to be had horse-riding, skating and sleighing in the winter, and the possibility of visits to Barnum's Circus to see General Tom Thumb and other entertainers.[15] A key influence during his childhood was that of John Parsons, whose Sunday school he attended with most of the village children on Sunday afternoons; Burroughs also played in Parsons's temperance band. Later in his life he 'frankly and freely acknowledged that he owed his success in life to the teachings and influence [of Parsons].'[16] The strong family ties and Medina community made a lasting impression: by accompanying his father on visits to relatives and the family farm, to cattle auctions and shows, learning about agriculture, trade and the local businesses, Burroughs came to know many in the district and was remembered as a boy of unfailing kindness. His affection for the place and its people remained, and he returned to Medina throughout his life whenever he could, praising its beauty and at times contemplating living there again.

Medina in the 1850s was far from being a peaceful backwater. It had started as a small settlement for Erie Canal workers in 1817 and was an excellent stopover point between Buffalo and Rochester, situated on a curve in the canal which created a natural basin and allowed boats to anchor out of the mainstream of the canal traffic. Water power was provided by mills on nearby Oak Orchard Creek, and fruit was grown in the area's fertile farming lands. Local sandstone, highly durable, its colour ranging from light grey to a deep reddish-brown, was much in demand in the building trade. Quarries opened and thrived, the stone being shipped all over America and Europe (today one can find Medina sandstone in the pillars of the Brooklyn and George Washington bridges and in the streets of Havana).

Medina's population rose steadily during the century. By the mid-1850s it had over 2,000 inhabitants and was still growing, creating a variety of work in a thriving community of workers. Burroughs daily experienced a lively and busy town, rivalling Albion, the county seat, and conscious of its own importance. There was constant activity and movement, with new faces at the sawmill on the Oak Orchard Falls and the salt works, gristmill hands at the corn mill, canal builders, operators, bargemen, mule-drivers and passengers, workers in the distilleries and packing houses, carpenters, builders and stonemasons, not to mention all the tradesmen and innkeepers to run the new shops and hotels.[17] These were boom days, farm settlers ushering in a wealthier class of bankers, merchants and property developers. The countryside around then was, and still is, attractive and gentle, with pasture, cattle and fruit trees, large barns with Dutch-style roofs and of course the canal. Lake Ontario and the Niagara Falls were an enjoyable horse ride away.

But Medina also had its rough side; among its mêlée of passing traffic and people, many of the inhabitants were immigrants seeking work or looking for easy money. The quarry men and bargemen were tough, and

3: Medina Main Street, c. 1882, looking southeast, as Burroughs would have known it.

drunken brawls were common. W.H. Davies, in *The Autobiography of a Super-Tramp*, described the Erie Canal men as 'the riff-raff of America and the scum of Europe; men who wanted no steady employment, but to make easy and quick stakes – for the pay was good – so as to indulge in periodical sprees. They came and went in gangs, for a week's work was so hard that there were few men that did not require a week's rest after a month's labour.' Some made a living out of robbing the workers, and murder was all too frequent, the canal being a handy place to dispose of bodies, lightened of their pay packets. 'Seldom a day passed but what a dead body was dragged out of the water, and more than two-thirds of these bodies bore the marks of murder.' In the 1850s the canal also served as a conduit for slaves escaping north to Canada, the horse barns along the canal supplying work. The mix of the free slave and canal worker sometimes led to serious fighting, most notably in 1858, when at least three people were killed and many injured.

Burroughs would have been well aware from an early age of his father's status, his support of the town's institutions and then his growing prominence on a wider stage through his political activities. He owned several properties in Medina and negotiated their exchanges for alternative use by the community;[18] with several others, he purchased land for the new Boxwood Cemetery.[19] An old school plot acquired at the back of the Walsh Hotel was given for use by the local arsenal, and, as a member and keen supporter of the state militia, Burroughs snr progressed from being colonel of a regiment to brigadier general in the 29th brigade of the New York State Militia (1848–58; he was referred to as General Burroughs).[20] His other civic duties included support for the establishment of a state agricultural college and his post as commissioner to investigate the drainage of the local swamp.

The house fire and death of Burroughs's mother did not end the turbulence of family life. In 1856 Burroughs snr was severely wounded in the head by the bursting of a pistol, a fragment of which struck his head, inflicting 'a severe wound and fracturing his skull'. The *Niagara Falls Gazette* of 20 August 1856 gave no other details of how this injury occurred and reported that the wound had healed and he was as well as usual. Just three months later the death occurred of Emily Bennett, Burroughs's aunt, who lived with them and must have played a key part in running the household before and after the death of her sister.

Yet death and upheavals did not stop the whirlwind lifestyle of a father whose political work occupied an increasing amount of his time and took him away from home to Washington, Kansas and further afield. He was a forcible speaker in spite of 'being quite deaf – an infirmity that is supposed to detract materially from the effect of oratorical display, but in his case, this embarrassment was surmounted to a great extent.'[21] It is not impossible that the deafness was occasioned by the head wound he had suffered. Highly principled in his public and private life, he assisted minority groups and championed those with rightful grievances. Amelia Bloomer, campaigner for women's rights and famed for advocating clothing reform for women – hence 'bloomers' – noted that it was the Hon. Silas Burroughs who, by prior arrangement, escorted her and two other women into the Albany Assembly ('an unheard of thing for women to do') in order to present a petition of 30,000 women on behalf of the state temperance societies for the introduction of a prohibitory law.[22]

Silas Burroughs played a key role in the bill to enlarge and improve the Erie Canal; this linked the Atlantic to the Great Lakes and cut shipping costs dramatically, bringing prosperity to the northeast of the state. Improvements were needed to enlarge the canal, which coincided with the building of railroads across the state. In spite of being urged to toe the party line, and knowing he would make enemies, Burroughs snr upheld a promise to support the bill. As a result of political battles over this issue, in 1851 he refused to stand for the Democratic Party, which he had supported for many years and which regarded him as their most able debater and recognised leader, condemning his opponents for the extent to which their ultra-partisanship and love of office deprived them of the sense of public justice and regard for the public good. He was returned triumphantly as an independent at the following year's assembly, lauded both for his 'manly, able, and independent advocacy' for the canal and for the independent freedom of the territories. He also performed a major part in a bill presented in 1858 to grant lands to aid the proposed Niagara Ship Canal.

Burroughs snr worked hard for the welfare and rights of Native Americans. He travelled extensively on fact-finding missions, including to a Kansas reserve in 1859 to safeguard the welfare of those whose rights and territories were being increasingly restricted at this time. On his death it was noted that the Indians of his state had 'lost as zealous a friend as they ever had'.[23]

When the issue of the abolition of slavery was debated in the assembly and in Congress, Burroughs snr wittily discredited suggestions that no congressional action was needed, mocking those who enjoined 'masterly inactivity' and non-interference in 'domestic institutions' (a euphemism for slavery). Slavery per se was wrong.[24]

Somewhere on Silas Burroughs's travels he met a 'beautiful and accomplished' young woman, Charlotte S. Brintnall, and in May 1858, four years after the death of Laura, she became his third wife. Little is known about her: the youngest daughter of Sewall Brintnall, she was a teacher in Watertown, New York, aged about 26, so some 21 years younger than her husband.[25] It is not known how Burroughs and his siblings and relatives greeted the news, but for an 11-year-old boy this cannot have been easy. However, on at least one occasion in 1860 Burroughs snr was joined by his family, as evidenced by a Mr Hamlin, his colleague in Congress, who recorded occupying 'with our families' the same house during the last session.

During his last term of office in Congress, Burroughs snr was unwell for several months but continued working and voting between January and the end of March 1860. His 'protracted and painful illness' turned out to be cancer of the stomach. He then returned to Medina, where he spent his last few weeks 'solaced by the kind and unremitting care of his wife' and 'cheered by the presence of kind and loving children'. He made his will on 13 May and died on 16 July, just before his 50th birthday.[26] His death was expected by fellow members of Congress, although it was said that he had hoped to return to Washington, not seeming to realise the gravity of his own condition or the 'inexorable disease which was upon him'.

Congress mourned a man who was 'eloquent, able and zealous ... generous without recklessness; exalted without pride or self-conceit; precise in conduct without the austerity of manner which repels and brave.' Keen to improve the lot of others, he investigated causes thoroughly, and when he had formed an opinion held it tenaciously. Yet he was kind and tolerant of others, unbigoted and highly esteemed as 'a most worthy recipient of the honours and confidence of the people whom he represented'; ... 'a warm, decided and ardent friend ... devoted to his family and cherished by a large circle of friends.'[27] A patriot, he supported the principles of liberty, equality and fraternity and was dedicated to education and philanthropic works. He had been 'cut off in the prime of life and in the midst of his career in usefulness' – words which were identical to those used when his son died.[28]

It is inevitable that Burroughs would have idolised his father, a larger than life figure who had achieved so much and was admired by all. It must have been fun, too, having such a talented and respected father, 'a gentleman in his deportment, a man of culture and varied and extensive information'.[29] Life was full of excitement and even glamour because his father enjoyed sharing his wealth, relishing in novelty – owning the first buggy in the village and entertaining in the grandest, most unusual house in the area.[30] Burroughs may not have heard some of his father's eloquent speeches, although he may well have travelled to the state capital, Albany, and, as we know, went to Washington at least once. But he would have heard his father's acquaintances discuss him and read reports in the press, and he knew of his father's hard work, passionate beliefs and principled stands. A wish to emulate such a father was natural, and in time many of his father's qualities would be attributed to him.

At the same time, for all three children – Emma (14), Burroughs (13) and Lina (8) – the death of their father, who was 'devoted to his family', was a traumatic loss. Their Uncle Isaac and Aunt Anna now became surrogate parents. From letters written later in life it is clear that Burroughs was extremely fond of them both, and it was during this period that he grew very close to his younger sister Lina.

Isaac, 'a man of calm judgment, strict integrity and generous heart',[31] was named as sole guardian of the children's nurture and education and given entire control of Burroughs snr's estate. Charlotte Burroughs, his widow, was left the use, during her natural life, of a third part of all her late husband's estate. The rest and residue was left equally between his three children. His executors (his brother, his brother-in-law Jacob B. Bennett, and Myron P. Hopkins) had authority to sell and convey or mortgage or lease any or all of his real estate at their discretion.[32] The only items specified were the piano he had bought his second wife, which was to go to his daughters, and all his clothes, which were to go to his son.

Charlotte is listed in the census less than two months after her husband's death as living in a hotel in Medina. Five years later, when Isaac made a final settlement of the estate, she was recorded as 'residing in Washington DC when last heard from'. This wording inevitably raises the question of how close the Burroughs family were to Charlotte, who had after all entered their lives only two years before Burroughs snr's death and had spent much of that time in Washington. She was a generation younger than Isaac and Anna, closer in age to her stepson than her husband, and would not have had much time to know her stepchildren. It is not impossible that the family may have regarded her as a gold-digger. Once she had received a payment of the third part of the estate due to her, there was no reason for her to maintain links with the Burroughs family: after five years she had remarried and was living in her home city again.

Burroughs snr had requested that his brother 'remove and reside in his mansion house', but Isaac did not do this, and instead the 10 acres that constituted the estate, including the mansion, were sold in July 1861.[33]

As executor, Isaac had a doubly difficult task, because his brother-in-law Jacob, as Laura's executor, had failed to do the necessary work to wind up her estate.[34] The complications of the wills of both Burroughs's parents occupied much of Isaac's time. Apart from the sale of the real estate (some 20 village lots), many goods were sold privately and by auction, and Isaac had to manage his brother's farm and estate, collect monies owing, handle numerous legal settlements and mortgages, and care for arable crops and their sales. Not until 1866 could a final settlement be made.[35] It must have been some comfort to Isaac and Anna to have their nieces and nephew stay with them and a distraction from their own sorrows: their eldest daughter, Cornelia, had died at the age of 27 in 1853, and their second daughter, Mary, married to Theodore van Heusen, was to die eight years later when she was 25.

The Civil War, or 'War of Revolution' as it was then sometimes called, started in April 1861 when Burroughs was 14 years old. Many young men volunteered and over 550 soldiers enlisted from Medina and Ridgeway, including Burroughs's cousins Samuel J. Hood and Silas M. Hood.[36] Several schoolfriends joined up, some of them never to return. One such was his closest schoolfriend, John Parsons, a 'very promising young man', the son of the manager of his father's farm and his Sunday school teacher and mentor. When Parsons died, Burroughs vowed to care for his father, a promise he kept by bequeathing a large sum in his will. Those scholars who did not serve in the military contributed to the war effort by staying after school hours to pick lint and prepare articles for the wounded. Whether Isaac conspired in keeping his nephew in Medina and safe from the war is not known, but not improbable. It was common for wealthy families to buy substitutes for their sons to avoid military service, but there is no evidence to support that this happened in his case. In any event, Burroughs continued his schooling and assisted his uncle, who would have found him useful in running the farm and merchant business.[37] Evidently Isaac saw no benefit of a university education for his nephew, although some fellow students went on to college: instead business and commerce beckoned.[38]

At 16 Burroughs was apprenticed to one of the local doctors, Dr Edwin Healy, who ran the drug, book and stationery store. This was a major step and the start of his involvement in pharmacy.[39] Work would have involved sweeping floors, washing up glasses and containers, helping Healy make up preparations and powders, learning dosages and running general errands. Two years later he moved to the nearby town of Albion to become a clerk and counter salesman to Ezra T. Coann, a dry goods merchant (selling textiles, clothing, hosiery and personal care or toiletries) and druggist, and he lodged with Ezra's elderly mother.[40] Here he was 'porter, storekeeper, book keeper, chemist and general factotum'.[41] In 1868 Coann closed his business to tour Europe, thereby forcing Burroughs's next move, which took him to Lockport, further west along the canal.[42] By now Burroughs was legally of age and presumably had control of his inherited money, which gave him greater independence.[43]

In Lockport, Burroughs was employed by Van Horn & Chadwick, one of the town's seven druggists, at 66 Main Street. Chadwick's reference for Burroughs's application to the Pharmaceutical College stated that he had worked over a year for him, from 1868 to April 1869,

4: Burroughs aged 18. This is the first known photograph of Burroughs. Studio photo taken by J.H. Kent, Rochester, NY, 1864.

and gave his 'heartiest approval' of Burroughs as a 'competent salesman, a straightforward upright and business man in every particular'. One of the main manufacturers in the town was Merchant's Gargling Oil laboratory, which expanded rapidly as a manufacturing business after the Civil War. By 1866 the firm was manufacturing a million bottles a year and packaging 125 cases a day, a success propelled by heavy advertising: it published almanacs and circulars and ran its own small printing press. Here Burroughs undoubtedly learnt important lessons about the power of advertising, which was to become a hallmark of his own business.

Now, at 23, Burroughs was determined to improve his position, and his next move was to Buffalo, some 30 miles west of Lockport at the western end of the Erie Canal. Buffalo had grown rapidly during the Civil War and by 1865 was the largest city in the area, with a population of 94,000. It had 26 druggists, and one of the oldest manufacturing and retailing druggists was Oliver H.P. Champlin, whose Champlin's

Liquid Pearl, a cosmetic compound, manufactured from 1869, sold well, as did Bells Specific Pills. Burroughs joined him and is listed in the 1869 *Buffalo City Directory* as a clerk living at 403 Main Street. Champlin later certified that Burroughs was in his employ from April to September 1869 and, 'so far as I know', believed 'his moral character was good and above reproach during that time.' Shortly before Burroughs left Buffalo, Mark Twain took over editorship of the *Buffalo Express*, though there is no evidence that the two men met.

At this time Burroughs was probably earning something like $80 to $100 per month, not a bad salary for an apprentice.[44] Working first with his uncle, then with a number of different merchants and druggists, he had acquired key skills of bookkeeping, finance, trading, marketing, manufacturing, competition, publicity and salesmanship. He now knew a great deal about drugs and was keen to learn more. His next move was to Philadelphia, to join the well-known pharmaceutical firm of John Wyeth and Brother. Before his departure he reaffirmed his faith and was admitted to full membership of the Presbyterian Church in Medina.

Chapter 2

On the Road

The truth is that when you are right and when you know
your preparation is as good and better than anyone
else's, it is pretty hard to put you down.[1]

Philadelphia, 'The City of Brotherly Love', was in the 1870s one of the largest cities of the world, an exciting metropolis of international importance with a thriving bustling commercial centre. It was proud then, as it is now, of its rich history, home to the Declaration of Independence in 1776 and holder of the Liberty Bell. During the 19th century it became the first major industrial city in the US, attracting many European immigrants; with the advent of railways it also became a major railroad hub. Buffalo had been big after Medina, but 'Philly' was vastly more exhilarating, and Burroughs could enjoy its vibrant social and intellectual life, with numerous libraries, literary, scientific and art institutions. He witnessed daily changes to the city, and many of the major buildings were constructed when he was there, one of the largest being the gigantic Norman-style Masonic Temple, which was situated virtually in front of one of his lodgings. For a time he lived in a comfortable row of terraced houses in an attractive, mainly Quaker area in the centre of town, at 1319 Arch Street. This was close to the College of Pharmacy, at 820 Arch Street, and opposite the Arch Street United Methodist Church; his Presbyterian church was not far distant, at 2014 Arch Street.

Wyeths presented Burroughs with a tremendous opportunity to learn about pharmaceutical manufacturing at a time when pharmacy was emerging as a dynamic and rapidly expanding profession. Philadelphia boasted the country's oldest school of medicine and the greatest number of physicians in America, and its College of Pharmacy, founded in 1821, was the first such college in the country.[2] In 1860 John Wyeth and his brother Frank opened a drugstore and small research laboratory at 1410 Walnut Street; their timing was fortuitous, coinciding with the new opportunities to pharmaceutical manufacturers created by the Civil War. The firm expanded rapidly, supplying a diverse range of products, including medicines and beef extract to the Union Army, and obtaining government contracts for basic drugs such as opium, quinine and ergot, which could be made using machinery. Before long they produced a catalogue, sold a wide range of elixirs and tonics, and by 1873 had started manufacturing compressed medicines at the suggestion of one of their employees, Henry Bower, who developed and patented one of the first rotary compressed machines in the US.

The firm soon found that, in Burroughs, they had a highly energetic employee whose work as their salesman, or 'detail man', involved travel all over America. A travelling agent or commercial salesman needed many talents, not least of which was a high degree of self-confidence, assertiveness and quick thinking. The travelling man also knew that his personality was his capital. As Arthur Miller wrote, they 'lived like artists, like actors whose product is first of all themselves, forever imagining triumphs in a world that either ignores them or denies them altogether.' The salesman (and it was very much a male-dominated occupation during the 19th century) also epitomised and spoke for many of the changes in society at this period.[3] Such was the growth in the numbers of this body of workers that in 1870 the US government introduced the occupational class 'commercial traveler' in the census for the first time.[4] 'Drummers', as travelling salesmen were known, became an important feature of post-bellum America's economic growth. By the 1870s their reputation had improved and they were no longer perceived as the hard-drinking womanisers who in earlier decades had peddled goods. One writer noted simply: 'he is less of an animal and more of a man.'[5] Advice given to the traveller by William Mather in his biography *On the Road to Riches* stressed that the salesman, in addition to being a good judge of human nature, must 'arrange his work well, understand his business and not misrepresent his goods, have knowledge of business law, and a good memory. He should be a gentleman with good manners, pleasant, dress neatly and create a good impression.' Importantly, he must be educated with an ability to talk intelligently about other matters than business: 'a man will not buy from a salesman he dislikes, no matter how low the prices quoted.'

Burroughs fitted all these requirements. He was handsome, 5 foot 6½ inches tall, and his appearance was compared to that of Kaiser Wilhelm; they shared the same shaped face and piercing light blue eyes. Photographs of him taken around this time show an intelligent, alert countenance with a fashionable handlebar moustache; he was fair haired and smartly dressed in a well-cut jacket and tie, often sporting a buttonhole flower. He always looked spruce and tidy in spite of the dirt and grime of travel. He once noted observing that the fingernails of someone he met were less than clean, so he clearly paid great attention to being well turned out himself. His voice was reportedly soft and pleasing, his American upstate New York accent being a gentle one. It was said of him that he had a 'keen and attentive eye … piercing in its glance … and when in a reverie, with a particularly dreamy introspection.'[6] His handwriting was large, bold and clear, with flourishes, suggesting an easy self-confidence.

Wyeths used a system known as 'detailing' to sell the firm's drugs, whereby sales were made directly to the medical profession rather than to the consumer, and Burroughs became a detail salesman. His work experience had given him all the basic knowledge he needed, added to which he had a way with words – remarked on by many – as well as a charming open and frank manner and an enjoyment of people and conversation. These traits, combined with a lively mind and natural curiosity, made him a good companion. He often acted on instinct, his trust inspired friendship, and on the whole his judgement was sound.

Travel was becoming much easier as railroad and telegraph opened up the country, creating the possibility of a new national market across America.[7] In 1870 the first trans-US rail service began, following the connection of the Union Pacific and Central Pacific lines at Utah, near Great Salt Lake, the previous year: it was said that the 'entire nation cheered' when this happened. Rapid progress was made towards the adoption of a standard gauge all over America. Undoubtedly journeys were still exhausting and uncomfortable but were relieved by the new Pullman sleeping cars, which were likened to 'first class hotels'. In 1865 the 3,000 miles from New York to San Francisco could be covered in six days and nights, and the journey would have taken the traveller through some of the most dramatic and beautiful scenery the country had to offer.

Burroughs always enjoyed travel, but it was far from easy. Journeying on from a railhead meant using stagecoaches, buggies, gigs, wagons and horses along rough roads and tracks. Hotels in the poor towns were basic, many simply small shabby houses, offering stale food in unsanitary conditions. As well as being physically and emotionally demanding, the travelling salesman's job was dangerous: accidents and attacks were always likely. Mastering the physical contingencies of road life and the props of the trade, such as baggage, product samples and catalogues, 'required practical imagination and knack for persuasive, sometimes histrionic self-preservation'.

Burroughs spent weeks and months at a time on the road, meeting people from all walks of life. His firm's samples were his vital baggage, and he would invariably have carried one of the latest new manuals and guides, such as Brockett's *The Commercial Traveller's Guide Book* or the Claremont Manufacturing Company's *The Pocket Companion*, which gave advice on how to get to any town and whether it would pay to go there.[8] Travellers recognised the advantages of mutual help, and after the Civil War many fraternal and insurance organisations developed: based on collective needs, they offered advice and assistance with issues such as discounted travel rates, better hotel services, and life and resident insurance. Burroughs probably joined one of the many newly founded national associations for commercial travellers, the first of which started in New York state around this time.

As Wyeths' agent, Burroughs travelled to California on at least two occasions, in 1873 and again in 1875–6. California was still frontier country: the Mexican–American War, the gold rush of the late 1840s, and America's expansion west were comparatively recent events. San Francisco was described as looking mostly like a sand heap in 1850, though it was fast changing, and by 1881 it had fine streets, shops, public buildings, a telegraph in every office, and one of the largest hotels in the world. Mining was giving way to agriculture and commerce, and people had more money to spend on medicines and toilet preparations. The social life in San Francisco was described by one visitor as having very little restraint, formality or stiffness: 'all may do as they like. Life is very public' – and the writer

5: Burroughs in San Francisco, aged c. 27.

also noted that everyone was out for money.[9] Los Angeles saw similar changes: the Clarendon Hotel, where Burroughs stayed in 1875, had been transformed over the previous quarter-century, from a basic single-storey structure surrounded by shacks occupied by Mexicans to a three-storey much improved building. Yet two years after his stay it was described as 'a low price lodging house, serving an increasingly poorer and diverse population'.[10]

Burroughs was clearly very successful, as he himself boasted some years later. 'When I first went to San Francisco I took or had sent to me $2,500 worth of goods which I had no difficulty in selling right off and the Drs began prescribing them the day they were distributed.'[11] Work did not stop him from enjoying the Californian springtime in the company of at least one young lady. The attractions of a certain Emily Bernal led to Burroughs picking her flowers and carving her initials on a tree. Clearly smitten, she wrote to him two years later, in 1878, when she heard a rumour that he had become engaged, to remind him of their romantic meeting under cherry trees. Although he had not kept in touch, young Emily nursed a hope that one day he would return, writing: 'Must my heart wither as those flowers, once picked wither to dry away! No, Mr Burroughs, your [*sic*] a man with a noble heart you know the feebleness of a womanly heart. I have loved … believe in the affection with which I cherished you.' In San Francisco he had his photograph taken by the celebrated photographers Bradley & Rulofson and took advantage of being near Yosemite to ride on horseback there, admiring the view and musing that when he married it would be a good place to honeymoon.[12]

During a hectic schedule Burroughs managed to return to Medina for brief visits to see his family and friends in January 1873 and again that March, possibly as a result of learning that his uncle had been seriously ill with typhoid. Given the hard living conditions, it is not surprising that, while in San Francisco, he himself was ill for several days with pleurodymia.[13]

In August 1876 Burroughs returned to Medina from California before heading back to Philadelphia, this time joined by his sister Lina and their friend Hattie Acer so that they could all visit the Centennial Exposition. As a child he may have attended the large 1853 Buffalo Fair, and he would have known of the sanitary fairs, held from 1863 to mobilize civilian support for the war effort. America's first world's fair, the Centennial Exposition, was on a different scale from anything seen before in the country. About 10 million visitors attended between May and November, equivalent to about 20% of the population. Modelled on London's 1851 Great Exhibition, it introduced exciting new technologies and machinery to the public and brought innovative designs and ideas to manufacturing and the decorative arts. More than 50 nations displayed exhibits in over 200 buildings in the 3,000 acres of Fairmount Park, and it was a huge success, attracting millions of visitors.

The main exhibition building was the largest in the world and dealt with mining, metallurgy, manufacturing, education and science – including pharmacy. Pharmaceutical firms from 51 countries were represented, including of course Wyeths.[14] The American Pharmaceutical Association (APhA) took advantage of the exhibition to promote the new changes in their industry, and its Exhibition Committee drew attention to pharmaceutical exhibits by sending out a circular to all exhibitors from home and abroad. Wyeths did exceptionally well and won five awards, its compressed powders being praised as 'superior to any other similar pills manufactured'.[15]

Careful planning ensured that those attending the APhA's 24th annual meeting could also visit the exhibition. Some members questioned whether they should be enjoying themselves in this way, but opposers contended that the display of the pharmaceutical, chemical and botanical items would be of great interest: 'We are now in the one hundredth anniversary of this country's independence, and on an occasion of this kind we can drop the usual routine of business without interfering with it; we can cultivate our minds ... this is pre-eminently an age in which we are taught more by object-instruction than by any other means!'[16]

Here Burroughs had an opportunity to meet manufacturers and learn about new goods and designs from all over the world. Here too he learnt much about the importance of high-quality displays, packaging and promotional literature and how exhibitions could be used in marketing, methods he later employed in his own business. His appetite for travel outside America and possibly a desire to move to London may have been born at this time. Before then, however, he had recognised that he needed to gain a professional qualification in pharmacy, a realisation possibly brought about by the APhA's publicity at the exhibition, but more likely because his employers supported such a move.[17] They described attendance at the College of Pharmacy as being 'almost essential', underlining the importance attached to salesmen knowing more about pharmaceuticals in order to work more effectively.

Before 1820 little was done in America to raise standards and instruct pharmacists: adulterated drugs with inferior remedies were common, a result largely of the poor training of druggists and apothecaries. That year the first *US Pharmacopeia*, laying down standards for the manufacture of drugs, was printed, and the University of Pennsylvania then passed a resolution to offer honorary degrees to a select number of pharmacists as a step towards improving the prestige of the profession. Spurred into action by criticisms of the trade, a group of Philadelphia pharmacists seized the initiative and recommended the establishment of a College of Apothecaries to put their business 'on a respectable footing'. This would ensure that quality products appeared in the drug market created by suitably trained qualified pharmacists. The college was established there, changing its name from 'Apothecaries' to 'Pharmacy' within the year, and the Philadelphia College of Pharmacy (PCP) became the first college of pharmacy in the country.

Some thirty years later, in 1851, the national organization, the APhA, came into existence – its creation again being mainly the work of Philadelphian pharmacists. Many Quakers were associated with pharmacy, and these included William Procter jr (1817–74), editor of the *American Journal of Pharmacology* and PCP professor from 1846 to 1874, Daniel B. Smith, a founder of the PCP, its president from 1829 to 1854, and president of the APhA in 1852, and the Wyeth brothers. Further developments at this time resulted from the immigration of German pharmacists, refugees from the failed 1848 revolutionary risings in Europe, notably John Maisch (1831–93), who arrived penniless in Baltimore.

Before the Civil War, not one of the few existing pharmacy schools had laboratories for basic chemical instruction, and science played a small role in pharmaceutical education in America. After the war some key individuals acted radically to allay public concern and continue the reforms started in the 1850s, Maisch being one. He and his colleagues drafted a proposed law 'to regulate the practice of pharmacy and the sale of poisons and to prevent the adulteration of drugs and medicines'. Although it was not formally adopted by the APhA, their action encouraged improved standards within the profession and ensured that any new state legislation was based on this proposed model law. Philadelphia was one of the first places to support the bill, which was passed in 1872, stating that no one in the city could engage in the business of compounding and dispensing medicines on the prescriptions of physicians or sell at retail any drugs, chemicals, poisons or medicines without a written certificate declaring him to be duly competent and qualified to do so. Druggists could not employ assistants in the compounding of medicines unless they were graduates in pharmacy, or unless they had served a minimum apprenticeship of two years in a store where medicines were compounded and dispensed, or had taken at least one full course of lectures on chemistry, *materia medica* and pharmacy. The editor of the *American Journal of Pharmacy* described it as the best pharmaceutical law yet passed in the US, and by the late 1870s nine states had adopted laws which licensed pharmacists.

In 1868 the college moved to larger premises, on 145 Tenth Street. Apart from its lecture rooms, seating 300 people, it had a library of 3,000 volumes, a museum containing *materia medica* and chemical and pharmaceutical specimens, an extensive herbarium of pressed plants, and a new laboratory 'fitted for practical instruction in analytical chemistry and pharmacy'. Instruction was given on certain evenings only, and the laboratory was open daily from 1870, the fee for each course of lectures being $12. Diplomas were awarded to those of 'good moral character' who had attended two lecture courses delivered in the college (or one course in the college and one in some other reputable college of pharmacy) and who had also 'served an apprenticeship of at least four years with a person or persons qualified to conduct the drug or apothecary business.' After passing a written examination, the candidate also had to present a satisfactory original dissertation or thesis on some subject of *materia medica*, pharmacy, chemistry or one of the branches of science immediately connected with them, written with neatness and accuracy. In spite of the strictness of the process, the 1871 examination committee felt it their duty to report on the 'growing laxity on the part of employers' who failed to supervise or instruct their apprentices adequately, giving them manual rather than educative duties.[18]

Following Philadelphia's new regulations, in 1872 the college received over 500 applications: many more attended lectures than graduated.[19] Lectures were delivered in the evenings, and most students worked at the same time as studying, so attendance meant that staff were absent from their routine employment duties and there was a financial cost to both student and the firm.

One early graduate who sat exams in 1874 was a young man from Wisconsin called Henry Solomon Wellcome who worked for McKesson & Robbins in New York.[20] Wellcome had applied to work for Wyeths in 1872, and at the time Wyeths wrote to him that they had 'almost made up our minds to take no more clerks who come to attend lectures as this winter we had six or seven and while we think it almost an essential for a Druggist it interferes very much with the surviving of our business.' They told Wellcome to answer their offer of employment at once as they had many applications.[21] In the event Wellcome did not accept their offer and took up a post in Chicago instead. Although there is no evidence of how Burroughs and Wellcome met, it is likely that their paths crossed in Philadelphia during a pharmaceutical meeting or through the college. What is certain is that the two men formed a strong friendship which was to have lasting consequences both for them and for the pharmaceutical industry.

Burroughs enrolled at the college in October 1876 and attended until February the following year.[22] The college obtained references from his previous employers, Healy and Coann, and John Wyeth vouched that he had 'been with them almost continuously since October 1869 and had exhibited a laudable interest in this business and has conducted himself in every way satisfactorily.'[23] His fellow students came mainly from Pennsylvania and New York, but there were also two from Germany and one from Sweden; 86 students were successful in his year, so the classes must have been packed.

* * *

The faculty teachers had excellent credentials. Joseph P. Remington, who became one of the foremost figures in the field, had recently been promoted to Professor of Theory and Practice of Pharmacy; he also practised pharmacy and owned an apothecary shop. His theory and practice course covered the weights and measures systems of the US, Britain and France; specific gravity; apparatus and manipulations used in shop and laboratory; all the preparations of drugs in the pharmacopoeia in their groups; classifications; preparations of animal substances; and the practical pharmacy of making pills, suppositories, ointments, etc. His impressive courtly presence, fluent and easy manner and geniality in address and conversation made him respected and liked. In his address to the APhA in 1875 he demonstrated Wyeths' compressed medicine, giving significant support to the firm by his recommendation. Burroughs and Wellcome kept in contact with him after they left the college and arranged sales of his textbook *The Science and Practice of Pharmacy* through their firm.

The Professor of Chemistry was Dr Robert Bridges, whose course presented 'a systematic view of the science, its improvements and condition to the present time'. Reportedly unselfish, loyal and painstaking, with kindly ways, he earned respect and, 'without being ready in debate or at all eloquent in speech, … was an admirable and efficient teacher.' One suspects that he was in fact rather a boring lecturer.[24]

John Maisch, 'the father of adequate pharmaceutical legislation' and at that time the college's Professor of Materia Medica and Botany, lectured on the best time and mode of collecting and preserving vegetable and animal substances used in medicine and the products obtained from plants in various ways. He gave students the means to recognise individual drugs and covered their botanical and commercial history. This relatively new course comprised one afternoon a week devoted to lectures and excursions in the countryside surrounding Philadelphia, giving the students 'a healthy recreation' as well as 'the best means of becoming practically acquainted with living plants'.

The examinations were not easy. A written exam required the identification of specimens and drugs and the answers to such questions as:

> *Chemistry* Give a process for the preparation of Iodide of
>   potassium and state the rationale for it.
> *Materia medica* Give a description of sweet and bitter
>   almonds. From what plants and from what countries are
>   they obtained? What are their medicinal products and
>   how obtained?
> *Pharmacy* Give a formula for preparing a castor oil mixture.[25]

Burroughs chose a highly topical subject for his thesis: 'The Compression of Medicinal Powders'. Handwritten, his essay covered seventeen pages.[26] He wrote that their history was of recent origin in America but had been employed in Europe for many years, and he criticised the use of the expression 'compressed pill': 'I consider the title of compressed pills, usually applied to them in this country, is ill chosen, as it may imply their preparation from a pillular mass, in which an excipient has been employed whereas if properly prepared they are merely dry powders, compressed without addition whatsoever, except in cases where an increase of bulk is demanded.' Starting with William Brockedon's work in 1843, Burroughs related how compressed powders had obtained some popularity among physicians in England and elsewhere.[27] However, the style in which they were 'put up',

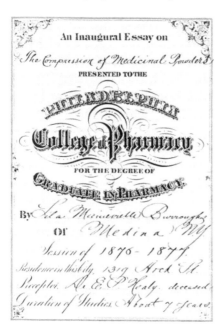

6: Burroughs's thesis, 1877.

or marketed, inhibited their employment by the profession, as the label claimed a patent for them. Burroughs made an important point here. Aware that Brockedon's discovery was undermined by the English medical profession's reluctance to purchase patented pills, he was later careful to reassure his clients on this issue in England.

The historical background section of his thesis demonstrated careful observation of developments in this field. Burroughs cited a German journal of pharmacy which alluded to the display of compressed pills at the Centennial Exposition and their use in Germany for some time. Quoting from a recent article in the *American Journal of Pharmacy*, he described the method employed by Professor Rosenthal of Berlin to create compressed tablets and noted that Wyeths had manufactured increasing varieties of compressed pills since 1873, mentioning Remington's recent work on compressing powders. The price of these pills was initially too high for the druggist trade to accommodate them, and Burroughs explained: 'Like most new products the price decreased considerably with increasing demand and improved facilities for rapid and economical production.' An additional objection – that they were liable to disintegrate on exposure to the atmosphere or by rough handling – 'seems now to be greatly obviated by careful regulation of pressure', although it was essential that they be carefully packed and handled. Burroughs's experiments were detailed, and his results led him to conclude that compressed powders dissolved quickly, acted more efficiently (since there was no excipient), were smaller, had a glossier surface, were easier to swallow, and were comparatively free from taste. They thus constituted 'a benefit to the Patient, a valuable aid to the Druggist, and to the Physician an advantage over former expedients in the administration of medicines, as well as a protection against Homeopathic practice.'

Burroughs's clear conclusion was that the future of the pharmaceutical world lay in manufacturing compressed pills. The thesis was well written and forceful, its fluency giving the impression that it was composed easily, almost casually; indeed, in parts it almost reads as a promotional report. Burroughs had done his homework well, cited practical experiments and included good examples. The fact that he failed to complete the year date for one work was an indication of a hastiness and inattention to detail, a failing in him later criticised by Wellcome.

Burroughs was regarded as an outstanding and popular student. To celebrate the passing of his exam in 1877 he commissioned a special photograph of himself, which he presented to Professor Remington. He was now 31, his face fuller, and his hair beginning to thin – a man in

7: Burroughs on graduation, 1877. He gave
this photo to Professor Joseph Remington at
the Philadelphia College of Pharmacy.

his prime. The following year he was elected to the APhA, and by May he had negotiated a fundamental change in his career – to act as Wyeths' agent in England.

Many years later, one of the Wyeth brothers was to say of Burroughs: 'he was the smartest boy I ever saw … he came into our employ at $20 per week, and when he left nine years later [in 1878] was getting $3,000 per year.'[28] The sum of $2,500 a year in 1878 is noted as being rather generous for a travelling salesman, so with $3,000 Burroughs had an excellent salary. By comparison, Wellcome's trial salary of $832 per annum in 1876 when he joined McKesson & Robbins in New York had risen to $2,500 by the time he left them in 1880, but then he was seven years younger and had less experience than Burroughs. Wyeths subsequently remarked to Burroughs: 'While you were in our employ we gave you more liberal compensation than was given to any other one of our travellers. You were active, energetic, and your efforts constantly received our commendation, for [the] above reasons.' In the same letter, referring to Burroughs's subsequent employment as their agent in the UK, they told him that he was still receiving more than others – double the equivalent, for example, of a Mr Thomas Brown, who received only $800. From all this it is evident that Burroughs was a sharp negotiator but was also valued by Wyeths.[29] They found him difficult to manage, with '"patent medicine impulses" and a predilection for advertising', and later complained that he gave them 'more bother than all our travellers combined – too hasty arrangements with our customers, often in a manner prejudicial to our interests, making statements and promises we could not fulfil.' That said, his easy manner and ability to make friends and maintain contacts stood him in good stead, and, as Wyeths admitted to him: 'the truth is that when you are right and when you know your preparation is as good and better than anyone else's, it is pretty hard to put you down.'[30]

How did the move to be Wyeths' agent in Britain come about? Was it because the firm was so impressed with him that they decided to send him to London as their representative, as Wyeth states in his obituary?[31] Burroughs's version of events is rather different. Many years later he wrote a friend that he had been disillusioned with Wyeths and that he had left the firm twice because he suspected things were 'not quite straight'. He added:

> You know also the reason why I went to England that it was because I requested it as a gradual severance of my relations with J W & Bro. I had observed the way JW disparaged every employee who left them & without any cause for speaking ill of the employee. I was determined to leave and requested the departure for England as the beginning of a final separation of myself from the house because it was my intention to sell out my half int[erest] in the London business after 6 mo[nth]s and then to return to the States. But I got interested in other business affairs in England & had to stay. I tried to sell out the int[erest] in JW&Bros business but John wouldn't buy it at any price. Perhaps the whole course of events has been most providential for me. I believe it is so.[32]

This is most probably the way events turned out: Burroughs saw an opportunity to move and managed to negotiate a deal with Wyeths. The prospect of a new challenge and going to England to explore the market there was one he would have relished. London, at the heart of the British Empire, was key to opening up new world markets and the ideal place to create a business. Working merely as an agent was clearly not his sole aim, though: he would make his own way, and his ambition, self-confidence, ability and unbounded energy augured well.

Chapter 3

London and S.M. Burroughs & Co.

I am sure I shall like to do business with Englishmen
for I learn they are reliable men.[1]

London in 1878 was the world's greatest capital, the hub of a vast empire, the global centre of finance, and an obvious place from which to launch a new firm and new products. The task facing the 31-year-old Burroughs on his arrival in May was a demanding one. He came armed with the inevitable introductions from Wyeths, his teachers at the College of Pharmacy and others, but ultimately success or failure rested on him alone. From the outset it was vital he initiate orders for Wyeths. First, though, he had to find his way around London and the country and rapidly understand how business and the pharmaceutical and medical profession operated in Britain. Attitudes, customs and financial arrangements all differed from those at home. What was likely to interest the market? How would the medical profession respond to the new compressed pills especially? Who were his competitors? How would he and his American goods be received?

The drug trade was expanding at a time of prolonged economic depression. The so-called Long Depression started in 1873 and affected countries across the world differently. It hit hardest at different periods in different places: in the US, trade revived in 1878, only to decline in 1882–5; in the UK, it is agreed that a 'Great Depression' lasted until 1896. This impacted in many ways. With higher imports of grain from the States, food prices in Britain, and consequently labour costs, decreased. Traditional British manufacturing – such as steel, shipbuilding and coal – continued to boom, but it anxiously confronted rising competition from the US and Germany. Most importantly, free traders lost their arguments over protectionism, which was reintroduced into all but two countries in Europe (Britain and Denmark). Resulting higher import tariffs made it expensive for UK manufacturers to export, while their overseas competitors faced no such barriers in importing into Britain. At the same time the 1870s and 1880s saw a fall in commodity and wholesale prices and a corresponding increase in purchasing power. The fall in drug prices boosted competition between firms, and demand for medicines and self-medication products grew: there was a fourfold increase in British chemists and druggists between 1865 and 1905. Such was the good and bad situation facing Burroughs, whose ambition was to sell not only in Britain but internationally.

The British pharmaceutical industry was dominated by firms which imported and processed basic raw drugs, serving domestic consumers and exporting to traditional markets. Leaders included Allen & Hanbury's, John Bell & Croyden, Savory & Moore, Whiffen & Sons, Lescher & Webb, Duncan Flockhart, Howards, May & Baker, and Thomas Morson & Sons. Most companies were small, with fewer than 100 workers, and with a couple of exceptions were not interested in scientific investigation or product development. Their typical product range included galenical preparations, alkaloids, numerous creams, infusions, dressings and miscellaneous medications in abundance. Dietary goods were considered medicinal and formed an expanding line for druggists at this time. Although there was some specialisation, products were difficult to differentiate, and firms also marketed the products of associated companies.

American pharmacy was perceived by the British as dealing in patent and quack medicine, and there was some prejudice against Americans and their 'boosterism'.[2] Although Americans were beginning to arrive in Britain in numbers, few American businesses operated here at this time, and it was noted that those that did faced special difficulties. One such businessman commented that 'an American's chances are by no means favourable in any line of business … the whole conduct and habit of business in England are entirely different from what is current in America. The currency differs, the methods of the people differ, and the conduct of men is entirely dissimilar.'[3] Henry Wellcome later wrote that 'Englishmen and Americans … do not always understand or appreciate each other's methods, and this is perfectly natural, for Britons are generally characterised by an underlying conservatism, sturdy persistence, and patient submission to precedents, whilst Americans are generally characterised by a quickened creative energy, almost breathless activity, and a disregard for precedents.'[4] Wellcome was probably thinking of Burroughs as well as himself when he wrote this, and it certainly describes the gusto with which Burroughs threw himself into his work on his arrival in London.

The first practical issues confronting Burroughs were lodgings and office space. He stayed in hotels or boarding houses, and his journals show that he moved around frequently. For a while he boarded with a Miss Warner in Torrington Square, Bloomsbury. On making friends, which he soon did, he often stayed with them at weekends. The Saracen's Head inn on Snow Hill, in between the City and the West End, was also regularly used. Much of his initial work and his contacts were in the Bloomsbury area, near the West End and conveniently close to two major railway stations, Euston and Kings Cross. The Pharmaceutical Society of Great Britain and its School of Pharmacy were located in Bloomsbury Square and Great Russell Street, and the well-known retail pharmacy and chemical manufacturers Thomas Morson & Sons had premises around the corner on Southampton Row.

Burroughs quickly rented office space in the recently constructed Great Russell Street Buildings. On the ground floor was John Morgan Richards, an 'export druggist' to whom Burroughs soon made himself known; it was the beginning of a lasting and useful acquaintance. Richards was a fellow American who had set up in business in London two years earlier and was to emerge as a leader in the patent drug-selling and advertising business: through him Burroughs was introduced to many Americans in London who became good friends. The new salesman made an immediate impression on Richards:

> In 1878 Mr Silas Mainville Burroughs called upon me in Great Russell Street with a letter of introduction. He was a handsome young fellow, of about 30 years of age, blonde of complexion, with fine pale blue eyes. He was full of enthusiasm as to his purpose to establish products of Messrs John Wyeth & Sons [*sic*] of Philadelphia, with whom he had been long associated. He rented a little office of two rooms on the first floor of Great Russell Street Buildings, and, with samples in hand, began a canvass among the London doctors and hospitals without delay. He had a magnetic personality, and the items he had to offer were new and important. He succeeded from the very first, at the end of a year taking quite large premises at Snow Hill and adding a factory for the manufacture of a

malt extract and beef wine and iron. He travelled constantly making friends and customers. … Mr Burroughs and I were warm personal friends from the day of his arrival.[5]

The agreement signed by Burroughs and Wyeths stated that Burroughs was appointed their 'sole agent for the sale and disposal of their goods and preparations throughout Europe'. For their part, Wyeths agreed 'not to ship or sell any of their said goods and preparations to any other party in Europe during the continuance of the said Agency.'[6] On his arrival Burroughs straightaway registered S.M. Burroughs & Co. as an independent agency with sole rights outside the US to sell Wyeths' products. He soon sought clarification of his agreement and confirmation that, henceforth, Wyeths' labels should state 'S.M. Burroughs & Co. sole European agent'. With an eye on markets further afield, he also asked Wyeths about their proposals for the Australian market and the role of other competitors.[7]

It was reported that Burroughs 'seemed to exude vitality', and the frantic pace of his work was evident to all.[8] After registering the firm he organised cash and finance transfers and investigated the complex matters of customs and excise arrangements and how they affected imports. An ability to make friends and contacts undoubtedly helped and led to an ever-growing business network as he continually gathered information about doctors, hospitals and major cities worth visiting across the country. Soon he needed to hire more storage space to accommodate goods and samples arriving from the US and their repacking and dispatch. During his first two years in Britain he had many business addresses: larger offices in Great Russell Street, a small office in a building on Southampton Street, a basement at 1 Cock Lane in the City, near St Bartholomew's Hospital, for use as a warehouse and packaging area, then a larger office at nos. 1 and 8 Snow Hill.

His approach to selling in Britain was as novel as it was effective. In order to build up interest and confidence in his goods he had to overcome resistance to American pharmaceuticals and convince the market that his products were superior to those of his rivals. At this stage most of what he and his competitors sold were not medicines in the sense that we now understand them. Burroughs recognised that there were elite chemists who were able to shun selling proprietary medicines, such as Beecham's pills, and there were also physicians and consultants who wished to separate themselves from 'sixpenny doctors' whose work looked ominously like a trade, selling cheap medicines themselves.

These physicians, consultants and quality chemists were potentially powerful allies in his fight to gain acceptance. In formulating his sales strategy he needed to stake out a claim for selling something new and beneficial while at the same time devising a distinctive approach that marked out his products from those of others.

British manufacturers traditionally did not mail product literature to physicians or make direct contact with them, relying on advertising through medical journals. In contrast, Burroughs employed the American method of 'detailing', which he had employed with Wyeths. Attention was concentrated on the medical profession, and 'medical items' were not sold direct to the general public. Instead, Burroughs and his salesmen, or 'detail men', visited doctors, surgeons, and chemists and druggists, explained to them the merits of the products – using technical language if possible – and left samples. After their confidence had been gained, medics were asked to request the firm's products at the chemists and subsequently to vouch for their quality and usefulness. The detail men ensured that the chemists had already been visited and stocked his goods for when the doctors prescribed them. Good-quality attractive information supported this approach. Price lists were sent to a range of chemists and doctors, followed up with further correspondence, visits and advertisements, this last for the medical press only. Trade cards were printed – more cheaply in London than Philadelphia, Burroughs noted – and samples distributed liberally. Samples were even sent to the medical press for testing and were reported under a 'New Inventions' column in *The Lancet* of 14 June 1879. The firm and its products, including 'ethical medicines', were pushed at every opportunity. This was not cheap, and Wyeths were unconvinced about the extent to which advertising was used, but Burroughs's aggressive salesmanship paid off. He communicated a conviction in his goods, persuaded with enthusiasm, paid attention to detail, and followed up contacts, building strong business relationships. Crucially, the strategy of selling via the medical profession rather than direct to the public set him apart from his British competitors at this period.

In early June Burroughs could report to Wyeths: 'All the physicians and surgeons give me a hearty welcome ... It is really pleasing to call on the Medical Gentlemen here. Their parlours & offices are art galleries of fine drawings and engravings ... The Druggists treat us first rate too.' Joseph Lister, 'the great surgeon', reportedly had 'a way of making carbolic acid remain in lint prepared according to his directions', and Burroughs planned to see him about this as soon as possible. Other eminent members of the profession contacted included Thomas Barlow at the Children's Hospital, Great Ormond Street, Hughlings Jackson at the London Hospital, and Le Gros Clark at St Thomas's. They and major hospitals received samples of Wyeths' Dialysed Iron, Parker's Paper Fibre Lint and other products and were asked to draw them to the attention of their Medical Committee for comment. To Dr Barlow, for example, Burroughs sent Saccharated Pepsin, Lint and Dialysed Iron, asking him to prescribe them where in his judgement they would be useful. A specimen of each was left in Barlow's consulting rooms and all items stocked by the dispensary. 'We believe that after prescribing these in your hospital practice you will then prescribe them extensively in private practice and recommend to your profession.' Consultants at all the main hospitals were approached in this manner.

By mid-July 1878 Burroughs could tell Wyeths: 'Gentlemen I am happy to inform you of my continued and uniform success with the medical profession here. I have yet to meet with the first rebuff or coldness. They all treat me first-rate, and all like the goods.' Yet he found the medical profession rather slow about writing and placing orders: 'hard work & patience & lots of both will be required to get up an extensive sale of the goods here but when once established the trade is sure & permanent as the English Drs are noted as good stickers to anything that has merit.'

Within a month Burroughs issued the first impressively long price list of the firm. It included elixirs; preparations of beef, iron and wine; syrups; liquors; wines; dialysed iron; Parker's Paper Fibre Lint; compressed powders or pills such as Peptonic Pills for the relief of dyspepsia or indigestion; compressed tablets of chlorate/potash for hoarseness, bronchial irritation, sore throats and croup; Papoma, a food for infants and invalids; suppositories; and also goods manufactured by other firms, such as Granulated Effervescent Salts (Alfred Bishop, London), cod liver oil (Marvin Bros, New Haven, USA), a concentrated extract of malt from Stuttgart, and Roberts's Asthma Cigarettes (cigarettes for asthmatics? what a marvellous concept!).[9]

From the outset Burroughs never intended to restrict his business solely to that of an agent for Wyeths, and he acquired other agencies and indeed marketed his own goods. He took careful note of potential products that would sell well and could be manufactured, sometimes simply following his gut instincts. Many agreements made at this time were to be highly successful and endure for decades. They included Professor Horsord's Acid Phosphate for headaches, stomach disorders and exhaustion; Fellows' Medical Manufacturing Compound Syrup and Hypophosphites; Bishop's Granular Effervescent Citrate of Caffeine; and

MEDICAL FORMULÆ.

THE
"BURROUGHS"
AMMONIA INHALER.

For Inhaling the Fumes of Chloride of Ammonium.

Price 12s. each, from any Chemist.

A great advantage of this Inhaler is, that not only does it remove Catarrh, but that after its use the patient is less susceptible to the effects of the weather than before, the contrary being the case with all steam Inhalers. It is not necessary, therefore, to take any special precaution, in respect to exposure or change of temperature, after the use of the "Burroughs" apparatus.

BURROUGHS, WELLCOME & CO., LONDON.

8: Advertisement for the 'Burroughs' Ammonia Inhaler that appeared in *The Lancet*, 1881.

Starr's Extract of Beef (acquired from the London Manufacturing Co. in New York). Hazeline, effectively a cosmetic made from witch hazel, became a long-standing earner for the firm.

The importance of having a brand name was not lost on Burroughs, and he began to market using his name: Burroughs's Beef and Iron Wine appeared in 1880. There was nothing in his agreement with Wyeths to prevent him from expanding his business in this way, although they were understandably aggrieved about Burroughs's Beef and Iron Wine, since it was in competition with a similar Wyeths product. Burroughs meanwhile was over the moon at the success of his wine, noting in his diary: 'Finished [bottling] the 2nd – 50 galls of Beef & Iron wine & it appears to be very good. The small labels looking very well. Hopefully I'll make a fortune out of this stuff.'[10] Other trade-marked products were registered using his name, such as Hazeline, Pepsin and Dextra Quinine. Crucially, Burroughs picked up on the British wariness of the word 'pill' and so did not push Wyeths' Peptonic Pills but registered 'tablet' as a trademark for compressed medicines. He later removed any mention of the American origin of his medicines from his labels. Calling on the conclusions reached in his thesis, he emphasised the reliability, standardisation, accuracy and solubility of the new tablets he sold.

Meanwhile he had hired an assistant, Theodore Young Kelley.[11] Kelley had tested the potential of a new 'blacking' product – a kind of saddle soap used for treating leather – and early in 1879 the Nubian Blacking Co. was established by the two men. Samples were sent out, and a whole-page advert placed in the *Chemist & Druggist* illustrated a dramatic profile of a black Nubian chief under the headline 'A Profitable Addition to a Druggists' Business / The New Discovery / Nubian Waterproof Blacking'. Nubian sold well, but Burroughs felt that Kelley's attention was occupied mostly with this and soon considered giving it up, as it was 'not in line of my legitimate business'. He withdrew from managerial involvement in 1880, although the firm continued to sell the item on Kelley's behalf for some years.

Burroughs's major new product was in malt extract. In July he alerted Wyeths to its potential market as a dietary tonic and asked them to use their influence to secure sole agency for him in Britain for some leading American brands. 'We are satisfied it will take here and if we don't ... somebody else will. Reed & Carrick are

9: Burroughs, Wellcome & Co. products, including beef and iron wine, cod liver oil, extract of malt and cotton wool in a sample case.

bringing out a mixture called "Maltine" but I think the name will go against it here. We want ... fluid extracts if there is money in them. At present we have no goods but yours.' As usual, Burroughs had seen an opening and acted speedily: he recognised the growing popularity of this new product. Maltine used extract of malted barley, wheat and oats and had a better flavour than other malt extracts obtained from malt alone. Philip Lockwood, chairman of the Condensed Beer Company, who held a patent for a malt extract, invited Burroughs to be managing director of a new company for its production. This would be a medicinal compound product and Burroughs would do the 'putting up' – that is, mixing, bottling, labelling and packing the extract, as well as taking on its marketing. In January 1879 the joint stock company Kepler Malt Extract Co. (KMEC) was registered at Burroughs's office in Russell Street. He held £1,000 in shares, making him the largest shareholder; Kelley was the company secretary and director, Charles Gardner was its chairman, and several others among Burroughs's friends were members.

This marked an important turning point for the firm. By taking on the processing of this Kepler product, Burroughs became a manufacturer as well as an agency. Kepler was to emerge as one of the firm's most important products over many years and a real money-spinner; Burroughs and Kelley had two-thirds of the royalties and Burroughs received 5% on sales. In the first full year of trading, sales figures reached over £5,000, and Burroughs could boast that KMEC was 'selling more than all the rest together'. Within two years he had 'masterminded' full acquisition of the company.[12]

Hired assistance was soon needed to help with the office work. Kelley supposedly manned the London office so that Burroughs could get on with visits to the drug trade. Finding suitable commercial travellers was not easy: 'We find the usual difficulty in getting a traveller who can do any good for us – it is almost impossible in this country, the commercial traveller is a stereotyped man. Men who could do what we want are not to be had & would be very expensive even if we could find them, so we have concluded to do as much as we can of the travelling ourselves, taking turns about.'[13] The following year, however, Burroughs reported having five full-time travellers on the road, some paying their own expenses and receiving 15% on sales. But not all were good at their job. Burroughs got on well with Kelley and reported his growing familiarity with their goods; he possibly contemplated him as a business partner in his firm. Wyeths meanwhile expressed doubts about Kelley's work: he had no pharmaceutical training and knew nothing about the medical profession. In subsequent adverts for additional travellers Burroughs specifically asked for 'one or two medical gentlemen who would like to assist the leading man in the profession in the principal towns in England and Ireland to introduce a new pharmaceutical preparation and surgical appliance of much merit and interest.'

Now additional office staff were needed. Two significant appointments in the firm's history were made early on by Burroughs and belie the accusation by Rhodes James, Wellcome's biographer, and others that Burroughs was not good at selecting staff. Robert Clay Sudlow was hired as a bookkeeper in February 1879 and went on to serve as general manager until his retirement in 1905. William Henry Kirby was hired in March the same year as a clerk and rose to become chief accountant and assistant general manager. Joseph Collett Smith joined the firm in 1881, aged 16, and on Burroughs's death in 1895 had become a member of the managerial staff.[14] Inevitably some of the appointments were less successful: one office boy took £20 from the office to go to the Derby. He returned repentant, and Burroughs, 'with his usual generosity', reportedly said, 'Oh well! But you must go,' and did not press charges.[15]

By the end of July Burroughs had 'pretty well' finished canvassing London, 'at least for the present', as the doctors had all gone to the country and the London season was over. He therefore attended the British Medical Association meeting in Bath and the Pharmaceutical Society's conference in Dublin, then went on to canvass Belfast. Such conferences were useful for making new contacts and business. From Ireland, Burroughs returned to London via Chester and in September headed to Paris to visit the International Exposition and negotiate sales in France.[16]

The Exposition Universelle of 1878, held to celebrate France's recovery after the 1870 Franco-Prussian War, attracted even more visitors than the Philadelphia World's Fair. Half the exhibition space was given over to France and nearly a third of the remainder to Britain and its empire. It should have been an enjoyable visit, but Burroughs did not have the best of times, writing to Kelley: 'on account of the chills and fever I have not been able to get round as lively as I otherwise would … I had another chill & fever last night and it makes me very weak. My cough however is much better.' Kelley replied: 'You must use great care or you will be on your back … I know you never think of your health until you are ill.' This comment was to prove perceptive: Burroughs always pushed himself too hard throughout his marketing tours and ignored his health.[17]

What added to the frustration of this Paris trip was the discovery that the French, in protecting their own pharmaceutical industry, would not allow any foreign drugs or medicines to be imported. Burroughs did not mince his words to Kelley: 'I have just returned from Paris yesterday and never was so thoroughly sick of a trip in my life.' Although some chemists had warned him about problems with French customs, he had thought that this applied to proprietary medicines, secret preparations, etc., but he found that even substances such as chlorate potash were prohibited. 'It is all very discouraging to try to make money by doing business with France & to do business with the French at all.' Burroughs had already discovered that the British customs made importing American drugs difficult and had got around this by changing Wyeths' name on the labels to that of his own firm, although payment of stamp duty was still necessary. It was a heavy blow to learn that French druggists would not give orders. After his return in October, Burroughs told Frank Wyeth, then in Paris, that he was not at all satisfied with the trip and mentioned a Parisian firm who might be able to get the drugs through. Changing labels on products sometimes facilitated imports and cut stamp duties, but protectionism in Europe was to prove a recurring problem.

Business was slow in August, with only £74 being taken, but sales in September doubled, and Burroughs pushed forward, promoting and advertising products in medical journals. 'Specimens free to Medical Men on application', his full-page advertisements proclaimed. The *British Medical Journal* agreed to sell him 12 pages monthly.

Burroughs had already been in touch with its editor, Ernest Hart, about advertising dialysed iron, and their business relationship developed into a close friendship. Burroughs also used *The Lancet, Record Times, The Examiner*, and the *Medical Press & Circular*, all of which he had found had a good circulation in India, Australia, Canada and the US, as well as in Great Britain and Ireland. 'I think it will be a good investment. Doctors pay a good deal more attention to advertisements here than in the U.S. and the editors give good notices to advertisers. Also they are very useful to quote in circulars afterwards.'[18] London having been largely dealt with, he planned more sales trips to Liverpool, Manchester, Birmingham, Glasgow, Edinburgh and Leeds. To Wyeths, Burroughs wrote of his concern about keeping ahead of the competition, especially with compressed goods.

With so much outlay, cash flow became problematic, especially 'owing to the long credits', and soon Burroughs needed larger capital than he had anticipated. He now requested the surplus cash he had left with Wyeths. Although he had investments in the US – bonds, mortgages and stocks – which were paying him large returns in dividends and interest, to realise these at that time would, he said, be a considerable sacrifice that he could not afford to make. He therefore proposed to make it attractive to Wyeths to take his acceptances – that is, his endorsed promise – instead of cash, by not charging them for the fine set of office furniture he had purchased or for the substantial shelving & fixtures he had erected in the store.[19] Wyeths wanted Burroughs's uncle to guarantee the new agreement financially, but he would not countenance the suggestion:

> I have not & will not ask him to indorse any paper for me as I am abundantly good for any debts I am at all likely to contract & because he is an old man who can't even see to write his own name. I think he would indorse for me if I should ask it but know he has not been in the habit of indorsing for others though he has often been invited to do so. I have never asked such a favour of him & don't think I ever will.

Wyeths decided the risk was worth taking and indulged his request.[20]

In October, Burroughs asked Wyeths to send over a small pill-making machine to use in a factory, a crucial move towards developing his manufacturing interests in the UK. 'Our business is increasing and the goods are getting a better foothold all the time. It takes time & experience however to convince an Englishman but when once convinced he stands firmly by the goods he has found good.' He warned Wyeths not to expect orders to come in quickly, justifying his outlay on advertising, of which they were critical. He also alerted them of his desire to return to the US:

> I would like to go home for a vacation this winter but it takes so long and there is so much to be done here. If I will stay here the year out that is till May '79 attending to the business will you not agree that in case my folks are wanting me at home on a/c of poor health to take this business of yours off my hands at what it has cost me if I throw in the year's time I have given it for nothing. To push the business properly it will be necessary to spend in advertising in Journals also samples etc all we clear for the next 6 months. By that time it will be well established and I think quite smooth sailing & show a fine monthly profit. In addition to the above agreement on our part I beg you will renew your proposition that I may turn the business over to Mr Kelley & leave the country if I choose furnishing another man in my place, retaining my interest leaving Mr Kelley manager or closing it out to him as you at first proposed. I trust you will see the reasonableness of the above and assent to them.[21]

This unexpected proposal may have followed from Burroughs's bout of illness combined with the disappointment over French sales. Or he may simply have wanted to see his family again and been concerned about his uncle's poor state of health. His letter was so worded as to win Wyeths' support for his method of doing business and thus make them consider the implications of losing an energetic agent. No copy of their reply survives, but they would have wished to dissuade him from giving up the UK business, not least because of their lack of confidence in Kelley and the absence of a suitable alternative agent.

In the event, Burroughs managed to get back to Medina in May 1879, but only for a few weeks. He returned to England in early July and moved the office into new space in Snow Hill. Clearly he was not giving up on his British business; quite the contrary, he was working harder than ever to ensure its success. In a comparatively short period between 1878 and 1880 the firm's long list of products and growing reputation speak volumes for his achievement. This had been accomplished in the face of a hostile market and obstacles which many others would have found insurmountable.

A snapshot of Burroughs's life in London at this time survives in his little notebook, a cross between a journal and a 'pocket letter book', as he called it. Burroughs glued a photograph of Horse Guards Parade onto the cover, and its flimsy pages hold his handwritten letters and diary notes. The letters are in fact the carbon copies of those he sent to his sister Lina and retained by him as an aide-memoire. Although it covers only the period from late January to mid-March 1880 and was not kept daily, the pocket letter book gives us our first real insight into Burroughs, revealing a man enjoying a tremendously busy working and social life with a large circle of friends and acquaintances. He describes his business affairs and meetings, new schemes and daily developments with the firm, his work and leisure time, and observations on the people and places he saw in London. Although London had been his home for nearly two years, he still had no settled address and moved frequently between different boarding houses in Torrington Square, Bloomsbury, Cavendish Street, Herne Hill, and friends' houses in the suburbs.

Burroughs took advantage of every spare second to jot down thoughts and ideas – a habit he was to employ on all his travels. He noted the weather and the notorious fogs of London: one day it was so thick that, as he walked down Holborn to the office, he 'could not see across the street or anyone on the sidewalk until he was almost up against them', and another evening he lost his way walking from Holborn to Montagu Place. His walks could be very late indeed – setting off for home one moonlit night and arriving on a clear frosty morning.

London hosted numerous American ex-pats, and Burroughs was introduced to some by John Morgan Richards and his wife Laura, who had become 'almost the patriarch and matriarch of the American colony in London'.[22] Many Americans attended the City Temple, one of the earliest nonconformist churches in London, used by Congregationalists, Methodists, United Reformers and Presbyterians. It had a splendid large interior in new premises next to the new Holborn Viaduct, a stone's throw from the firm's Snow Hill office. Burroughs frequently attended lunchtime or evening services and lectures and met friends there. Laura Richards introduced him to its celebrated pastor, the Rev. Dr Joseph Parker, whose sermons attracted huge crowds and whom Burroughs soon befriended; Burroughs later presented the Temple with a stained-glass window in memory of David Livingstone.

Through Laura Richards, Burroughs met her sisters Susie Arnold and Mrs Terry, 'two of the best women in the world kind hearted, jolly, sensible'; Mr Terry was a manager and tobacco manufacturer. Burroughs spent many Sundays with the family of Mr Gardner, a commission agent, later a glass manufacturer, delighting in playing with the children. Their daughter Anna said that he was like a brother to her, and Burroughs wrote of them that they were 'just the right sort of people to have as friends ... kind hearted sincere and true.' Other acquaintances were Mrs De L'Isle, who lived in Montagu Street; Philip Justice, an iron and steel merchant whose son was a patent agent; Mr Gosnell (whose face resembled pictures Burroughs had seen of Prince Albert); Mr Gladstone, a soap and perfume manufacturer ('a prudent business man' and 'one of the best specimens of a fine old English gentleman I have ever seen or known'); John Moss, a manufacturing chemist and merchant shipping agent ('a very good fellow'), who wanted to join Burroughs in business and had a 'cosy home' in Croydon; Mr and Mrs Bishop, in whose 'kind and genial company' he always had a very pleasant time (Alfred Bishop joined him in Kepler and later gave a large loan to the firm); and the Wilsteads. Others were encountered at his lodging houses: when 'a whole cargo of young ladies from Boston' stayed at Miss Warner's lodgings in Torrington Square, Burroughs greatly regretted missing them.

A typical weekly routine saw Burroughs getting up early to get into work ahead of everyone else. If possible he walked or took a bus part of the way, and when further out he caught the train to Holborn Viaduct and crossed the road to arrive at the Snow Hill office at about 9am. There he sorted out orders for Beef and Tonic Wine, filtered and bottled the wine, dealt with general finances and sales with Mr Kelley, and then set out to visit various doctors, hospitals or pharmaceutical firms. In town he might attend the City Temple at noon, then lunch with Mr Kelley, Mr Sudlow, or a business acquaintance such as Mr Gardner, or he might cut lunch 'to be economical'. Some weeks he took a train to provincial cities to attend meetings and visit doctors and hospitals to make contacts and get orders. In the evening he was frequently invited for dinner with friends, followed by games and dancing, or he might return to the City Temple and then dine, for example, at the Holborn Restaurant. Alternatively there was the theatre, a concert or an opera or a more formal supper or ball. The walk home could be very late – after midnight – and Burroughs must have been exhausted at times. On Saturdays he would often work in the office and spend the weekend as a guest of friends enjoying outings, with Sunday morning church service, walks, concerts and high teas. One Sunday he reported hearing Charles Spurgeon, the famous preacher, give a sermon at the Great Metropolitan Tabernacle. Business acquaintances, their wives and their relatives swept Burroughs into their circles, and he forged lasting friendships. Life was full and enjoyable and he was having 'a jolly good time'.

Many diary passages dwelt on the attractions of the fair sex, and it is all too evident that Burroughs – now aged 34 – was contemplating marriage if he could find the right woman. He took care with his appearance, on one occasion making 'as perfect a toilet as possible for the sake of a good impression' on a young lady. Pretty Miss Pocock had a 'very amiable expression, though not as positively amiable as the beautiful Miss Smith whose smile is like the gentle sunshine whose eyes look like the soft stars in the evening'; he missed seeing Miss Frost at the City Temple and felt 'lonesome and disconsolate at missing seeing Susie Arnold too'. Acquaintances with attractive wives or charming fiancées elicited comment. Mr Kelley was 'lucky to have such a splendid good wife. So sensible, straightforward, & true every time … so very good looking & not a bit of a flirt'; Mrs Whitmarsh was 'a model mother & wife & if I could get such a wife I would surely have every reason to be happy in this respect.'

Friends tried to pair him off: 'Dr Whitmarsh is going to introduce me to a lovely young lady whom both himself & Mrs W say would make a model wife.' One sunny Sunday he met an acquaintance, Miss Taylor, and they went to Westminster Abbey together. 'She looked very pretty, such red cheeks & lips she has a pleasant manner of speaking … the service most impressive.' But his mind did not stay on the service, or even on Miss Taylor, as he noted: 'I think of the beautiful lady in grey I met there with Miss Fairchild in September & I wonder if I'll ever see her again.' He was similarly inattentive when attending a church service with the Wilstead family and their dog: 'I like the big dog, but the clergyman is such a bore. A brawler without the least life or enthusiasm, whose sermon is a rehearsal of old proverbs & tame exhortations. Such a pretty young lady sat with us. Black hair and eyes and a Madonna-like face and dear soft complexion.'

It was the independent modern American woman Susie Arnold, however, to whom he came closest at this time. A Bostonian studying music and art in London, she invited him to join her at concerts and sent him a Valentine and box of peanuts she had roasted herself. 'Had a lovely time at the [Prince's] theatre … Miss Arnold's always agreeable company and such a nice ride taking her home in the moonlight and stopping to say goodnight on the porch.' At lunch at the Richards, Burroughs notes that, 'in spite of plans to get me on the other side of the table alongside of Miss Pearl [their daughter] – very nice but so quiet – I did get a seat by Miss Susie – and had scraps of chats with her while smuggling off her napkin under the table cloth.'[23] It was very mischievous and fun. The quiet Miss Pearl went on to become Pearl Craigie, a celebrated writer who wrote under the pen-name John Oliver Hobbes.[24] Burroughs later wrote of Susie as a splendid girl, ambitious and independent: 'Lucky man who gets her for a wife'.[25]

Burroughs was excellent company, and his presence was in demand at social gatherings. He loved dancing and attended countless balls. A certain Miss Scott, 'although a vicar's daughter', was fond of dancing (there was still an aura of disapproval about dancing in some circles), and he delighted in having a partner who danced well but was unhappy when intermissions between dances were too long. He knew his steps too and commented gleefully on a male dancer making a mistake in the Lancers. An evening's entertainment in private homes might include dancing as well as magic-lantern shows, table croquet, music and amateur dramatics.

His love of pretty women was matched by his pleasure of being with children. Clearly Burroughs loved his times with the Whitmarshes. He described Dr Michael Whitmarsh and his wife as 'a model married couple', and they reciprocated his warmth for them. They had three children, and Burroughs enjoyed 'romps' and outings with them. 'Not all children do I fancy but these three little chicks and I are always going to be the best of friends.'

London's buildings and parks impressed Burroughs. Mention is made of Queen Victoria Street, 'which is built up new & handsomely like the Viaduct to the Bank', and the streets in the West End which looked lively in the evenings. A January evening found him on the Thames Embankment, which looked 'very brilliant' illuminated by the new 'Russian Electric light': 'the long line of electric lights down the noble Embankment gleam bright and shine with the changing colors while they flash and dance upon the broad river in tremendous reflection.'[26]

Good meals were consumed at the Swiss Café, the Grosvenor Hotel, Brentinis, the Willis Rooms and the Holborn Restaurant, a favourite haunt, where he would join the chemists' assistants, who introduced him to several 'good fellows', all of whom he wanted as friends. Excursions took him out of town to the Crystal Palace, Kew Gardens and Windsor, where he rode through attractive countryside – his prose turning rather purple: 'velvet green fields and roads lined with old trees whose trunks were like huge pillars whose boughs like Gothic arches, met and overtwine high overhead ... the good birds' song a pretty welcome to the returning spring, while flocks of bad black crows were reconnoitring the newly planted cornfields.'

Public displays of affection surprised him. A walk in Hyde Park prompted the observation that it was a 'common & rather monotonous spectacle to see a soldier or anyone else with his sweetheart, with his arm round her waist, squeezing her hand with his disengaged paw at the same time … It is perhaps a sure sign that the red coats are loyal not only in their duty to Her Majesty but in affectionate regard of all her sex.' It would amuse the Americans, he thought, if this were done in broad daylight in Central Park, New York, or Fairmount Park, Philadelphia. As well as walking, Burroughs kept fit visiting the gym[27] and rowing up the Thames from Hammersmith or on the Serpentine, preferably with a young lady in tow.

Exciting sights and famous people were to be spotted. One day he saw troops of cavalry just home from Zululand; another day he went with the Misses Terry and Susie Arnold in a hansom to the Royal Chapel to see the Queen open Parliament. Clearly his American republican sentiments were suspended by the possibility of catching a glimpse of royal pageantry, and he took advantage of a friend who arranged a good platform for them to see the procession as it came from Whitehall gate and turned to Parliament: 'The carriages and Equipages were elegant and the horses superb. The Queen looked very amiable and bowed right and left to the crowd – The Prince of Wales was like his mother heartily cheered – the Beef eaters wore the costume of the olden days & trot their spears up from the Tower with them. The Queens band on horseback played [Gilbert and Sullivan's] Pinafore & Carmen while Her Majesty was in Parliament.'

All the exercise, dancing, rowing and walking agreed with Burroughs, who reported that he thought he was 'getting stronger and Mrs Terry says I'm getting fat & wants to know what has made my hair grow out so nicely.' He was happy and popular, with a large network of English and American friends and business contacts who drew him into their lives and sometimes gave him a substitute home life. They came from many walks of life, and it is notable that Burroughs emphasised their goodness rather than their wealth or usefulness when he wrote of them. Many of these friendships were to last throughout his life, despite onerous work and travels that took him away from London. Although he was clearly sorely tempted by the prospect of a wife and family of his own, Burroughs knew that he still had a great deal to do to place his business a long-term success.

Chapter 4

Brotherly Love and Henry Wellcome

I think we would make a pretty lively team in the
pharmaceutical line.[1]

Organising the business was difficult given Burroughs's frequent absence from the office to drum up customers and sales. In spite of Kelley's administrative abilities, his lack of training and knowledge in the pharmaceutical business hampered his effectiveness. Burroughs was aware soon after he arrived in London that he needed someone with knowledge of the trade to help him, especially as he wanted to create a market for the firm's goods overseas, and he realised that Kelley was not the man. Towards the end of 1878 he decided to approach his American friend Henry Wellcome to persuade him to come to England and join him.

Wellcome's background was very different from that of Burroughs. He was born in 1853 in Almond, Wisconsin, and his family suffered, as many others did, following failure of the potato crop in 1861. Believing that there was more wealth further west where Indian land was available cheaply, the family moved when he was eight to the small frontier settlement of Garden City, Minnesota. There his father, Solomon, went into part ownership of a drug store with his brother Jacob, and Wellcome helped his elder brother George in the shop. Solomon was not a good businessman, and he gave up store work to become a minister at the Adventist Church, subsequently becoming a Second Adventist preacher, which took him away from home for long periods. Adventism and its 'fanatical doctrine' were not to Wellcome's liking; though dutiful, he was not deeply religious. His father's letters after he left home were full of stern injunctions to obey the Lord, to be cautious of others and careful with his spending. He was much closer to his mother, to whom he wrote of 'striving to live a truly Christian life'. Garden City was a happy but strict religious community which did not make for an easy upbringing. Schooling took place in a log cabin, but this modest education did not prevent several of Wellcome's schoolfriends doing exceptionally well in their careers.

Despite hardships, there were hunting, shooting and fishing excursions, and Wellcome enjoyed aspects of frontier life, including spending some time with the local Winnebago Indians. He was very close to his uncle Jacob, a highly respected doctor/surgeon who operated on the wounded following a Sioux uprising in 1862. The Sioux, Winnebago and other Native Americans were appallingly treated, and Wellcome recognised the injustices done to them and developed a lifelong respect for them. Having left school at 13 to work in the family store, he decided that a career as a farmer or doctor did not appeal. Indication of the aspiring businessman can be seen in his 'invention' and manufacture at the age of 16 of a magic ink, which he promoted as 'The Greatest Wonder of the Age'. His interest in chemistry and pharmacy was stimulated by two Englishmen: H.J. Barton, who opened a pharmacy in Garden City, and William Worrall Mayo, a friend of Solomon. Stifled by the rigid community and keen to move on, in 1870 he found work in Rochester as a prescription clerk for the pharmaceutical chemist Poole & Geisinger, where Mayo also worked.[2] The testimonial that he took with him from Garden City described him as 'honest as the day is long and no bad habits of character about him'.[3] Mayo urged Wellcome to obtain a qualification in pharmacy. While he initially considered going to the Philadelphia College of Pharmacy, he did not wish to commit to working there for two years. Instead he opted for the Chicago College of Pharmacy, which he attended until the following summer, at which point he changed his mind and in 1873 took a post with an apothecary in Philadelphia and enrolled at the Pharmacy College there, four years before Burroughs.

After leaving home Wellcome supported his family whenever he could, but his father had to loan him $20 to start his pharmacy course. He did not make many friends in Chicago and was sometimes lonely, but he enjoyed Philadelphia more. One of his fellow students there was Frederick Power, who had been a close friend since boyhood. Power went on to become director of the Department of Pharmacy at the University of Wisconsin and later still was employed by Wellcome. One particular anecdote reveals Wellcome's ambition to escape poverty. He had stayed with the Power family for Christmas 1874 and showed his worn-out wallet to Power's mother, telling her, 'You see this Mrs Power? A pretty poor showing; only a few cents in it now; someday it will be bulging.'[4] Wellcome and Power went so far as to consider the possibility of going into business together and discussed plans to do so with their tutor, Professor Remington.

Wellcome's college thesis was an essay on urethral suppositories, in which he argued the case for good design, composition, and manufacture using a mould. His ideas were subsequently taken up by others, and he probably regretted not having patented his invention, a mistake he was careful not to repeat. After qualifying in 1874 he applied to McKesson & Robbins and Caswell Hazard & Co., two of the most important pharmaceutical firms in New York; he joined the latter firm for two years before moving to McKesson & Robbins.

Writing did not come easily to Wellcome, as he himself admitted, and his early letters are stilted and contain grammatical errors. Nevertheless he learnt quickly and contributed usefully to pharmaceutical literature, producing nine papers in American and English pharmaceutical journals between 1874 and 1880. He undertook several exploratory missions and reported on his travels in America, Canada, Mexico, and Central and South America. In Ecuador he studied the native cinchona forests (cinchona bark was at the time the source of the active ingredient quinine) and published a highly regarded account of them in the *Proceedings* of the American Pharmaceutical Association. His rapturous descriptions of the wildlife and forests, where 'balmy, zephyr-like breezes gently fan us into a dreamy fanciful mood that we could easily have imagined ourselves transported into a fairyland', echoed the similar flowery descriptions found in Burroughs's travel writings.

The two men had much else in common. Both had seen their families affected by problems and ill health and had lived in small communities where mutual support was necessary. Both had fathers who were absent from home for long periods, and both developed strong affections for their uncles who mentored them in their youth. Both were quick-minded men with a background of many years' experience in pharmacy, having worked in their family shops and as clerks. Both had travelled extensively for pharmaceutical firms where they were respected as good salesmen/detail men. Both trained at the Philadelphia College of Pharmacy. Both were attracted to the company of women. Most importantly, both were keenly aware of the changes in society around them and highly ambitious to be movers and shakers in the rapidly changing pharmaceutical world.

That said, their backgrounds also contained great contrasts. Family and community were key to Burroughs, who enjoyed a very close relationship with his aunt, sisters, and others in Medina, and he stayed there until he was 19 despite, or indeed partly because of, the tragedies of close family deaths. Medina was larger than Garden City, with an ever-changing population, and the Burroughs family were the wealthiest in the town. Wellcome, on the other hand, had suffered the trauma of an early move at the age of eight; his father was a failed shopkeeper, and his family one of the poorest in a town which evidently lacked the Medina community spirit. Tellingly, Wellcome wrote that he liked Rochester because people there seemed to take an interest in him that he never experienced elsewhere – unlike Garden City, where 'you know how it was ... everyone for themselves (unfortunately).' A vast difference in their fathers and family life inevitably coloured their attitudes to others. Burroughs's father was a highly successful politician, knowledgeable and well respected, who shared opinions with his family and women friends, admired independent thought and was a role model to his son, who learnt trust and openness from him. In spite of difficult times Burroughs had not suffered real hardship, had had a very good education, and his career had been comparatively straightforward; he was self-confident and made friends easily. Wellcome, in contrast, had no sisters, and his was a male-dominated household without close female companionship. He lacked Burroughs's easy-going manner, and some found him stiff and hard to engage in conversation. His father instilled in him a suspicious nature, advised caution and wariness of those around him, and warned that too much female society would lead him to be fickle-minded (girls being 'fickle as the wind as a general thing'). Burroughs's Presbyterian belief dictated his lifelong desire to serve others, whereas, although both his parents were deeply religious and Adventism dominated his upbringing, in maturity Wellcome's faith was not particularly significant. He suffered a tougher struggle to rise in the world and was always acutely conscious of his position and status. These differences conditioned the two men's attitudes to work, friendship, marriage and the conduct of their lives and in time were to affect their relationship. For now, however, all was brotherly love and friendship between them.

Rather surprisingly, there is no record of the first encounter between Burroughs and Wellcome. It is possible that they both attended the APhA meeting in Boston in 1875.[5] An alternative suggestion, made by Robert Rhodes James, is that they came across each other in

Philadelphia when Burroughs was in Wyeths' employ there and Wellcome attending college. This is likely, since both men were in the city at the same time in 1873–4, although Burroughs was often absent. Later, while working for McKesson & Robbins in New York from May 1876, Wellcome sold their range of drugs, which included their new gelatine-coated pills, and was therefore then in competition with Wyeths; Burroughs's thesis of 1877 on compressed medicines would thus have been of great interest to him. Both men travelled the same pharmaceutical trail and attended meetings of the APhA, and Wellcome almost certainly attended the Philadelphia Centennial APhA meeting, which had been largely organised by their college teacher and mentor Professor Remington. Clearly by 1876 their paths had crossed, and they became acquaintances and then good friends. This is confirmed by their first recorded correspondence – a letter dated 31 October 1877 from Burroughs to Wellcome.[6] In this letter Burroughs recommended friends on whom Wellcome might call on his commercial travels and suggested a joint holiday the following summer and/or a journey of some kind in England. The letter was jocular, friendly and personal, suggesting that they had known each other for some time. Wellcome himself regarded this period as one when he and Burroughs were 'bosom friends'.[7] It was with this background of friendship at the end of his first year in London that Burroughs invited Wellcome to join him in business.

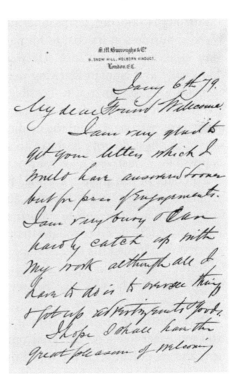

Wellcome initially expressed a cautiously positive interest. He indicated that he would like to visit England and took up Burroughs's suggestion that while he was attending an APhA meeting in Toronto he would visit Burroughs's

10: Letter from Burroughs to Wellcome, 6 January 1879, discussing Burroughs's work and expressing his hope that Wellcome will join him.

family in Medina. Burroughs subsequently reported that his sister was 'much pleased' with his 'too short visit' and that his uncle and aunt were much encouraged by it. 'My dear Friend Wellcome', he wrote:

> I am very glad to get your letters which I would have answered sooner but for press of engagements. … I hope I shall have the great pleasure of welcoming you to these hospitable shores at an early day as soon as your engagement will allow you to come. You need not say to McK&R that you certainly will never come back but rather that you are coming over here to spy out the country or prospect it. And my opinion is that you will report so favourably that you will decide to unite your fortunes with mine. I think we would make a pretty lively team in the pharmaceutical line.[8]

Burroughs laid out terms offering 'to give or sell an interest' in Wyeths' business at its cost to him and get him some stock in Kepler Malt at about 10% advance. He went on to cite figures confirming that Kepler and Nubian Blacking were doing well and reported on his agencies and foreign trade. Possible new products were mentioned: 'I think that good goods of this sort would take immediately & get permanent patronage from the medical profession. We are on the right side of the best doctors & mean to strengthen our position as much as possible … Just you take your next vacation over here & I haven't much doubt of you staying a while.' He asked Wellcome not to discuss his plans with any in the pharmaceutical trade: 'I don't want anyone to know what we are up to.'[9] Business talk was combined with chat about shared friends. Burroughs thanked Wellcome for sending photos which now adorned his office: 'hope you saw the little darling Miss K in Toronto', he tantalisingly noted, and referred to their mutual friend Maggie Steers, who was a go-between for some of their letters as she lived in New York.

Over the following year similar letters were sent by Burroughs, who was eager to encourage Wellcome, emphasising the success of the firm and its potential in the world market and offering various deals: Wellcome was the only person with whom he felt that he could work, success beckoned, and once Wellcome had come over and seen matters for himself he would agree to join him.[10] Along with the friendly banter about business contacts and mutual friends, Burroughs appears to have assumed a partnership by the directness of his approach. Since

Wellcome's side of this correspondence has not survived, we cannot judge how he responded, but friendly exchanges continued; Wellcome even sent over some birds (probably parrots) from Peru for Miss Graham and other lady friends of Burroughs.

The carrot of prosperity was constantly dangled in front of Wellcome. 'Think there is a big show for manufacturing Ph[armaceutical] preparations & if we go into it will be about the 1st in the field. Our house is the only one in the kingdom making a <u>business</u> of calling on doctors with samples of new things.' Only after Wellcome had seen for himself should he decide: 'I would not want you to do so till then. I think we can make big fortunes over here if we work things right & we ought to know how to do this with our combined experience.'

In addition Wellcome could 'join him or not' in Wyeths' malt extract and he would 'let him in at just cost to him charging nothing on personal account time etc.' Burroughs was also keen to manufacture a line of fluid extracts and elixirs, believing that quality goods of this sort would immediately find a market among the medical profession.[11] To do this he reiterated that he needed a competent man to assist him in the business and take turns with him in travelling. 'We have travellers out but I find the trade like to see one of the heads of a concern they are dealing with.'[12]

An important letter of August 1879 from Burroughs went astray, so he wrote again that October. 'I am making money already pretty lively in some branches of my business. Keep this quiet though as we don't want to encourage Americans to come over here to start in competition with us.' He expanded on his offer: Wellcome could have an interest in Wyeths and Kepler on account of his services, and without putting in capital, and join him in the manufacturing business, or he would do the manufacturing if Wellcome would assist in the management of the business for a salary and an interest in the profits – 'In fact I am open to make any sat[isfactory] offer arrangement with you.' And he reiterated the suggestion of a short vacation when Wellcome could look around: 'I have no doubt [it] will lead to your going into business with me.' He threw in the bait of Miss Graham again: 'I am sure Miss Graham would be delighted to see you. She will probably stay here all winter so you will have to come over to see her anyway.' He concluded with the suggestion that Wellcome obtain agency rights from McKesson & Robbins; he would offset Wyeths' business to them and they could go into business equally. There was a final plea: 'I have no partner here. You are the man I want to pull with & we have confidence in each others ability & straightforwardness.'[13]

Eager to move plans forward, he now offered to pay Wellcome's fare for a proposed trip to England in April the following year, adding that Maggie Steers and her mother and sister might join him on the same steamer. Then Burroughs could go to America with the Steers a month or two later, or, alternatively, if the Steers travelled later he might return with them from the States in late summer or early in the fall. He sent Wellcome and Maggie photographs of London. 'I expect to see you over here soon. Don't fail to come ... I want to take a trip through India & Asia for our goods next winter at latest or else someone from our firm should go round the world. The Malt Ext[ract] business promises to develop into a big thing & our other articles take well too. We want a good line of gelatine coated pills also & then will have enough.'[14]

Wellcome could not have doubted Burroughs's abilities, energy and determination, though he might well have questioned how easily he could work alongside such a strong-willed and forceful personality. But crucially he was unable to finance joining Burroughs on an equal basis, or even on a one-third basis, while he presumably did not want to come for a salary. For these reasons, and because he was cautious by nature, Wellcome did some homework, asking Wyeths and others about Burroughs's prospects, and he took his time.

Finally, in February 1880, Burroughs was delighted to hear that Wellcome intended coming over. To Maggie Steers he wrote: 'I just read a very wellcome [sic] letter from our dear friend W H Wellcome whom I am happy to say is coming over here and with a prospect of uniting his fortunes in business with mine. He is one of my very best friends & in whom I have perfect confidence both as to integrity friendship & business ability. ... Wellcome is just the one & I think the only one I would care to have join me here.'[15] To Wellcome he replied:

I am not the sort of a chap to flatter anyone but I would rather have you for a business partner in my present business than anyone I know. At present there are such a multitude of things to be attended to that require experience in this particular branch of pharmacy & medicine that I am constantly kept in the office & warehouse when I would like to be on the road half the time. I don't like to be in town all the while any more than I like or travel from January to December, but think that a division of labour in my present business not only pleasant but much the most profitable ... Even if you do not decide to remain here with me I don't think you will ever regret the trip to this country & the Continent. I will be glad to go with you if possible to Germany & France. I am doing some business with those countries already and ought to have a very large trade with them.

This was followed by a stream of suggestions about possible additional agencies and American contacts: Wellcome should call on Messrs Lanman & Kemp (with whom he had been negotiating) and, if it seemed suitable, tell them of his proposed partnership. Burroughs concluded: 'come over here as soon as you can conveniently, as I wish to visit America in the spring but not till you have been here. Perhaps I shall come early & return here with you God willing.'[16]

Meanwhile Wellcome started negotiating with McKesson & Robbins about becoming their agent in Europe, and they offered him a salary rise if he stayed with them. By the beginning of April, before setting out for England, he negotiated a contract with them which not only gave him exclusive agency for McKesson & Robbins's preparations in Europe, Asia, Africa, the East Indies and Australia but granted him the status of an associate with the partners. Interestingly, Wellcome hedged his bets on the success of working with Burroughs, as the contract included a clause that the agreement would apply to any firm while Wellcome was with it. Wellcome's Uncle Isaac opposed his move, but, undeterred, he set off, writing of his uncle to his mother from the Atlantic steamer SS *City of Berlin*: 'he cannot judge of my projects as well as I can … I do not expect to fail.'

When Burroughs and Wellcome met in London in the spring of 1880 the *Chemist and Druggist* carried a note that 'Henry S. Wellcome is now we believe in London with Messrs Burroughs & Co and is likely to stay among us', which might have been rather premature news but was good publicity. Wellcome's biographer states that this meeting was unsatisfactory, but does not say why, and the men soon reached an understanding. Wellcome undertook a brief inspection of English chemists after his arrival and then set out on a tour of the major cities of Europe, returning in mid-August after an enjoyable visit, although over-exertion and excessive heat in Rome and Naples had caused him 'nervous prostration'.[17] Burroughs meanwhile set off for America in mid-May to visit his family and talk to the Wyeths; he was away until the end of August.

He left the office in the charge of the two invaluable new staff members he had appointed the previous year – Robert Sudlow and William Kirby.[18] Sudlow's abilities were already evident, and he soon became an essential part of the firm, running it in Burroughs's absence. Writing to Wyeths from Vienna, Wellcome explained why the two men had not finalised their partnership at once and that, although they had 'arrived at a general understanding', they thought it right that Burroughs lay the matter before [Wyeths] and his Uncle Isaac for consideration and advice. Both also wanted Wyeths' advice concerning relations with Mr Kelley, which they now proposed to sever.[19] John Wyeth, in a later letter to Wellcome, praised Burroughs, whose 'energy is exceptional, and his assiduity most commendable', but noted that the firm had not received the expected remuneration anticipated from the greatly improved sales of their goods. He put this down to Burroughs trying to do too much and being distracted by other agencies: they preferred him to canvass physicians and druggists personally rather than advertising in medical journals. They added that Burroughs had not asked for advice on his proposed deal with Wellcome but had intimated instead that he 'would like some change or modification' with them, adding 'We do not know what he wanted nor did we think he knew himself.'[20]

It was inevitable that Wyeths would consider the many sidelines in which Burroughs engaged as interfering with their agency work. In fact Burroughs was quite sure of his plans but deliberately did not say too much to Wyeths, since they centred on the growth of his own company, which would manufacture and sell goods. He used many methods to sell his and Wyeths' goods, had a greater knowledge of the UK market and its workings than they did, and some of his agencies, especially Kepler, were already proving good money-earners for the firm.

On the return from their travelling in August, the two men finally thrashed out the detail of a partnership, and a Deed of Partnership was signed on 27 September 1880. Wellcome brought to it a five-year agency for McKesson & Robbins's sugar-coated pills and other products for sale outside the Americas, although other British firms also had agency rights with them. The terms of the deal are revealing. In Wellcome, Burroughs was convinced he had someone he could trust to help run the show and was prepared to pay heavily for him. Partnership capital of the business was set at £2,000, a significant amount for such a new firm. Burroughs, as senior partner, held two-thirds (£1,200) and Wellcome one-third (£800). But, as Wellcome literally could not raise more than £400, Burroughs lent him £550 (at 10% interest) to allow him to get established. Profits and losses were to be divided according to the ratio of each partner's investment. The agreement was for ten years, but at the end of five years either partner, by giving the other six months' notice in writing, could end the partnership. At any time after two years Wellcome could, if he so desired, increase his capital

Silas M. Burroughs   Henry S. Wellcome

11: Photographs of Burroughs and Wellcome taken around the time they became business partners in 1880.

holding until it became equal in amount to that held by his partner. Kepler Malt Extract Ltd was adopted by the newly named Burroughs, Wellcome & Co. (BW&Co.).[21] Burroughs retained his interests in the Nubian Blacking Company, though he now shed his management of it, and Kelley's contract was terminated.

The significance of Burroughs's achievement before he went into partnership with Wellcome has been noted by Roy Church. Had it not been for Burroughs and the strong foundations he laid based on a good marketing strategy, the later achievements and scientific advances of BW&Co. in the 1890s would not have occurred. An observer commented on his 'singular mastery of detail', which he demonstrated time and again in his management.[22] It was Burroughs's innovative marketing skills that introduced American products as 'New Inventions' and recognised what the market wanted (and at this time it was the consumer, not modern science, that dictated the market). To underline the point, it was the Burroughs brand name under which the firm sold its goods – with the exception of the McKesson & Robbins range brought by Wellcome. In the event, the latter goods sold poorly, undermining further Wellcome's contribution to the new firm, and their products were given up after five years without profit. It was Burroughs, too, who made two of the most important staff appointments for the firm – Sudlow and Kirby – flying in the face of accusations that he was a poor judge of character. Indeed, his choice of Wellcome as a partner showed an appreciation of the latter's many abilities, and the ultimate failure of their relationship can be attributed to many causes. Wellcome has been portrayed as the steady hand which controlled a wayward, extravagant Burroughs, who was a good salesman but lacked imagination and both practical and business sense. These supposed failures were far from true, as we will see.

Meanwhile – thanks to Burroughs's loan – Wellcome rented rooms near St James's Square, employed a cook–housekeeper and male servant who worked as valet and waiter, and enjoyed London life. His friends included many actors and actresses and the celebrated comedian Frank Lincoln. He left for America at the end of the year to discuss matters with McKesson & Robbins, returned in January 1881, and wrote to his mother that all was going well with the work, praising his partner: 'Burroughs is an American – and a real energetic one too.' The only thing that worried him was his debt, but he promised to send his mother

12: Display of products at the International Sanitary Exhibition, 1881.

$50 soon,[23] and that summer he moved to a larger house in Marylebone Road. He was rarely in the office before 10.00, took a long lunch and left the office shortly after 4pm.[24]

During 1881 the firm continued to operate as it had before, its products being mainly those of Burroughs & Co. Burroughs continued to travel around England, and both men reportedly had 'a pleasant time' attending the annual meeting of the British Association for the Advancement of Science in York in August. By now there were enough travellers for the firm to introduce a centralised information system recording their visits to medical men and chemists for use in future approaches. A code was used to distinguish the class of shop, the reception given to the salesman, the attitude of the shop/medical professional, and the state of their business and its order and stock, including blunt personal notes such as 'old fogey', 'useless' and 'toney'.[25]

The International Medical and Sanitary Exhibition at South Kensington held in July 1881 was a major success. A photograph shows the BW&Co. stand with a magnificent display under draped American flags, with 'American Improvements in Pharmacy' emblazoned in large letters above the name of the firm. Yet, in spite of praise from the medical press, no prizes were won by the firm, leading Wellcome to cable Burroughs: 'no awards, simply disgraceful'.[26] This example of hostility towards an American business was recognised as unjust, and the ensuing publicity turned out to be good for the firm. BW&Co. now had an assured place in Britain and, with a partner and a management structure in place, Burroughs could concentrate on the next stages of his ambition – to break into the international market.

Chapter 5

'A Little Excursion'

I think I can do well by working up and more firmly
establishing our trade in more distant parts.[1]

On Wednesday, 26 October 1881, Burroughs took a cab to his lodgings in Leinster Terrace, off the Bayswater Road, where he hastily breakfasted, packed and rushed off to catch a train to Southampton. With 15 minutes to spare he wrote to Wellcome asking him to forward his overcoat and 200 business cards – mentioning that a spare ticket to a ball that Friday would now be unused. His decision to travel had been made on the spur of the moment after learning that the SS *Ceylon*, a steam yacht, was due to sail on a world voyage: he had intended to travel to build up a market overseas for some time; now he spotted an ideal opportunity and acted with alacrity, planning initially, as he later said, simply on 'a little excursion to the South of France'.

The occasion was a historic one, for this was the first commercial 'around the world' cruise. Undertaking a world tour for pleasure had become easier and cheaper as the century progressed, with new routes and ports opening up. Crucially, the opening of the Suez Canal in 1869 meant going east was now much simpler. Such changes had enabled Thomas Cook to organise his first round the world tour in 1872, inspiring Jules Verne to write *Around the World in Eighty Days*.[2] 'Globe-trotting' was the new attraction in the 1870s and 1880s: affordable and no longer quite as dangerous or uncomfortable as it had been previously, 'ocean yachting' enabled the traveller to see the world through their own eyes.[3] Businesses could also take advantage of the improved communications, and there could not have been a better time for Burroughs to use the opportunities this cruise presented.

The *Ceylon*'s voyage was unusual in that passengers would be able to leave and rejoin it at different stages. Should passengers unanimously wish to visit any place not included in the programme, this would be permitted – providing it did not delay the journey beyond the estimated time. Thus Burroughs could make contacts in new places. He was probably also attracted by the advertisement for the cruise, which pushed all the principal places of interest around the world that would be visited 'at a cost greatly inferior, and with a comfort greatly superior', to those using ordinary mail and passenger steamers. Passengers had 'subscribed' rather than paid £500 each for the voyage, evidently to underline that it was an elite party. Since the yacht was delayed loading stores at Southampton, Burroughs had been able to get a berth at the last minute and almost certainly booked at first to go only to Marseille via Spain and Portugal, at a cost of £25 for 19 days.[4] The flexibility of these arrangements thoroughly suited him.[5]

The *Ceylon* finally set off on 29 October and was soon crossing the Bay of Biscay bound for Lisbon. Burroughs busily noted tasks to be done by Wellcome.[6] In Lisbon he was pleased to get samples through the custom house without difficulty – no duties were payable on

13: The SS *Ceylon*, c. 1880. Burroughs sailed on the yacht from Southampton to Bombay at the beginning of her round the world cruise.

medicines there – and during the two-day stopover he visited doctors and chemists. The only English doctor was in the British Naval Hospital, and he had hardly any private practice; none of the chemists spoke English, so Burroughs relied on an interpreter. He complained that they were 'rather a slow lot'; he called on one half a dozen times, always to find him eating or taking some recreation. When his money ran low he requested two more £20 cheques from the firm, plus a copy of Thomas Henry Huxley's *Lessons in Elementary Physiology* (1866).

At Gibraltar orders were taken from all the good chemists and samples given to most of the doctors. In Malaga Burroughs contacted the American consul, a standard method of making trade contacts at this time and his usual procedure when travelling.[7] He heard that the Spanish were enthusiastic medicine-takers but that the drugs there were very unreliable, the problem being the bad quality of the chemicals used rather than the dispensers. Use of translations and labelling of the firm's products preoccupied Burroughs throughout the trip. He suggested having a pamphlet printed in Spanish carrying the best parts of the firm's recent reports and a complete list of all their goods wrapped around each bottle of Hazeline, Beef and Tonic Wine and Malt. His easy-going manner and engaging personality led to invitations to people's homes: he made several good friends, was entertained by the family of the British consul, and on his last evening in Malaga enjoyed a very pleasant ball on the *Ceylon* attended by some local ladies. With the exception of Bordeaux, Burroughs reckoned on good prospects for the firm in each of the towns he had visited.

Apart from the Bay of Biscay the weather had been fine, but when the *Ceylon* left Malaga for Marseille on 13 November she nearly did so without Burroughs. He recounted to Wellcome the dramatic incident which occurred in Malaga Bay:

> I was returning to the ship just before the time she was to sail. There was a wind and heavy swell against us, and I took an oar with the boatman. It was a heavy boat for two, and we got on slowly with hard work. While we were pulling away, giving all attention to the oars, the Spaniard suddenly cried out, and looking around I saw a big white ship coming right down upon us in full sail. At first I thought she was going for the open bay, and backed water to head for the mole on her right, when she headed for the same direction, and would be smashing through our boat in another half-minute. I was so bewildered I hardly knew what to do, and pulled away without hardly knowing it. She passed us barely, her anchor

swinging within a hand's breadth of us, dipping in the huge waves, and then leaping swiftly and high into the air as the ship rose and fell, for they were making ready to drop anchor. One of those great ugly hooks was pointed toward us; a stroke less by my unwitting hands on that oar would have left us before the swift and solid bows of the ship, which would shiver our boat in a second; half a stroke less and that terrible anchor would have torn through us, lifting our boat like an egg-shell and dashing it under the waves. Our escape was most providential – apparently almost miraculous. My life was saved by God, and henceforth belongs to Him; therefore, in my future, may it be the great aim and study of my life so to labour as best to serve Him, and do good in the world.[8]

This brush with death reinforced Burroughs's determination to devote his life to the cause of doing good, and from this date his copy of the New Testament included annotations and underlining of passages which he now studied more closely than ever.[9]

Burroughs was frustrated at being unable to land samples in Marseille and was obliged to tranship them to a steamer going to Barcelona, which he planned to accompany.[10] At Marseille the American consul arranged for his business cards to be sent to consuls at some of the towns he was to visit, and Burroughs appointed an agent there. Then on the following day he determined to continue on the *Ceylon* to Genoa, Naples, Palermo and Malta, 'where I will probably stop … perhaps will go thence to Alexandria as I hear there is a good chance to sell drugs there.'[11] At Malta he expected to learn if Wellcome needed him in London: if not he would go on to Athens, Smyrna, Constantinople and Alexandria, hoping to secure local agents in each place. Informed by Wellcome that all was fine, he pushed on. Quarantine problems at Genoa delayed the *Ceylon* landing, and with only two hours there he accomplished nothing. In Palermo, his next stop, he secured as an agent Ottavio Dotto, the son of a professor of chemistry.

The *Ceylon* tied up for several days in Naples, where Burroughs hoped to appoint another agent.[12] With time on his hands, he wrote a long, mainly personal letter to Sudlow, describing his journey and his visit to Pompeii. A night view of the city was a high point, and from his porthole he could see electric lights along the railway leading nearly to the summit of Vesuvius looking like 'a ladder of stars'. On the work front he enquired whether Dr Power had arrived in London yet and, if so, whether he would assist Sudlow in correspondence relating to scientific or professional inquiries 'which medical men may sometimes make'.[13] He generously offered during his absence the use of his room and furniture at 24 Leinster Terrace to Sudlow, or Dr Power, Mr Hine or Mr Kirby, should Wellcome not have returned from Paris to share with him. Copies of the periodicals [*Christian*] *Commonwealth* and *Fountain* were requested, and he sent his proposed new itinerary: Alexandria to Brindisi, Venice, Bologna, Florence, Genoa, Marseille, then back home via Milan, Switzerland, Germany and Belgium. Sudlow had to handle these complicated travelling plans.

There were persistent difficulties in landing samples. The captain had been able to unload only at Malta and nowhere else before or after. Burroughs now determined to stay longer on the *Ceylon*, since he might have difficulty in catching steamers from port to port, whereas the *Ceylon* usually stopped long enough in each to enable him to do his business. His new itinerary now included Cairo.

The journey continued through 'the loveliest seas and weather'. In Malta Burroughs considered it unlikely that sales would do well, as there was only one English chemist, all the doctors were locals, and 'the native population too poor'. A short stop at Piraeus – the port at Athens – at the beginning of December was followed by another at Constantinople, where he reported being very busy, adding enthusiastically that Turkey offered a 'splendid field' for the firm.[14]

As he travelled, Burroughs managed to take in key sights in Athens and Rhodes, delighting in an evening waltzing on board while the ship sailed into the narrow harbour at Rhodes. He reflected not only on the beauties of the scenery but also on imponderable questions posed by faith, and he jotted down reflections on biblical proverbs. In his small notebook he recalled reading a history of the Jews and being deeply impressed with their industry and thrift, which had enabled them to overcome apparently insurmountable disadvantages with every man's hand against them. 'I am now convinced', he noted, 'that if I would make that progress in a useful life which is my ambition, living to the Glory of God and the credit of my good name, accomplishing something besides the mere drudgery of life I must be up & doing in the morning, not later than six o'clock, when there is time for thought and preparation and the higher labours of life. So make it be.' Similar resolutions were repeated throughout his journey.

From Alexandria Burroughs took a train to Cairo, where he visited the only English pharmacist and appointed an agent to represent the firm in Egypt. After ordering more samples for India and pamphlets to be printed in several languages, he enquired of Wellcome how the balance was looking: 'I hope on the right side lately?' Presents were purchased for his family in the bazaar, and sightseeing notes mention the primitive irrigation system of a windlass for hoisting water, the huts of the Egyptian farmers, the tropical gardens of the hotel, the dark rich soil, the Pyramids and, on a less exotic note, the fact that the eyes of babies were full of flies. One Sunday he found some of his friends from the *Ceylon* in the garden of the New Hotel. The evening air was so delightful that he joined them visiting the Pyramids again, rather than attending church as intended. Guilt set in afterwards, and he vowed that in the future he would spend the day more quietly in the work of God. To his friends he wrote: 'My journey as you will expect has been of the greatest instruction and enjoyment and also made me more than ever grateful that I am a citizen of our great Republic and a descendant of the pure blood of England which is so far removed from the oppression of these benighted lands.'[15]

In Alexandria, Burroughs heard from Wellcome, who wrote that business was going well and suggested: 'Now that you have gone so far and at such heavy expense it would be little extra to go to India where you might do a profitable business if you adhere to our regular terms.'[16] Burroughs responded with far more ambitious plans: 'I am thinking that it may pay to canvass Australia and New Zealand while I am down in that direction. What do you think about it and returning home by way of China, Japan, S[outh] Islands, and San Francisco. This is a job that must be done sometime and the sooner its off our hands the better perhaps.'[17] His 'little excursion' had now become a journey that would take him all round the world.

The rail journey to the port of Suez from Cairo to rejoin the *Ceylon* took eight hours, and her arrival was delayed a couple of days by the volume of shipping in the canal. After hot cloudless days the night of 20 December saw a torrential downpour – the first rain there for ten months – and the yacht set sail for Bombay the following day.

By now passengers knew each other well and had developed a fondness for the *Ceylon* during their voyage.[18] Acutely aware of the opportunity that travel afforded him, Burroughs decided to try to publish some of his observations, based on his journals and letter books. On board he wrote to Pearl Richards – who by now was an increasingly successful author – reminding her of her earlier suggestion that he write about the places he visited. He suggested that Pearl try to publish one of his articles in the *Medina Tribune* 'or your *Orleans American* or some other unambitious country paper'.[19]

The Christian Commonwealth for the Advocacy of Good and Right and Truth throughout the World also regularly published articles by Burroughs. 'We are fortunate', the *Commonwealth* announced, 'in having on board the *Ceylon* a very intelligent correspondent. He will accompany the ship part of the way, at least, on her voyage round the world, and will, from time to time, give our readers the result of his observations, in special letters to the *Commonwealth*.' One of its editors was Henry Varley, Burroughs's friend and a preacher at the City Temple. The journal was non-sectarian, evangelical in tone, chatty and informal, covering American news as well as political issues such as land nationalisation, and it took a strong line on temperance.[20]

To his Medina friends Burroughs wrote of the perfect sailing weather in the Gulf of Suez and across the Red Sea – not too hot, with a gentle breeze – 'like our July or August at home'.[21] They passed Mount Sinai the morning after setting off from Suez. Some passengers would get up at three or four in the morning to see the sunrise, with brilliant tints of colour on the mountains; sunsets were equally stunning. Canvas

1. The Dining Saloon. – 2. The Ladies' Boudoir. – 3. Deck View of the Vessel Looking Forward. – 4. General View of the Vessel.
THE YACHT CRUISE ROUND THE WORLD – NOTES ON BOARD THE INTER-OCEANIC YACHTING COMPANY'S STEAM SHIP "CEYLON"

14: Drawings of the SS *Ceylon* from *The Graphic*, vol. XXIV, no. 618, 1 October 1881.

awnings were spread over the deck to give shade, and only the slightest swell gave motion to the ship. On Christmas Day it was nearly 90 degrees Fahrenheit in the cabins and flying fish were spotted for the first time. The usual festivities were observed, with roast beef and plum pudding. Instead of the church service being in the cabin or saloon as usual, it was held on deck. Burroughs reflected on his proximity to Bethlehem and Medina, 'the ancient town from which our beloved village takes its name', and imagined the Medina of Arabia to be as beautiful in the east as his village was in the west.

Much of the voyage was delightful. Time was passed sitting on deck in the shade, reading, writing, drawing, painting, listening to the ship's orchestra, or simply looking at the changing colours and the sea, the 'delightful languor' induced by the weather, interrupted now and again by playing a lazy game of quoits. People fell asleep in easy Indian reclining chairs, and after dinner 'our excellent band of twelve plays to us, and occasionally couples are seen gently dancing under the soft moonlight: over any flirting of which some of our amorous pilgrims *may* have been guilty we will draw a veil,' Burroughs wrote. When not writing to his family and friends, reading, annotating passages from the New Testament, musing on the stars, or strolling on deck, he participated in the organised entertainments, including play-acting, and photographs show him with passengers and crew in fancy-dress costumes. At the end of the year he wrote to Wellcome that he was 'getting strong and healthy as ever thank the Lord', the implication being that he had not been too well.[22] The New Year was seen in by all the passengers gathered on deck for a prayer meeting, and after midnight they sat and sang in the moonlight until 2.30 in the morning. The heat increased as the voyage continued, and some passengers took to sleeping on deck. By the time the *Ceylon* docked at Bombay on 5 January 1882, it was 86 degrees in the shade. His delightful sea voyage over, it was time for Burroughs to face more marketing in a very challenging new country.

Chapter 6

'A Superficial Jaunt'? India and Ceylon

*I am very hopeful of laying the foundation for a big trade
in our goods in India.*[1]

While the SS *Ceylon* remained docked in Bombay, Burroughs recorded
his first impressions, and he admired its 'splendid big harbour, well
protected forts, public gardens and wide streets ... The public buildings
are very fine & the English part of the city is as beautiful as any town
I have ever seen.' He took detailed notes of the scenery, the people and
their customs.

The Esplanade Hotel was beautifully sited, overlooking the seafront
near the polo ground, and in the evening Burroughs could watch 'a
hundred games of cricket going on at the same time on the mile smooth
grounds between ... long avenues of trees'. The sun set over games of
lawn tennis, and Parsees – adherents of Zoroastrianism – assembled
in knots on the green or squatted on the grass on square bits of carpet
to play cards and other games. Mark Twain stayed at the same hotel in
1896, noting many of the similar sights and marvelling at the 'shining
and shifting spectacle'.[2] Carriages of Europeans with liveried footmen
sped by, and at the same time Burroughs was painfully aware of the
poverty around him, the 'miserable huts' of the natives and the hard
work of men and women alike. After nine in the evening scores of
local people were sound asleep along the street and under the awnings
of the hotel, servants lying in the hotel hallways or on the balcony.[3]
Although the mornings and evenings were cool and pleasant, it was
'like walking between furnaces' on the sunny side of the street at
noon.[4]

New contacts were made in Bombay. One evening Burroughs attended a lecture at the Town Hall given by the Rev. Joseph Cook, a New Yorker and a Congregationalist, internationally famous as a writer and lecturer.[5] His teachings on Christ and the Gospel truths impressed Burroughs: 'the more I hear & see of this man the more he becomes one of my heroes and good examples to follow as best I may.'[6] They met and corresponded, encountering each other several more times during Burroughs's travels in India and Australasia.[7] He also befriended the minister of the Scottish Presbyterian church and was entertained by English friends in their large tent overlooking Malabar Bay. They served home cooking, which had much more flavour than the monotonous hotel dinners and reminded him of 'the good old times'. Over supper he found one guest to be 'a very intelligent woman bright talker', with sound ideas on politics, and wished that she had been viceroy instead of Lord Lytton: 'India would be millions better off and England would have thousands of her now dead ... alive.'[8]

After hearing a band playing 'Home Sweet Home', Burroughs wrote to Lina that, in spite of the kindness of strangers, he missed home and friends. He took comfort in writing when a visitor in a foreign land, 'where all or nearly all are strangers whose language is unintelligible to me whose customs are in many things offensive to every Christian.' Lina was updated on his busy schedule: how polite the government officers had all been, especially those connected with the Medical College and Army Medical Department, who appreciated the medicines he had introduced, and how he had refused the offer of an honorary membership of the Bombay Club because he was too busy with business and social engagements – and anyway his dress suit was heading to Calcutta on the *Ceylon*. Burroughs managed to take in many sights on his travels, and his notebooks and letters record his enjoyments of the wide streets of Poona, which he compared to Washington, the scenery of places such as Mount Abu and the Dilwara Temple in Rajasthan, the Eden Gardens in Calcutta and the beauty of Bangalore.

During the five months he was in India, Burroughs covered a vast area, using railways where possible and travelling north and east from Bombay to Baroda, then Jaipur, Delhi, Benares and Calcutta, before heading down the west coast to Madras and on to Bangalore. Some places were out of the way and, while he visited the main hill stations of Mount Abu, the Nigiri Hills, Ootacamund and Darjeeling, he failed to get to the hill station of Simla, or to Hyderabad or Secunderabad, though he noted names of people to contact there instead. India presented entirely new challenges: 'I am working like sixty here with good and present prospects. It's a bigger job than I thought for however doing India.'[9] By early February he was a month behind his planned schedule: he had expected to be in Bombay for a week but had been busy for nearly a month. 'I have already reaped a fair harvest for my labors & with great hopes for an hundred fold yield next year and in other years to come. For the seed is good, may the sower be worthy to sow it.'[10]

As with all the countries he visited, Burroughs needed to cover a wide range of tasks: find suitable interpreters; appraise the general situation; learn about existing markets; determine what the medical profession and the public wanted; discover what prices the markets would bear; determine which doctors, dispensaries, merchants and people he could rely on; explore customs and excise taxes and legal constraints; find suitable agents; check that goods were not damaged by long journeys; ensure plentiful supplies of samples; and make arrangements that orders would be fulfilled after he left. This was far from easy work and called for experience, sharp thinking, flexibility and charm, all virtues Burroughs had in abundance. His work was boosted by supreme confidence in the quality and value of his goods, his philanthropic outlook and his Presbyterian faith.

The important market in India at this time consisted of the British middle-class expatriates, the service industries supporting them, and the British Army. Indigenous medicine was based almost exclusively on Ayurveda and Unani ideas, and pharmacology had a tradition of eclecticism, but Indian attitudes towards Western drugs and medicine were complex and changing at this time. When Burroughs arrived there were more Western-educated Indian practitioners, and a growing number of middle-class Indians used Western medicine.[11] There was a long tradition of charitable medical provision: Jain merchants, for example, distributed relief to the poor, and missionaries played a key role in medical care and tried to provide access to 'English medicine', or 'doctoring' as it was known, via hospitals and 'dispensaries'.

Apart from smallpox, malaria and epidemics of the plague and cholera, the most common illnesses suffered by the population resulted mostly from poor diet and conditions such as ulcers, itch, ringworm, skin diseases, worms, abscesses, tumid spleen (sickle cell anemia) and eye diseases.[12] Furnished with his 'new and improved chemical and pharmaceutical preparations', Burroughs had in fact very little in his product range that was really new to the subcontinent – his goods were typical of agents in use at that time. What was novel to India was that many of BW&Co.'s drugs were of reliable standard doses in compressed tablet form and were packaged and marketed differently.

Unaware of – or perhaps simply too busy to investigate – the numerous varieties of practitioners, doctors and drug vendors and the many different systems of medical treatment used by the indigenous population, Burroughs observed that the majority of local people were very ignorant: 'when sick [they] send for the native doctor or priest who performs incantations and administrations of bugs, reptiles and native roots and herbs enough to frighten or kill any but the natives who have got used to such things.'[13] Indian remedies, he noted, were cheap and popular, whereas Western medicines were expensive and scarce and, if used by 'native practitioners', were not infrequently diluted or adulterated; drug vendors sometimes practised as well as prescribed. Of Calcutta he wrote: 'I don't think much of these native drug shops ... their customers are all ... of the poor classes & no use for our drugs.'[14] He considered Jaipur native drug shops to be 'of the crudest sort', without any European medicines.[15] One of the two chemists in Darjeeling was a general merchant who did not know how to read a prescription. Cawnpore had two 'good native doctors', but Burroughs noted that the natives there were 'no good ... as their record in the mutiny proved very bad indeed.'

Having secured an interpreter and visited the British or American consul, Burroughs used introductions from senior doctors, members of the church and others to gain access to important leading local doctors, hospitals, dispensers and merchants. Dr Bhalchandra Krishna, chief medical officer of the state of Baroda, for example, was 'a gentleman ... very courteous ... a very intelligent and progressive physician', who was already well informed about the firm's products through the medical journals and ordered everything on Burroughs's list. Burroughs ordered a medicine chest to be made for Dr Krishna's private use, and when he travelled with the royal prince it was to be charged at cost, in the certainty that it would result in large orders from Baroda's Medical Department. Such procedures were not unusual: Burroughs gave generously, believing that it would be repaid with orders. Particularly important people would be sent special medical pocket cases or other goods.

The firm's goods were promoted through the distribution of samples to the medical profession, advertising in medical journals and a supply of picture cards for customers. Detailed instructions were issued to merchants to distribute samples immediately before the approaching wet season to all doctors in their area – selected from local gazetteers or directories. Not infrequently samples were also given to missions and schools, along with private donations of money by Burroughs. Towards the end of his Indian trip he considered sending samples or donating the firm's medicines to all Christian missionaries or medical missionaries. It is not clear whether he did so, but certainly the line between his desire to make money and also be charitable was at times a thin one.

Castigated by Wellcome for not keeping notes following his visits to date, in India Burroughs made detailed records on pre-printed forms, the sort already used at home by doctors ('medicos'), chemists and dispensers. His comments reveal much about the Indian drug trade. For dispensers he noted the class of establishment; the state of its shop; the reception given – 'cordial' to 'refused interview'; the characteristics of the boss – 'enterprising' to 'indifferent'; and their disposition to the firm's goods – 'will push' to 'prejudiced against our goods'. Merchants were the most important group to do business with, so orders placed and the state of their stocks were noted. For 'medicos' he noted their specialty (physician, surgeon, homeopath or general); class ('toney', 'moderate' or 'leading man'); age; the reception given; and the source of goods.

Sometimes his remarks were derogatory or humorous. In Bombay, Kemp & Co., although leaders in introducing pharmaceutical preparations, were 'a little tight fisted'. One dispenser was 'drunk, lazy, or not one to do business with'; another 'not up on the latest pharmaceutical news'; a third an 'old fogey'. In Madras a merchant was 'a little off his nut'; O'Hara & Co. in Bangalore 'seemed sleepy people – too lazy to exist & always putting off.' Messrs Scott-Thompson in Calcutta he described as 'a precious lot of old fossils. No more enterprise about them than in an old cow.' But he was much taken with Dr Kernot of Smith Stanistreet & Co. in Calcutta, who had the largest wholesale trade and stock of goods, and he left with them 100 boxes of samples to distribute among their best doctors and chemists. Burroughs was treated well by many doctors and merchants, who entertained him and showed him local sights. Dr Kernot was one such, and Wellcome was commanded that, when Kernot and his wife visited London, they were to be taken for a drive in the park to see the new theatre (the Savoy) lit by electricity.

Medical journals and their editors also came in for comment. Dr McLeod, editor of the *Indian Medical Gazette*, was considered 'an offish sort of man, very conceited … the idea that anyone could show him anything he didn't already know about seems quite impossible to him. He is the only doctor of this sort in Calcutta.' In general doctors thought highly of *The Lancet* – very few of them took any other journal – and Burroughs was pleased that Wellcome was keeping up advertising with a page in nearly every issue; 'it will pay I think,' he counselled. In

England, on the contrary, he had seen a lot of country doctors who did not take the wrappers off the *British Medical Journal*: 'they get it for nothing and perhaps don't appreciate it as much as a journal which they must get something out of for their money.'[16]

The marketing potential of travelling medicine chests and cases in India was quickly recognised by Burroughs. His journals teem with ideas, designs, doodles and detailed instructions about improving their appeal, layout, contents and pricing. Wellcome has wrongly received credit for being the partner with the eye for design and for pushing the medicine cases and chests. In fact it was Burroughs who introduced one of the most successful innovations of BW&Co. – the portable or pocket medical case. Acting on a suggestion of his 'particular friend' Dr Valentine, superintendent at the medical mission in Agra, Burroughs wrote: 'I think we can sell a lot of pocket cases all filled with our medicines if we get them up of this metal – for the reason that they will be strong, light, handsome and we can get them up at such a reasonable price that Druggists will buy them already filled to sell to their regular customers instead of the old fashioned pocket cases of leather which cost as much empty as ours would full.'[17] He instructed Wellcome to get a sample case made up and sent to Valentine for trial. It was a suggestion by Surgeon General Moore that also led Burroughs to direct that each case made by the firm and sold everywhere should be supplied with a handbook or manual on modern medicine for use by the practitioner yet comprehensible to the man in the street: when published the following year, it 'took the medical profession by storm'.[18]

Burroughs spotted untapped markets for their goods. The doctors were 'ripe for fluid extracts', and if BW&Co. could get army contracts for pills, fluid extracts or concentrates, and compressed drugs they would have 'a jolly business'. Phosphates in concentrate form would bring a 'whaling big business' to a firm that brought out a reliable line, since there were many temperance people in India and 'nerve tonics are much indicated'. And Hazeline was another product he rightly believed would sell well.[19]

The Indian climate created serious problems. Dread of the anticipated hot weather drove Burroughs to finish his work in Jaipur, and after completing correspondence and orders to his agent in Bombay, Mr Ballantine, he headed for Delhi. From Kellner's Hotel he took more orders from doctors, military surgeons, missions and the Civil Dispensary.[20] A week later he was drumming up trade in Lahore. It was now the middle of March and the heat was unbearable. In a long letter to Wellcome on the train from Cawnpore to Allahabad, Burroughs told of his concerns about the impact of the climate on their goods, graphically describing how 'eggs can be cooked by putting them in the sand in the middle of a summer day and bare feet will be blistered by walking through it.'

Soon Burroughs noticed that goods deteriorated in the heat and humidity after long journeys and poor storage. Ants ate their way through corks and gelatine. Temperatures he erroneously claimed were sometimes 130 degrees Fahrenheit in the shade: this figure is an exaggerated one, but certainly goods in transport would suffer in a heat 'nearly enough to set fire to them', and his metal portmanteau got so hot he could hardly touch it. He considered this issue the most serious obstacle to the firm establishing a big trade in India: 'An insurance company formed to insure the safe keeping of the merchandise in India would be about the riskiest spec[ulation] one could take stock in.' He proposed trials at home of pills at high temperature and suggested compressed goods – rather than any coated pills – were best for the army in India, as they were free from moisture and the least affected by heat. In future, samples for India would need to be stored in metal cases, otherwise ants and rats made short work of the boxes, labels, wrappers, capsules and corks. The case should be as air- and moisture-tight as possible and also attractive – 'not like the ones Savory and Moore used in the Afghan war'.[21] Goods not suitable for hot climates should be marked 'Not for Export' to prevent wholesale companies sending them abroad, and such labelling would facilitate keeping track of their foreign trade. Interestingly, no mention was made of the impact of religious sensibilities on demand for some of their products, such as beef and iron wine.

Another major difficulty faced by Burroughs was the delay in receiving post and samples. Inevitably this led to misunderstandings with Wellcome and the exchange of sharply worded letters. In mid-March Burroughs had not heard from Wellcome since leaving Alexandria in the middle of December. He subsequently received a letter posted by Wellcome in January or February, which was highly critical of Burroughs's handling of affairs. Its contents did not make cheerful reading: 'When we agreed that you take a trip around the world that would last some one and a half or two years, I did not favour a "superficial jaunt", and still less so now.' In other words, it was no good Burroughs appointing sub-agents and then moving on, leaving them to do all the really important work; if this happened the firm would bear an enormous expense for very little in return. Personal work with the medical profession was essential for success. 'No chemist, no agent can place articles before the profession as intelligently as you can and they will not take the interest.' Wellcome added that he hoped that Burroughs would stop in India and work the doctors and chemists as hard as he could, visiting every accessible trading post of consequence and calling on all important medical men and chemists.

He then went on to say that sending samples was a waste of money, and that Burroughs had been deceived by the agents he had appointed so far. He had failed to make proper enquiries before appointing them, had sent no authority for statements to be made to the company and supplied no references. Problems could rise should agents go bankrupt and not pay for goods, especially as Burroughs had given two months' credit to at least one of them. He had written previously on the subject and very much regretted that Burroughs treated the appointment of agents with 'such indifference', urging caution. 'It is rather disheartening that you should entirely ignore my opinion and go on continually committing us to such rash contracts.' Burroughs's 'extraordinary carelessness' made it his duty to express himself plainly and tell him that he emphatically objected to Burroughs 'committing to any more foreign contracts and binding the firm to the payment of exorbitant commissions – or the allowance on travelling expenses – incidentals postages … etc.'

Moreover, Burroughs had sent little information about the business firms in the various towns visited, instead writing in a 'social nature … In fact from first to last it seemed … as if you had forgotten all about the business part of the trip and that your mind and thoughts were wandering elsewhere. The fact is from the time of your leaving London until your arrival at Bombay there was nothing in the shape of profitable results to distinguish your journey from a pleasure trip – I hope that this cannot be said of your trip through India.' Wellcome wanted a careful record kept of all the chemists visited, and he strongly favoured Burroughs completing the trip via Australia and New Zealand, and even China, Japan and Manila, providing he did them all in proper detail. He ended that he had written 'as a <u>warning</u>' and ended with 'all good wishes and brotherly feeling'.[22]

This long, repetitive and bullying letter must have irritated and upset Burroughs, who, after all, had been doing a great deal of work under difficult circumstances for the previous three months. Its harsh tone displayed a lack of understanding or indeed of friendship. Burroughs drafted a response from Allahabad but softened it in his letter sent the next day from Benares, in which he concentrated on the practical issues of supplies and refuted criticisms with justification of some of the costs – for example, his telegram omitted the names of the four principal cities Calcutta, Bombay, Madras and Colombo to save cost – adding his own grievances about the lack of goods:

> I think that 200£ worth of our goods could have been sold in Bombay if I had had them with me or if they had been shipped on receipt of my telegram and 300£ worth of them I think would have been consumed during the three months before they could get them on order. It seems very discouraging to me after working hard and getting up a healthy demand for our goods that you pay no attention to my telegram for goods and thus throw cold water upon the enterprise. There is no difficulty in settling the goods for cash down if they are on hand but they will not order out as liberally because they say the Doctors will be over the notion of prescribing them by the time they arrive ... It is too late now to send any on to Calcutta or Madras or Colombo but do not delay to forward good [samples] to Adelaide Sydney Melbourne Christchurch etc and afterward to the Sandwich Islands and Hawaii. The latter with the samples as I expect to be there in September. I will write on another page what I think should be sent with spls [samples] to various places ...
>
> Yours truly B, Awfully sunny & hot.[23]

A few days later, by this time in a similarly furnace-like Calcutta, Burroughs confided to his journal: 'In rather ill humor on account of Wellcome who is in want of a dose of liver pills a turkish bath & shampoo sleep diet Pil Phos Nux Iron and Quin Val Zinc &c. A thorough reorganizing in fact for I believe he has got the [jaundice?] bad and sees things green and black with no end of snakes in the grass and blue devils everywhere.'[24] Sensitive to financial implications of his request that Wellcome visit his aunt and uncle when in America, Burroughs told him to recover the $50 or so required for this from him personally, the firm paying only the cost of his business trip.

After a few days of visiting hospitals and doctors in the Calcutta heat, Burroughs set off on the train for Darjeeling and the Himalayas, enjoying the cooler air and the landscape of tea estates, orchids and magnificent trees, several species of which he had seen in Calcutta's botanical gardens. There he reflected on his goals and methods of achieving them and wrote a long memo on the subject; Wellcome was sent futher explicit instructions. The memo dealt with his sales strategy and demonstrated how effective he was in his transactions with clients, making them feel they were part of a mutually supportive deal. Money was certainly not the only factor: honesty and industry were fundamental, and his notes confirm the resolute belief Burroughs held in his goods and the improvements they would bring.

From Darjeeling he rode to Jalapahar and received a cordial reception from the surgeon major at the military hospital. Finding that he would not be able to catch his intended steamer to Ceylon, and with two weeks to spare, he sailed for Burma, where he found more to do than expected: it was a rich country and Rangoon a promising town with a better harbour than Calcutta.[25] After a brief return stop in Calcutta, where his schedule was revised again, he set off for Madras. Wellcome was told not to send samples to the Sandwich Islands until instructed as he might not get there: he now intended going to China and Japan.

The presidency of Madras in May was at its hottest. There Burroughs pushed himself too hard, as he himself admitted. His daily routine involved hiring a carriage for the whole day, even when the weather was at its most oppressive, between 11am and mid-afternoon. He subsequently thought that this caused his unexplained fever. He told Wellcome that he was 'on the jump to get out of this red hot country at the earliest possible moment', and on the same day told another friend he 'had a touch of fever the other day but it seems all gone now that the Lord and I am harty [sic] as usual again.'[26] Three days later he scribbled rambling thoughts in his journal, in a very faint and in some places illegible hand, showing that he was extremely ill and hallucinating and far from recovered.

For a week Burroughs was on the sick list, suffering first with pleurisy, then chills, fever and dysentery. To Sudlow he later described his symptoms as 'altogether too much like cholera to be pleasant' and was grateful that 'by prompt treatment … and the mercy of God in sparing a so far unprofitable life I am able to be about as usual.'[27] Three days after the worst night, he felt 'pretty comfortable', though not as 'frisky' as he liked. He took a ride in a tonga (a 'curious cart') and hoped that he would be well enough to go on to Bangalore the next day. His own poor health prompted him to enquire of Sudlow if Wellcome was well and taking proper care of his health, since he was 'not much given to do so'; he advised a horse ride in Hyde Park every morning.

Fortunately the weather in Bangalore was blissfully cooler and rain cleared the air so that, while visiting doctors in his carriage, Burroughs was able to enjoy the many gardens, parks and fine public buildings, 'mostly of the Corinthian style'. All the European residences were

surrounded by large gardens and lawns, full of flowers and varieties
of tropical trees and characterised by 'magnificent distance', woody
parks, green commons and parade grounds, similar to Madras and
other military or garrison towns of India. He believed that the English
had 'taught the natives a good lesson about architecture and landscape
gardening', which, he patronisingly suggested, 'they have much needed
to learn', since most of the old native towns were very crowded, with
streets too narrow for carriages to pass (though he admitted that Lahore
was built long before people thought of riding in carriages).[28]

Burroughs's conviction as to the superiority of the new pharmaceuticals
chimes with what one historian has described as 'the peak of European
confidence in the superiority of western medicine in the 1880s and
1890s'.[29] He had the advantage, too, of being there when India was seen
as a potential new market. In his reports and instructions to 'Bro[ther]
Wellcome', Burroughs recognised the likelihood of an excellent market
in India, where sales would mostly be to the European market. The
quantity of drugs sent there by the British government was enormous,
with civil and military servants receiving medical care and medicines
at the expense of the state. While this was not helpful for the firm
at present, Burroughs realised that, as long as the Indian Medical
Department adopted their goods and lists, they would 'hardly need any
more business'.[30] He also appreciated the importance of missionaries
and of using Indian practitioners, who were well placed to give an entrée
to the native population. Missionaries used to give the goods away, but
'now sell them at a profit.'

In spite of finding India 'an interesting and remarkable country to
travel in', Burroughs considered it too hot and 'hardly desirable for
business to reside in permanently'. More work had been required than he
anticipated, and, notwithstanding bouts of illness, he reckoned he had
made the very most of his time. He would have prolonged his stay but
for the weather: 'Never knew what hot weather was till my experience
here and now have had enough to satisfy me all the rest of my days.' He
could, though, look back with huge satisfaction on his achievements in
India. He had sold in every town he visited, all the dealers gave him
orders, and he had made an impression in a highly competitive drug
trade, which, as he himself said, was conducted very differently from
that of any other country with which he was familiar.[31]

Of particular note was the pocket medical case and handbook which
originated from the Indian visit, and these became effective and popular
promotional tools. Knowledge gained about packaging, conveying
and storing goods in tropical climates paid valuable dividends and

led to new ideas for sales and marketing. Burroughs recommended a follow-up visit within a year or 18 months and a representative of the firm to visit India two years later to consolidate his work and forge new links. 'We know the trade and profession together better than any other house in the world', Burroughs boasted to Wellcome, 'and have greater facilities for introducing specialties in pharmacy etc than any other house.'

The firm could now respond with speed and flexibility to the unique situation operating in colonial India. In spite of the enormous expense – mainly on samples and advertising – which Wellcome estimated in excess of $4,000, the huge investment paid off handsomely, and the brand name Burroughs, Wellcome & Co. had been established. Visits and contacts in India laid down a vital foundation for the firm's long-term success there, and it went on to exhibit at the Calcutta International Exhibition in 1883 and display goods at the Delhi Durbar of 1903. It advertised regularly in the Indian medical press, even to the extent of advertising in Urdu in order to reach Indian practitioners. In 1912 the firm's depot in Bombay was converted into a branch, and by the turn of the century the Indian market was recognised as 'offering almost unlimited possibility of business'.[32]

After two days back in Madras, Burroughs sailed for Ceylon, where he arrived at the end of May. It was lush and green after the heat of India, and Burroughs fell in love with it at once. In Galle – which was on the point of losing its importance to the new capital, Colombo – he stayed at the fine Oriental Hotel. His letters are full of descriptions of its beauty: 'A splendid place for a jolly picnic here on the smooth grass or for a stroll on a moonlit night.' Colombo he found prettier than any of the Indian cities, with its new wide streets, smooth green lawns, splendid barracks and hospitals.

The surgeon general described the financial cost of sickness to the army: a soldier's passage to Colombo at a time when soldiers were 'not so easily got' cost £100, and too many died in India, so the army could not afford to ill-treat or neglect them, even if there was a disposition to do so. Burroughs learnt that, in the opinion of old settlers, it was drink, not the climate, that was the real problem. He was told that hospital statistics were reckoned to show that the teetotallers in the ranks had much better health than even moderate drinkers, and that drink taken with impunity in England was 'quicker & deadlier in its effects under the influence of the tropic sun', where it brought 'an enlargement of the liver that endangers the whole system putting it all out of order making it an easy prey to fever cholera & dysentery'.[33]

In a relaxed and cheerful mood, Burroughs wrote a long and amusing letter to Wellcome about his adventures and, knowing Wellcome was enthusiastic about botany and medical botany, about the luxuriant foliage of Ceylon. He was particularly struck by the Tonga tree, a screw pine tree which flourished there and which he had thought grew only on the Fijian islands. Its properties were of interest to pharmacists on account of its 'incalculable benefits … upon suffering humanity'. Botanists and the public insisted on calling the tree the Pandanus – a 'horrid' name, he thought. Its appearance was peculiar, with 'roots that forget to start till the tree has got well on so that they look like props', graceful branches with a 'touzled bunch of long leaves, and a truly precious top-knot', making it look like a joke in *Punch, Judy, Funny Folks* and other weekly comic papers. 'I mention the name [Tonga] merely as conclusive evidence that I am thoroughly au fait … there you are. I am always well up in the profession you see and don't you forget it,' he quipped. Warming to the theme, he regaled Wellcome with stories of tonga rides with a Miss G in the Nilgiri Hills and a decidedly risqué and racist joke.

In mid-June Burroughs took the train from Colombo into the mountains. Such a journey would have been impossible a few years earlier, but now the jungle had been cleared: 'one of the excellent features of English civilization is that they help forward the march of progress by building good roads and railways.' At the same time he noted that near the towns the roads were 'lined with miserable mud houses of the Singhalese Tamils and Moormen or Mohammedans all of which are dirty smoky and bad smelling.' He briefly visited Kandy, which he found 'rather hard up', since coffee, the principal crop, had failed for several years and seemed to be dying out, whereas the cinchona plantations were flourishing and he hoped would make the island rich again. Since cinchona was used for making quinine, Burroughs took detailed statistics about its sales and shippers, sending them later to McKesson & Robbins: this trade was highly lucrative, and exports went to America via the UK.

One of his happiest days was spent in Kandy. Here, after enjoying an early morning ride with a friend, accompanied by 'joyous' birdsong, he went on to explore the mountains. In the evening he investigated the sound of music from a nearby temple (the celebrated Lankatilaka Temple) and observed the service. Later the *Christian Commonwealth* published his vivid description of the ceremony – the crowds, the traditional procession with an elephant, the priests and worship of the great carved Buddha, the flowers, the smells, and the music of the drums and orchestra. Burroughs's intense dislike of this worship contrasted with his expressions of delight at the beauty of nature around him, and he formed the opinion that Christian children were very well educated – 'a happy contrast to the ignorance depravity and superstition of their heathen brothers and sisters who are worshippers of a false religion and belief.' His attitude that Christianity was superior to Indian faiths was quite common among Westerners at this time, and some of his remarks would be considered offensive now. He was even convinced that only Christians could be truly happy, and he was proud that the first missionary sent to India – presumably the Rev. Dr John Scudder snr – was from one of America's Christian churches. He praised Queen Victoria's intervention, which encouraged missionary teaching after the governor of Bombay had at first forbidden it.[34] Burroughs was equally hostile to the Mormons and Brigham Young, their leader and director of the settlement at Salt Lake City: they 'are as dangerous to our country [America] as cholera or snake bite to human flesh.'[35]

After a month in Ceylon, where good sales to the major practices had been made and business contacts forged, it was time to move on, and Burroughs boarded a steamer bound for Adelaide.

Chapter 7

The Antipodes

This is a splendid country for Biz.[1]

Burroughs arrived in Adelaide in early July 1882 and found plenty of work to do, 'prospects fair or good, all doctors favourable but wholesale trade not very ready for new things.'[2] He liked Australia and the Australians immensely. After the heat of India the Australian climate – it was midwinter there – was invigorating and renewed his energy: 'This old boy seems younger and fresher than ever before.' Green grass, flowering roses and graceful eucalyptus flourished; everyone seemed healthy, happy and wealthy and the young ladies were charming. Such sights were 'reviving indeed after the monotonous sights of dusky natives and washed out Europeans in the depressing atmosphere of Hindustan.' The people seemed 'like our Western states people – go-ahead jolly & with lots of money. ... Everyone here seems to be comfortably well off except the drunkards and idlers. This country is much like our own – prosperous ... and with great resources. It is a good country for us to work.'[3]

To his friend Frank Mattox he wrote revealingly: 'I must get over the way I have of putting things off. Somehow when there are any doctors chemists or nice young ladies whose society is readily available I leave the letter writing to a more convenient season so to give proper attention to correspondence I find the only way will be to get up early in the morning.'[4] He planned to follow the examples of Gladstone and Napoleon: sleep less, read and study before breakfast.

Adelaide, with its impressive new buildings and wide streets, had become a showcase city, and Burroughs was smitten by its grandeur. It had numerous churches, and the large majority of the people took a lively interest in religious matters, 'which no doubt is the foundation of their general intelligence and well-being.'[5] It was going through a period of exceptional prosperity: although crops had been small in the two previous years because of low rainfall, farming was easy and inexpensive in southern Australia, with good pasture and water for sheep and cattle. The first successful commercial shipment of frozen meat from New Zealand to London had taken place two months earlier, and Burroughs noted that this new idea of using refrigerators was already a source of considerable wealth and promised great results for the future. 'The last shipment to

15: Burroughs: studio photograph taken in Adelaide, 1882.

London arrived in prime condition ... With Beef Steak at 15d per lb in New York the Australians will have the English market pretty much to themselves.' Generally speaking, he found southern Australians to be industrious, temperate, enterprising and thrifty. 'There was not a white beggar in the whole place and those who were not too lazy to work had enough to spare.'[6]

While there, Burroughs read of the persecution of Jews in Russia and other Eastern European countries and wrote to Wellcome asking him to send 2 guineas from his personal account to assist those who lacked the means to leave their country: 'I am proud of the action of the US Government having the justice to speak on behalf of those oppressed subjects of the Czar even while all other nations were silent.'[7] Joseph Cook was now lecturing in Adelaide, and both men attended a lecture by Archibald Forbes on 29 July on 'The Inner life of a War Correspondent', further arousing Burroughs's sympathy for those who suffered persecution and his admiration for the power of a writer who could influence with the pen and be the 'mouthpiece of truth'.[8]

Burroughs next sailed by steamer to Melbourne, a booming city, its population having doubled in the previous ten years to half a million. Whereas Adelaide was like a 'big beautiful model village', Melbourne was 'a faster town, a big city', its suburbs dirtier than those of Adelaide. While there Burroughs admired the new big Swedish four-masted iron barque, the *Routenburn*, and went to the theatre to see the famous actress Jennie Lee in *The Grasshopper*. He wrote censoriously that 'she was very nice & lively in it but like 9/10ths of the modern plays the moral tone was almost extinguished and put out of the play by looseness sordidness and occasional profanity.'[9] He was also critical of a comic opera called *Billy Taylor*, 'a melancholy affair ... as insipid, nasty, and bad a piece as any scoundrel without wit could have written ... a contemptible imitation' of Gilbert and Sullivan's *HMS Pinafore* in parts, but unlike *Pinafore*, which had 'innocence, true affection and wit'. His reading was Thomas Carlyle's *On Heroes and Hero Worship and the Heroic in History* (1841), and he reflected that these were men who were true to themselves and were led by the spirit rather than the word of the law.

Not surprisingly, with his Presbyterian beliefs and work ethic, Burroughs had much to say on the subject of drink. The temperance movement in Australia was at its height at this time, and in Adelaide he had talked to a couple who had sold their public house and were very critical of the Salvation Army trying to 'cram religion down people's throats'. Burroughs observed that their animosity was probably connected with the fact that they had lost customers. He considered that, whatever might be said against them in Britain, the Salvation Army had achieved a great deal in southern Australia, and initially he stayed at Melbourne's YMCA. Burroughs took detailed notes of Joseph Cook's Melbourne lecture on the evils of drink.[10] The city had a large number of temperance coffeehouses and hotels, many being far grander than the pubs. One of the first was the Victoria Coffee Palace, opened by a temperance league in 1880. Impressed by its comfort and style and by other such places there, Burroughs wrote about temperance hotels for the *Christian Commonwealth* – 'a subject of interest to the travelling community in particular and the whole community in general' – urging that they be built in London. A similar venture could be both a financial and moral success in London. 'No doubt there are hundreds of thousands of people who visit London who would much prefer a first class temperance hotel at the same price to stopping at the Grand or the Langham or the Alexandra but the trouble is every temperance hotel in London is of the cheap and nasty style and temperance people are forced to the whiskey drinking palaces.'

Burroughs calculated the costs of room and board and dining in British hotels, comparing British and American hotel policy on drinking, and observed that much money was to be made from a well-run enterprise.

At this period large luxury hotels were being opened everywhere, and he spotted potential investment opportunities. Years later he was to befriend Russell Cotes, who made a fortune from the Royal Bath Hotel in Bournemouth.

Concern about the damage drink could inflict led Burroughs to question the firm's Beef and Iron Wine, which physicians had found to be a beneficial stimulant and useful in dipsomania, but which he feared might lead some to drink. One doctor had suggested that it be made with pure alcohol in place of wine, but he had been thinking of dropping it altogether or of putting some caution in the directions. He sent Cook a copy of *The Lancet*'s comments on the product and asked for his advice on the subject.[11] To Wellcome he wrote: 'I am sure we don't want anyone to use this preparation except as a medicine' and suggested substituting the word 'Elixir' for 'Wine', or simply calling it 'Beef and Iron', listing the content/formulae in small text or using the names *Elixoid Carnis Comp* or *Elixoid Carnis et Fer.* 'This would be a handy title for doctors to use in prescribing as they often like to use Latin phrases in Prescriptions and the public think they are not getting the value of their money unless some Latin is thrown in as a general mystifier,' he noted cynically. He also argued that excise authorities might wish to charge if they thought it was a drink rather than a medicine.[12] Wellcome changed the name to 'Beef and Iron'.[13]

Burroughs also suggested introducing 'Equaloids', 'Pil-Ovoid' or 'Pilovoids' for their compressed tablets. 'How would that do for a trademark – this would be easier to write and easier to remember.' They discussed these and other names, all similar to the 'Valoid' and 'Tabloid' names that Wellcome was to register as a trademark two years later, in March 1884. While Wellcome had been credited with coming up with the celebrated name 'Tabloid', Burroughs had by then recently returned to the UK, so it is highly likely that they both discussed and agreed to his doing so.

The partners exchanged lengthy business letters. Wyeths had agreed to give permanent sole agency rights to BW&Co. in Europe, Asia, Africa and Australia, and Burroughs reported positively to them of his trade in Australia. At the same time he told Wellcome that there was nothing to stop their firm now manufacturing for themselves, since Wyeths' inventions were not their own – moreover, other patents (Bucheron and Dunton) had lapsed, leaving the field open to all. Burroughs proposed that, in future, Wyeths' name should be omitted on the goods they imported to Australia and that labels might now read 'Burroughs, Wellcome & Co.' or 'BW&Co. (late Wyeth) Tablets of chlorate', etc. He asked whether it would be good to buy some of Wyeths' goods if they would sell at a low figure and then put their own labels on them. It is a suggestion which sounds decidedly underhand.

Endless financial and marketing proposals were sent to Wellcome. They included getting excise to remove the 25% duty on Kepler's goods, since duties on proprietary medicines were the same as those on patent medicines; establishing a depot or agency for the firm's goods in New York or Philadelphia, where their Hazeline and Malt would do well; and writing to medical societies across the world, sending specimens of their goods and asking for results to be reported for use as publicity. Should they get into the market with a line of fluid extracts and not let Parke Davis and others get ahead of them? Perhaps Squibb would make goods for them, since a few years previously he had been anxious to sell his laboratory as trade was falling off. Burroughs considered that Wellcome had exaggerated the cost of malt extract apparatus and suggested asking Allen & Hanbury's about where theirs was made. Allen & Hanbury's were friendly, not jealous, and indebted to BW&Co., who had made a sale for their malt extract without their having to do anything. More marketing suggestions were proposed, such as a calendar for 1883, blotting pads, and a portfolio printed with the firm's name, which would please the medical profession and be their best advertisement – 'beat medical journals out of sight'. Most importantly, Burroughs raised the possibility of expansion: did Wellcome agree with him that they would have to get other premises before long for a malt factory? If so, should he look for a place with a level ground floor and a lift – as such places were the only ones suitable for wholesaling and manufacturing?

He suggested the appointment of a permanent salesman or traveller in Australia to look after their interests, warning that otherwise Warner or Parke Davis (who both had people looking after their interests) would get a start on them. He had his eye on one such person and was careful to ask Wellcome's opinion. His opinion was justified: numerous agency agreements were made across Australasia. His heavy advertising campaign paid off, a resident representative was appointed in Melbourne in 1883, and the firm's first branch opened there three years later.

Australia was a high point in Burroughs's travels, and he later drafted an article proposing that millions of people 'of the old country' (England) would find it to their advantage to settle in Australia and suggesting that the chief hindrance to emigration was ignorance of the resources, progress and climate of Australia. An attractively illustrated little book should be printed, distributed and advertised in newspapers in England, where there was a great lack of literature and information on the subject of the colonies.[14]

In mid-December 1882 Burroughs sailed to Auckland. New Zealand was enjoying an economic boom at this time, having seen massive immigration in the 1870s; the city of Auckland doubled in size between 1878 and 1886, and there were many fine new buildings along Queen Street. Burroughs, who saw it in good weather, was struck by its beauty and reflected on his good fortune with the weather on his travels in pursuit of business (the heat of India being ignored).

As usual new friendships were soon made. On Christmas Eve he sailed from Auckland with fellow boarders Mr Macarthur, principal of the teachers' training school, and his Irish wife, 'both very intelligent and agreeable', to Waiwera, a resort with bathing and hot springs houses by the sea. Burroughs wrote business letters to Wellcome and the Wyeths on Christmas Day, but on the whole he spent his holiday break with a houseful of congenial people, thoroughly enjoying simple pleasures. In the morning he bathed in the hot springs then swam in the sea, joined by other men, including Macarthur and the eminent politician and ex-prime minister of New Zealand Sir William Fox.[15] Early-morning walks gave him a hearty appetite for a good breakfast, and there were delightful boating trips. His reading, other than the newspapers, included *The Life of Richard Cobden*, whom he admired because he tried to make the most of his opportunities and improve them all in a sensible and energetic manner. He also studied the sermons of Charles Spurgeon, the celebrated Baptist preacher whom he had heard lecture in London.

Serious study, though, was quickly relinquished when the ladies invited him to join them in gathering wild flowers and watching the steamer arrive with 'excursion people'. In the evenings there were tennis or ball games, games of musical chairs, French Tite (whatever that might have been!), recitations, band music, polkas and waltzes. On New Year's Eve, following a ball and rocket display, Burroughs discussed hopes and prospects for the future with his female acquaintances and, yet again, resolved on abstention during the coming year or in the future 'as long as I live'. Yet again he berated himself for not working harder. He would be more useful, devote more time to reading the Bible and write more about his travels – at least a letter a month to the *Christian Commonwealth*, *The Chronicle*, the *Chemist and Druggist*, the *Chemist's Journal*, and the *Chicago Pharmacist*, and, if they published them, a letter to some American daily or weekly newspaper.

Before leaving Auckland, Burroughs made a special journey to see one of the scenic marvels of New Zealand, called by some the Eighth Wonder of the World. Lake Rotomahana near Rotorua was a region celebrated for its volcanoes and geothermal activity, a dramatic landscape of geysers, springs and hot pools. Here the famous Pink and White Terraces, with their huge cascades of springs, were painted and photographed by hundreds of tourists. Burroughs was very taken with them if the number of photographs he purchased is any indication. Four years later the terraces would no longer exist, completely obliterated when Mount Tarawera erupted.[16]

Burroughs's personal notebooks and letter books covering the next two months in New Zealand have not survived, but his correspondence records his journeys to all the main cities and towns on the North and South islands.[17] Railway lines were still being developed, so he would have travelled mainly by boat and horse and carriage. After his idyllic Waiwera break he returned to Auckland on 3 January 1883, was in Wellington by 12th and in Christchurch in late January and early February. From there he went to Dunedin and Invercargill, seeing Mr Rankin whom he had met in Sydney (a 'first rate fellow'), who would take orders for BW&Co.'s goods on his travels to the Straits and India. In early March Burroughs took a steamer to Tasmania and stayed at Hobart and Launceston during most of the month. From Hobart he wrote to Wellcome after a week that he had 'about got through with business' there, and that 'all the chemists except for one drunken good for nothing fellow, go in for our goods and the doctors are as usual delighted with them.'

At this stage he was still working up the Indian market. To Wellcome he wrote about issues such as the design and content of medical cases; improvements for the design of bottles (an indentation in the base would help with pouring); their relationship with Fellows & Co. (whom he considered were mistaken in consigning goods to India, since the Indian trade preferred to buy from London); the need for Beef and Iron Wine of a consistent standard; and his intention to register the firm's trade names to protect their use (which, as we have seen, was actually accomplished in early 1884 on his return to England). He considered that the firm ought to be represented at the Calcutta International Exhibition and that someone ought to go out to India and then on to Burma. To Wellcome's enquiry about cinchona he responded with a long list of suggestions and useful contacts in India and Ceylon who could advise on prices, markets and shipments. His aspirations were growing.

If our business is very prosperous we may find it desirable to start a laboratory in NY for distilling the Hazeline and for making the equivalent Fluid Extracts. My ambition goes even so high as to hope we may be able to buy or rent Squibbs Laboratory and buy his business. The old gentleman told me ten years ago that he wanted to sell out ... Alcohol being cheaper in America than in England it might be desirable to make all fluid extracts & Tinctures there ...

Squibbs was a long established reputable firm founded in 1858 (now Bristol Myers Squibb), and it says much that Burroughs could contemplate buying the firm out at this time.[18] Wellcome's reports on negotiations for the new Snow Hill building as their offices excited him, and he suggested that a lift be put in the building: 'I shall be satisfied with your decision in the matter.'

By Easter 1883 Burroughs had returned to Sydney, where he visited the international bazaar at the Exhibition Buildings and a model farm where calves were inoculated and calf lymph obtained. The company's goods continued to sell well and 'would have sold much more if they had been obtainable in the market', but supplies from London were not keeping up with demand. However, the high opinion of the doctors for the firm's goods gave him confidence. Good Friday was spent with work associates sorting out orders by phone and packing, even though it was a holiday. 'What a lot of time I do seem to waste in packing up my clothes books and chattels,' Burroughs grumbled; 'such a confusion and variety of things I hardly use once a month but still imagine I want them all.'

He enjoyed a swim in the sea and noted a race where 'all swam on their sides with one hand and arm out of the water half the time as an oar' (evidently the crawl was new to him). At nearby Port Phillip sharks were a danger, and Burroughs saw the protective enclosures of spikes with narrow apertures built around the bathing places. There were also theatre visits: the Irish American Minstrels and more serious theatrical productions too, although 'legitimate drama' seemed unpopular given the empty benches at Sheridan and Shakespeare plays, which he considered splendidly and perfectly interpreted.

After revisiting Melbourne and Adelaide Burroughs moved on to smaller towns in southern Australia, getting orders in each one. To Wellcome he sent a couple of long letters on business matters (one 48 pages long) covering a huge number of issues. Now he intended going to the Calcutta Exhibition himself. If he got through Queensland and the

Straits in time he would return to Colombo, Madras and Bombay before the exhibition, stopping long enough only to canvass the chemists and hospitals. He had written to his uncle and sister asking if they wanted him to come to America in August, and if they did he would telegraph from Sydney using the code word FRISCO. If instead he decided to go to the Straits, China, Japan or India, he would use other codes – the use of codes being economical.

During the next two months Burroughs was continually planning and replanning his schedule, and he now had personal reasons for wishing to finish his travels. At first he intended leaving Australia in April or May, to arrive in America 18 months later via Singapore, China and Japan.[19] That would have been three years after leaving London and nearly five years from the date of his last visit there. He now wished to let Mr Rankin and others cover northern Queensland, Java and the Straits (samples had already been distributed), and he would leave for San Francisco in early August, spend a month in America, and return to Bombay in October or November via either London or San Francisco (the London route being much the most practical). Such a timetable was completely unrealistic, even had he been using today's air travel.

On second thoughts, Burroughs realised he was pushing his luck, and a further proposal was sent to Wellcome: 'Perhaps though you will consider me very selfish in absenting myself from London for so long a time and so preventing you from getting a breath of fresh air or a little trip combining pleasure information & business. If so my dear partner, you may be sure I shall be <u>willing</u> and happy to resign in your favour if you would like to go to the Exhibition & round the world.' Wellcome's reply when it came was decisively negative. 'I do not entertain this [suggestion] for a moment, & it is hardly likely that I shall ever be able to make that trip, nor is it practicable for me to attend the Calcutta Exhibition.'[20] Burroughs made clear that he would like to make another trip to Australia in the next five years and anticipated a large trade there if properly nurtured.

All his plans collapsed, however, following the arrival of a telegram from Wellcome at the end of June, which read simply: 'Your Uncle very ill.' Wellcome had received a letter from Medina marked 'Sickness' and had taken the liberty of opening it. It enclosed a letter from Lina to her brother, saying that she feared their uncle would not survive his illness and left Burroughs to decide if he wished to return to Medina. Burroughs, already looking for a way of shortening his trip, made up his mind at once and took the next fast steamer to America. He replied to Wellcome's telegram, 'Leaving first Frisco mail', and subsequently wrote

'I decided in this way for the reason that my uncle is very old and as this may be his last illness I should feel duty bound to sacrifice if need be some business interests to go home to see him. He has been a great benefactor to me and if I can do him any service in his illness I should take pains to avail myself of the opportunity even though difficult to attain.' Wellcome, anticipating this, had written to Burroughs: 'I believe that on receipt of it [the telegram] you will take the first steamer for America, as I think that under the circumstances you should go to your uncle at once.'[21]

Before leaving, Burroughs made arrangements for Rankin to continue his work and engaged a traveller in Australia. On 14 July he left Sydney for San Francisco on the SS *Australia*. The steamer called at Hawaii, and, although there are no letters describing his stop there, Burroughs purchased some 20 photographs of the island, its royal family, palace, buildings and places of scenic interest.[22]

In San Francisco Burroughs was greeted by the news that his beloved uncle Isaac had died.[23] It must have been a cruel blow, especially given the guilt he felt at not having visited his family for so long. Now his concern was for his 86-year-old aunt Anna. Wellcome sent him a kind letter:

> I know that you will feel most keenly the deprivation and when you return will fully realize the great changes that have occurred in your family circle during these past two years. Please accept the most sincere sympathy from the depths of my heart for your sad bereavement and believe with me that the Lord has only relieved your good uncle from affliction to place him in a happier world free from pain and sorrow. ... With repeated expressions of sympathy my dear friend and believe me, ever yours faithfully Henry S Wellcome.[24]

Although Wellcome had planned to visit America in August, he now wrote that he was preoccupied with work.[25] He hoped to sail by 1 September and possibly see Burroughs in Medina, believing at this stage that Burroughs would be back in England by early October. As things turned out it was to be still longer before the two partners met again.

Chapter 8

'This Lovely Opposite Sex'[1]

*… you are very impressionable and have fallen
in love many times …*[2]

Apart from work and travel, another issue that preoccupied Burroughs when in India and the Antipodes was his solitary status as a bachelor. 'Very lonesome very often,' he wrote, and the sight of happy families and pretty women made him long for a wife and family of his own.[3] Photographs of Burroughs, now aged 36, show a handsome man with a bright intelligent face and cheerful happy smile: his hair was thinning, but he was a smart, if somewhat unconventional, dresser, had charisma, was gregarious, and enjoyed dancing and sports. A fund of stories of his life and travels made him an entertaining and fascinating talker, with a 'silky voice', an 'extraordinary fluency of ideas and charming manner language', and 'the quaint and original forms' in which he conveyed his thoughts and beliefs made his conversation particularly attractive.[4] At last he could begin to believe that his hard work and world trip had paid off, and that orders being placed with the firm would turn BW&Co. into a success, bring him wealth and enable him to settle down.

Burroughs found women attractive and fell in love many times. Before leaving America he had proposed to Carrie Davis, who lived outside Boston. She refused him, in spite of her parents' urgings, but they continued to correspond, and he continued to hope.

While in London he was drawn to his 'dear and practical friend' Susie Arnold, whose company he enjoyed. He told a friend:

You may have seen that I was very much struck after Miss Susie Arnold and proposed to her. 'Didn't love me enough' she candidly told me so it was all up and we are to be very good friends as long as we live ... I shall always have a very high regard for Miss Arnold and a great respect for her. During our long and intimate acquaintance there was no use in presuming upon friendship for even so small a favour as a single kiss though I think she might have granted me one at least when I left on this long journey. Keep your distance young man was the motto she always gave to me and I respect her very highly.[5]

Burroughs remained on good terms with Susie and wrote to her from India about a romantic quandary he faced: he had managed to fall in love with both 'Miss A and Miss B the lovely daughters of two of the principal medical men in Bombay', and now asked Susie what she would advise a fellow like him to do when he was leaving town the next day for good, and 'when I am so very desirous of continuing such pleasant acquaintance.'

Susie was worried enough to pass on her concerns to Wellcome, who in turn quizzed his partner about his romances: 'there is a slight rumour current here that you are enamoured by a beautiful Indian princess worth 8 million rupees – how is it? Miss A[rnold] is anxious about it.'[6] It would seem that Burroughs did nothing to pursue this attraction, although stories of his infatuations circulated. Although it is unlikely that he had any serious romance in India, Burroughs retained an intriguing informal photograph of an unnamed Indian woman – perhaps a servant, as she is shown squatting on the ground cleaning pans: on the reverse is written: 'from your Bombay flame'.

Meanwhile Carrie's friends encouraged her to consider Burroughs, in spite of her engagement for two years to a man from the West Coast of America. On St Valentine's Day 1882 Burroughs wrote from Gujarat to his 'dear and lovely friend Carrie', his letter revealing his fondness. He recalled their meeting at Niagara, wished her angel presence was with him, and said that there was none whose esteem he valued as highly as hers.[7] However, in July he received a letter from Carrie putting paid to his hopes. He gave Wellcome the news of 'the Little Darling of whom you have heard so much from me' and commented that it was as well he had not heard much from her, or it would have 'gone hard for him ... for the little acquaintance I had was enough to give me a most exalted estimate of her.'[8]

After Carrie's second and final rejection Burroughs wasted no time. He wrote to a third American lady with whom he had corresponded: Olive Chase. They had exchanged letters 'in a friendly way for some time but without any matrimonial intention', though Burroughs told Wellcome he reckoned that 'she thought differently of my intention'. Her letters were 'wonderfully nice' and had 'more than kept alive the regard he always had for her'. One letter must have been particularly wonderful as it elicited this response:

Dear friend Olive

Have we not been long enough good friends that I may now venture to call you by the name which shall ever be dear to me … I wish instead that we may be the dearest lovers in the world and married too for a long and happy life.

I haven't the presumption to think myself worthy of your hand but I daresay I would improve with astonishing progress if very much in your good company. But of your dear heart I would prove worthy. I think our tastes and temperaments are alike for this reason that I like everything that you do so there would be no chance for disagreement. Besides you are so good and amiable that no-one could or would think of quarrelling with you – and you would sure to be always right so that none could rightly disagree with you. You may think this a funny way of paying myself a compliment but I do flatter myself I haven't at all of a bad disposition and would soon become a perfect saint like yourself and I feel sure if we were joined together in wedlock the cooing [?seated] doves would be nowhere in comparison to us for uniform affection and our honeymoon would last as long as life.

Do you remember my letter written from a horseback in the Yosemite valley. I said to myself then that is the place for a wedding trip and I'm sure if you will say the word I'll do my best to make it agreeable to you and also a long and happy life's journey afterward please God.

And now my dearest Olive (I beg your pardon) if you'll just write me the little word 'yes' and a long long letter too, but that word at least – very easy just you try it – then I'll work like a Trojan to finish my business in Australasia China and Japan and marry you the Lord willing in nine months – if you will consent to make me completely happy.

I must say a good word for myself also as to prospects –
which thank the Lord appear to be very promising so that I
hope to be a rich man before long if I may share the blessing
with you its enjoyment will be a thousand fold increased ...

Affectionately, Mainville[9]

Burroughs realised that a reply to his proposal would be long in coming
and, desperately impatient to know Olive's response, wrote again after a
few days, this time sending a copy of this 'momentous' letter eastwards
via San Francisco, hoping it would arrive sooner. He would send a
recent photograph of himself. Meanwhile, as his 'splendid photo' of
her was in London – he had not anticipated his journey being longer
than a month – would she send him her picture? His work would keep
him away for some time longer, but would she join him for part of his
journey and meet him in San Francisco? Wanting her decision as soon
as possible, he requested that she reply by telegram to Melbourne rather
than by letter, asking her to use a code (telegrams being expensive).[10]
If Olive agreed, she was to send the code OLIVE, if 'no', PHINEUS,
if undecided, ATALANTA. He signed off: 'Till I hear I shall wait and
hope. Affectionately and fervently yours, Mainville,' adding that he was
arranging a paper he had written to be sent to her.[11]

This combination of detailed practical instructions with distinct
anxiety make Burroughs's letters both moving and amusing. Clearly
Carrie's rejection was the trigger for his proposal, while Olive's sensitive
and intelligent communications ignited the necessary spark when
he was feeling so lonely. Quite possibly he would have proposed to
someone else had Olive not written when and as she did, since one
gets the sense that, at this stage, he was working through a list of
his lady friends. Frustratingly, neither Olive's 'lovely letter' nor the
correspondence in which they engaged before this proposal have
survived. What is evident, however, is that Burroughs and Olive hardly
knew each other. They had first met by chance seven years earlier in
America, had last met four years previously and had 'occasionally
corresponded' since.[12] Burroughs was making a decision based on his
recollections of Olive, his great 'admiration' for her, and was influenced
by her letters to him. As was so often the case, he relied on his instincts
rather than on the experience of a close or lengthy friendship.

Burroughs described Olive to Wellcome as 'just the sort of girl you
would be glad to see my wife. Good looking though that's not her chief
attraction for she is so very lovely in her character & manner an angel

on earth – sure – intelligent … You can judge of her character from the photograph of her splendid face … a grand face,' and he asked Wellcome to retrieve her picture from his album at the Terry's house. The photograph he sent to Olive shows a good-looking man who cut a fine figure, well dressed in a smart suit, with high collar and a tall hat, looking intently at the camera and leaning against a pillar.

So who was Olive Chase? Born in New York state, she came from a large family. Her father, Benjamin Chase, was variously described in the census over the years as a millwright, miller, manufacturer, mechanic and farmer; he owned and operated a number of mills in Broadalbin, some 250 miles east of Medina, near Saratoga Springs. Broadalbin, like Medina, was a farming community, and besides corn-, paper- and sawmills, there were tanneries and glove-making businesses. Benjamin was a prominent citizen in the community and relatively wealthy.[13] Like Silas Burroughs snr, he had married three times. In 1848, within just six months of losing his first wife and two young sons, he married Hannah Taber. Olive, who was born two years later, had two older half-sisters, Mary Louise and Phebe, and a younger sister and brother. She was 13 when her mother died and 17 when her father remarried for the third time – his bride, Jerusha, being 21 years younger than him. Olive was very fond of her father, and she seems to have formed a close relationship with her stepmother, referring to her as 'mother'. With this family experience she differed from Burroughs, but otherwise there were striking similarities; both had parents who had lost children from their first marriage, both had lost their own mothers when they were in their teens, and both had seen their fathers remarry much younger women.

Olive's half-sister Mary Louise became a schoolteacher but continued to live with her father and stepmother, reflecting convention of the time, but Olive's ambitions took her far from home. After two years in elementary teacher training at Oswego, New York, she graduated in 1871 at the age of 21 and took up a teaching post, first in Potsdam, then in Gloversville. From there she moved even further away, to Kansas City, Missouri, for a further three years, and after that to Minneapolis, where she taught for five years. In 1883 she was appointed principal of Everett School, Minneapolis – though it is unclear whether she took up this post before marrying Burroughs. Such promotion indicates that Olive was highly regarded and had enhanced her status, as well as her salary. It also made her decision to marry a hard one, as it meant turning her back on a profession that she enjoyed.

Teaching was not a highly paid profession, and Burroughs said as much to Wellcome. Initially Olive's annual salary was $500, but as a principal she might have earned as much as $2,500. She enjoyed a very independent life in Minneapolis in the household of a travelling salesman from Connecticut, and among her fellow borders were a dressmaker and another schoolteacher, Sophia Lewis, a lifelong friend. Olive by now had a circle of close feminist friends of her own age. These included Dr Mary L. Swain, a gynaecologist, and Dr Adele Hutchinson, both formidable pioneer women physicians.[14]

This, then, was the Olive who now dominated Burroughs's thoughts, a thoroughly independent modern American woman, articulate and intelligent, with a circle of successful professional women friends. She was also attractive and warm-hearted and fitted Wellcome's description of the sort of woman that would suit Burroughs: bright, charming, full of sparkle and wit, who had something to say for herself.[15] Having proposed, Burroughs immediately planned Olive's future should she accept him, and his subsequent letters are full of ideas which might well have overwhelmed a less practical and sensible woman caught up in such a whirlwind. He soon wrote again, trying to reassure her that, although his prospects might not be as secure as he might wish, he believed they were good and that he trusted in God's providence, his motto being 'to be diligent in business fervent in spirit serving the Lord'. Although his work would take him another six months, he was impatient to be married, so would Olive travel to San Francisco and meet him there, where he knew a minister who could marry them? Her terms of engagement as a teacher might end in May or June, so would July the following year be too soon for them to wed? Would she write a long letter telling him about herself?[16]

Unable to restrain his impatience, he wrote again the following week, desperate to know her feelings and flattering himself that his sympathies and tastes were like hers. 'I feel like a stupid boor when I compare myself to your lovely disposition and character,' and described himself as a 'duffer' and 'conceited numbskull' in comparison with her.

Olive was to tell him about her school, which he imagined must be hard work, but did she still like teaching or did she get tired occasionally when there were 'stupid urchins'? He planned to get his life insured for her and to settle on her some shares in the New York Central Railroad. He supposed that she had told her parents of this proposal and they would be anxious for her welfare, so would she tell them from him that on their wedding day – 'if that should come please God' – he would give her these railway shares, which were then worth about $7,000. His business prospects he thought good enough to support her comfortably.[17]

Olive cannot have doubted Burroughs's serious intent, and here was evidence of the singlemindedness with which he pursued his goals. Before even receiving an acceptance he had suggested when and where they would marry, explained his financial position, offered Olive his valuable railway shares and suggested she give up her work as a teacher. This and subsequent letters also demonstrate that he was in awe of Olive's intellect despite the shortness of their relationship: while this could be interpreted simply as flattery, the tenor of his letters underlines a genuine regard and admiration. By now he was daily anticipating a telegraphed reply, and he made sure that the Victoria Coffee Palace informed him of any telegram addressed to RANIMANZO, which would mean that Olive loved and would marry him.[18]

Finally, on 20 September, after an agonising wait of seven weeks, the answer came. Burroughs replied at once, this time to 'Dearest Olive':

> Your dear message came two hours ago – Bless your dear heart I have almost believed you would accept me all the while. Perhaps I am too much inclined to hopefulness when I saw the dear word Olive my heart gave a big bounce and has been going on pretty lively ever since. I feel about ten pounds lighter. Got a smile on all the while and can't help it. There's one more happy and conceited man in the world and I'm the man.

He wanted to send her a nice engagement ring, but the duty payable on diamonds would be excessive and it would not be right to send it in a letter – besides which he did not know her size. So would she use some or all of the cheque he was sending her – and he would gladly send another if need be. His generous offers were seemingly endless.

Olive had mentioned her physician friend Mary Swain, and Burroughs wondered whether Olive would like to study medicine, in which case he offered to pay for her course. Such a study would also complement her 'useful scientific knowledge'. He was thinking of taking a course in medicine himself as soon as he could, and maybe they could study together: 'Any study would be pleasant if I could have one hand around your waist dear.' He did not propose 'turning Doctor' or leaving his present business, which he liked immensely, but as it had much to do with the medical profession and with medical literature a knowledge of medicine would be helpful. 'I have sort of knowledge of it as far as *materia medica* goes but not up in physiology surgery … which I am desirous of know[in]g.' Qualifying in medicine would also raise his standing with the medical profession and be 'a worthy means of social advancement', and since he and Wellcome wanted to start a medical journal soon it would help to be qualified to do so.[19]

Burroughs wrote frankly of his financial situation:

> As things are going now I suppose the Good Lord has given me for my own about 35,000 dollars. That's what I meant when I spoke of being a rich man … Mr Wellcome writes me that our business is flourishing. The last 3 months being the best we have had yet both in sales & profits. Sales over $50,000 profits over $5,000 net. Our business is however speculation and risky to a certain extent but I hope will soon get beyond this to a safe & substantial reality for your dear sake more than for my own.[20]

Burroughs's next short business letter to Wellcome included a paragraph wedged between work matters that must have come as a bombshell. 'You will be glad to learn of my successful proposal. Miss Chase has accepted me and I wish to marry her as soon as I get to the dear old US.' He described her as 'very intelligent, good looking, amiable and true as steel. A perfect lady and used to the best society.' He said he was marrying her not for money but for love and admiration, both of herself and her character. 'You will like her immensely I am sure.'[21]

After their first encounter, Burroughs had visited Olive and her father in Kansas City, and he wondered if Olive would have thought him presumptuous if, after only a few days' acquaintance, he had expressed the admiration he felt for her. He had felt an immediate desire to have her confidence, esteem and friendship and now went so far as to ask if she had not always thought he was in love with her and suspected it from his long continuous attentions to her. In spite of his loving letters to Olive, or maybe because his thoughts now turned to romance, Burroughs still had a roving eye, and women preoccupied him.

Shortly after his proposal he wrote about the 'Lovely Miss Murray' in Adelaide. In Sydney, he encountered a Miss Garran, with whom he seems to have been infatuated: 'one of the prettiest girls in Australia or anywhere. Very lovely manners too … her look seems now to charm my eyes and melt my heart … how when my hand grasped hers did her touch thrill me. I think I must be in love with her for I find myself thinking of her every day and hour and her face and form are always before me.' Olive might have been still more concerned to know that, the day after confiding this in his journal, her fiancé anonymously sent flowers to Miss Garran, 'to tell her in their own sweet language that I love her and shall always wish her joy – peace – happiness', hoping that 'some day we shall meet in good time and be near & dear to each other.'[22]

To be fair, he wrote the same day to Olive, wishing she were with him to enjoy the area around Sydney, the temperance picnic grounds at Cremorne, the harbour, grass, sea breeze, birdsong and nature. There is a month's gap in his diaries, and when they recommence he is in Auckland and makes no mention of the lovely Miss Garran. Her place had been taken by the beautiful Miss Baker, with whom he waltzed in the art gallery, 'where the lights were nearly all out', and who was 'the homliest girl in the room and she sold soap!'[23] And in Waiwera he admired the daughter of a missionary in the Friendly Islands who was known as the princess of Tonga.[24] Yet he wanted Olive with him to share his enjoyment. 'I want to come to you as soon as I can without neglecting my business ... I am very anxious to get our business on a strong foundation by the time I come for you dear so that when we are married I can take jolly good care of you and give you everything you want.'

Burroughs's New Year's resolutions included the hope of marriage to Olive before the year's end and that he would make a good fortune in the meantime. A busy social life and new acquaintances only reminded him of his solitary state, and he was envious of the couples that strolled together in the moonlight, 'talking so confidentially and close together. ... I felt so lonely – so lonely ... The perfect life is only found in wedlock. May that good time come soon ...'

A few days after his proposal, Burroughs received the sad news from two old family friends in Medina that his elder sister Emma had died from typhoid pneumonia not long after the death of her son, Burdett. Emma Dean was a year older than Burroughs and was not as close to him as Lina. She had been unwell for several years and had nursed her son so devotedly 'as to injure her own feeble health'.[25] Burroughs was filled with remorse for not having been a better friend and brother to her and felt guilty that his absence from home had prevented him from supporting his family at this time. Losing a close relative and unable to share his grief with friends and family emphasised his loneliness. He contemplated his 'Dear suffering patient loving sister Emma ... When I think how seldom I wrote to her how few thoughts I gave to her I grieve to think I did not requite her fond affection and that without meaning to be so I was guilty of unkindness toward her ... She suffered long and was kind.'

Burroughs's thoughts now turned inwards, and he questioned his conduct and the purpose of his life. Jottings in his notebook record a day of 'sunshine, of life's joys and smiles, the showers of penitential tears, the mists of doubt ... I begin to fear I am not doing right in giving myself so entirely to the business I am in, to the comparative neglect of those who have the strongest claims upon me to whom I am under the greatest obligations.' To his Medina friends and to Carrie he had justified his world trip by emphasising the foundation of the business and raised the possibility of establishing a branch house in New York or Boston, where he could spend his life nearer home and his friends 'in his own dear country', with a trip occasionally to England and his friends there.[26] He felt a particular obligation to his uncle and aunt, who had cared for the family for many years in times of need.

In this melancholy frame of mind Burroughs wrote an emotional letter, full of self-reproach and regret, to 'My dear old friend Wellcome'. After discussing Emma, he responded to Wellcome's previous criticisms in one of the most friendly and open letters the two men had ever exchanged. He also wrote to his pastor, asking to be remembered in his prayers, and around the same time corresponded with Dr Parker at the City Temple, with his church in Medina, and with the first Presbyterian Church in Philadelphia, as he wished to be formally adopted as a member of their church in London.

In the spring of 1883 Burroughs kept chopping and changing his mind about his travel plans. For personal reasons he did not now wish to prolong his journey to Japan, China and the Far East. Later that year he devised a short-lived and impossibly over-ambitious proposal to leave Australia in August, spend a month in the States and then return to India by early October or November via San Francisco or London: he would spend only a month in America, during which time he would court and marry Olive.

He received a long letter from Wellcome, who had visited his family in Medina again.[27] Off his own bat, Wellcome decided to call on Burroughs's 'old flame' Carrie Davis to learn if her engagement had been broken off and, if so, why. 'Knowing how strongly you were attracted to Carrie and remembering that you had said you loved her more than any girl you had ever met I thought it a duty to you as a friend to learn if, it was really true, that she had broken off her engagement on your account or was disposed to do as requested by Mrs Davis.' Wellcome learnt from Burroughs's aunt and Lina that Carrie's parents had intervened in her affair with her fiancé, successfully inducing her to end it with the promise of a generous present, and Carrie had briefly broken off her engagement: subsequently she had resumed it, and the couple were soon to be married. From his brief visit he heartily endorsed Burroughs's description of Carrie: 'she appears to be a most loveable girl in her personal appearance, manners, amiability and in the sunshine of her face.'

The final and longest section of Wellcome's letter told of his visit to none other than Olive Chase, not only to introduce himself but to see for himself what sort of a future wife his partner was to marry. He had previously warned Burroughs to be wary of a woman choosing him for his wealth and was evidently suspicious of Olive's motives. His comments say little about Olive but reveal much about himself and his assessment of his partner's character.

> Now about your Olive branch – While in Minneapolis I called on Miss Chase and had about five minutes conversation with her – she is undoubtedly a smart intelligent instructor, otherwise she could not occupy her present situation. ... I presume that you have considered well before asking for her hand and are quite satisfied. Only two persons should either make a match or break it and those are the contracting parties.
>
> I want to see you marry a good true noble christian woman – one who is intelligent, refined, cultivated and above all is patient, affectionate, sympathetic and will love you with her whole heart and being – devoid of wish to wear the trousers. If the above describes Miss Chase then I congratulate you with all my heart.
>
> ... but in falling in love you have not looked deep into the soul of the object of your admiration ... you judge too liberally and too readily accept compliments, gush and flattery as sincere expressions while you resent criticisms which are really sincere and honestly beneficial in guarding you against error – I mean to say that the complimenting acquaintance ruins your heart while you repel the frank critic. ... I have seen this repeatedly when you trusted those who flattered you ... while their sole object was to use you or gain some selfish end.
>
> I have always feared that you would marry a woman whom you did not know and that you would sadly repent it at your leisure – or that *by* your polite attentions you would allow some woman to fasten herself onto you with the plea that you had encouraged her into the belief that you meant matrimony & would finally marry her out of charity.

...

Your personal acquaintance and association with Miss Chase seems very slight for an engagement, and especially that you have not seen her for more than four years. ...

...

Regarding Miss Chase I will only add that I hope you will become acquainted with her and she with you <u>before</u> marriage. It is far better for both to become acquainted before than after. You are absolutely strangers to each other and you do Miss Chase as <u>great wrong</u> as you do yourself by even encouraging her and especially by marrying until you are familiar with the disposition of each other ...

There is certainly no hurry for either of you to get married and there are several very good reasons why neither of us should marry for several years to come and I hope you will not hasten yours too quickly – at any rate I want to be present even if it be in Borneo.

As regards my prospects to matrimony I have <u>none</u> and am not at all anxious.

I expect to meet the one someday, until then I am a contented bachelor. With warm regards Yours faithfully, Henry S Wellcome.[28]

What did Burroughs make of this letter and of Wellcome? It shouted – Do not marry now and do not choose a woman who is going to take the lead in a relationship or who lacks warmth – the clear implication being that Carrie had the necessary qualities that he had not seen in Olive. Yet Wellcome's own judgement was based on only a five-minute meeting with Olive. The letter may possibly have made Burroughs consider his hasty proposal, but it might also have led him to trust his instincts that Olive would make him a good wife. He knew that his engagement was at this stage only an engagement and, indeed, had written to tell Carrie about it, saying that his regard for Olive continued to grow with their better acquaintance, so he was 'hoping to marry her' on his return home.[29] Wellcome was right – it had been years since he had met Olive and he did not know her well – yet the suggestion that there was no need to rush into wedlock may have irked him. Clearly he had no wish for a long engagement, and in all likelihood both he and Olive wanted children. Olive's letter to Burroughs describing this meeting – which had evidently been very unsatisfactory for both parties – would have made interesting reading had it survived. The brevity of the encounter might be explained simply because Olive was unprepared for Wellcome's unannounced arrival or had been busy with other appointments. Being no fool, she might well have resented being checked over or patronised, especially as their conversation would almost certainly be reported to her fiancé. Burroughs received Wellcome's letter some two months before his return to America in time to plant doubt that longer should be spent with Olive before they married.

In any event, Wellcome's visit and letter had repercussions. It is not impossible that at some point Burroughs revealed some of its contents to Olive; if so, it would not have endeared Wellcome to her. This crucial first contact reveals that Wellcome did not take to Olive, and one strongly suspects that the feeling was mutual. It also marked a turning point in Burroughs's relationship with his partner. The two men had previously shared details of their private lives and desires but had very different expectations for an ideal wife. Wellcome had decided Olive was not right for Burroughs because she was not the sort of woman that *he* would want to marry, insensitive to the fact that Burroughs was seven years older than him and now wanted a family. The letter also made clear that Wellcome did not trust his partner's judgement, which might well have rankled. Wellcome could hardly have played his hand more badly: henceforth Burroughs would not communicate his innermost thoughts to his partner. Neither man was to know that Wellcome's future marriage, for all his careful planning, was to be an absolute disaster.

Burroughs left Australia hastily in July to return to his uncle in America. On his arrival in San Francisco he learnt that Isaac had died and so hurried to Medina. From there he made his way to Olive in Minneapolis to find that the speedy wedding he had hoped for would not happen; the decision about marriage was to be a joint one. They both spent time getting to know each other better, and Burroughs met Olive's family and friends; he continued to work and travel on the eastern seaboard.

Wellcome originally intended sailing to America by 1 September and to meet Burroughs in Medina, but business events led him to change his mind. In early October he wrote, urgently requesting more funds for the firm. Burroughs immediately left Medina for Rochester, taking with him 56 New York Central Railroad shares to use as collateral against a loan. 'I hope this will see you through,' he wrote to Wellcome.[30] Meanwhile, Kirby, the firm's chief clerk, informed him that Wellcome was ill through overwork. Burroughs responded at once: perhaps he should have returned to the UK sooner to relieve his partner of some or all of this extra work for a while and given him the opportunity of taking a vacation in America – actually he had offered to return if required only the previous month and on other occasions.[31] Alternatively he suggested that the firm could employ a young physician to stand in for Wellcome, Burroughs happily bearing the cost of his salary.[32] Wellcome dismissed this idea out of hand, acknowledging the generous spirit that had prompted it but declining to accept compensation in any form. In fact, he asked in turn if Burroughs wished to stay in America a few months longer.[33] At the same time Burroughs reiterated his wish to remain in America all winter, partly to support his widowed aunt and also to establish a branch or corresponding house in America as long as she was alive. He mentioned the possibility of attending medical lectures 'for the purpose of increasing my efficiency in our medical & pharmaceutical business'. This he could do in Buffalo and get home to see his aunt afterwards. Wellcome responded: 'I recognize that a course of medical lectures would be of great value to you and to our firm – ... I leave the matter to your own judgement & feelings – I shall be perfectly content to accept your decision.' At this stage it is clear Burroughs was torn between obligations to his firm and his family and keen to settle and marry Olive. The idea of staying and working in America appeared to offer a solution, but he wrote to Wellcome that he would be glad to comply with Wellcome's wishes and respond to the demands of the business.

Burroughs now kept from Wellcome the progress of his engagement, either because the situation was uncertain or quite probably because he knew of Wellcome's real feelings and wanted no more advice on the subject. Wellcome was moved to write, 'You don't say anything about Miss Chase,' and tentatively enquired whether perhaps he had upset Burroughs. 'I hope you are not annoyed because I answered so plainly over the subject of matrimony. I feel a deep interest in anything that interests you – hope to always enjoy your confidence in such matters.'[34] His letter crossed with one from Burroughs, who told him: 'Now my dear old fellow. I want you to let me know by return mail if our business prospects are sufficient to warrant my taking a life partner to share them with me. I should exceedingly like to be married this fall or winter and to bring my wife with me to London.'[35] Unsurprisingly, the answer when it came was not to Burroughs's liking. After explaining how busy he was, Wellcome went on to say 'no' to a possible wedding in the fall or winter and strongly urged Burroughs to postpone marriage until next autumn. He wanted to be present at their wedding and thought it better if Burroughs took time preparing a nice comfortable house for his wife somewhere other than in 'charmless London'; this was hardly the strongest of arguments for postponement.[36] Wellcome added that it was unlikely that he himself would marry soon as he had never met a woman with whom he wanted to share his life, although Burroughs might be able to find one for him from among the great number on whom he had 'been sweet'.

In the meantime, what was happening between Olive and Burroughs? Rumours abounded. Wellcome had 'learned from outsiders here that you had stated that you & the young lady were not quite certain whether or not you were suited for each other & there were prospects that the match wd be broken off – that you were very much puzzled over the subject etc.' Yet again he warned against the marriage and wished that Burroughs would write with a little more freedom on this subject.

Wellcome's intrusive advice went unheeded and the rumours proved groundless. On 2 January 1884, some four months after his arrival in America, Silas Mainville Burroughs and Olive Augusta Chase walked down the aisle at St Paul, Minnesota. Burroughs wrote to Medina friends a fortnight later that 'Olive says she is happy (and she always tells the truth). As for myself I never was so happy, and what more could any man want in a wife than I have in Olive. There <u>never</u> was a <u>better</u> girl in the world.'

In the cold winter weather the couple enjoyed warm and comfortable railway sleeping cars and hotels as they travelled from St Paul to Medina. There they stayed in one of the town hotels, spending their time visiting family and numerous friends. Olive liked them, and they certainly all liked her: Burroughs's aunt and sister took a great fancy to her and thought he had been exceedingly fortunate in getting such a lovely wife.

A very different life faced the newlyweds, who planned to travel to England within the month. Burroughs's work and travels continued to take him far and wide, but despite long periods apart their marriage was to prove a loving and successful one.

Chapter 9

'Bones of Contention'[1] and Brotherly Strains

We blame each other for various things which are not our faults –
but due to the failures of the past ...[2]

It might be supposed that the shared achievements of Burroughs and Wellcome would have drawn them closer together. They had, after all, known each other for many years; undertaken the same training at Philadelphia; had similar experiences as travelling salesmen; shared many mutual friends and business acquaintances on both sides of the Atlantic; and, not least, shared the same ambitions. Yet, even in these early years, strains in their relationship and bickering can be detected, exacerbated by their separation during Burroughs's lengthy travels between October 1881 and March 1884. Disagreements arose from simple misunderstandings, aggravated by delays in communications and differences in their working methods; at times both men were under great stress, depressed or unwell. Financial worries and arguments over the partnership agreement compounded this, and resentments and grudges emerged in these early days which went unresolved and therefore festered.

Wellcome had not been idle during Burroughs's absence and felt justifiably proud of all he had accomplished, implementing the many suggestions Burroughs had sent him, liaising with agents, dealing with official bureaucracy over taxes and patents, attending meetings of the British Medical Association and handling office moves and building works. He had travelled to France, twice to America, and wintered in Spain in 1883–4.

Sudlow, the general manager, and Kirby, the chief clerk, were proving invaluable assets, and they kept in touch with Burroughs throughout his travels. More travellers were employed, two in Britain and two abroad, their expenses monitored assiduously by Wellcome. Leaflets, sometimes drafted by Burroughs, were translated, printed in London and distributed internationally as Burroughs instructed; trademarks were registered abroad and in London; doctors in Britain continued to be visited; and eminent medics were solicited for endorsements of the firm's products. Imitation tablets and other goods were noticed increasingly by both partners, necessitating stern letters and threats of prosecution by Wellcome. Advertising in medical and other journals in England, India and Australasia continued to be identified as crucial to the firm's success, and the scale of the firm's promotions was stepped up. In addition to advertising in *The Lancet*, a *Medical Formulae* book was distributed to 'the grand Mogul Drs' in a sales campaign which took the medical profession by storm.[3] Burroughs, 'much pleased', now considered the possibility of printing a book on modern medicine and pharmacy.[4] As we have seen, the important Kepler Malt Extract Company had been acquired after long negotiation,[5] and Fellows Manufacturing Co., New York, producers of Hypophosphite Syrup – who looked likely to give up their agency when Burroughs was in India – had been persuaded to remain. The two partners communicated at length on how to achieve the highest standards for their products and worked closely on producing attractively packaged items, as well as on the content and design of new medical cases.[6] The firm's agencies were reassessed and renegotiated, and American agencies were reminded that distribution and marketing in England or India differed from their own practices. All this was essential in order to keep ahead in an ever more competitive market.

During Burroughs's absence Wellcome had successfully negotiated with HM Customs & Excise over the firm's interpretation of the Stamp Act, boasting to Burroughs of his 'ingenious and exhaustive defences', something Burroughs would have done well to remember in his later legal dealings with his partner.[7] The partners knew that it was now imperative that the firm should develop its own manufacturing capacity to head off competition from newly established manufacturers in Britain and from lower priced imports from Europe and America.[8] Initially they had used Wyeths tablet-making machines sent from America, on which a much resented 20% royalty continued to be demanded. Attempts to renegotiate the agreement with Wyeths and manufacture their own compressed tablets continued: Burroughs feared being made a 'catspaw' and mistrusted them, and Wellcome agreed that they were 'greedy spirited'.[9] This prompted the dispatch of their chemist, Otto Witte, to America and Germany to report on new machines and design a prototype, leading eventually to the installation at the firm's Wandsworth factory of improved machines capable of greater output. With expansion in production and staffing came a need for more office space, so an additional floor was rented in their Snow Hill building. Then in March 1883 Wellcome leased buildings, a private dock for barges, and a fresh water supply at Bell Lane Wharf, Wandsworth,[10] to accommodate the manufacture of their own compressed tablets in what amounted to the firm's first chemical works; it was managed by Otto Witte.

Yet more office space was now essential. When a recently constructed and still unoccupied building became available opposite their Snow Hill offices, Wellcome informed Burroughs but said he considered it was too expensive. Burroughs, however, was very enthusiastic. He thought that the location was perfect and they should take it if the business could stand it, using it for offices and storage. If a lift was installed, another large floor could be added to the roof for a laboratory. 'We shall need large premises as large as Wyeth in Philadelphia someday,' he counselled Wellcome.[11] A lease was taken and fitting-out put in hand; it all took longer than thought, and the firm moved in early in 1884.[12]

Some English competitors derided the firm's achievements. As Wellcome said, 'the English people as a rule detest progress & novelty – whatever we have won here has been by persistent fighting.' He put down their success to the effort, patience and money that the partners had invested in it: no entrepreneur should attempt to follow in their footsteps in bringing American goods to the European markets without ample capital (which of course was what Burroughs had supplied) and the patience to wait for results. He reckoned that four times the personal labour and expenditure was needed in England to produce the same results as in America.

Burroughs's world journey had been costly, provoking Wellcome repeatedly to raise concerns about it. He urged Burroughs when in Turkey to adhere to their agreed regular terms of business because the firm was skating on thin ice and needed every penny of profit.[13] Although there are lamentable gaps in the firm's financial records, they reveal what turbulent times it faced. Despite excellent growth in sales during the early years, good profits did not follow. There were various reasons for this, including relatively low capitalisation; the cost of carrying stock; the convention in the UK drug trade of long credits; the need for

16: Burroughs, Wellcome & Co., Snow Hill, in the 1880s.
The impressive new headquarters of the firm opened in early 1884.

investment in order to expand production; and the cost of acquiring the Kepler Malt Extract Co. A number of measures were needed at this time to keep the business afloat, among them the provision by Burroughs of a large personal loan and the extension of an existing loan.

Both men oscillated between expressing serious worries and steady confidence, depending on to whom they wrote. When communicating with Burroughs's aunt and uncle for example, Wellcome was always very positive. 'Our business is steadily improving,' he assured them, adding that without expenditure on advertising the business would not advance.[14] Yet he was far less optimistic when writing to his partner a month later, reporting the extraordinary strain of heavy payments since Burroughs's departure. The enormous cost of Burroughs's trip added to these.[15]

Was Burroughs excessively lavish in his expenditure? Wyeths had once complained of this, and Wellcome criticised the quantity of free samples and literature he distributed.[16] An assessment of any extravagance on Burroughs's part is hard to make, but the returns from it were substantial. Undoubtedly the firm's massive promotion spread its name and reputation at a key moment both for it and for expansion in pharmaceutical products.

Wellcome's concern about his partner's expenses was the cause of only one of many areas of friction between them. Simple misunderstandings were made worse by poor communications. They relied heavily on the telegraph, but this was expensive, not always available, and in any case did not allow any intimacy. Once Burroughs was hurt by a curt telegram; Wellcome agreed that the word 'please' might have helped but claimed he had deleted it on the grounds of cost. Another time Burroughs told Sudlow that he thought Wellcome had misinterpreted his telegram, 'which was much too brief for the sake of economy'.[17] Inevitably postal problems occurred, such as letters going astray, being returned or crossing the Atlantic twice. Samples and leaflets did not arrive in time, leaving Burroughs irritated and frustrated that his sales orders could not be supplied – blaming this on Wellcome's inefficiency.[18] The problem was compounded by his being continually on the move, changing his route and dates according to whom he met and what he found. Such flexibility was essential in allowing him to tailor his marketing and act on leads and instincts, but his hastily written orders and instructions, often jotted down on the move, were not always clear or easy to interpret. Wellcome's request that Burroughs report more systematically and use pre-printed forms provides an insight into their different approach to handling business.[19]

Stress and hard work began to weigh heavily on both men. Wellcome complained of feeling poorly and lacking strength during Burroughs's absence, although exhaustion from a busy social life may partly explain this; Burroughs told him to take better care of himself. At the same time Burroughs experienced several bouts of illness, in particular severe malarial fever when in India. He too suffered from exhaustion, and by the time he left India he was homesick and depressed. Physical and mental strains impinged on their business and personal relationship.

Shortly after Burroughs left on his travels, Wellcome warned him against undertaking a 'superficial jaunt', criticised his 'happy go lucky' manner in setting up agencies and appointing sub-agents overseas who were expensive and not always effective, and advised against opening direct foreign accounts and giving credit.[20] His subsequent complaint about the meagre information Burroughs sent back unsurprisingly irritated Burroughs, who by then was working hard in India, needed to cover a lot of ground and was desperate to receive samples. Unless Wellcome paid attention to his orders, he wrote, his work was 'nullified or destroyed', and he might as well have stayed at home and avoided the considerable expense of the trip. When he failed to hear from Wellcome for three months and no samples had been sent to Calcutta or Bombay, he wrote: 'It seems very discouraging to me after working hard and getting up a healthy demand for our goods that you pay no attention to my telegram for goods and thus throw cold water upon the enterprise.'[21] This was a stern rebuke, but two months later he mellowed and addressed Wellcome as 'Dear old boy', sending greetings to a long list of their mutual friends.[22]

His reply crossed with a 24-page letter from Wellcome: its tone was conciliatory but firm. He had written as he did with friendly motives and never in an 'offensive or dictatorial manner' and in turn had accepted when Burroughs had written plainly to him on several occasions noting his faults. They both knew each other's qualities well enough and did not need to exchange compliments. He was glad to know that Burroughs had intended to discover India thoroughly, that his costly telegram was unnecessary, and that he had not needed to repeat his advice about appointing agents but wanted figures and/or statements of facts, 'deeming it only proper that you should know the "whys and wherefores".'

To Burroughs's suggestion of bearing the expense of his voyage himself, he responded that he would 'positively never consent', although he agreed to being credited £2 per day, presumably for his extra workload.

And he denied saying anything that indicated that Burroughs had not worked most energetically: 'in fact I know full well that to canvass the towns in the brief time allowed by the brief stay of the Ceylon at each port would require mighty lively work' – a statement that sits at odds with his use of the expression elsewhere in the letter of 'pleasure trip'. While he acknowledged the difficulties of doing business in a proper manner when travelling, he asked why Burroughs had not used sailing time to write out full tabulated lists of doctors and chemists visited. And in emphatically pointing out how barren of profitable results the trip had been until India, he impressed on Burroughs the importance of changing tack and doing the rest of his trip thoroughly.

> In our friendly acquaintance, and in our more intimate relations as partners you have never found me niggardly nor inclined to shrink my burdens – I have only a feeling of liberality towards you, I speak plainly and always shall – you have found me most severe face to face. ...
>
> Sometimes my persistence may appear to you like conceit – but you cannot say that I am boastful ... You may not fully appreciate it but nevertheless it is a fact that if I had coincided with & put through all of your schemes for advertising, such as picture cards, show cards, handbills show cases etc we should have been in a tight squeeze long ago. You must more seriously consider that <u>money</u> is the motive power of business.[23]

Burroughs in response also bared his soul:

> You know I am rather impulsive ... perhaps too much given to saying and doing things in a hurry, and so may injure the feelings of others without any thought or wish to do so. ... True friends are not so many that one can afford to lose any, and I have for some time regarded you as my dearest and best and always true friend. It is therefore with regret and grief that I apprehend any lessening of the old friendship between us. If at any time I express myself strongly on any business matter, upon which we have different opinions, I hope you will not find in this any source for personal offence, but if I have given such occasion, I am very sorry, and ask your pardon for it, though you may be sure it has been an act of thoughtlessness on my part.

He went on to say that, after consideration, he agreed to short credits and the avoidance of foreign credits, concluding that Wellcome was right that this was the only safe policy, especially since the business was increasing faster than their capital. 'As this has been the bone of contention, we can now consider it disposed of thoroughly.'[24]

The relationship had been patched up. Yet this exchange reveals how fundamentally the partners differed in their approach to work and relationships; this difference was entrenched. Wellcome's natural caution, his desire for statistics and evidence before taking decisions, and his more formal, severe – even lecturing – manner were completely at odds with the methods of Burroughs. Wellcome asserted that everything he had done had been for the good of the firm, and he could not be blamed for lost letters, misunderstandings and the rest. Burroughs, while recognising his tendency to be impulsive, did not push justification of his actions in the way Wellcome did and was more generous in apologising. His attitude remained one of warmth, the emphasis being on friendship rather than on 'friendly acquaintance'. Significantly, Wellcome's belief in money as the essential ingredient of a business was not entirely shared by Burroughs, who was strongly influenced by his faith and the poverty he witnessed on his travels; he had higher motives of being able to improve mankind's lot.

Their most serious difference of opinion arose out of discussions over their 1880 partnership agreement. This stated that the original distribution of profits (3/5ths to Burroughs and 2/5ths to Wellcome) could be amended at any time after two years if Wellcome's capital equalled that of Burroughs. Burroughs wanted Wellcome to postpone his claim to equal partnership until September 1884 and also that a 'verbal understanding' made previously between them concerning the purchase of Kepler shares be conditional on delaying this partnership change: 'I think this will be agreeable to you especially as the two years here referred to in agreement will be up [to] my return to London to talk it over,' wrote Burroughs. He completely misjudged how this would be received.[25] Unsurprisingly, Wellcome was not at all enthusiastic: he told him that he found the suggestion 'insulting' and had taken advice from a QC. He also pointed out that not only was Burroughs's agreement with Kepler out of date but he had never signed it and had no right to claim royalties under it. As for the delayed equal partnership, his fury was emphasised with much underlining:

> I must express my <u>very serious regret</u> and <u>chagrin</u> at your proposal ... <u>You know</u> as <u>positively</u> and <u>clearly</u> as man can know any <u>fact</u> that I have worked as sincerely and devotedly

for the success of this business and have spared no effort and care to gain that end. You know that when the management fell into my hands the business was in such an entangled snarl that had you gone on in the old ways you would have been ruined. You know that as the result of my care and hard work the whole snarl has been cleared away. You know that the policy which was adopted by the firm under my management (though such policy was strongly opposed by you) has been thoroughly successful – while if the course urged by you had been carried out we should have been ruined and I have proved such to you in figures.

For good measure he added that, although Burroughs had worked hard, he had shared very little in the conduct and responsibilities of the firm, in particular handling the difficult negotiations with Kepler. 'You must not entertain the fallacious idea that you alone have made the success of BW&Co.' He concluded that he hoped that Burroughs would read and re-read his letter. 'I am very sorry that such a matter should arise between us for our relations have been unmarred by any serious misunderstanding but I cannot with any self-respect permit my rights in this matter to be treated as lightly as you seem to.' At best such differences were 'not pleasant'.

In spite of these words, Wellcome's letter enclosed a new draft agreement in which he offered to accept the delayed partnership arrangement until the following year – September 1883 – if by then he had made his capital equal. He had 'sacrificed' certain parts of his rights rather than endangering their relations by allowing differences to arise. It is not inconceivable, however, that this postponement actually suited Wellcome, who at this point did not have the funds to add to his capital and make it equal to that of Burroughs, a requisite of equal partnership.[26]

Two weeks before Wellcome wrote this angry letter, Burroughs was in Adelaide, reacting with grief to the news of the death of his sister Emma, who, unwell for years, had died in April. His diary noted that he had written to 'dear old Wellcome' that morning before breakfast and in the evening received a long, most kind and friendly letter from him. 'I had great hope and joy in the Lord today.' After discussing Emma he reflected on his dealings with Wellcome and opened up his heart. He apologised for failing to write social letters, believing Wellcome would be too busy and not bothered about this, taking for granted that their friendship and mutual regard was understood. 'In future we will be as brothers … Let me hear soon of your forgiveness and the renewed confidence and dear friendship of the old days. … Ever your friend and Brother – Maineville.'[27]

Soon he wrote again in a more cheerful, almost flippant vein, invigorated undoubtedly by his marriage proposal to Olive and his move to Melbourne:

> Hope you will write and tell me all about your trip and visit and flirtations if you ever should go for anything of the kind. I think we once started what we called a little flirtation which ended as such affairs sometimes do. I was smitten of course as I might have expected but as you were not it ends in a friendship that is very dear to me and which I hope will grow deeper and stronger as the years go by. I mean to write to you again by the next mail. Hope you'll do as much for me.
>
>   Your affectionate old bean, M.[28]

It is hard to know how to read this intriguing reference to 'the little flirtation': does this refer to the relationship with a third party or between the two of them? If the latter, then it indicates that Burroughs's feelings for Wellcome were quite deep and Wellcome's for him less so and is evidence that Burroughs's desire that Wellcome join his firm was based on a very close friendship as well as being a business decision. Although more letters from Wellcome remain than from Burroughs, Wellcome sometimes repeated the latter's comments. Burroughs wrote in haste, often changing his mind as soon as he had written; Wellcome's letters have been given more thought and are carefully worded, the impression being that they were penned with an eye to the future when they might be produced in evidence.

When the SS *Ceylon* returned to Southampton from her world cruise in August 1882, with Burroughs still being abroad, a curious Wellcome took the trouble to go and look her over. Christmas gifts were exchanged: Wellcome said he would always treasure his fine writing desk and slippers, and Burroughs received a magnificent travelling trunk. Early in 1883, on his return from America, Wellcome reported to Burroughs on their many mutual friends who enquired very specially after him and took pains to congratulate him on all his hard work, complimenting him on the style of an advertisement and an 'exceedingly well written' communication for *The Lancet* in March 1883; Wellcome reckoned they did Burroughs 'much credit' and sent copies to Wyeths and the Burroughs family. When Burroughs planned to return from Australia via America, Wellcome considered a further visit there, where together they could attend the American Pharmaceutical Association meeting in Washington or meet up in New York or Medina. In the event, a fire in the firm's offices in the Saracen's Head inn and delays to the building works at Snow Hill persuaded him to cancel this trip.[29]

Despite all these efforts to smooth over their differences, more discord arose in the autumn of 1883. Burroughs's ambitions for the firm were as bold as ever; he wanted the best firm and the best headquarters in London. That included customer service, and he placed great importance on achieving the highest standards. So he was furious when he thought that Wellcome had been negligent in completing orders and had written imprudent letters to customers – thereby causing some reputational damage. Back came Wellcome's riposte, condemning Burroughs's 'thoughtless impertinencies … You treat me as if I were one of the errand boys of the house to deliver your messages … These rash expressions do not harmonize well with the opening clause of your letter wherein you manifest a desire that nothing shall mar our cordial relations.'[30] Burroughs's irritation mounted when he discovered that Wellcome had not paid attention to his letters from Australia regarding Eucalyptia, although Wellcome had said he could see some potential for it. As things turned out, Eucalyptine, produced the following year, was to become a popular product of the firm.

In late 1883, uncertain when Burroughs would return, Wellcome nevertheless planned a reception for him. It was from their mutual friends the Terrys that he was to learn that Burroughs had arranged his passage on the steamer from America. He now looked forward to their meeting – the first for over two years – when they could 'discuss things verbally and communicate much better than by letter.' For their part, Wellcome's letters betray a range of emotions at this time: on the one hand, keen to have Burroughs home to discuss matters; on the other, displaying an underlying nervousness about their changed relationship and its implications for both of them and for the firm. 'I am very anxious for your return,' he wrote, yet went on to add: 'but there is no urgency.'

Ahead of their meeting he wrote Burroughs a very long letter, covering business but focusing on personal matters; it was one of unusual frankness and openness. He hoped to be able to attend Burroughs's wedding, while reiterating that he was more than likely to become an old bachelor looking at Burroughs's fireplace with envy. Maybe Burroughs could find a suitable woman for him? Was this a serious suggestion, or, more likely, was Wellcome attempting to elicit sympathy and renew the old friendship? An apprehensive Wellcome admitted some of his own failings and uncertainties. The last two years had been long ones for him, as he had not been able to discuss issues with Burroughs and had had to rely on his own judgement. He was anxious that Burroughs should recognise that no difference of opinion between them had for a moment ever changed his feelings from the warmest and sincerest friendship and hoped that this would continue.

'On reflection', he wrote, 'I sometimes think I am too angular and that I take too much liberty in criticizing my friends in a manner that they regard as severe & unkind. I fear that I have sometimes [?treated] you in this way.' He emphasised how hard he had been working, starting his letter with a pronouncement that his health was good, but ending it by declaring that he was fatigued, with a nervous weakness and needed a complete change.[31]

Other letters followed in which Wellcome justified his neglect in writing sooner on business matters because he thought it best to wait until Burroughs returned, and, besides, Burroughs overlooked his letters and rarely answered them. Further criticism ensued:

> While you are excessively sensitive yourself, you unintentionally but very often do say things which cause others a good deal of pain ... I say the above as a friend to a friend whom I love with all my heart and with a hope that you may give it more than a passing thought. For your own happiness as well as for the happiness of our friends you must think more carefully before you speak – wait & consider both sides ... I sincerely hoped that this long voyage around the world would prove to you how much easier life could be passed by avoiding friction – haste makes waste and a deal of unhappiness. ... You may rest assured that whether referred to or not in my letters everything you write is carefully read, weighed and considered. I have sometimes wondered if you ever carefully read my letters.[32]

Hurt sensibilities and resentments surface, almost as though they were the squabbles of a married couple! Their see-saw relationship by correspondence continued. Burroughs responded regarding Wellcome's health: 'I am very glad to read in the beginning of it your comfortable health and sorry that at the time of closing it that you are suffering from another attack of prostration. Dear old fellow you have had enough on hand to tire you out. You have had such labours & responsibilities to tackle and then the discouragement of my unreasonable fault finding besides. I know you have done your best and am satisfied with everything you have done.'[33]

Such friendly words were all too soon replaced by stern ones, once again over their partnership agreement, although this time the context had changed and Burroughs provoked their next disagreement. Concerned that it would be difficult for him to leave America before the spring because of his aunt's health, and aware that Wellcome needed help, Burroughs now suggested that John van Schaak should become Wellcome's assistant. John was the son of Peter van Schaak, an old business and social friend of Wellcome from his time in Chicago, and his son had joined him in business. Burroughs also knew them both and reckoned that Wellcome would be pleasantly surprised with arrangements he had discussed with John, whereby the latter would be involved at a senior level in their business on the continent, holding out an inducement of partnership in the main business. 'He seems to be just the man to assist you in carrying out important details which you have not time to attend to owing to the growth of the business.'[34]

Predictably, Wellcome angrily rebutted the whole scheme: he did not need another partner or a representative on the continent and should have been consulted. John might be clever and active, but he was 'in no way suited to our business'. Burroughs had placed him in a very awkward situation, since John was also his friend, and it would be difficult to extract himself from such a compromising agreement. He added: 'I look upon partnership as next to matrimony in serious importance and there are very few men in this world I would associate myself with as a partner ... I am afraid that you have been somewhat indiscreet in holding out a partnership – I am quite certain that you did it thoughtlessly and without intent to do me an injustice ... It seems to me that you have too light a view of partnership matters.'[35]

Although Burroughs's agreement with John was conditional on Wellcome's willingness to accept it, he undoubtedly overstepped the mark in acting in this high-handed way without prior consultation. It demonstrated a failure on his part to appreciate Wellcome's contribution to the firm in his absence, still regarding him as a junior partner and subordinate. Wellcome insisted that Burroughs withdraw from the arrangement and tell John there was no opening for him. In the event a compromise was reached: John came over to England and Wellcome admitted that he had much improved. After discussions John agreed to join the firm without the encouragement of a partnership: he worked for BW&Co. on the continent for a period before returning to the US. Fortunately, friendship with the van Schaak family was retained.

By the end of 1883 a great deal of business needed to be discussed. With Burroughs still in America, Wellcome determined to sail there as soon as possible and meet him in Medina. Burroughs almost certainly dissuaded him, since Wellcome instead spent the winter in Spain, leaving the steadfast Sudlow to manage the firm. Burroughs married Olive on 2 January 1884, and the couple left New York on the SS *Gallia* on 14 February. He had been away for nearly two and a half years.[36]

Burroughs's absence abroad was an astonishingly long period for the business. Undoubtedly his world tour was hugely successful, but it created more than simply a physical distance between the partners. During that time both men had developed and changed: each of them had, in a sense, been able to carry out their work with some independence. Their first serious difference of opinion came with the suggestion of a revised partnership agreement. Irritations and angry exchanges kept surfacing, only to be repeatedly patched up. The London office meanwhile became accustomed to working with Wellcome, and a pattern was set for the future when the partners would increasingly take turns in being absent from the office. The fundamental personal and business reasons which caused disagreement between them were not likely to be resolved with Burroughs's return to London. Quite the contrary, they would reappear in the future.

Chapter 10

Atlantic Crossings and Divided Lives

*His firm cut out a path for themselves, and made of
it a great highway.*[1]

So much had changed since Burroughs left England in 1881. He returned
with a wife, which brought more personal responsibilities, to an awkward
and at times tense relationship with his business partner, and to a firm
which had developed dramatically. A visit to the magnificent new office
at Snow Hill was his first priority on arrival in London in February 1884;
he wanted 'the Boss premises of the Drug business in London' and he
got it.[2] The *Chemist and Druggist* sang its praises: 'everything about
the exterior of the building has a solidity which seems to say, "We have
come to stay", and this is no less apparent in the interior.'[3]

Enthusiastic about the site from the start, Burroughs saw the
opportunities for 'gilt-edged advertisements' on large windows. The
imposing seven-storey building of red brick and stone with Corinthian
columns was no less magnificent inside. Wellcome had gone overboard
with his attention to detail: he had ensured the highest standards of
workmanship to create a 'rich and artistic' appearance by employing
the celebrated art decorator Christopher Dresser to design and direct
the works. The wood used was American walnut, with a Moorish
design for desks and windows, suggesting flamboyance. The mosaic
floor of the vestibule pictured Commerce and Industry; chairs and
settees were upholstered in alligator hide; bound volumes of medical
and pharmaceutical literature lined the walls. In the general office an
American eagle sat on a huge American safe, and there was a small-scale
model of the Statue of Liberty, supposedly modelled by Bartholdi's own
hand. Clearly the firm recognised its American roots as a marketing asset.

The office was overlooked by a half-moon gallery used by lady clerks. The first floor had an en-suite set of three rooms, a library and a writing room: soon a grand piano and an American organ were added for staff use (often played by Sudlow). Here Burroughs's triangular-shaped room had 'little of pretension', being furnished with a writing cabinet, a revolving bookcase – holding mostly modern medical and pharmaceutical works such as Lauder Brunton's *Materia Medica and Therapeutics* and Remington's *Pharmacy* – and a chemical test cabinet. Wellcome's room, by contrast, looked more like a 'bachelor's den' than a commercial office, with a library which included general literature, hunting trophies, works of art, and a statuette of Henry Ward Beecher: it underlined his keen interest in the collection of objects. In all of this there was a style, if not a functionality, which stood out from many other London offices and must have made a big impression on visitors.

A brand name was now required for the growing range of compressed tablets that the company has started to manufacture in 1883.[4] Various alternatives had been mooted when Burroughs was in Australia, such as 'Pil-Ovoid', 'Equaloid', 'Equoid' and 'Elixoid'. On his return the name 'Tabloid' was decided on and registered as a trademark in March 1884.[5] Wellcome did the actual registration and has been credited as devising the name, but Burroughs was back in the office at this time and the decision was almost certainly a joint one. 'Tabloid' was also applied to other products such as lint and medical chests. The effectiveness of the name is shown by the fact that over the years other firms tried to hijack it, and much time and energy was spent in thwarting them. Ultimately the term 'tabloid' became shorthand for other products, notably for smaller format newspapers.[6]

Burroughs was worried at seeing so many imitations of BW&Co.'s compressed tablets, some even having metal boxes and label wraps similar to theirs, and their trade risked falling into the hands of competitors. As if that were not enough, Customs & Excise's recent stringent application of import duties on foreign drugs continued to be a concern. The firm could not compete if handicapped in this manner, and Burroughs wrote despairingly: 'It may be four years and it may be forever before this cursed stamp law is repealed. We certainly cannot hold our trade on the pills 6 months if we have to stamp them … that just as seems as if about to turn them around and make a profit on the pills, the laws of this stupid country step in and rob us of our earned reward.'

In March Burroughs caught a cold and suffered 'a slight attack of pleurisy', so on medical advice he delayed a planned journey to Switzerland until June, when he and Olive set off, combining a belated honeymoon with work. The next two months set the pattern for what was to become Burroughs's usual travel schedule. He zigzagged back and forth across the continent with Olive, then on his own, mixing work with leisure.

In spite of minor irritations the partners got on reasonably well and participated in social events together.[7] Both offered sympathy and practical support to one of their travellers – a family friend of Burroughs – who had blotted his copybook though personal indiscretions. It showed their liberalism, and the person in question, Corning Weld, went on to be a useful employee of the firm.[8] In late summer Wellcome's health gave rise to concern, but despite this he travelled to America in early August. Burroughs wished him a pleasant and prosperous journey, hoped that the sea air and voyage would do him good, and passed on an invitation from his sister and aunt to visit them, so their cordiality continued. At the same time he chided Wellcome for his grudging hospitality to their mutual friend Miss Steers when she was in London, despite the kindnesses Wellcome had received from her and her family in New York.

Yet Burroughs was in fact undecided about his future and, ever unpredictable and full of surprises, from Kiel wrote to Wellcome – now in New York – with a startling proposal: 'I should be willing to close out my interest in the business to you or to sell to you the larger part of it and to take up my home again in the United States. The good will of this business I suppose would be considered very valuable but I would not set any price upon it ... I await your reply to this letter with considerable interest and perhaps anxiety also.' His reasons centred on his wish to be nearer his widowed elderly aunt, although it seems likely that both he and Olive missed America. He also asked Wellcome to send some money from America as early as possible, reminding him that the railway shares which he had previously offered as security for the firm were no longer available as he had settled them on Olive when they married.[9]

Wellcome's reply is not known, but inevitably he would have wanted further discussion on his return from America: Burroughs did not refer to this suggestion again in his following letters, though he was clearly concerned about the financial position of the firm and considering other options. Liquidity was now a serious problem, as the firm's funds were locked up in the factory, storehouse and office, as well as in consignments overseas. They therefore needed more capital for their large business, and soon. 'I have been thinking it might be advisable to form into a stock company as with double our present capital we would be able to conduct it to the best advantage.' This was the first time Burroughs had suggested adopting joint stock company status, a corporate form increasingly used by growing and forward-thinking businesses at this time to spread financial responsibilities. Not unreasonably, he asked for repayment of some of the money Wellcome owed him as he had personal use for it. He would be glad if Wellcome paid him 'the amount of his note of £800 and over' soon, and wrote at that opportune moment, since Wellcome was

> among friends and relatives in America where I believe you have loaned out money. I don't suppose you are aware of it but last May I am credited with over £9,000stg while your a/c on our books credits you with £500 odd. I am therefore confident that you will at the earliest possible moment make your investment in the business equal with mine by putting in £400 and allowing me to withdraw £4,500, or if I leave this in then you will be glad to make your investment equal to mine.[10]

The figures underline Burroughs's far greater financial stake in the business relative to Wellcome's investment. Two days later he wrote again and launched into an analysis of the proportionate capital invested by both of them, reiterating the need for more capital, the suggestion of a third partner and the possibility of his selling out. He suggested that McKesson & Robbins would help Wellcome in raising some money, unless Wellcome preferred to look elsewhere for the funds.

There seems now more than a hint of urgency in Burroughs's urgings, as the business – typical of many expanding and ambitious enterprises – was suffering a lack of liquidity; it had inadequate cash flow. This problem may have been at the heart of a small incident that occurred at this time and which mortified Burroughs. Wellcome had failed to make a payment into Burroughs's account at the Bank of Medina. He pointed out to Wellcome that he always took great pains to pay all his debts promptly and would be sorry if his reputation and financial standing among his old friends in his home town was damaged.

Wellcome failed to respond to letters, and Burroughs complained of not hearing from him for over ten days. By mid-October Sudlow was also concerned and wrote: 'Not being able to comprehend the silence maintained by you in the face of the exceedingly urgent letters I have lately addressed to you I at last cabled "Important letters … and reply".' Wellcome this time responded promptly by telegram: 'Letters answered – advise situation.' Meanwhile Burroughs had at last heard from Wellcome, who was making arrangements 'to relieve the pinch' and planned to return to London by 1 November.[11] It was a laid-back response, and Burroughs remained worried; in mid-October he again urged a conversion to a joint stock company. The options were simple: the firm could continue by Wellcome increasing his capital contribution, by issuing shares to friendly investors and employees if converted to a joint stock company, or by being bought out by Wellcome.

Still no decision was made. On Wellcome's passage to London – now delayed to late November – Burroughs telegraphed him on the SS *Umbria* with an invitation to go straight to the Lymans in Norwood, 'make himself at home' with Olive, and join them for Thanksgiving.[12] Doubtless urgent discussion was also on the agenda. In any event, the longer-term issues and cash-flow problem did not go away, and the New Year ushered in the first really difficult discussions over continuation of their partnership.

In January 1885, Burroughs took a key step and instructed his solicitor, George Radford, to send Wellcome – as arranged by him and Burroughs – a formal statement of his claims under the deed of partnership. It stated that the accounts of the firm kept during Burroughs's absence from October 1881 were drawn up in a manner prejudicial to his interests. Annual turnover had increased hugely, and although capital in the business had also risen it was clearly insufficient to finance their very great increase in turnover. Moreover, most of the additional capital had been contributed by Burroughs, not Wellcome. Wellcome's contribution of £1,000 in 1883 in the form of an 'acceptance' had never been cashed and the current capital figure was 'wholly fictitious'. The accounts needed to be rectified, and Wellcome was informed that he should, 'without delay', contribute to the business a capital proportionate to two-fifths share of the profits under the terms of the partnership deed. Privately Radford told Burroughs that a resolution of differences would be difficult, since Burroughs had determined that Wellcome was to have only two-fifths of the profits, and Wellcome's mind was equally made up that he was to receive a half.

Wellcome in reply said he could not admit that the manner in which he kept the books of the firm had been erroneous, though it was quite possible he had made 'errors of judgement', but agreed to honour the £1,000 acceptance. He was 'extremely desirous' of coming to an amicable arrangement and to increase his capital on the understanding that his share in the profits be agreed. Negotiations continued and quite possibly contributed to Wellcome's ill health in the spring of 1885.[13]

In April, in an effort to break through the stalemate, both men spent a few days together in Bournemouth. There Burroughs wrote to Olive about their negotiations and his 'big talk with Wellcome'. Although initially there was no definite basis for a deal, he hoped for one on the following day (a Saturday, as he 'did not like to talk shop on a Sunday'). That Saturday they walked down the pier together, and Wellcome was 'very desirous to come to some definite understanding which would assure him an interest in BW&Co. for five years.' Eventually they settled on an arrangement for a fresh partnership contract.

Olive was now pregnant and had remained in London making preparations for her imminent journey to America, where she wanted her child born; Burroughs was keen to return to London to help her pack and join her in America as soon as possible. However, Radford counselled him against this until a formal agreement with Wellcome had been reached. When Wellcome returned from Bournemouth, he boarded with Burroughs at Miss Warner's in 32 Dorset Square. Burroughs told Olive: 'He wants congenial company & there are some pleasant people here from California including one young lady who is rather good looking. ... I don't notice any trouble in making the new partnership contract. W don't appear so self assertive as heretofore.' He closed his letter: 'I miss you very much my dear.'[14] A few days later the story had changed again: 'W still very seedy & has not gone to Ireland yet. Perhaps it would have been better if the partnership had been allowed to terminate. W can be of much use to the business if he will attend to it. I hope he will not continue to show a grasping disposition.'

Both men visited Radford, where Wellcome now agreed to a 70/30 split and to pay some of his debts. But now new doubts about Wellcome's failure to attend to business in the office were underlined by reports Burroughs received from Dr Burrows, the physician who treated both men. Evidently he had no qualms in passing on medical and private information that Wellcome's old habits of late nights might damage his health and prevent him from working.[15] The deal looked uncertain again.

> Cannot yet say whether we will continue together. He [Wellcome] is giving better attention to business & is very polite to me. If we settle at all it will be on a strictly business basis & I shall require him to pay up all indebtedness by 1st September when the 850£ note falls due. If he cannot do this he will have to take a smaller interest than the 30% or none at all as I am not going to lend him money in order that he may draw more profits.

A further look at the figures with his accountant had so perturbed Burroughs that he told Olive he was indifferent to prolonging the partnership. If they continued he hoped that Wellcome would consent to making Sudlow a partner.[16] Not only was he unsure about working with Wellcome, but he himself was undecided about the best way to go forward.

On 29 May 1885 a decision was finally reached and a new partnership agreement signed. Wellcome capitulated and accepted that the capital be substantially increased to £15,000. Burroughs increased his share to seven-tenths (£10,500), while Wellcome had three-tenths (£4,500), with profits divided pro rata as before.[17] The deed was to last until 1895. An additional agreement allowed for any further capital invested to be treated as a loan at 5% interest. Wellcome had been unwilling to approach American contacts and unable to raise additional funds to make a larger capital contribution. There was no provision for him to increase his share in the firm at a later date, which must be seen as a recognition that he did not have the necessary finances to do so. At the same time new clauses were introduced. The partnership could be terminated after five years – six months' notice in writing being necessary – when the continuing partner could buy out the other. In addition neither partner could engage in any business outside the firm without the other's consent. Both these clauses were to become vitally important in the future.[18]

The Edward's Hotel off Hanover Square was a private establishment run by three sisters and used by many 'highly respectable' Americans. It was maintained 'in the most aristocratic way imaginable' and had large beautifully furnished rooms, well warmed with coal fires. It was here that Burroughs and Olive spent a week in March 1885, probably to shop in the West End, before Olive set off for America accompanied by her good friend Mrs Perry. She was six months pregnant.

Although Burroughs now lodged at Miss Warner's boarding house in Marylebone, he preferred the homelike atmosphere of his friends the Terry and Gardner families. His never-ending discussions with Wellcome and solicitors were relieved by social events with friends and by the occasional concert at the Albert Hall. He frequently cycled to the office and factory, in London parks or into the countryside, enjoying the spring blossoms. On his new tricycle, which was twice as fast as the old one he had sold to Mr Kirby, and was 'as good as a horse', he sported the latest cycling gear, boasting that he had 'the suit all bar the knee breeches'.[19] To Olive he suggested that, on her return, they could settle in Norwood.

Unfortunately Olive's crossing was a bad one. In Boston she stayed with Mary Swain, which Burroughs considered very sensible; there she would get proper attention. Few of Olive's letters to him survive, but one, from Boston at the end of May, reveals her strong character and sense of humour. Addressing him as 'Mansie', she told him of meeting their many friends, making buttonholes and buying dainty silver smelling salts for Mrs Perry's return voyage. Dr Swain was taking her out in her carriage nearly every morning. When someone noticed her pregnant condition and spoke kindly about missing her husband at such a time, Olive wrote: 'My Mansie boy, just as if I should care anything about having you here but everyone seems to think I do.' She added, however: 'be a good boy and come as early as you can. I <u>do</u> want to see you. Lovingly yours.'[20] When she praised Burroughs's charity, he replied: 'Such nonsense as you write about my life a sacrifice. Right the other way. You are the one to be the object of sympathy having married such a duffer.'

Then Lina sent him news that Olive was unwell and missing him but had not wanted to trouble him. Burroughs, agitated that Olive might be lonely or needed him, resolved to sail to America within the week if he could change his ticket. His negotiations with Wellcome were dragging on and on, taking far longer than anticipated, and he now decided to 'wrap things up' with him. He told Olive he would 'give his undivided attention to completing an understanding with Wellcome, so that no complications would arise during his absence … I told Wellcome of your poor health at which he was much ashamed for having detained me. He will now hurry up and settle things as soon as possible so as to let me off … he sends you his kind regards & sympathy.' His disenchantment with Wellcome, however, was serious, and he made a new will, replacing him with Mrs Perry.[21]

At the end of May, with the new partnership deal agreed, Burroughs sailed on the fast steamer RMS *Servia*, which docked in New York on 8 June. In Boston he was delighted to find Olive better than at any time since her arrival in America, with a 'capital nurse'. She had now moved to Union Park, South End, an attractive area, and a short walk from 'her dear Dr Swain'.[22] While there he attended an exhibition at the Massachusetts Medical Association meeting, then headed to Medina, where Aunt Anna was at her gate to greet him. He planned to return to Boston on 24th, but on 21st Olive gave birth to twins, and he departed hurriedly to join her.[23]

The twins were named Anna Lucille, after Burroughs's aunt, and Gladys Swain, and notices of the birth were dispatched to staff and friends.[24] Wellcome commented on their charming names. Feeling especially cheerful at becoming a father, Burroughs paid for every employee to have a day's visit to the International Inventions Exhibition in London.[25] A month after the birth the family travelled up the coast from Boston to Swampscott, where they had enjoyed their honeymoon. But their happiness was short-lived, for on 5 August little Gladys died. Olive had had problems getting her to feed, and the baby died from a condition called marasmus (severe undernourishment).[26] Shocked and grief-stricken, the couple now regarded their surviving child Anna as even more precious. A sad family returned to Boston, then to Broadalbin to visit Olive's parents. A month later Burroughs told the firm that, since Olive and their baby were now getting stronger, he could return to London when wanted.[27]

Wellcome wrote how 'very grieved' he was at the death of Gladys, but he was engrossed with his own important news. He recounted that he had nearly drowned while rescuing a woman from their canoe in Boulter's Lock on the Thames. Burroughs wrote at once from America congratulating him on his narrow escape and on his 'successful efforts to save another from a similar threatened fate', hoping that the shock and strain to his nervous system had passed. Privately, however, his reaction to this news was very different, and his comment to Olive reveals the extent to which he doubted his partner's truthfulness: 'No news from London except a couple of papers from HSW dilating upon his heroism. There is a big query in my mind as to why he should have so endangered the young lady's life by allowing the boat to upset ... could it be a put up job between them to secure notoriety and enjoy a swim on a hot summer day without appearing eccentric in going bathing with all their togs on.'[28] In fact the incident was witnessed by a large number of people and widely reported in the English and American press, and Wellcome was later awarded a bronze medal by the Royal Humane Society. Unsurprisingly, Wellcome subsequently had a 'very severe' reaction from this experience and later said it had caused peritonitis. An aggravated fistula and inflammation of the bowels made him more susceptible to the shock, and Dr Burrows successfully operated on him.[29]

At the end of September Burroughs returned to Medina on his own. His aunt wanted Olive and Anna to visit them or go to nearby Auburn, where Lina lived in a larger house.[30] Medina activities now occupied Burroughs: gardening, picking peas and helping put up a coal store, and visiting the sadly overgrown local cemetery with John Parsons, father of his old schoolmate, and John Coleman, his father's old foreman. Soon he settled down to an easy-going country life, a world far removed from the pressures of travel and work: and yet again, in spite of the generally poor international communications, he contributed to the firm's affairs.

Many friends hoped that Burroughs would settle in America. Much to the delight of his aunt, he contemplated selling out and leaving England before long. 'If I can close out to good advantage and come back here', he reasoned, 'I ought to be able to manufacture goods cheaper in Medina than in a large city but would have a depot in Boston or NY for which the trade could be readily supplied.'[31] Burroughs, perhaps tongue in cheek, tried to interest Olive in moving to Medina, saying she could enjoy the attraction of sermons by Mr Gardner (which he admitted were monotonous) and join a newly established Literary Society and Chautauqua Circle;[32] Olive resisted the enticement.

Meanwhile baby Anna, who was a delicate child, was put in the care of an Irish nurse, Miss Maggie. Olive worried about her decision not to visit Medina, where Aunt Anna was not very well and where space was tight.[33] Her letter led Burroughs to comment: 'You write very lovely letters my dear but once in a while mix up "great imagination" in them – such as fancying I did not miss you here nor regret your absence. Fact is you didn't want to come if I guess right because you thought the baby & nurse would make too much trouble in Aunt Anna's house.'[34] Olive's health concerned him, and he advised her to get 'fat & strong' with rest. Olive had now decided to winter in America and agreed to meet Lina at Syracuse and spend time there before heading to Medina. Burroughs thought she would be comfortable at Lina's in Auburn or return to stay with Dr Swain's lodger Miss Lougee. The decision was hers: 'I am sorry I cannot advise you anymore than you can advise me which place to choose in London.' He missed Olive, though: 'What a treat it will be for your little ole man to see you again after so long a separation' (in fact it was less than three weeks). After further delays, husband and wife met again in mid-October, but Olive, baby Anna and nurse Maggie stayed less than a fortnight in Medina, after which they moved to Lina's.

In November, after receiving a wrongly worded cable, Burroughs became worried that his presence was needed again in London: 'Perhaps O.M.W. [Old Man Wellcome] is sick or the firm in difficulties.'[35] It transpired that there was no urgent necessity to return, but Burroughs was now convinced that his presence was needed in London.[36] So baby Anna was hurriedly christened; Burroughs said his farewells to Olive and headed to New York for a few days to visit friends and business contacts.[37] As usual, his days there were hectic and he had no time for a planned trip to Philadelphia. He sent a steamship ticket to Olive, suggesting that if she did not use it he could exchange it to a return ticket for himself.[38]

Cunard's SS *Etruria* turned out to be very uncomfortable and the crossing a bad one, with two big storms. Burroughs was seasick for a whole day, the cabins had no heating and he caught a cold on the voyage. Wellcome met him at the station in London and they spent the evening together at the house of Mr Miller, one of Burroughs's friends, where he had decided to lodge. London had recently suffered one of its blackest and filthiest November fogs, the weather was dreadful and everyone seemed ill. It was a far cry from Medina. Burroughs felt better, though still hoarse from his cold, whereas Wellcome was 'pretty feeble and run down'; he nearly fainted in the office, at which Burroughs urged him to go to the seaside until he felt stronger.[39] In fact Wellcome's 'neuralgia of the bowels', or peritonitis, which had dogged him in 1885, was to get far worse the following year.[40]

Apart from a month, Burroughs spent the first half of 1886 alone in London, the first such period since October 1881, and he reverted to his old routine of a busy work and social life. Initially he lodged at 56 Torrington Square, Bloomsbury, although he planned to move back to Miss Warner's house, where he would take some of his meals and cycle to the office and back every day. On Saturday afternoons, after the clerks and Wellcome had left, he was sometimes alone with Sudlow, packing and marking up cases for dispatch. He was rarely alone otherwise, being in demand as a guest for musical evenings, dinners and weekends with friends.

In January 1886, Burroughs boarded with the Varleys in Elgin Crescent, Paddington, rather than with Miss Warner: 'I do dislike her looks & ways so much.' Henry Varley was a well-known evangelist, and Burroughs enjoyed chess games with Miss Varley and the company of Varley's eldest son, 'a minister and a man after my own heart, a thorough radical'. Dancing was still considered rather immoral by some, and Mr Varley had not always been keen on it, but Burroughs delighted in changing his mind: 'he probably saw that his young folks were missing lots of good times & much hindered in social engagements by not being allowed to dance.' Theatre-going was also not always deemed correct: the Misses Varley considered it alright to see *The Rivals*, since it was performed by amateurs, 'but when professionals are actors then its all wrong.'[41] Amateur theatricals were very popular, and there were many balls to raise money for charities. One, for the Hospital for Women, was 'a beautiful sight with so many beautiful and well-dressed ladies', and he noted Pearl Richards, Susie Arnold's niece, who 'had grown into an intelligent and vivacious lady, combining her mother's volubility with her father's caution in speech.'

Evenings at the Central Club, whose members came from a wide-ranging background, fuelled Burroughs's interest in taxation, and land reform and political interests increasingly occupied his attention. His letters to Olive were frequent, sometimes covering his work but more often his social life and mutual friends, some of whom would visit her in America. At times she struggled to work out who was who, so large was his circle of acquaintances. She also complained, as Wellcome had, that he sometimes failed to address her questions, to which he admitted that he forgot as he seldom re-read her letters when replying. He found Olive's letters 'very lovely', especially when not too short. His letters to her covered several pages and burst with affection.

Olive had made a strong impression on his friends in London, who regretted that she and baby Anna were not wintering in England. Employees enquired after them and photographs were proudly displayed; places were even set for Olive at dinner tables where her health was proposed. In fact Olive, like her father, was suffering from rheumatism and feared the return boat journey. Burroughs urged her to go to dancing parties for exercise and social enjoyment and was glad that she would join Dr Swain in Boston for Christmas. 'If dancing does you half as much good as it does me it will cure your rheumatism in a hurry.' Lina visited her there, and Burroughs encouraged them to go to operas, theatres and pleasant places of fun. Lina, who suffered from depression and frequently had 'neuralgic headaches' (almost certainly migraines), reportedly improved two months later under treatment from Dr Swain and another doctor.

Olive had put on weight, and her husband congratulated her: she would not look any the worse for it but rather better, and being tall could stand it. He expected to see her looking 'heartier & stouter & handsomer than ever' when the warmer weather came and he returned to the States or she came over to England. Her rheumatism and poor circulation, especially in her feet, remained a concern, and Burroughs recommended brisk friction with a towel, exercise, oil and malt, Turkish baths, early nights and calisthenics, believing that this last had immensely benefited him. He had 'never felt better in his life than at the present time', and his use of malt, or oil and malt, agreed with him. He urged Olive and Lina to find warmer weather, somewhere like Florida or Bermuda, or, if they preferred, Washington or further south. He subsequently ensured that £500 was available for their trip to Bermuda.

In London that winter it was cold, and one Sunday, after several days of snow, Burroughs went to the East End to hear Henry Varley preach at Dr Thomas Barnardo's church; Barnardo by this time was already well known as a philanthropist and founder of children's homes. Burroughs found him 'quite a different man from what I had imagined. He is short fat slightly deaf very energetic in manner & speech and has a clear ringing voice.' In his sermon Varley spoke of remembering to help the poor and prayed to God to come quickly and settle the land question and the Irish question. Afterwards Barnardo, 'in a joking yet sincere way', said that the prayer and sermon 'savoured of communism and a division of property'. An argument started which lasted through dinner and until they left Dr Barnardo's 'hospitable roof'. Burroughs assured him that his 'conversion to the truth of the gospel of freedom from Landlords' was only a question of time.[42] Both men had much in common, although politics was not so important to Barnardo. Both were philanthropically motivated, passionate about trying to improve people's lives, deeply religious and self-confident, with a flair for publicity and business. In addition, both worked long hours and supported the temperance movement. Burroughs may also have met Barnardo's youngest daughter, Gwendoline (known as Syrie), who was seven years old at the time. He would never have imagined that years later she would become Wellcome's wife.[43]

The arrival of spring and the blossom always made Burroughs happy, and he loved cycling, which was becoming ever more popular. He saw the Oxford and Cambridge boat race on the Thames and attended a popular adaptation of Goethe's *Faust* at the Lyceum, with Henry Irving and Ellen Terry. He also managed to get a good view of the opening procession at the new College of Physicians, where he described Queen Victoria as looking 'quite up to the average fat cook. There's an awful lot of bosh going on about Royalty ... and as people get more intelligent and less selfish they will seek to do away with it.' Although not a supporter of the monarchy, he did not turn down the opportunity to see them.

One evening his friend Mr Fellows took him to the Beaconsfield Club of Tory supporters. Burroughs described Fellows as a liberal, whose wife was 'struck after the aristocracy & royal family and so [he] goes the Tory ticket and associates with the swells.' His interest in political issues continued to grow. On Whit Monday he travelled with friends to a mass meeting of agricultural labourers at Yeovil, knowing that there would be much talk about land tax and criticisms of landlords. He sent Olive a copy of *The Democrat* and a circular from Frank Verinder, secretary of the English Land Restoration League: 'You will see ... that

times are getting hotter every day for the Landlords and I do assure
you my dear that any unprejudiced person can be convinced that the
Landlordism which takes ground rents is robbery of the people. I am
sending copies of this issue of *Democrat* to all our principal customers
but they will not know who sends them.' In doing so he showed both
naivety and impulsiveness.[44]

Soon afterwards he wrote about a meeting on the land question at St
Pancras vestry hall. Several MPs had spoken, and Burroughs was invited
to second a motion and send a copy to Gladstone, the prime minister.

> The temptation to magnify the Grand Old Man [Gladstone]
> was too strong. It was late in the evening and many were
> getting up & leaving but, I assure you before I had said the
> word they all turned around and listened to all I had to say
> with open eyes & mouths as well as ears. They gave me a good
> cheering too when in a few words I told them the plain truth
> about landlordism and its plain truth in the misery & poverty
> of the rent paying public. I gave them a regular rouser and
> no one seemed to think I went beyond the mark though my
> comparisons of landlords with pirates & highwaymen were
> not flattering.[45]

The episode provoked his confidence and his appetite for public speaking.

Burroughs was keen to return to America that spring or summer,
but Wellcome's health, combined with pressure of work, made this
uncertain. He hoped instead that Olive would come over once the
weather improved in April or May, possibly travelling with Lina or
with Maggie. He planned for Olive's return; possible places they might
live together in London were mooted. Like many others at this time,
they intended to rent rather than purchase. Would Olive like a pleasant
furnished house in Denmark Hill, Dulwich or Notting Hill? Would
she prefer the countryside in the summer? He could acquire one for
a few months or a year at a very reasonable price. They could have the
charming house off Park Lane of his friend Dr Field; it overlooked
Hyde Park at the back, which was 'almost equal to the country with
300 acres of meadow'. Alternatively, his friends were still looking out
for a furnished house or a boarding place with a family in Camberwell.
Mrs Perry had located some pleasant houses in Camberwell Grove
which would also be close to their good friends the Huttons at Bealair,
Dulwich, and he would try to make her 'as cosy as possible'.[46]

Then news came that Aunt Anna was gravely ill, and Burroughs determined to hurry through business and go to Medina as soon as possible. He booked a passage on the SS *Servia*, which sailed on 17 April.[47] Perhaps significantly, with his departure his partner's health improved, and Wellcome was to spend most of May and June on the Isle of Wight.

The fine seven-day voyage to America was one of the fastest yet. Six months had passed since Burroughs and Olive had been together. If news of Aunt Anna was good, he would stay in New York for a day, then meet Olive in Boston and travel with her to Medina. In the event he headed for Medina alone. His 80-year-old aunt had probably had a small stroke and was confused and forgetful, but much improved by mid-May, when Lina, whose health was now better, joined him in Medina.

This now made possible their return to England; Burroughs had intended it would be a short visit, thinking he was needed in London and believing Wellcome to be ill. The couple planned to travel together and for Olive to book one of the best rooms on the SS *Egypt* or the SS *America*, 'the best ship afloat', and their berth should be near 'amidships' to reduce the chance of seasickness on the voyage. A new nurse was to be hired for the journey, since it had been discovered that Maggie had a tendency to tell lies.[48]

On a trip into Albion, Burroughs met an old employer, Mr Coann, who encouraged him to take the big works by the railway station and set up a factory in Albion. Burroughs favoured Medina and asked Olive which she would prefer. The answer almost certainly was neither; Olive evidently entertained not the slightest interest in living in upstate New York.

Baby Anna was teething, and a powdered milk for babies was discussed. Infant nutrition was of special significance following the death of Gladys, and at Burroughs's suggestion Dr Witte had created a drink which Burroughs thought would be nourishing baby food – a mix of milk with extract of malt.[49] Burroughs considered Fairchild's powdered milk excellent and fulminated about Robinson's 'Groats' brand of baby food, which infants had difficulty digesting, mainly because it was full of starch. He believed that if peptogenic milk powder had been given a trial they would still have both twins. 'I insist upon nothing. I only tell you what I believe and yourself and Dr Swain may do just as you please as heretofore.' This passing remark hints at a possible resentment by Burroughs towards Olive's belief in the judgement of her friend Mary Swain rather than in himself.[50]

Gladys had died in August the previous year, yet strangely only now did Olive raise the question where the baby should be buried. One suggestion was in Dr Swain's family plot in Boston. Burroughs responded: 'Dr Swain is very good as she always is' and offered to pay for the ground:

> If you will only tell me what your wish is regarding a burial place for little Gladys it shall be done. I have no choice nor opinion in the matter whatever and hope you will believe me when I tell you so. If you prefer that she should be buried in the cemetery in Boston I am quite willing but do not wish to buy a large & expensive lot there having already a cemetery lot here in Medina worth a thousand dollars. I think that perhaps it will be best to bury little Gladys at Boston cemetery.

He held strong views on burial, however:

> I am not though in favour of a vault or even a grave inclosed in bricks. 'Dust to dust' is the law of nature and if this be allowed the frail mortal body soon becomes part of the earth from whence it sprang. I dread to think what condition physically will be those poor bodies at the resurrection morn which have been sealed up in metallic caskets defying the absorptive powers of the earth and left to fester in their own corruption.

Such radical ideas of burial were being discussed at this time, but as in other things Burroughs was in advance of public opinion.[51]

Burroughs planned to join Olive again in Boston after brief local trips to Lockport and Auburn, travelling via Philadelphia and New York, while Olive visited her father in Broadalbin. He remained concerned about Lina's mental state and sent her $250, instructing her to use it to get well and not to put it in the bank. As usual his schedule slipped, and at the end of May he was still in Philadelphia, where Wyeths seemed 'in a mood to make a deal' about royalties.[52]

On 6 June, Burroughs and Olive sailed for England; she had been away for 14 months and he for two.[53] On their return they appear to have stayed in Norwood with the Lymans, and from August until the end of that year they rented and stayed in hotels in Brighton, with an interlude in Margate in September. Burroughs was able to make rail journeys up to London from both places easily, staying in town during the week if necessary.

For a very brief period from late June into July Burroughs and Wellcome were in London at the same time, but in early August Wellcome set off for America. It was as though physical separation was their preferred arrangement, but one that brought dangers and did not bode well for their relationship. In spite of the attraction of America – especially for Burroughs – Britain was the best place for them to do business.

Chapter 11

Partnership in Crisis: The High Court

*I have long feared that your failure to fulfil our partnership
obligations would render a dissolution imperative.*[1]

The transatlantic separations of Burroughs and Wellcome from 1885
led to increased mistrust between them which was to culminate in a
dramatic crisis over their partnership in 1889. Differences of opinion
hinged on proposals for establishing a joint stock limited company to
run the firm and Burroughs's enlightened ideas on profit-sharing. When
the firm needed larger manufacturing capacity, the partners disagreed
over the purchase of a new site in Dartford, a quarrel that was to create
future financial conflict.

Yet while business in general was in 'a most wretched state
throughout Europe and the Colonies', the firm held its own, and in
May 1886 it was in a much healthier financial position than in the
previous quarter, helped by the public's 'unquenchable demand for put
up medicines'.[2] 'Business is much better than for the past two months
and we are anticipating good trade this winter,' Burroughs reported.[3]
By 1888 the *British Medical Journal* noted that Burroughs, Wellcome &
Co. had consistently introduced more new drugs than its major British
rivals Allen & Hanbury's, May & Baker, and Parke Davis. New agency
agreements were made, mainly with American suppliers. Murray &
Lanman's Florida Water sold well, as did Lundborg's perfumes. Important
deals were also struck with Fairchild Bros. & Fosters, manufacturing
chemists in New York, for their digestive preparations such as peptin
and pancreatic extracts. There was a very successful alliance with a
German firm, Benno Jaffé Darmstaedter, when BW&Co. acquired the

sole agency to sell Lanoline, a soap made from wool fat which was very popular. The *Chemist and Druggist* spoke highly of the firm's 'entirely new class of business in what seemed to be a sufficiently crowded trade by their novel methods.'[4] The partners in turn boasted of their 'remarkable progress and success', thanking 'those intelligent members of the medical and pharmaceutical professions who have recognized the merits of our products and the benefits of our improvements', and describing would-be imitators as following in their wake 'like a pack of hungry wolves, ravenous for our substance'. They remained competitive, and the pages of advertisements for their tabloids and compressed drugs were proof enough of the growing scale on which the firm now operated.

In spite of the new partnership agreement, Burroughs continued to agonise over profit-sharing, bonuses for the employees, and converting the partnership into a joint stock limited company. Profit-sharing (dividing among all employees a fixed percentage of the net profits as a present or bonus in addition to salary) was very uncommon in businesses at this time, and Burroughs was in the vanguard of employee welfare in wishing to introduce it. In spite of Wellcome's indication in April 1885 that 5% of the net profits be divided among the employees and the possibility of Sudlow becoming a partner, the Sudlow partnership proposal was subsequently shelved, probably because Burroughs was then contemplating a joint stock company and selling shares to the employees in proportion to their contribution to the business. By the spring of 1886 Burroughs believed that Wellcome had finally agreed to a joint stock company, although this too was not realised. Wellcome did, however, agree to profit-sharing 'when he saw that I was bound to carry it through', and a circular announcing the scheme was sent to all staff.[5] In addition there was a large increase in wages of 15%. In high spirits, Burroughs wrote of his grand vision to Olive:

> I think when it is all settled that we should get the Wandsworth Town Hall some evening and give a dance in honor of the new profit sharing basis of business which gives everyone an interest in the business like a partner without any investment of capital or risk of loss ... Mr Sudlow should be Sec[retar]y, Mr Kirby Treasurer and both of them with Dr Witte on the board of directors. Mr Wellcome should be managing director and as for your humble servant who at present owns 3/4ths of the business should be permanent chairman of board of directors as well as manager.

Feb. 2, 1889

THE CHEMIST AND DRUGGIST.

SUPPLEMENT

vii

"TABLOIDS" OF COMPRESSED DRUGS.

Prepared by Burroughs, Wellcome & Co.

THE "Tabloids" present many and very substantial advantages over all other forms of medicines yet introduced. They are portable, easily carried in the waistcoat pocket, and can be taken while following the daily avocations. A most noteworthy feature about them is that accidents are not apt to happen, for the dose of each is accurately appointed.

The "Tabloids" are compressed with due regard to the purpose for which they are to be used. Those designed for dissolving in the mouth, like Chlorate of Potash, "Chlorate of Potash and Borax," and Voice Tabloids, are made very hard; while those destined for internal administration are less dense, and quickly disintegrate, such as Bismuth Subnitrate, Manganese Dioxide, Charcoal Tabloids, &c. Other of the more lightly compressed Tabloids dissolve with the greatest readiness; for example, the soluble Quinine Tabloids dissolve almost as quickly as they touch the water. The Sodium Bicarbonate "Tabloids" and the Potassium Bicarbonate "Tabloids" are both eligible preparations, pure and reliable—the latter salt, as is well known, enjoying precedence over Sodium Bicarbonate in those cases where the "acidity of the stomach" is ever recurring and chronic. This is the salt *par excellence* in the indigestion from fatty acids, to alkalize the urine, and eradicate the causes of "chronic acidity."

Dr. J. A. Marston, Deputy Surgeon-General, in his official report on the recent International Medical Congress, held at Washington, says:—

"These Tabloids are not more expensive than the ordinary forms of administering medicines, as they can be made at a very small advance on the crude drug.

"They keep well in all climates and are unaffected by heat or moisture. Specimens were examined which had been round the world in S.S. *Ceylon*. Mr. H. M. Stanley, in his work, 'The Congo,' vol. ii., pages 325 and 327, refers to their value."

LIST OF "TABLOIDS" (B. W. & CO.).

Aconite Tinct., 1 min.
Aloin, 1-10 gr.
Anti-Consti-{Aloin, 1-5 gr.
pation. {Strych., 1-60 gr.
{Belladon., Ex., ⅛ gr.
{Ipecac., 1-16 gr.
Ammon. Bromide, 5 and 10 gr.
Ammon. Chloride, 3, 5, and 10 gr.
Ammon. Chloride with Borax.
Antifebrin, 5 gr.
Antimonii et Potass. Tart., 1-100 gr.
Antipyrin, 5 gr.
Apomorphine Mur., 1-50 gr.
Arsenious Acid, 1-100 and 1-50 gr.
Atropia Sulph., 1-100 gr.
Belladonna Tinct., 1 min.
Bismuth Sub-nit., 5 and 10 gr.
Caffein Citrate, 1 gr.
Calcium Sulphide, 1-10 gr.
Capsicum Tinct., 1 min.
Cascara Sagrada Ext., 2 gr.
Cathartic Comp. U.S.P.
Charcoal, 5 gr.
Chloral Hydrate, 5 gr.
Chloramine.
Cinchonidia Salicylate, 2 gr.
Cocaine, Potash and Borax (Voice).
Digitalis Tinct., 1 min.

Digitalin, 1-100 gr.
Dover Powder, ½ gr.
Euonymin Resin, ½ gr.
Hydrarg. Iod. Rub., 1-20 gr.
Hydrarg. Iod. Vir., ⅛ gr.
Hydrarg. Perchlor., 1-100 gr.
Hydrarg. cum Creta (Grey Powder), ½ gr.
Hydrarg. Subchlor. (Calomel), 1-10 gr.
Hyoscyamus Tinct., 1 min.
Ipecac. & Opium (Dover Powd.), 5 gr.
Ipecac. Powder, 5 gr.
Iron and Quinine Cit., 3 gr.
Laxative Vegetable.
Lithia Carbonate, 2 gr.
Manganese Dioxide, 2 gr.
Morphine Sulph., 1-20 and ½ gr.
Nitro-Glycerine.
Nux Vomica Tinct., 1 min.
Opium Tinct. (Laudanum), 2 min.
Pepsin, Pure (Fairchild).
Pepsin Saccharated, 5 gr.
Peptonic.
Pilocarpin Mur., 1-20 gr.
Piperine, 1-20 gr.
Podophyllin Resin, ½ gr.

Potash Bicarb., 5 gr.
Potash Chlorate, 5 gr.
Potash Chlorate with Borax, 5 gr.
Pota h Nit. (*Sal Prunella*), 5 gr.
Potash Permanganate, 1 and 2 gr.
Potassium Bromide, 5 and 10 gr.
Potassium Iodide, 5 gr.
Quinine, 1-10 gr.
Quinine, ½, 1, 2, 3, and 5 gr.
{Quinine Sulph., 1 gr.
{Ferri Hypophos., 2 gr.
{Acid Arsenios, 1-50 gr.
Strychninæ Sulph., 1-50 gr.
Saccharin, 1-100 gr.
{Quinine Sulph., 1 gr.
{Arsenios, 1-20 gr.
{Strychnine Sulph., 1-30 gr.
Rhei Comp. (Pil.), 3 gr.
Rhubarb, 3 gr.
Rhubarb and Magnesia (Gregory Powder), 5 gr.
Rhubarb and Soda, 5 gr.
Saccharin, ⅛ gr.
Salol, 5 gr.
Santonin, ½ gr.
Soda Bicarbonate, 5 gr.
Soda Chlorate, 5 gr.

Soda Chlorate and Borax, 5 gr.
Soda-Mint.
Soda Salicylate, 3 and 5 gr.
Soda Sulpho-carbolate, 5 gr.
Sodium Bromide, 5 and 10 gr.
Sodium Iodide, 5 gr.
Strophanthus Tinct., 2 min.
Sulphonal, 5 gr.
Tannin.
Test Tabloids.
Tinct. Camph. Co. (Paregoric), 2 min.
Tonic Comp.{Fer. Pyrophos., 2 gr.
{Quinine, 1 gr.
{Strychnine, 1-100 gr.
Trinitrine (*Nitro glycerine*), 1-100 and 1-50 gr.
Trinitrine and Amyl Nitrite.
Trinitrine {Trinitrine, 1-100 gr.
Comp. {Nitrite of Amyl., ½ gr.
Trinitrine {Capsicum, 1-50 gr.
Comp. {Menthol, 1-50 gr.
Urethane, 5 gr.
Voice (Potash, Borax, and Cocaine).
Zinc Sulph., 1 gr.
Zinc Sulpho-carbolate, 2 gr.
Zymine Tabloids.
Zymine Comp. Tabloids.

B. W. & CO. COLONIAL MEDICINE CHEST.
Fitted complete with Tabloids of compressed drugs, from 50/.

B. W. & CO. CONGO MEDICINE CHEST,
as supplied to Stanley and other distinguished travellers and explorers. Fitted complete with Tabloids of compressed drugs, from £7 to £20.

B. W. & CO. LIVINGSTONE MEDICINE CHEST.
Fitted complete with Tabloids of compressed drugs, from 80/.

BURROUGHS, WELLCOME & CO., Snow Hill Buildings, LONDON, E.C.

23

17: An advertisement for BW&Co. products and their tabloids in the *Chemist and Druggist*, 1889.

During the latter part of 1885 and early months of 1886 Wellcome had been much absorbed by the publication of a translation of Flaubert's *Salammbo* by May French Sheldon. Burroughs had agreed to Wellcome having a business interest with the Sheldons in the small publishing firm Saxon & Co., and the translation appeared in April 1886, just before Burroughs left for America. Wellcome, who had postponed his planned trip to America because of his poor health, left his Montagu Street flat to move in with the Sheldons. At this time he went into the office very little, and Burroughs was advised that he was very sore about the kidneys and liver and would 'have to keep pretty shady for a while'.[6] The situation was so grave that it was reckoned that he would not get better unless he was very careful and moved out of London to fresher air. 'Poor fellow', Burroughs told Olive, 'he's much too young to leave this world,' although he went on to say, rather casually, 'I dare say he will be ok if he gets out of town soon.'[7]

It was August 1886 before Wellcome finally sailed to America. The partners had worked alongside each other since June, but it had not been easy against a background of uncertainty about the firm's future management and the time this had absorbed. Neither of them could have imagined how long Wellcome would stay in America (in the event, until June the following year), during which time the relationship between the two men was to deteriorate still further. The firm meanwhile continued to function and prosper, underlining the vital role played by Sudlow, Kirby and the office staff during these prolonged absences of the partners.

It was during his time in America that Wellcome became deeply involved in research on a group of dispossessed Native Americans, the Metlakatla Tsimshian, and much of that winter was spent researching and writing a book, *The Story of Metlakahtla*.[8] Glad to be away from the stress and worries of

18: Robert Clay Sudlow's commemorative medal. Sudlow was general manager of the firm, without whom it would never have survived the differences between the partners, who both recognised his contribution. On Sudlow's retirement in 1905 Wellcome had this gold medal struck.

business, and preoccupied by his new project, he failed to respond to
letters sent by Sudlow or Burroughs, much to Burroughs's irritation.
Then in the spring of 1887 Burroughs heard that his beloved Aunt
Anna was seriously ill and immediately booked passage on the SS
Alaska, hastily making a will before he left.[9] He arrived in Medina on
2 May and, almost as though she had waited for him, his aunt died the
following day.

To Sudlow, Burroughs had written that he felt quite easy that
everything would go all right in his absence: 'I do not say publicly what
I go over for beyond a vacation and a visit to see my aunt who is ill.'[10] A
New York newspaper posited that both Burroughs and his wife wanted
to return to their native country;[11] a further reason was to explore the
feasibility of locating some of the firm's manufacturing activities there.
Burroughs took with him the firm's work manager, the German chemist
Dr Otto Witte, to advise on possible locations and finances for malt
extract and malt milk manufacture. 'If we cannot make the goods to
considerable better advantage over here we shall have to locate the malt
ext[raction] factory in England & perhaps give up the idea of doing an
American business also,' he told Sudlow. Dr Witte had been appointed
in 1883, but by this time he and Wellcome were on bad terms.[12]

Now, on learning of Burroughs's 'hasty decision' to visit America,
Wellcome contacted him, sorry to hear of Aunt Anna's serious illness. He
was wary and non-committal about the establishment of an American
factory, saying that he had given the matter careful consideration and
taken advice on the subject ever since his arrival in America and was not
fully satisfied that it was wise to take such a step yet: he wanted to discuss
the matter fully first.[13] The two men met in New York: 'I have seen Mr
Wellcome who looks pretty hearty,' Burroughs wrote to Sudlow, but he
did not mention their discussion about the factory.[14]

Burroughs looked at a number of factory locations in New York
state and around the Hudson River up to Poughkeepsie, but exorbitant
prices were being asked for the land. Cold Spring he found to be rather
dingy, and the people 'shiftless & seedy'. If a tidy pharmacy factory was
located there it might encourage the people to 'pull up their weeds, scrub
& paint the houses & brush their teeth, so it may be we have a call to
settle there,' he joked to Olive.[15] It became clear, though, that not only the
sites but also the customs duties chargeable on the materials required in
manufacturing in America were too costly. After two months searching,
Burroughs accepted that the figures did not stack up. As usual, time
constraints defeated his plans, and his intention of visiting the Van
Heusens in Albany and Olive's family in Broadalbin had to be shelved; he
now intended to sail for England as soon as possible. Wellcome informed

Burroughs that he was 'ready for duty' and left America on 25 June, saying he wished they could sail together on the SS *Etruria* but giving him scarcely any notice. A further meeting of both men in America thus failed to materialise, and Burroughs returned seven days later.[16]

Not long after their return, Dr Witte put his job on the line when it became clear that he had copies of the firm's compressing machines for his own use. When confronted by the partners, he told 'one lie after another', to such a degree that Burroughs lost all confidence in him and he was dismissed. To rub salt into the wound, Burroughs, who had been so supportive of Dr Witte and had loaned him furniture several years before (some of the articles being keepsakes), now discovered that Witte, 'bent on reprisal', would not return it. His 'contemptible ingratitude cured me of sentimental ideas of helping him,' Burroughs wrote, adding that Witte would be 'honest in his dealings until there is a chance of making 6d more by being dishonest ... [He] has made a most egregious ass of himself, followed farthing wise, pound foolish policy.'[17] Night watchmen were employed to ensure that Dr Witte did not enter either the office or the factory.

During Wellcome's absence in America from August 1886 to June 1887, much of the time incommunicado in Maine, Burroughs had acted increasingly independently, and in the summer of 1887 it was evident that the survival of the partnership was in doubt. Burroughs was openly disenchanted and mistrusted Wellcome, who, only too aware of this, tried to explain and justify events: 'I have now returned to business with fully restored health and am prepared to make up for lost time in extra exertion to promote our mutual business interests.' His illness had been 'beyond question more severe and prolonged on account of long and close application to business ... particularly when during your absence of two years and a half of the most critical period of our business history, the burden of worry and care fell mainly upon me ... Our business is prospering, and its future looks very bright. I trust that with united feelings and united strength we may realize our best hopes.'[18] He straight away paid a cheque to Burroughs for £100 to settle an outstanding debt which had dragged on for many years, excusing his failure to do so before because Burroughs had never clarified the exact amount or interest required.[19]

If Wellcome hoped to encourage his partner to put past disagreements behind him, he had failed to do so, causing irritation rather than confidence.

Burroughs responded in late July: 'I am sorry not to be able to accept the explanations of the past, and the assurances for the future, contained in your letter. I have long feared that your failure to fulfil our partnership obligations would render a dissolution imperative, and I have now come to the conclusion that this can no longer be avoided or delayed.'[20] A formal letter followed from his solicitor, demanding dissolution of the partnership. In August Wellcome wrote a confidential letter to Sam and Ben Fairchild, making clear that he too considered the partnership would be broken up:

> In all probability Mr B & I will separate ere long ... While I have not told you yet you must, from your pointed comments, have observed that we are far from being in harmony in our views on business matters. While my illness was directly due to the relapse caused by the river incident yet it was the more grounded and agravated [sic] by over work and then the worry caused by friction and disagreement. I will not enter into details but simply state that either one or the other of us must purchase the business and one retire as discord will only ruin the business ...

Wellcome claimed that it was he who had organised the business and brought it from its 'shaky embryo to its solid basis', in spite of his partner's attempts to introduce 'erratic and wild cat projects'. He had resisted Burroughs's and Dr Witte's American factory schemes and other equally absurd projects, and things had come to a crisis. His partner had lately disregarded his views, entered into business contracts and made extensive expenditure without mentioning the matter to him, and it had urged him to take a prolonged trip to America until he recovered his health. He went on:

> Now Burroughs taunts me with this – though it was the first considerable absence I had taken since I came over and he did not hesitate to spend eight months of pure pleasure and love making in America after his trip of two years & a half around the world ... I feel a great relief that things have come to a climax and whatever the issue I shall be content whether buy or sell – If I buy I have no fear for results. I have now the fullest measure of health and value it sufficiently to conserve it. If I sell I shall have enough substance to make a good strong fresh start ... Please do me the favour to burn this letter at once after reading it. PS Nothing may be done for some months.[21]

Word spread of a possible dissolution. In February the following year, J.J. Fellows of the Fellows Manufacturing Co. of Montreal and New York wrote to both partners: 'In the name of all that is good, do not spoil your grand business built at the cost of much industry and exertion. Why not find a basis for Arbitration.'[22] In April Wellcome wrote again to the Fairchild brothers that the aggression continued and was likely to do so for some time; he had taken the best legal advice, which would be expensive, but he had no fear of the ultimate result. But at this point he was saying that he 'had not the slightest intention of selling' and was quite prepared to purchase. 'I may tell you that Mr B. has been a very subtle worker against me.'[23]

To add to his grievances, Burroughs now doubted Wellcome's honesty in his private life as well as in the business. He had, quite wrongly, questioned Wellcome's account of his near drowning at Boulter's Lock in 1885. Then, in the spring of 1888, Wellcome's landlady told him that Wellcome's illness was 'humbug' – that he played sick yet was well enough to entertain in the evening. In addition Wellcome's own doctor and their mutual friend, Dr Burrows, raised doubts in Burroughs's mind by commenting on Wellcome's behaviour towards May French Sheldon; at the very least Wellcome was being indiscreet.

There was a whiff of scandal around May Sheldon, the attractive wife of the American businessman Eli Sheldon; he was known to chase women, and it is possible that the couple had an open marriage. May became close to the explorer Henry Morton Stanley when the latter lived in the same building as the Sheldons in Sackville Street, London. She once wrote to Stanley: 'I also know the benediction of a harmonious union and therefore am safer for a score of experiences!' When Stanley met Dorothy Tennant (whom he subsequently married) he thought it better to see less of Mrs Sheldon. Wellcome had known the Sheldons since 1882 and in the winter of 1885–6 took an apartment in their house at her invitation, partly on the grounds of his poor health, since May had medical training. Before travelling to Maine in 1886, he had stayed at the hotel used by the Sheldons, then with May Sheldon's mother at the seaside and then at her sister-in-law's in Philadelphia; they had returned to England together on the same steamer in 1887, when Wellcome continued to reside with them. A brief correspondence between Burroughs and May Sheldon from the summer of 1886 survives, in which May expressed regret that they had not been able to meet when both were in America that year and asked for a copy of his views on the land question.

In March 1888, Wellcome, learning that Burroughs had spoken of misconduct by him, informed the Sheldons, whose solicitor warned Burroughs that his remarks regarding Mrs Sheldon were false and slanderous: Mr Sheldon trusted it was not true, but that if he heard anything more of the sort 'he would hold Mr Burroughs legally and otherwise responsible.' Burroughs responded through his solicitors that he had made no such statements affecting Mrs Sheldon and presumed that Mr Sheldon had been misinformed. A discreet line was now drawn under the subject, but questions remained unanswered, and the episode certainly raised doubts about Wellcome's lack of judgement, if not morals. Wellcome makes no mention of having raised the matter with Burroughs, but he should have anticipated his partner's strong disapproval over any dalliance with a married woman.[24] The fact that they did not discuss this reflects the distance between the partners that now existed; once they had shared observations and dreams of the women they thought would make good companions. The rumours, combined with unfavourable public comment about Flaubert's *Salammbo*, led Burroughs to look again at May Sheldon's translation of the book: having initially praised it, he belatedly rated it an indecent work.[25]

During October and November Burroughs undertook another five-week stint in America. The firm's work continued, although the atmosphere in the office must have been at the least strained. Formality entered into how the partners addressed each other – 'Mr Burroughs' or 'Mr Wellcome' replacing previous 'Brother', 'Friend', or simply 'Burroughs' and 'Wellcome'. Both men later claimed that they did not speak ill of each other in the firm, although this is contradicted by a statement Wellcome later obtained from a member of staff.[26] But nevertheless some residual formality of friendship remained. At the end of the year, when Burroughs suffered a bad chest cold and stayed with his close friends the Huttons in Dulwich, Wellcome, though too busy for a visit, relayed his concern.[27]

It was a highly stressful situation for both partners, and documents highlight their frustrations as negotiations – now conducted by lawyers – dragged on. How would the partnership dissolution be effected? How would Wellcome's loan be repaid? Would Burroughs pay Wellcome his interest in the business? How would trademarks be divided? What was the situation regarding goodwill? These were complex matters, and wrangling over the terms of dissolution of the partnership continued month after month, with accusations and grievances escalating. Burroughs believed Wellcome was deliberately procrastinating and referred to him as 'a snake in the grass'.[28]

In February 1889, Burroughs's solicitors, Radford & Frankland, informed Wellcome that their client now found the position unbearable and, with reluctance, was about to serve a writ. Wellcome was alleged to have neglected the firm's business when he was in America and continued to do so; following his return to London attempts had been made to induce him to consent to a dissolution by mutual agreement on reasonable terms or move to arbitration, but he had delayed the negotiations by every means in his power.

19: Firm outing to Crystal Palace, 14 July 1888. Outings for work staff were held annually from 1886. This one is rare in that it shows both Burroughs and Wellcome together, though not side by side. Burroughs is in the middle of the second row with the white cap, Wellcome to his left, with an unknown woman between them. The photo was taken by Kirby, the chief accountant, who was a keen photographer.

In response Wellcome raised the issue of the time Burroughs spent on his political work, devoting his time to various 'Socialistic societies' over several years. He had frequently entered into heated discussion in the firm's public offices; placed literature in packages of goods it sent out; and the firm's office and address had been included in an advertisement in the *Christian Commonwealth* for the Society for the Propagation of the Gospel amongst Landlords.[29] Burroughs's attendance at various political demonstrations, such as recent ones in Trafalgar Square, and his making of incendiary speeches was calculated to do injury to the firm's business, especially in the eyes of those who held contrary views. In Wellcome's view, business and politics should never mix.

Burroughs in turn questioned the validity of Wellcome's claims to ill health, since 'a person' (Dr Burrows), 'who had excellent opportunities of observing Wellcome's habits of life', had told him that, before 30 July 1886, Wellcome's stay in bed all day was 'hum bugging'; he was always well enough to get up for dinner at 7 and to sit up till 3 or 4 o'clock in the morning. He denied having encouraged Wellcome to go to America for his health, although he had consented to his doing so.[30]

How had things come to this serious turning point? Crucially through lack of trust and respect, compounded by disagreements over financial issues and how the firm should be managed. While the world trip of 1881–4 created problems between them, especially over the partnership renewal, continuing lengthy separations led to poor co-operation and misunderstandings. Key issues for Burroughs were Wellcome's failure to repay loans to him while living a lavish personal lifestyle. Other concerns were how Wellcome handled finances and his vetoing of or failure to implement suggestions. Principles that Burroughs held dear, such as profit-sharing and bonuses, were hard fought for. Attempts to spread the financial and administrative burdens by taking on a third partner or by creating a joint stock company had been thwarted at every turn. Both men felt they carried the firm on their shoulders. Burroughs believed that Wellcome did not always pull his weight; Wellcome believed that his contribution was undervalued and deeply resented Burroughs's long journeys abroad, especially the time he had spent in America courting Olive. He was offended that Burroughs still regarded him as a junior partner and failed to consult him or take him into his confidence. Social links and common friendships had dwindled, and with them bonds of friendship; and, finally, Burroughs considered his partner not just unsupportive but mean and lacking in moral principles.

There could be no amicable settlement, and now it was for the Chancery Division of the High Court to rule on the dissolution of the partnership on the grounds that Wellcome had broken his partnership articles and neglected to perform his duties as a partner.[31]

The court met on 24 and 25 June 1889, and the case was reported in *The Times* and other national papers. The evidence and verbatim court transcripts revealed the very different approaches both men took towards work and how they handled the legal process.[32] To discredit Burroughs's claims, Wellcome carefully accumulated documentation, extracts of letters going back to the start of the partnership, and witness statements. At one point he said he mentioned his thoughts of counter-suing for dissolution but was advised against this. Burroughs on the other hand was poorly prepared, had not done his homework, failed to keep a good record of what he had previously stated, and gave evidence lacking documentary backing. Indeed he was admonished for not having made a better search and study of the office files for relevant letters and telegrams. His evidence relating to the firm's dealings with Wellcome in the America period was incomplete and did not stand up to scrutiny, whereas Wellcome had noted every occasion he had communicated even the shortest messages. Wellcome's close personal attention to detail was completely at odds with Burroughs's laid-back style of management, trust in people and, one suspects, dislike of the whole process of giving evidence against his partner and old friend.[33]

Wellcome had his detailed evidence and documentation collated, printed up and retained by his solicitors, whereas Burroughs's papers are patchy. The upshot is that a somewhat one-sided view of the court case survives as historical evidence. Burroughs claimed that Wellcome had 'entirely and utterly neglected the business for twelve months when in America' (from August 1886), and since his return his application had 'not been such as Burroughs was entitled to'. He raised Wellcome's opposition to attempts to establish a factory in America as well as the question of Wellcome's health and his relationship with Mrs Sheldon; he asserted that Wellcome's interest in the publication of the translation of *Salammbo* by his publishing firm, Saxon & Co., took up a great deal of his time.[34] A litany of other serious accusations followed: that Wellcome's failure to pay off his debts in 1886 had resulted in the office being 'haunted by gentlemen who required payment'; that drawing funds as permitted by the articles of partnership had been extended by Wellcome; that Wellcome had effectively been a manager of the American entertainer Frank Lincoln (a charge dropped with the realisation that this happened outside the time of the active deed of partnership); that he had failed to visit Cuba or Mexico as agreed in 1886; and that when in America had merely attended a meeting of the Pharmaceutical Society and replied to some enquiries about the drug strophanthus. Most importantly, he had gone to America in part over his health but soon after arrival had taken an extended hunting tour in the forests of Maine. *The Times*, tongue in cheek, reported: 'Not only did the smell of drugs but even the mention of them, seemed detrimental to Mr Wellcome's health,' and he was 'out of the reach of letters and [tele] grams ... During the intervals of hunting he found time to compile a book called *Metlakahtla* ... and when he was not following the moose or paddling his own canoe he spent much of his time at the "Lotus" Club in New York.'

Wellcome's response was vigorous. During the first nine months of his absence he was prevented by illness from giving complete attention to the business – his trips to the forests had been undertaken for his health, not his pleasure. He had not travelled to Cuba or Mexico as the papers had reported cholera in the Spanish-American states and the ports were under quarantine.

When interrogated, Burroughs was unable to say exactly on which dates Wellcome had gone to the Isle of Wight or been in the office; nor could he say how many samples had been sent abroad or kept for Wellcome and how many were unusable. He could only say that Wellcome's lack of communication with the firm caused problems and that he 'believed' Sudlow had not heard from Wellcome for 'months and months at times'. Burroughs had gone to America mostly to attend to some business about which he had written to Wellcome and to which he considered Wellcome had not given adequate attention. On Wellcome's return to the UK, Burroughs had been dissatisfied with his attendance to business. Whereas Burroughs usually visited the factory at about 6am and again in the evening, being in the office from about 8.30 or 9.30am until between 4.30 and 7pm, Wellcome rarely arrived at the office before 11am. Mr Prevost the journal keeper gave evidence that Wellcome attended between 11 and 12 and left at all times, often in the early afternoon. In his evidence Wellcome reckoned that attendance between 10.30 to 11 in the morning until 4 or 5 in the afternoon was reasonable, but contradicted Prevost and Burroughs by saying that he very often stayed until 6 or 7. He was aware that Burroughs had worked longer hours in the last two years and had been arriving very early.

Asked if customers had complained to him about Wellcome, Burroughs said that he knew several who thought Wellcome was a myth in their business, 'never having seen him, or never having heard anything personally about him. He has lived in a literary atmosphere separate from the drug business.' Had employees ever suggested that Wellcome had failed to give assistance or direction when asked? Burroughs responded that it had never been the custom in their business for any employee to find fault to one principal about another; Mr Justice Kekewich acknowledged this was a very good thing.

On the issue of a factory in America, Burroughs stated that he thought he had met Wellcome two or three times when they were both in America and that he had yielded to Wellcome's opinion on the factory, though he considered that his own reasons were as strong as Wellcome's.

As to their joint interests in other firms, it was pointed out that Wellcome had agreed to Burroughs's interest in Terry & Co., a tobacco company, and Burroughs in Wellcome's interest in Saxon & Co. He had thought that Wellcome had two or three partners in Saxon & Co. and a third or quarter interest in it, but in reality Wellcome was the sole owner. On the other hand, Burroughs was merely a nominal director of Terry's; he had attended only one board meeting, had not spent five minutes on it and had speedily retired from the directorship.

Burroughs explained the position about petitions made to the firm regarding Wellcome's debts while he was in America. One creditor had come to the firm's office to explain that he needed repayment of around £150 and Burroughs had felt it incumbent on him to settle the debt. He robustly defended doing so: 'I do not see why I should apologise [for interfering in the matter of Wellcome's arrangements]. It was contrary to the interests of the firm that he should have debts long overdue and still unpaid.'

Wellcome was cross-examined only briefly and successfully countered many of Burroughs's claims. He was able to show that, while in America, he had been in touch with the firm more often than Burroughs had claimed and that he had done some business while there, 'never knowingly having neglected a single thing that was placed before [him].' He denied that there was ever a firm commitment to go to Cuba and Mexico and gave ample evidence that he had been genuinely unwell for some time: Burroughs, he insisted, had agreed to his journey to America for his health. Moreover, he had not delayed returning because of work on his Metlakatla book, which he could as easily have written in London as America. He had learnt from outside sources that Burroughs and Dr Witte were coming to America and, although he did not see Burroughs on arrival, he did see him 'several times ... on many different days, on some days several times a day at his hotel and at the business offices of Fairchild's'. On one or two occasions he had also gone to the sites selected for a possible factory and discussed the finances with Burroughs.

Wellcome agreed with Burroughs that no discussion had taken place between them concerning dissatisfaction with his work; nevertheless he claimed to have heard rumours about this during July after his return from America. It seems unlikely that he would not have sensed Burroughs's concerns when they met in America.[35] Significantly, four key employees – Sudlow, Kirby, Collett Smith (correspondence clerk) and Spratlin (assistant accountant) – were willing to give depositions for Wellcome.[36]

The responses made by Burroughs to some questions ('to the best of my knowledge' and 'I understand') infuriated the judge, who, not surprisingly, found it rather odd that Burroughs had not confronted Wellcome about his performance.

> B: I observed that he had not given much attention to
>   business while he was over there. I am not of a fault-
>   finding disposition, and therefore I said nothing.
> Q: You did not say anything?
> A: Not that I remember. I simply went over and attended to
>   it myself when I was there.
> Q: Do you mean to say it had not been done when you went
>   there?
> A: The goods had been delivered to Fairchilds but they had
>   not been properly advertised and the business had not
>   been properly pushed. So they told me. They told me it
>   was very difficult to get an interview with Mr Wellcome,
>   or to hear from him at all.
> Q: And you never mentioned that circumstance to
>   Mr Wellcome until now?
> A: I did not. I am not in the habit of finding fault with him
>   or with anyone else if I can help it.[37]

Mr Justice Kekewich reached several conclusions. He agreed that 'the charms of hunting' had 'tempted' Wellcome, 'in the pursuit of health, to spend a little time longer than perhaps was absolutely necessary ... and that [unanswered] letters accumulated ... beyond what was convenient', but he did not think this was serious. As for Wellcome's debts, they were too trifling to worry about. The judge considered that Burroughs was 'the willing horse in the firm. He goes to work early in the morning, and probably takes intense pleasure in his work, and he no doubt has devoted himself very earnestly to it. Mr Wellcome on the other hand, does what he thinks is a fair share of work, and his ideas of work are not so extensive.' He suggested that Wellcome's constitution would not allow of the exertions which Burroughs could bear without fatigue, and that there was no evidence that Wellcome had neglected his duty. It had become clear to him that the business was still making a good profit, that plans for a new factory had continued satisfactorily, and that both partners continued to see each other frequently. Cross-examined, Wellcome had stated that 'practically we have business conference daily, and we frequently lunch together.' The judge found it 'certainly strange' that, notwithstanding the writ issued and claims and counter-claims, up until recently both partners had communicated, either directly or indirectly, but effectively, through their agents about the development of a new factory at Dartford, its terms of purchase, and so on. Kekewich ruled that there was not 'the slightest ground' for a dissolution. Wellcome agreed to give up his interest in Saxon & Co. and costs were to be debited from the partnership accounts, borne by both in proportion to their shares in the firm. The judge hoped that the two partners would join in lunching together again soon.

'Partners Shake Hands' was the banner in the newspaper the next day. Wellcome sent his mother a telegram with the single word 'VICTORY'. Evidence of Burroughs's reaction has not survived, although Rhodes James asserts that he felt the defeat and public humiliation keenly and his wife even more so; but he would inevitably have been depressed at the prospect of continuing to work with a partner he neither trusted nor liked. The prospects did not bode well in spite of Judge Kekewich's comments about lunching. Burroughs had certainly anticipated an alternative verdict, and in mid-May, shortly before the case was due to come to court, he had in fact signed up to become a medical student at St Bartholomew's Hospital. Although he had earlier discussed with Olive taking a medical degree, this action may have reflected a desire for an alternative focus in the event of a dissolved partnership. It was not to be, and there is no evidence that he ever attended any lectures.[38]

The unexpected verdict set extraordinary challenges for both partners. At some point after the court case they no longer spoke to each other, communicating instead via their staff and written memos. Exactly when this situation arose and who was responsible is uncertain; the only source is the biased word of Wellcome's first biographer, Haggis.[39] Such lack of direct communication – at a time of further substantial expansion of the firm with unresolved financial and management issues – would put the partnership under huge stress.

Regardless of his disappointment, Burroughs hardly had time to consider the implications of the judgement, as he now turned his attention to the imminent opening of the new Dartford factory which he had striven so hard to acquire.

Chapter 12

Henry George and the
Phoenix Mills Philosopher

*The association of progress with poverty is
the enigma of our times ...*[1]

As Judge Kekewich noted, both partners had worked hard to make
the firm the success it had clearly become, and extraordinarily, while
legal battles were taking place, they continued to make detailed
arrangements for the firm's expanded manufacturing. Clearly both men
recognised that, whatever the outcome of the court case, the business
would continue. Burroughs's determination to find a new location to
manufacture BW&Co.'s products took up much of his attention in 1888
and 1889. Yet at the same time he increasingly devoted more of his time,
energy and financial support to promoting numerous radical causes.

Within a week of the court verdict on the partnership, the firm's new
works were opened at Dartford. Their location was on the site of the
disused Phoenix Paper Mill by Dartford Creek, with access by river
to the Thames 3 miles away and next to the main railway line. These
excellent transport facilities strongly influenced Burroughs's wish to
purchase.[2]

However, the move to Dartford created further tensions between the
partners. Wellcome wanted to lease with an option to purchase, but
the owners wished to sell. After negotiation a sale price of £5,000 was
agreed, and Burroughs offered to pay £4,000 if Wellcome would put up
£1,000. This Wellcome objected to, so Burroughs felt compelled to buy
alone. He leased the works to the firm for 49 years with the option that

Wellcome could require him to sell them to the firm within seven years at the sum Burroughs had paid for them. This unsatisfactory financial arrangement would create problems in the future.[3]

The mill purchase was a bold and very shrewd business move by Burroughs, allowing the firm to expand with speed and flexibility at a critical time. Within four years it was operating at full capacity and expansion was required. Without Dartford the firm's manufacturing capacity could not have coped with the increasing demand, and, crucially, when the Wandsworth factory suffered a severe fire, the firm was able to continue production. Only two months after the Dartford opening, on 12 September 1889, a blaze swept through the manufacturing building at Bell Lane Wharf. The cause was never discovered, but the outcome was serious; the chemical works building was destroyed, along with much machinery and stock, and a fireman was killed. Compensation was paid to his family by the partners, who assessed the whole issue of safety and spent several thousand pounds on fire apparatus at the mills.[4] Fortunately insurance covered much of the losses; there was a large stock of goods at the Snow Hill warehouse, and significant amounts of the machinery had already been relocated to Dartford. Had it not been for Burroughs's insistence on acquiring the Phoenix Mills, the Wandsworth fire might well have engulfed the whole business.

When the mill had been advertised in 1888, Burroughs asked his friend Charles Hutton to survey the site. It covered 8 acres, of which about half was water, and had wharfage facilities, many well-constructed buildings with excellent light, and plenty of space for expansion. Hutton reckoned that putting these premises into working condition would require about £1,500 and recommended purchase.

By November work was well advanced, and the partners appear to have worked together on the plans. The *Dartford and West Kent Advertiser* published an upbeat description of the proposed changes: the ponds would be restocked with fish and new trees planted; a new turbine engine would replace the waterwheel; there would be electric and gas lighting; separate departments would handle malting, shipping, printing and bottling; and there would be a boiler house, engineers' and fitters' workshops, storage, a steam barge, and a library. About 300 workers would be employed, some of whom would relocate from Wandsworth, but most would live locally in Dartford. The town's workers, unemployed since the closure of the old mill, greeted news of the new factory with enthusiasm, and Dartford looked forward to a brighter future.[5]

Advance publicity and a tour led by the Dartford manager Walter Herbert Hutton (Charles Hutton's son) ensured a good press at the opening, which was a splendid affair enjoyed by many hundreds of people from Dartford and beyond. Burroughs's friend Henry George, the celebrated American champion of single taxation and free trade, was touring England at this time, and Burroughs had invited him to visit Dartford and open the factory during his 'Henry George Campaign'. The use of the large Conservative Club for a meeting was refused outright, so instead Burroughs invited George to use the Phoenix Mills factory. Wellcome was

20: Henry George, c. 1885. He and Burroughs became close friends over the following decade.

understandably concerned that the occasion would be used to promote George's economic and political beliefs. After discussing the matter, it was agreed that George would not use the occasion for 'politicking'; instead it was arranged by Burroughs that he would address a later separate meeting, to which all the workers, townspeople, pharmaceutical representatives and dignitaries would be invited.

At 3pm on Wednesday 3 July 1889, 1,000 people were seated in the shipping room, which was 'charmingly adorned' with a banner proclaiming 'God save our Queen – great and good' and with posters emblazoned 'Welcome to Henry George', 'Free Trade' and 'Free Land'. The impressive gathering included major local dignitaries, representatives from the pharmaceutical world, eminent doctors, MPs, engineers, and journalists from London and America. After several preliminary speeches, Henry George praised the firm for its introduction of an eight-hour working day: its employees were not mere 'hands' but fellow human beings. When Sudlow spoke on behalf of the employees and called for three cheers for the heads of the firm, the cheers were 'enthusiastically enlarged to five'. Light refreshments were then provided in the hypodermic room, and the town band played music in the grounds to accompany tours of the building. Burroughs, who had 'spared neither time nor money to make the undertaking a success', was seen the whole day 'welcoming his guests and shaking hands in good hearty fashion with everybody that came to see him.'

The next part of the programme, the 'Henry George meeting', started at 8pm. By this time the crowd had more than doubled, and in the excitement police feared a stampede as people surged through the doors. Someone, 'rather unwisely perhaps', played a water hose on the people to beat them back. Some 2,000 packed into the main factory, requiring an overflow meeting to be held in an adjoining shipping room. The room was stiflingly hot, so 'amidst great cheering' Burroughs gave instructions for the top window panes to be knocked out and welcomed everyone as 'friends and citizens of the world'. George's speech lasted over an hour and covered taxation, free trade, and the firm's attempt to obtain a factory site in America, where the great cost of land and punitive American duties had made it prohibitive. A resolution, 'that this meeting considered the Land Question the most important social question', was carried 'amid wild enthusiasm', and a vote was passed thanking Burroughs for use of the room; the meeting concluded with a rousing rendition of 'For he's a jolly good fellow'. The party then started, with the lake and islets lit by Japanese lanterns and fairy lights; over 10,000 people witnessed one of the finest firework displays Dartford had ever seen. It culminated in a huge illumination of George surrounded by the slogans 'The Land for the People' and 'Our Greetings to Dartford'. The shipping department was then turned into a dance hall, and it was 1 o'clock before Burroughs, Hutton and a few friends adjourned to the Royal Bull Hotel for supper, and 3am before the last exhausted but happy dancers left. The Dartford Works grand opening was over.

21: Fireworks and speeches at the grand opening of the Dartford works by Henry George, 17 July 1889.

However, one person – namely Wellcome – was singularly unhappy at the way the factory had been opened. He had not attended the George meeting, perhaps because he felt unwell, though his hearty disapproval of the event probably had more to do with it. He complained bitterly that Burroughs had broken his pledge by allowing political issues to be raised in the workplace, to which Burroughs responded, somewhat disingenuously, that the actual opening ceremony had been devoid of politics. To make matters worse, Burroughs had George's speech printed and circulated to the firm's clients. It was a forlorn hope on Wellcome's part that no political rally would take place: George's fame and the chance to promote his beliefs was too good an opportunity to miss. The publicity for the firm was tremendous, however, and in adopting an eight-hour working day BW&Co. became a pioneer as one of the first firms in the country to operate this policy. But in the midst of this a new bone of contention between the partners was born, mentioned later by Wellcome as one of many indignities he had to bear.[6]

When sailing from Australia in 1883, Burroughs read Henry George's *Progress and Poverty*. He was immediately attracted by George's argument, that the primary cause of poverty lay in the systems of rent, and that a single tax on land value would resolve social injustices. The single tax movement was to dominate Burroughs's thinking for the rest of his life and led to his increasing involvement in radical politics.

George was described as a man of modesty and sincerity and as having 'an almost mystical religious conviction'. An American newspaper owner and editor, his involvement in local politics arose from witnessing the economic effects of land speculation and corrupt politicians. *Progress and Poverty: An Inquiry into the Cause of Industrial Depressions, and of Increase of Want with Increase of Wealth – The Remedy*, published in 1877, was a huge international success, selling over 100,000 copies in Britain alone. George became famous almost overnight, and it was claimed that his popularity was surpassed in America only by Mark Twain and Thomas Edison; sales of the book exceeded that of the popular *Uncle Tom's Cabin*. Many celebrated figures supported George's views, including Alfred Russel Wallace, friend and rival of Charles Darwin and author of *Land Nationalisation: Its Necessity and Its Aims*, who headed the Land Nationalisation Society. Wallace described *Progress and Poverty* as 'the most remarkable and important book of the present century and tried, unsuccessfully, to interest Darwin in it. Tolstoy supported his views; Joseph Chamberlain introduced some of the ideas into his policies, and George Bernard Shaw declared that Henry George converted him to socialism. When George died in 1897 more than 100,000 people attended his funeral in New York.

The single tax was a simplified and equitable tax based on land value; its premise was that the economic value derived from land, including natural resources, should belong equally to all residents of a community. George contended that the economic problems of the world arose from concentrated ownership of land, compounded by land speculation. By land he meant the exclusive right to use natural resources in a specified place, including timber and fishing rights, water, mining, road and rail rights, and some patents. Since such land was owned largely by speculators and owners who sometimes let the land remain underused or idle, labour was forced onto marginal land and wages were driven down. The solution was to cut all taxes except those on land values, thus bolstering the economy and making land available to those who would use it. This 'single tax' would be a fairer tax than income tax, since land ownership was (and still is) heavily concentrated among the wealthiest; social justice and all other advances would stem from this.

George's ideas were not entirely new: the evils of 'land monopoly' had been identified by earlier economic theorists, but he was able to popularise his theory and soon developed a large following on both sides of the Atlantic; indeed, his ideas still gain supporters today. In 1880 his fame was at its height, and his views on the 'Negro Question' gained him the backing of the black community; more significantly, he won support from the New York Republican Irish. At the same time, he saw private enterprise as acceptable – there was nothing wrong in businesses owning the means of producing wealth; as a result he was increasingly at odds with socialists. In 1886 he ran for mayor in New York as a candidate of the labour organisations, coming in a close second (Theodore Roosevelt came third). By the late 1880s his support had fallen, many also being afraid of the revolution they believed would follow from such a drastic change in land ownership and taxation.

After reading *Progress and Poverty*, Burroughs wrote to George, introducing himself as a fellow American who was sympathetic towards George's efforts to stop the greedy from getting wealthy at the expense of the community and urging him to continue to fight land monopolies. Writing of the great majority of the English who suffered from poverty, he described the condition of 'semi-serfdom' that existed, suggesting that societies should be formed in England and other countries as had happened when Cobden and Bright worked together to repeal the corn laws: if such a society were formed, he would become a member and subscribe to a fund to distribute literature so that the public could be better informed and cast their votes for Members of Parliament accordingly.[7]

Burroughs and George met in 1885 during Burroughs's prolonged stay in America that year. Both men passionately believed in creating a fairer society and soon became good friends: George said of Burroughs that, 'the longer you know him, the truer you find him, and the better you like him.'[8] Burroughs always called on George when in New York, George always visited him when in England, and both were to visit Ireland together.

Since land ownership, tenancies and poverty concerned him, George was inevitably drawn into discussion on the Irish problems. The potato crop failures, famine, evictions and agrarian violence fuelled debates on land rights and Home Rule, and Irish nationalism was a burning topic among America's large Irish community. George drew parallels with social injustice and land taxation in America. Soon after finishing *Progress and Poverty* he published *The Irish Land Question*, and the radical paper *Irish World* commissioned him to go to Ireland, where he worked alongside Michael Davitt.[9]

Burroughs made several trips to Ireland in the 1880s, some of them with George. On one occasion George recounted his mischievousness:

> Mr Burroughs, a Member of Parliament [almost certainly William Saunders] and I went to Lough Neagh, a celebrated lake ... one day when there was a great Orange celebration. We stopped at Belfast and while there a great crowd of Orangemen stood about the station. They seemed to furnish Mr Burroughs with much fun, and he made some jokes at their expense. Just as the train started he put his head out of the car window and yelled 'Hurrah for the Pope!' Of course the Orangemen made for the train and him with a rush, but Mr Burroughs had calculated the speed of the train and the distance they were away, so they didn't get at him.[10]

After attending a medical exhibition in Dublin in 1887, Burroughs took a cycling holiday in Ireland with his brother-in-law James 'Jai' Riggs and friend Dr Alfred Gubb. The Irish landscape, especially in that region, was stunning, but Burroughs was appalled by the poverty: 'The villages are but huddles of miserable houses, and the peasants' homes are not fit for pigstys [*sic*]. The landlords' houses <u>are</u> palaces, that of the Earl of Kenmare costing over £200,000.'[11] Once, during a train journey to Limerick, he addressed a 'car full' of Irish constabulary, delivering 'the strongest doctrine [on landlords] which the soldiers pretended not to agree with at first, but which they quietly assented to when their captain was looking the other way.'[12]

Heated debates took place about land reform, led by the Irish Land League, and there were frequent public meetings in England over the Irish Question. Burroughs was prominent at the large demonstration in Hyde Park in 1887 of 45,000 people who opposed government legislation on Ireland.[13] Public demonstrations were more frequent as the unions grew in strength, and protest marches took place for better working conditions, pay and social justice. From the late 1880s Burroughs participated in further marches and rallies on other issues, such as the eight-hour working day, opposing the licensing laws and supporting the right to protest.[14] He later stated that the labour question in England equalled in importance the slavery question in America.[15] His increasing political activities were recognised by his election in 1889 as president of the Dartford Liberal and Radical Association.[16]

From the mid-1880s Burroughs recruited followers to the concept of the single tax at every opportunity he could, mentioning it in correspondence with many people, including President Cleveland. In 1885, when sending Henry Morton Stanley a sample medicine chest, he took the opportunity to comment on a report that stated that the Congo was no place for Americans because all desirable lands there had already been acquired, and he urged Stanley to consider the benefits of a single land tax for the Congo's future. Stanley did not take the bait, though after using the medicine chest in the Congo he subsequently praised it in his book *In Darkest Africa*; it gave the firm no end of good publicity. Both Burroughs and Wellcome became good friends of Stanley and his wife.

In 1887 Burroughs met George again and joined the Anti-Poverty Society and the Anti-Slavery Society, the former having just been set up by George.[17] In 1888, after the two men had visited Shanklin on the Isle of Wight, they travelled together to America to vote for Cleveland as president. The crossing was rough and Burroughs ended up with a broken arm. Immediately on arrival, however, hiding his considerable pain, he joined 'the drug trade boys' in a demonstration supporting Cleveland.[18] George returned to the UK at the invitation of William Saunders and on this visit addressed Dr Joseph Parker's service at the City Temple, undoubtedly at Burroughs's suggestion.[19]

Along with other single tax supporters, Burroughs pressed George to return to England very soon to undertake an extended lecture tour. This George did in 1889, bringing his family with him. He was greeted by the socialist and economist Sidney Webb with advice about how to handle the current complex political minefield. When Burroughs was in Paris he visited some of George's family, reporting back to George on the eldest daughter who was ill from a malignant form of scarlet fever. On his next visit shortly afterwards, Burroughs took them to the Exposition Universelle.

A few days after the factory opening, Burroughs and George travelled together to Ireland, where Burroughs spoke on the same platform as George at a meeting in Belfast. Burroughs made a considerable financial contribution to promoting George's theories – including financing a weekly American journal, *The Single Tax*, speaking frequently at public meetings and writing regularly for the press, his quick humour winning many laughs.[20]

Influenced by Gilbert and Sullivan's popular *The Pirates of Penzance*, Burroughs, under the name 'Mainville', printed a semi-historical comic operetta for landlords and tenants entitled *The Good Pirate*. It poked fun at taxation and abuses in the political and economic system, using the story of pirates wishing to charge for sailing the seas. With a rally cry 'Yours for the single tax, and consequent free land, free trade, and free men', BW&Co.'s products were jumbled into the chorus lines, which featured a Lord Fitz-Noodle, the Duke of Loo, Captain Jinks, and the Good Ship *Law and Order*:

> O I'm not sea sick
> Happen to have any of the Tabloids about you?
> I'm not sea sick
> Introduce me to your Anti-pyrine.
> Don't forget the Primrose League that's patronised by peers.
>
> Over-population is the question of the day.
> What to do with all the people is more than we can say.
> A war or epidemic, a handy thing would be
> To clear the discontented population from the sea.
>
> To strengthen our position and to shut up competition
> From the sailors of the Great Pacific Sea
> We must go in for protection, and allow of no connection
> With the oceans, seas and rivers that are free.

The single tax a blessing is to landlords good and bad,
The good ones will be better off, the others will be mad.
They must use the land or sell it, for taxes they must pay,
These dog-in-the-manger landlords too long have had their
    day.[21]

Another work written and privately published by Burroughs was *A Strange Dream*, recounting a singular dream in which the doings of a peculiar people in a strange country are observed. Amusingly told, his story promoted the single tax.[22] It was probably the closest that he came to voicing a socialist outlook.

Back in New York, George stated in his paper, *The Standard*, that Burroughs had two businesses: the first was running the drug company, in which he 'gets a living and makes money, and which he seems to thoroughly enjoy. The other business is one in which he spends money, but which he seems to even more enjoy. It is the diffusion of the single tax idea. About the only time when he is not at either one or the other of these businesses is when he is asleep.'[23] There is no doubt that the single tax movement now governed much of Burroughs's life, and he supported it financially as well. He contributed to *The Standard* and in 1887 arranged for the publication, illustration and distribution across America and Europe of 60,000 complimentary copies of George's *Protection or Free Trade*, with a covering note citing his own credentials.[24]

His family was not exempt from this obsession. Burroughs recounted asking his daughter Anna if she remembered his golden rule ('Do unto others as you would be done unto'), to which she reminded him that two years previously he had taught her 'Down with the landlords!' His conversation on the subject must have become well worn, and the local Dartford newspapers were increasingly outspoken about his being 'absolutely engrossed' by it.

Some found it hard to follow his arguments, and to be fair the theory of single tax is not easily understood. The *West Kent Advertiser* printed a letter in which Burroughs attempted to clarify how it would operate, and its editor commented that not everyone was convinced: 'Mr Burroughs keeps on hammering away at the subject and we fancy that his own colleagues on the Council of the Liberal and Radical Association find it rather a bore.' While he had a 'peculiar literary style', and some passages might amuse, there was 'the same old trick of walking round the subject in which this agile Yankee is proficient.' It was noted that Burroughs had wisely decided not to try to enter Parliament, at least at that time, but was 'manifesting considerable interest in local matters'; it would be much better if he was elected to the Dartford Local Board, and he would be 'a capital man to hurry up the steam-roller and the scavenger. Moreover he ought to prove a tough and reliable buffer in the brunt between public and private interests, which so frequently occur in local government.'[25]

An audience in Dartford, made up largely of operatives from the Crayford Gun Factory, heard Burroughs speak, 'in his quiet manner', on 'How to Advance Wages' and 'heartily agreed with the deduction', but they were unable to follow his reasoning.[26] His audience tolerated him, in part because he was so likeable, well-meaning and sincere, but also because he wanted to improve their lot. As one observer put it: 'it pleases you greatly to find that a keen man of business like Mr Burroughs, "single-tax crank"[27] though he is, is not too deeply immersed in money-making to be impervious to the demands of humanity.' Another newspaper said simply: 'His politics are nebulous, but he has a good heart, and he manufactures most excellent soap.'[28]

A certain hostility greeted Burroughs's support of Henry George from those who viewed him as a 'professional agitator', stirring up the discontent of 'ordinary people'. The local press deemed his letter on 'How to Advance Wages' as

> interesting, if only as an example of the utter rubbish which a clever man may write or talk when he has become a crotcheteer. Mr Burroughs appears to be possessed of Henry George to such an extent that he is blinded to actual facts ... A great deal of harm is done by well-intentioned people, and we are not sure that local mischief will not result from Mr Burroughs' talk about advancing wages, especially as [it] was countenanced by another considerable employer, in the person of Mr Hesketh. We have had quite enough strikes in this neighbourhood.

Burroughs was considered to be well meaning though misguided. 'We are all for free discussion, but [his] glib platitudes and false logic do not help us one iota towards a solution of the problem', noted the Dartford press, concluding that 'Mr Burroughs is an amiable fanatic, with a feminine fluency of words, which he mistakes for argument ... We only wish we could believe in the inspiration which has come to the Phoenix Mills philosopher.'[29] The implications of his philosophies about the economy and political and social order created unease among many, though people liked him and he made no enemies.

Employers 'whose chief aims are to line their own pockets without any anxiety for the welfare of those dependent upon them' were, Burroughs declared, 'unhappy in comparison with himself and his partner, who knew that every employee held them in the highest esteem and regard: their employees discharged their duties in the same way as they would were they working a business of their own.' The business 'had been a great pleasure to himself and Wellcome', and, 'even if he were to become a rich man [which of course by then he was] with plenty of leisure', he would still like to go on with the business 'as a matter of pleasure'. The partners flattered their staff, but their paternalism and concern for the welfare of their employees won them genuine appreciation and loyalty. Significantly, there were no strikes at the factory throughout the late 1880s and the 1890s when a crisis in the economy gave rise to general disaffection and the growth of the modern trade union movement. The match girls' strike at Bryant & May in 1888 was followed by the dockers' strike of 1889; in both cases the workers won considerable public support. In 1893 Charles Booth conducted a survey of working conditions, and the surveyor of BW&Co. told him that there had never been the slightest trouble with the unions and that drunkenness was not an issue. The firm was not subject to absenteeism for 'recovery' after a bank holiday as was frequently the case in factories at this time – a large percentage of the workers sometimes being absent for a whole week.[30]

The town on the other hand did not have a good reputation. 'The Slough of Despond' was one description, and a well-known ditty went: 'Dirty Dartford / Horrible people / Bury their dead / Below the steeple.' Burroughs wrote to the local press that, although Dartford was 'undoubtedly one of the ugliest' towns in England, he would like it to be 'one of the most beautiful'.[31] In this he was undoubtedly influenced by the 'progressive era' of social activism and political reform which swept America from the 1890s. Improvements, notably municipal reform there and in Britain, resulted from a growing investment by local government. In London, vestries and the newly formed London County Council accomplished major advances: most of London's parks and open spaces, for example, were developed in this period. In Dartford, Burroughs faced a difficult task, but, undaunted, he achieved changes in a wide range of schemes to enhance the environment and amenities. He was joined in this by a fellow manufacturer, Everard Hesketh, who thought similarly about town improvements, although the 'apathetic' attitude of the local board to their suggestion of assisting financially with a promenade around the factory lake was frustrating. Nor was the suggestion by Burroughs of public bath provision pursued by the local councillors.

Yet life for the people of Dartford started to look up. They benefited from the firm's paternalism and Burroughs's philanthropic generosity. All manner of local organisations approached him for support, from the Dartford Wesleyan Day Schools to those trying to establish a free library.[32] He helped finance projects such as the Dartford Memorial Hall. The locals could boat in summer and skate in winter on the lake in front of the factory. A keen tennis player, Burroughs set up tennis courts for use after work by staff and their friends. He encouraged participation in musical and social evenings through the Phoenix Literary and Musical Society. Entertainments were combined with efforts to improve sobriety, support being given to the Dartford Young Men's Bible Classes and the formation of a local temperance society. Burroughs chaired and lectured at numerous meetings of the Young Women's Christian Association.[33] Together with Hesketh, he established Dartford's Free Lecture Society, and both paid fees for their employees to attend classes.[34] It was noted that 'nothing rejoices Mr Burroughs' heart more than to see his employees thoroughly enjoying themselves after business hours,' and Burroughs himself commented that, 'when he directed his affairs by the teaching of the Bible, they invariably prospered.'[35] Similarly, at Snow Hill there was a library, a piano and a 'Liberty Club', which met regularly at the Anchor restaurant in Cheapside for talks and musical evenings with both partners in attendance.

Special events included the Balaclava Fête. In 1890 a public appeal in support of survivors of the Crimean War's Charge of the Light Brigade, by then suffering from penury and destitution, caught Burroughs's attention. He immediately suggested that the townspeople make a contribution varying from 1s. to 2/6 each towards a concert or ball, or both, to raise a 'handsome sum'. His idea was taken up with enthusiasm, a committee formed, and the Balaclava Relief Fund Fête took place at Dartford that summer. Coloured lamps on the island read 'Honour the Brave', and inside was displayed Burroughs's favourite motto: 'All work and no play makes Jack a dull boy.' Over 1,500 people attended, along with some of the Balaclava survivors. Between noon and midnight there were boating, concerts, dances, walking the greasy pole, swimming, and egg and spoon and other races. Tennyson's ballad 'The Charge of the Light Brigade' was recited, and a temperance refreshment tent quenched the thirst of the public (alcohol being carefully excluded). The finale was a grand firework display. It was all a huge success, with much money raised, causing one reporter to comment: 'When Mr Silas M. Burroughs puts his hand to anything, he carries it out on a scale which is truly American, and with a spirit and enthusiasm which is particularly his own.'[36]

From 1884 the firm ran an annual summer excursion for its workers. Among places visited were the Crystal Palace, Margate, Hastings and Southsea, this last being the most popular, as it enabled many to take a boat trip to the Isle of Wight. Railway coaches were chartered from London and Dartford, lunches, teas and even cigars were provided, and dancing, singing and general fun was the order of the day. On one trip Burroughs alighted at Horsham station, famous for its roses, and distributed a basket of roses to the occupants of each carriage. Employees would return late in the evening, thoroughly uplifted by the generosity of the partners and pep talks on the success of the firm. The local press gave the excursions extensive publicity, and both partners attended if they could. Two of only three known photographs of the partners together – but, tellingly, not seated next to each other – are those taken at the Crystal Palace and Southsea outings.[37]

Public success masked private upheavals. Sudlow as general manager needed both his wits and diplomacy to keep both partners informed on important issues and must have played a heroic role keeping the business running smoothly while retaining their mutual respect and confidence. The Wandsworth fire and Dartford Mills expansion brought new challenges, and to some extent work kept both men so busy that they had little time to consider their business relationship. But mutual gnawing distrust meant that minor problems and misunderstandings could and did grow out of proportion. The court settlement of 1889 did not alter Burroughs's desire to dissolve the partnership and set up a joint stock company. It was the elephant in the room, inhibiting all their discussions and now non-existent friendship. In the face of all this, Burroughs, not surprisingly, chose to spend more time abroad marketing and building up useful networks, thereby avoiding the unpleasantness that now characterised his relationship with Wellcome. For two men who set such store in the happiness of their employees' lives, it was a strange and miserable situation for them to have reached.

Chapter 13

Citizen of the World

He made his business a pleasure and his pleasure a business.[1]

Was Burroughs's restless travelling born of a desire to escape from the tensions of the office with Wellcome? Did he feel himself sidelined by Wellcome? Or was it simply that he believed that his most effective contribution to the business was to meet people face to face, push the firm's products abroad and check out competition? Over the next three years, between 1890 and 1893, his travels took him to Egypt and the Holy Land and on many occasions to cities across Europe; as always, he mixed business with pleasure. He became an 'omnivagant traveller' and 'inveterate globe-trotter'.[2] Whatever the cause of this travelling mania, it is clear that his frequent absences from home led to tensions between him and Olive, although she did on occasion accompany him. He also had a brush with the law, which revealed a more intemperate side to his character.

Unusually, in 1890 Burroughs went abroad only twice, both times to Germany in connection with the 10th International Medical Congress. The first visit, in May, was within three weeks of the birth of his younger daughter Daisy, so it is probable that he intentionally stayed in the UK while Olive was expecting. This was a journey that Wellcome referred to disparagingly as a 'pleasure trip'.

On his return Burroughs applied for and was granted British nationality. What prompted him to make this move? The death of his aunt and his failure to find a manufacturing base in America, as well as his commitment to the factory in Dartford, meant that he had finally decided he wished to live permanently in England. Now, as he said in his application: 'being engaged in an industrial pursuit & having made a careful study of labor questions I wish to have the privilege of voting.'[3] Another reason might have been an interest in holding public office, for which he required British citizenship. Possibly he was prompted by Wellcome's complaints about his bringing politics into the firm's business and criticism of his signing a petition against Charles Bradlaugh – who had been refused permission to enter Parliament on the grounds of his lack of faith. Wellcome, on the other hand, declined to sign the petition and took the opportunity to draw an analogy with his views on Henry George: although an ardent admirer of Bradlaugh, he did not agree with his religious theories; he respected George's integrity and honesty of purpose yet did not accept his political views any more than Bradlaugh's religious ones. 'I don't think foreigners should interfere with the domestic policies of a country unless the people of the country are incapable of managing their own affairs,' Wellcome pronounced. He hoped his letter saying this would lead to 'a better understanding' with Burroughs, but a better understanding between the men did not follow.[4]

The family was expanding. Anna (the surviving twin) was now five, her brother Stanley Mainville ('Junie') was born in July 1888 and named after the explorer Henry Morton Stanley, and a third child, Frances Margaret ('Daisy'), was born in February 1890. The family moved frequently, renting a number of properties, including Pitfield in Eltham and 9 Craven Hill, Bayswater. In May, Burroughs took a summer lease on 16 Highfield Road, a small semi-detached house within easy walking distance of the factory, for use as a Dartford base; meanwhile Olive and the family remained in Paddington. That October Burroughs was unwell and the winter was one of the coldest on record in London. When the Serpentine froze he went skating and was slightly injured by another skater. A few days later he left London for the warmer climes of the Riviera. In thanking Olive for her excellent packing of his cases, he hoped that she would join him but supposed 'domestic arrangements' would detain her, a comment that not only suggests a lack of communication between them but indicates that they were leading somewhat separate lives at this point. In writing home, he painted an idyllic scene, describing the view through his window to the sea – the sound of lapping waves on the rocks a hundred feet below, and the sight of two small fishing boats – aimed at making Olive wish that she was with him to enjoy its beauty.

Olive meanwhile reported that their friends the Mattoxes had fallen out, and Burroughs urged her to try to act as peacemaker: 'They must each have patience with one another and each be very careful lest they should say or do anything that might be a cause of pain or sorrow to the other. Anything that might fill the life of the other with ceaseless regret.'

He went on to reflect on his relationship with Olive. From this it is clear that all was not well between them, or at least not from Olive's point of view. She had evidently told him of her unhappiness with their marriage and even indicated that at times she had wished to separate from him. Burroughs now wrote an impassioned plea:

> I thank God and your good angels that you have changed your mind from the insane idea which you say has possessed you sometimes. If you are not at any time happy say what you wish and I will deny you nothing but for heavens sake and your eternal happiness never think of leaving us. What would become of the little dears. If you think I did wrong to marry you it can certainly be right for each of us to do what we can to make the other happy afterward. You have a very stupid foolish husband. I have got a very sensible & good wife and ought to improve rapidly so don't despair of making me a man after your own heart. With an earnest desire which both of us possess to please the other our lives should be a blessing to ourselves and to the world.

Burroughs intended to write a book on the land question, hoping to show the evils of the present system of taxation and bring about social justice. Then he suggested that, since Olive had read widely, she could take up writing.

> I think you could write a good one [story] & if it took well you would have your ambition gratified of making a lot of money yourself. It would be a profitable & diverting occupation for your mind. You would soon forget all your unfounded notions of leaving poor me and get over your super-sensitive imagination ways of looking at things. We have never had any differences of opinion excepting on some trifling mode of procedure or careless word here & there soon repented & forgiven. Neither of us mean to give cause of sorrow or trouble to the other. I am sure you do not want to make me unhappy by doing anything rash or foolish and I will do anything that you say will tend to your happiness.

What lay behind Olive's unhappiness? Her letters to Burroughs have not survived and so Burroughs's replies and the evidence of her own life are the only information available. Five years previously Burroughs had alluded to Olive's imagination leading her to draw unfounded conclusions and tried to reassure her of his desire to have her with him. Olive was intelligent, educated and articulate, and she may well have desired and anticipated the independent career and success enjoyed by Mary Swain, Amanda Lougee and others of her female friends in the United States.[5] In many ways her education was superior to that of an English woman of her own situation in this period. She did not marry for money; had that been the case their courtship would have been a speedier one. When wooing her, Burroughs had expressed concern about Olive giving up teaching, a profession she loved, and pondered on ways in which she could continue to use her skills, proposing medicine as a possibility. A totally modern woman, she epitomised the new liberated attitudes of some American women at this time. As Burroughs's friend John Morgan Richards observed: 'there would be great difficulty in finding an American woman who would be prepared to take a back seat: and if she were placed in one, no long time would elapse before she would march into a front one.'[6]

Since marriage, Olive had experienced huge changes in her life. Living with Burroughs could never be dull – meeting many interesting people in a hectic social whirl and travelling abroad. She was popular with his family, acquaintances and colleagues and made many new and lasting friends. Significantly, she shared and discussed with Burroughs the problems of the business and of his relationship with Wellcome. Together they entertained the firm's staff, friends and visitors from all over the world and not infrequently hosted and attended events such as the Conversazione held at Holborn Town Hall in December 1890. By now Olive had her children to care for and, even with a nanny and domestic help, carried the responsibility for their upbringing on her own. She was the accommodating wife, entertaining guests and visitors and supportive of Burroughs's career. His workaholic, frantic lifestyle and lengthy absences on business meant that, even when at home or on holiday together, they were frequently in the company of others. Accompanying him on his journeys, which would involve frequent moves with three children, was impractical, and leaving the children behind with a nurse for a long period clearly did not appeal to Olive. She also suffered increasingly from rheumatism and, having experienced difficult voyages, resisted crossing the Atlantic.

It is more than likely that Olive felt that her husband was turning into a stranger and now, after seven years' marriage, had some regrets about the direction her life had taken. Burroughs for his part was uxorious: close ties and frequent contact with his relatives are evidence of the value he placed on family, and he was deeply fond of Olive and his children. Although Olive evidently changed her mind about leaving him, Burroughs was at pains to set down reasons why it would be wrong. He blamed himself for any failure of communication; *he* was the stupid one, *she* the sensible good wife, and Olive must consider the children, her own eternal happiness and his happiness. He in turn would do what he could to become the husband she wanted.

After writing these emotional words, Burroughs immediately moved on to practicalities: where might the family live the following summer? Could Olive look at places around the Hamptons, Kingston and Sunbury, 30 to 50 minutes by fast train from Waterloo and near the river (rowing would be good exercise for her)? Or would she prefer to live in town or winter on the Riviera? 'I will do as you like,' he wrote in January 1891, signing off 'with lots of kisses for you & the children & kind regards to mutual friends. Your affectionate Mainville.'[7]

Discussion must have cleared the air, and a compromise arrangement was reached. They stayed together, but it is significant that in future the family spent more time abroad, frequently based at one location in Switzerland, where Burroughs joined them when he could: it is likely that London's poor air quality and Olive's rheumatism influenced this decision. Olive became closer to her friend and companion Alice Miller, and Burroughs's frequent business travels continued. After a flying visit home in the spring of 1891 he undertook a long journey to Egypt and Palestine.

On his first trip to Jerusalem, in 1881, Burroughs was fascinated by the biblical stories and places he had seen while travelling. Now he had the chance to go to some of the places he had not had time to visit then. The opportunity presented itself when his sister and brother-in-law, the theologian Jai Riggs, planned to join a party of ministers from New York state for a tour of the Holy Land. The group included some of the ministers' wives and old family friends from Lockport. Burroughs joined them on the continent, from where the party of 15 men and four women sailed from Brindisi to Alexandria. Two weeks were spent in and around Cairo and Ismailia and travelling via the Suez Canal to Port Said, the route Burroughs had taken on the SS *Ceylon* ten years previously. The group arrived in Jaffa, traditional gateway to the Holy Land, on 23 March and headed for Jerusalem for the start of their 500-hundred mile, 37-day expedition. Essentially a package tour for pilgrims, it was organised by the unlikely named Mr Rolla Floyd, an American contractor who had made his living there for 25 years by taking parties through Palestine and Syria. He supplied tents and good horses and a Syrian dragoman (guide) called Habib Saibah.[8]

We can retrace Burroughs's travels from his letters to Olive, rough notes kept in tiny diaries (into which he tucked wild flowers), reports in the American and English press, articles in the *Chemist and Druggist*, and lectures given on his return. In Syria, the usual tourist attractions were visited, but most of his time in Alexandria and Cairo was consumed by visits to chemists and doctors. He anticipated a large trade in Egypt: leading European chemists in Cairo had given good orders, and he expected the civil and military authorities would do the same. Otherwise, armed with his *Baedecker Guide*, Burroughs and his friends explored Cairo, its pyramids and the Sultan Hassan Mosque. As with modern tourists, the group was mobbed by children demanding backsheesh, and Burroughs bemoaned the poverty, inevitably blaming the taxation system. He gave donations to several missions and hospitals, including Dr Harper's Medical Mission in Old Cairo and the Municipal and Rothschild Hospital in Jerusalem. In typical imperialist thinking of the time, he considered that living standards were steadily improving and that if the English stayed in Egypt better times would follow.[9]

Burroughs's familiarity with the Scriptures is evident from his notes on the places visited, and he knew that Medina (in present-day Saudi Arabia) was not far away. The pilgrims would be woken at 4 in the morning and ride on horseback all day, pitching camp at about 5 or 6pm. Had they tackled their journey the following year, a railway would have taken them from Jaffa to Jerusalem. Long days on horseback and camping proved hard going: on the first day 26 miles were covered in gruelling heat. Inevitably, religion preoccupied most of the party: Jerusalem was described as a sacred city, though anything but a religious city. One minister found 'people were kept in menial and moral darkness' and that women were kept in ignorance, slavery and drudgery; 'this is true of every land where the gospel of Jesus Christ is not taught and lived.' The abject poverty, miserable dwellings, wild dogs and, at times, hostile receptions made a deep impression.

In Beirut, Burroughs heard that his children had been seriously ill, though were now recovered. He wrote of his relief about the excellence of the family nurse and doctor, telling Olive he had the utmost confidence in her judgement.[10] After the tour Burroughs travelled to Smyrna (where some of the party split off), Constantinople, Venice, Athens, Brindisi, Naples, Rome, Florence and Milan and then headed for home. On the voyage from Athens he humorously described the lack of manners of fellow passengers, whose platefuls of chicken and rice were so large he 'thought the dishes would crack'. In Naples, Burroughs with his friends

22: Visit to Pompeii, 1891, on his return from the Holy Land. Here Burroughs is leaning against a pillar in the Temple of Isis, with his sister Lina in front of him, her husband Jai Riggs on the step and three family friends from Lockport, May Gardner Jackson, Jessie Schuler and Anna Gardner.

explored Pompeii; they were photographed resting on the steps of the Temple of Isis, with Burroughs looking away from the camera as though in his own reverie.

The Holy Land trip was a success for business too, and Burroughs, in buoyant mood, wrote: 'our goods seem to catch on pretty well wherever they get a show & they have I think got a good start in each of the countries I have visited which have never been "looked up" except by us.' He had sold all the goods sent out in Constantinople for cash to the leading chemist there and was sure of a good trade, as all the doctors (the physician to the sultan especially) were delighted with the goods. Were it not for the 'unspeakable Turk', whose taxes enabled people only to exist, he believed that Turkey would be prosperous.[11]

Experiencing only two days of bad weather in three and a half months away, Burroughs had never felt so good in his life: 'England is a good place to get out of in the winter especially if one can also make the getting out profitable in a pecuniary way as I trust I have done.' He looked forward to his homecoming, imagining that Olive had settled on a house upriver or somewhere where they would be 'cosy & make our friends the same this summer ... Guess up river is about the jolliest place to live especially in July Aug & Sept ... it beats the sea shore. Rowing will do you lots of good & you can air the kids that way & I can row you out Saty afternoons or perhaps Sunday afternoons too if you don't think it wicked & I don't see the harm if the disposition is right.' Olive rented Leigh House in Surbiton, close to the station and the Thames, and the family did indeed enjoy frequent outings on the river.

That summer of 1891 the firm's annual excursion was to Southsea: attended by Burroughs and Wellcome, it was larger and more splendid than ever. Both partners also attended the British Medical Association meeting in Birmingham in the summer and the International Medical Congress in Berlin shortly afterwards, where Burroughs demonstrated the now celebrated Stanley medicine chest to the empress of Russia. In November he departed for Paris, then Rome for the 3rd Universal Peace Congress, where he spoke on the two great determinants for peace – free trade and free travel.

Free trade was passionately defended by Burroughs, who criticised the United States' protectionist policies throughout his life: 'America's mistake is England's opportunity, which we may reasonably expect will be duly improved by English merchants and manufacturers.'[12] Taxation in Britain of course also affected the firm's business, and when the budget of 1890 proposed a rise in taxes on spirits Burroughs quickly sent off a letter to the *Chemist and Druggist*, urging chemists to oppose this by lobbying their MPs.[13]

Burroughs gave papers at the 7th International Congress on Hygiene and Demography in London on furnishing steam from central districts for heating and power in towns and cities, arguing that it should be possible to supply steam from mains laid under the streets, as well as on the topic of how taxation affected housing, especially of the poor. Free travel also joined the long list of issues which Burroughs proposed could be solved with a single tax which could fund utilities such as railways. Transportation issues had concerned Burroughs throughout his life, influenced in part by his father's involvement in the Erie Canal, by the dramatic development of railways in the United States and, not least, by his personal experiences of travelling. Travel was a political issue at this time, when major cities were expanding, more people were displaced from city centres, and workers had difficulty meeting travel costs from their wages. In London, the Cheap Trains Act of 1883 removed passenger duty on any journey costing less than a penny a mile and obliged railway companies to operate a larger number of low-cost services. Burroughs supported both the 1889 Central Railways Bill to construct a new London underground line to run from Shepherd's Bush to Liverpool Street and a proposed line from Uxbridge Road to the Tower of London, claiming that it would it be advantageous to tradesmen and would increase the value of land in the adjacent areas. He noted that a line under Broadway in New York was planned with extra tracks to allow for fast through trains and thought a comparable system was possible in London, for which he made various arguments around cost, convenience and land values.[14] The Woolwich Ferry was free: was it not possible to have free transport as well? A Free Railway Travel League was formed in 1891, and Burroughs gained a platform to speak on the subject to the august audience of the British Association for the Advancement of Science.[15]

Burroughs's critics were quick to poke fun. Was he also including free conveyance of goods in his scheme? If by free travel he meant passengers only, would there be adequate space for goods traffic? – the Woolwich ferry, for example, would be full of old women, along with their 'perpetual … knitting and gossip'. These were just more 'pet theories', with Burroughs acting like a 'good fairy' bestowing benefaction, his critics claimed, but he ought to carry his theory through to its logical conclusion. Why not free food and clothing? The Dartford press mocked that Burroughs was 'fascinated by the word "free"' and followed it as if it were a 'Will o' the wisp'. 'Let us first try free medical tabloids, or something of that kind … and what about free beer?' A letter signed by 'One who would like to travel free' asked where the money would come from if the state took over the railways and granted free travel. The following poem also appeared:

> Oh why should anybody cavil
> At those who offer us free travel?
> To journey free o'er land and ocean –
> It surely is a glorious notion!
>
> But if the Nation pays the Nation
> None gain, and that's a revelation!
> And so, perhaps, when all is ended
> The present plan will not be mended.[16]

To the critic who accused him of talking 'plausible socialistic nonsense', Burroughs retorted that this idea would sooner or later take root. After all, people used to pay to travel on roads and to cross

Thames bridges, but such tolls ceased when it was recognised that more satisfactory methods existed of constructing and maintaining roads and bridges. Cheap travel was a step in the direction of free travel, just as a reduction in road tolls was a prelude to their abolition. In Melbourne, Australia, children travelled to and from school without charge on railways owned by the state, and this genuine experiment in free travel had not been deemed 'socialistic nonsense'. In his paper to the Universal Peace Congress in Rome that year, Burroughs argued that free trade and free travel were linked: free travel would be a powerful agent in bringing about that 'harmony of tastes, aspiration, and interest which are a sure guarantee of peace', while direct taxation would 'tend to promote peace and goodwill by removing tariffs which are a constant source of friction.' By increasing travel facilities, the railways could become a vital factor in securing universal peace, an acquaintance with the habits and customs of foreign countries being 'the best antidote for absurd and irrational or radical prejudices, which constitute an excellent medium for the cultivation of diplomatic dissensions.' The notion that railway transport would lead to global harmony had been a liberal cliché since the 1840s, when Lord Macaulay was propounding it, but Burroughs's advocacy of free transport was more unusual. His resolution was unanimously adopted, expressing the hope that 'the day is not far distant when freer communication by railways, commerce, &c, may become, in the words of Mr Gladstone, gigantic looms to weave the nations into one.'

Like Henry George, Burroughs rejected socialism, but he believed that the best interests of all would be served when 'the suffering people' had all their rights. 'I am a radical in the sense of desiring to go to the roots of injustice, and in believing in the radical as distinct from the palliative treatment of injustice.' In addition to serving as president of the Dartford Liberal and Radical Association, Burroughs belonged to numerous other organisations. He was, for example, on the executive committee of the Tenant Tradesman's National Union (which opposed exactions by unjust landlords) and a member of the Reform Union. He supported Home Rule in Ireland; shortening the length of the working day; introducing employee profit-sharing; correcting wrongful monopolies of gas and water; and exempting machinery from rating. He wanted change to the House of Lords (a nest of monopoly and 'often fouled with iniquity'); tithes to become national property; the disestablishment of the Church of Wales; government by the people for the people; one vote for one man (there is no indication of his opinion on votes for women, although he believed in well-paid work for women); public assumption of election expenses; payment of members of legislative bodies; free education; and the removal of all customs duties. His thinking was well ahead of his times, and in time many of his causes were to be taken up and adopted.

It was unsurprising, then, that in 1890 it was suggested to Burroughs that he stand as a Member of Parliament for the Liberals in Dartford; although he was 'highly complimented', he rejected the idea. 'I think a member of Parliament should be in a position to give his time chiefly to the public interests which he is elected to attend to. My work would not allow me to do this.' This was despite his conviction that any 'thorough radical candidate' could be elected without difficulty.[17] A friend, H.G. Somerville of Twickenham, wrote to the local paper to make known that Burroughs had no intention of entering Parliament 'just yet at any rate … He is a tremendously busy man … and his chemical business necessitates his attention early and late, and every moment he can spare is devoted to the amelioration of the condition of the working classes.'

The winter of 1891–2 found Burroughs in southern France again in what was becoming a regular pattern of avoiding the fogs and cold of London, and again he was there without Olive. By now his circle of friends there, consisting mostly of doctors and pharmacists, was close. He returned briefly to London in January, then set off again for the continent, thereby avoiding Wellcome, who returned to London from America in early February. From Marseille he continued to Valencia, Madrid – where he met Mrs Sheldon at St George's Anglican Church and socially – then to Tangier via Cadiz.

In Tangier, Burroughs dropped into a Moorish café and had some coffee and then experimented with a drug he did not know by taking a few whiffs of a pipe of hashish; it instantly carried him off to a 'seventh heaven of imaginary delight':

> The music, or the hashish, or both … makes you feel so light that you could run up the jagged sides of the pyramids … without the sinewy Bedouins tugging at our hands or pushing you behind. From the secure but dizzy height you seem to see the Nile flowing among the green fields. … You are transported like Aladdin, to the moonlit Alhambra, and hear the music of its fountains and streams, or down the Red Sea … And the next morning … you try to collect your thoughts, and there are none to collect. The best thing under the circumstances is to try something as an antidote to the combination of hashish, tobacco, coffee, peppermint and green tea, so you enquire if there is any English chemist in Tangier where you can get something cooling.

The following day he made his way to an English chemist, comically describing the route past a dead donkey and turning up his trouser legs to get through the muck. There he learnt that the effect of hashish was less bad than that of opium, but that taking it was a slavish habit; the drug could be made into a confection, and its consumption caused bursts of laughter. All of this he carefully recounted for the *Chemist and Druggist*.[18]

Miss Dietrichson, a Norwegian, was introduced to Burroughs in Rome in 1892. At the request of mutual American friends, he called on her when she visited London that May and invited her to join him at a meeting of the National Homes for Refugee Children at Exeter Hall. After the meeting he decided to escort her by hackney cab from the Strand to her lodgings off Tottenham Court Road. Their enjoyable evening then took and unpleasant turn. He described to Olive what happened next:

> After the meeting, cabs were scarce and I took the 1st one that came without looking to see what sort of phiz [physiognomy] he had. He was as it turned out not exactly a credit to the nation. ... He drove furiously & I told him he needn't on our account punish his horse so. He stopped at the wrong side of the street. I handed him half a crown & told him to take 1/6 out of it tho I knew the fare was 1/- he said the coin was 2/- I told him he was mistaken & he was. Said he couldn't make change. I then said I shall only be able to give you a shilling which I did. He then remarked as I was going across the St with Miss D: 'I hope you'll pay the lady better than you've paid me.' I was dumbfounded at the man's awful insult. Didn't know he could be punished by law. Thought it over while crossing the street & turned back from near the opposite pavement went up to his cab & gave him some whacks on the arm with the stick you gave me. I then returned to the curbstone opposite where Miss D was waiting for me. I had not quite got to her when I became convinced I had not thrashed the man as much as he deserved & so returned to him & gave him some more & heavier whacks. Then escorted Miss D to the doorstep & bade her good night.

The cabman followed him and said, 'I have you now,' and struck him with his whip, although not hurting him. When Burroughs asked what he wanted, the cabman replied: 'To give you in charge' [have you arrested], to which Burroughs said that he had no objection. A policeman arrived, Burroughs did not deny use of his stick and explained his reason, and the cabman did not deny use of offensive language. At the police station Burroughs was charged on remand for assault and bailed out by a friend who 'happened along'. A week later he appeared in Bow Street Magistrates' Court, where the cabman at first denied fast driving, Burroughs having cautioned him, and having said anything provocative, although he finally admitted he might have done. Burroughs did not call Miss Dietrichson as a witness (she said later she was sorry he had not done so) and tried to justify his behaviour. His lawyer pleaded that Burroughs was a gentleman deeply interested in philanthropic movements, 'a man of peace' who 'never quarrelled with anyone', and that, had the cabman made offensive remarks about Burroughs, he would simply have ignored them and pitied him. However, on that evening he felt called on to punish the man for his 'entirely un-called for and gross insult' to Miss D; he had taken his responsibilities as her guardian seriously: her countrymen were very chivalrous, her brothers occupied senior positions in the army and civil service, and so on.

The magistrate was unsympathetic. No provocation justified an assault, and the prosecutor was entitled to compensation for being laid up for a week. Burroughs was fined 20 shillings with costs to cover the cabbie's loss of earnings. He later said: 'I had no wish to inflict serious injury upon him, but to let him know that such treatment would not go unpunished' … better for 'me to thrash him so that he would be laid up for a week rather than that some more violent person on a similar occasion should lay him out for good, and past all hope of recovery.' The incident reached the popular evening paper the *Pall Mall Gazette*. Burroughs told Olive: 'You may see by the Pall Mall Gazette that I have been enjoying myself in drubbing a cabman for insulting language … Everybody says he deserved the thrashing & I guess he won't use such language again in a hurry. What do you think about it. It was worth what it cost to have the satisfaction of punishing that fellow in the way he could feel punishment.'[19] What indeed, one wonders, was Olive's response to all this?

Burroughs also wrote to the Dartford newspapers, anticipating the interest of his employees. His position was entirely unrepentant. 'After mature consideration' he could not say that he was at all ashamed of his conduct, especially as he had received letters and messages from many friends and from doctors and chemists assuring him that under similar circumstances they would do exactly the same. At the same time he was careful to add that he had no animosity towards cabmen, heartily sympathised with them for their long hours of labour and low incomes, and had sent £5 to cabmen's charitable associations. Miss Dietrichson's brother turned out to be none other than the vice consul for Sweden and Norway at Gibraltar, and he in turn wrote to the Dartford press to confirm all Burroughs's account of the event and that, in his opinion, Burroughs's punishment of the cabman was the proper thing to do.

The hansom cab incident illustrates that Burroughs could have a quick temper and react physically where he took offence. His abhorrence of ill manners, concern to defend a woman's honour, and desire for justice led him to take instant retribution instead of the more measured response of appealing to the police. Possibly he would have had a more sympathetic response to his drubbing of the cabbie in America. Luckily for him, the incident did no damage to his reputation.

During the summer of 1892 Burroughs's negotiations with Wellcome over the transfer of the Dartford property to the firm continued, but much of the time he now spent in Switzerland with his family and on sales trips in Europe.

In August the family all set out together. They stayed initially with a doctor friend near Interlaken and then at the famous Hôtel du Cygne, on the edge of Lake Geneva, amid glorious scenery; it was a good base for local business trips and for longer ones into Germany. For some of his travels Burroughs was joined by Mr Mattox (evidently he and his wife were reconciled), and in September Dr Gubb joined him to cycle from Baden-Baden to Dieppe, some 420 miles away. He sent his family postcards almost daily. In one card to his son, Burroughs noted that Olive had been crying. Although he did discuss the reason, it is not impossible that this was a result of another hurried arrival and departure. Olive and the children joined him for some of his trips, but she was not without company; a group photograph taken in Thun shows her with many old friends from the UK, including the Lymans. It was during the 4th Universal Peace Congress in Berne, which Burroughs attended, that Alfred Nobel asked another participant to be kept in touch with developments in the peace movement and that, if he heard that it was moving along the road of practical activity, he would help it on with money. This indeed happened with the later establishment of the Nobel Peace Prize.

In mid-October Burroughs was off again, first to Paris to attend the annual meeting of the Anglo-American Medical Society, then to Hamburg, where he met his business acquaintance Mr Hertz and made an important deal for the firm over Rosbach mineral water.[20] From Frankfurt he returned to Montreux, where his family were still residing, for ten days, then suggested to Olive that she accompany him to Budapest.

'It is a very interesting journey. If you think you wouldn't enjoy it alone
with only us two for company you can bring Miss Green along or Anna
if she could stand the journey better than the trip she took with us
to Lucerne.' Why, one wonders, should Burroughs be concerned that
Olive would not be happy with only him for company? Would work
have taken up much of his time? Evidently Olive did join him on a trip,
and they got as far as Genoa (BW&Co. were exhibiting there), where
she wrote to Junie at the Hôtel du Cygne on 10 November that they
expected to be back soon. But, as he was unable to stay long in any one
place, Burroughs's return to Montreux was punctured by frequent day
or overnight trips to other European cities – all this covering 14 cities
in a whirlwind 20 days before arriving in Paris on New Year's Day 1893.

During 1892 Burroughs had been in the UK for only four and a half
months. The travels of the 'ubiquitous' Burroughs were commented on
by his friends, and Dr Gubb declared: 'writing to you is like starting on a
paper chase.' His appointment diaries and notebooks give evidence that
he continued to work when he was away, and clearly he felt he could also
trust those in London and Dartford to carry on the regular running of
the firm. Yet this lifestyle of frantic travelling must have been exhausting
and raises questions about the stress this caused, with constant upheaval
on his family life. Little wonder, then, that Olive may sometimes have
been unhappy, however much she enjoyed the company of good friends
and a comfortable hotel life in Switzerland.

Chapter 14

Partnership in Peril

*I will not put up with your false and slanderous statements
or treat you as a gentleman when you cease to behave
yourself as a gentleman.*[1]

By the early 1890s Burroughs must have felt great satisfaction at
the achievement of the firm in only a decade. By dint of hard work,
innovative selling techniques and fast responses to changing markets,
it had managed to keep ahead of its rivals and was established as a top
pharmaceutical manufacturer both in the UK and internationally,
winning medals and prizes at all the major international exhibitions.
In 1893 it was to achieve still more success at the Chicago World's Fair,
where, with its ever-growing range of Tabloid lines, it won many prizes,
gained excellent publicity, and secured a deal to sell Rosbach mineral
water. To the business world, BW&Co. seemed the model of success, yet
beneath the surface the relationship between Burroughs and Wellcome
worsened, becoming increasingly hostile and tense and threatening the
future of the partnership.

As well as Kepler, Hazeline, Beef and Iron Wine, saccharine
preparations and hypodermics, the range of products now extended
to over 100 Tabloid lines, and the frequency with which it introduced
new products – such as Tabloid Tea (basically the modern-day tea bag)
and Tabloid photographic chemicals – was unmatched. There was no
end to the clever promotional ideas used by the firm. In 1893 the prime
minister, Gladstone, was presented with a Tabloid medicine chest from
the employees of the firm; copies of his letter of thanks, reproduced on

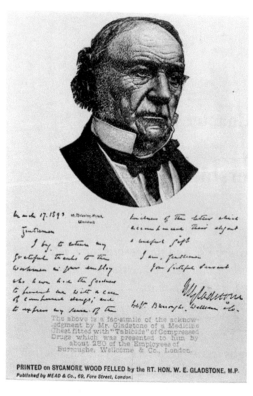

The above is a fac-simile of the acknow-
ledgment by Mr. Gladstone of a Medicine
Chest fitted with "Tabloids" of Compressed
Drugs which was presented to him by
about 250 of the Employees of
Burroughs, Wellcome & Co., London.

PRINTED on SYCAMORE WOOD FELLED by the RT. HON. W. E. GLADSTONE, M.P.
Published by MEAD & Co., 69, Fore Street, London.

23: A facsimile of Gladstone's letter to
BW&Co., thanking the firm for his case of
compressed drugs, 1893, printed on sycamore
wood he had chopped down and used
for advertising.

thin sheets of sycamore wood from a tree that Gladstone had felled, were circulated for advertising purposes.

After the previous year had been marked by hectic travelling, 1893 was marked by greater success. Burroughs was briefly in London before setting off for America in mid-January to prepare for an event of major international significance – the World's Columbian Exposition in Chicago. Travelling with him first class in the RMS *Majestic* (which he considered the best ship he had ever used – 'steady with a splendid promenade deck') was Mr Collingwood, who was to assist in negotiations to sell Rosbach mineral water, which Burroughs hoped to sell there.

On the first leg of his visit, in New York, Burroughs met up with Ladd and Coffin, manufacturers of Lundborg perfume, then visited the Fairchild family – pharmaceutical manufacturers – at their grand new house overlooking Manhattan. Sam Fairchild met them at the station with a double cutter sleigh, and they passed a delightful day in the snow, despite Burroughs feeling homesick for want of playing with his own children. It was one of the coldest winters in America for some years, but he stood up to the weather better than he had expected, feeling and eating well. Burroughs and Collingwood were so busy that they exhausted themselves and usually retired to bed at 10pm, although there was time to dine with Henry George and his family. Burroughs went on to Philadelphia, then Auburn, where Lina joined them, and they travelled to Chicago.

The scale of the fair was extraordinary; it covered 633 acres and was still under construction. Although Burroughs had attended previous world's fairs in Philadelphia in 1876 and Paris in 1889, he was greatly impressed by what he saw. The buildings were enormous and splendid but not so gaudy as in Paris, and he imagined that the grounds would be very handsome, as indeed they proved to be. First and foremost the fair aimed to educate and inform, but its entertainments were endless and included a huge ferris wheel (the first of its kind in the world), an amusement ground, and Buffalo Bill's Wild West Show – making it a forerunner of the later permanent fairgrounds at Coney Island in New York and present-day Disneyworld and Disneyland. Pavilions were planned for 23 countries as well as for each of the 44 American states, American goods understandably predominating.

24: Burroughs, Wellcome & Co. exhibition stand at the Chicago World's Fair, 1893. Wellcome has been identified as the man on the left wearing a hat, but Burroughs was also present, standing, hatless, at the back immediately behind him.

For a fortnight, preparations preoccupied the two men. Burroughs gained important concessions, including one for Rosbach Water, which he thought would do very well, since people would not want to drink the contaminated water from Lake Michigan; he negotiated the erection of a handsome pavilion where visitors could try the water.[2] Another site was acquired to accommodate an elegantly furnished house where medical and pharmaceutical friends could meet, write letters, and network. When finished, the firm's stand was impressive.

Burroughs was much taken by Chicago. Many people urged him to live there, and the idea appealed to him: 'such a nice live go-ahead sociable town'. He told Olive that it would be a good place to manufacture their goods and obtain a deal on Lanoline goods in America, as they had in England. Once the London business was a joint stock company he wanted to start a business in Chicago for the whole of the United States. 'It is a first rate centre & taxes are very light, everybody has got money, new things are all the go.' He found it strange that, although people were buying immense quantities of goods from outside the country, there wasn't a single factory there in their line of business. A manufacturing site at Chicago Heights had been offered, free and exempt from taxes, but he would be 'mighty careful' before deciding. What he could not have guessed was that America was on the edge of one of its worst economic depressions, one that would last for two years. Yet the fair was a huge success, boosting the morale of the country, and Burroughs was correct that Chicago did expand rapidly, becoming a base for much new business.

After returning briefly to Medina and Auburn with Lina, Burroughs hastened on to New York to seal the Rosbach Water deal, failing to get to Boston or to see Olive's family.[3] In New York he somehow found time to canvass again for Cleveland – who was elected president on 4 March – and before leaving America gave an informal dinner at the Fulton Club to those who had helped him on his short visit. Among the guests was Henry George, and the meal was followed by a discussion on the ethics of taxation and the possibility of establishing an American society to fight for the abolition of the tax on alcohol and medicine. Burroughs found his guests 'a sober set' and that teetotalism agreed with him 'muchly'; he 'never felt better in his life, never weighed so much as now, 153 lbs, & all the old friends say I look younger than a year ago. So I am of opinion that water is the thing for me ... for life.'

RMS *Teutonic* made record time to Liverpool in mid-March. Meanwhile Olive and the family were still in Geneva with her friend Alice Miller, and Burroughs planned to see them as soon as possible, before travelling via Milan to Genoa and then returning to America before the fair opened. Olive would not be persuaded to go to Chicago in the spring or summer despite his telling her about some pretty houses, moderately priced, near the fairground. Lina now had a big house so could put them up, and he could take a house near Chicago so she could visit the show often with her friends. Olive's dislike of an Atlantic crossing undoubtedly influenced her, and after a brief week with 'Chicksey' (his nickname for Olive) and his 'little darlings', who were unwell, Burroughs decided to delay his return to Chicago until he was sure they were out of danger. Although he found the business 'flourishing and everything looking favourably', there were the usual disagreements with Wellcome, who had written to him listing all his faults, and Burroughs complained bitterly of his meanness.[4] In the event Burroughs let Collingwood return to Chicago without him.

All their friends enquired after Olive and 'the chicks', and Burroughs saw them again on a quick business trip to Paris. He suggested that the family stay in Bournemouth or Eastbourne that summer, but they ended up renting a house in Surbiton, and when not there Burroughs stayed in town at the National Liberal Club or at the Saracen's Head near Snow Hill. His energy levels were restored to their usual high. As usual, Burroughs burned the candle at both ends, often being in the office before 8am, travelling between Dartford and Snow Hill and combining work with his charitable and political activities. Although he was keen to return to Chicago before July's heat, it was early August before he managed to depart, leaving Olive a long list of duties: to host a visit from his friends the Heitshus;[5] to make things lively for the Lymans in Surbiton; to invite friends over to play tennis; to contact Sudlow about a possible situation for the son of a friend; to 'kiss the little dears for their daddy'; to distribute the valuable souvenirs left on top of the clock in his room; and to give kind regards to all the servants.[6]

Wellcome had already gone to America in mid-June, so both men were now there at the same time, and appear in the same photograph with others, at their Chicago stand. Both attended the International Pharmaceutical Congress held in Chicago immediately afterwards, and Burroughs spoke at the 5th Universal Peace Congress and the International Arbitration and Peace Association.[7] Before his return he stayed with Henry George jnr in Washington, visited Detroit, and spent his last fortnight in upstate New York. Had it been possible he would have stayed longer, but Sudlow alerted him to the need to return to the UK to give evidence in the forthcoming 'Lanolin case' lawsuit on patent infringement.[8]

INTERNATIONAL PEACE CONGRESS,

CHICAGO, 1893.

Proposition by S. M. Burroughs,

Delegate from the International Peace and Arbitration Society, London.

USTOMS Tariffs cause unfriendly feelings between states and nations. Freedom of trade tends to bring states and nations together in bonds of mutual interest, prosperity, friendship, and peace.

The general adoption of free trade would powerfully aid in preventing war by making peace a matter of common and universal interest.

Taxation, which restricts industry on the one hand, and creates special privileges on the other, tends to poverty of the industrial classes and builds up an aristocracy upon unearned wealth. It tends to social discontent, leading perhaps to violations of the peace.

The single tax on land values created by the

25: Proposition at the International World Peace Congress, Chicago, 1893. Burroughs spoke on peace, free trade and taxation at the congress, which was held at the same time as the Chicago World's Fair.

It is hardly surprising that by the end of 1893 Burroughs was exhausted. His diary noted regular trips to Dartford, where a new building for manufacturing tabloids was nearing completion. Early in December he came down with a severe cold that developed into flu, which kept him indoors in Bournemouth, although this did not stop him writing to his many correspondents. Feeling better, he recorded: 'Thank providence my health seems to be already much improved. Shall try a cycle ride this morning.' His last appointment of the year was the Chemists Assistants' Association musical and social evening, and, although still unwell, he travelled back to London especially for it.

The partners' relationship now deteriorated still further: characteristically, they squabbled over minor disputes and had acrimonious rows over finance and the running of the firm. Arguments arose over instructions issued by one partner without the authority or knowledge of the other. Sometimes issues were almost laughable for their pettiness, but they demonstrate the extent of tension between the two men. For example, Wellcome wanted company managers to have 'Esq.' rather than 'Mr.' on the firm's envelopes, whereas Burroughs considered Esq. to be a 'very un-American & un-business[like] title … nowhere used in business circles in America excepting among persons who wish to put on airs … As for myself I have no hankering after empty titles, especially those which smack of courtiers and waiters upon Lords and

Barons, for if I mistake not the title "Esquire" was given in some such.' On envelopes printed for his use, his name would appear as Mr S.M. Burroughs.[9]

They bickered over the value of printing desk calendars; Wellcome thought them excessively expensive and not a profitable form of advertising, whereas Burroughs found that travellers and doctors appreciated them highly. He was not at all surprised that Wellcome objected, he wrote, as they were not his invention. Wellcome's curt response that he had distinctly refused his consent to their issue led Burroughs to offer to meet the cost himself, make a gift of the calendar to the firm and send them out with his own compliments. 'Your statement that the proposed calendar is useless as an advertisement, in the contrary opinion from everybody else, is very similar to that of the … juror who declared that he never knew eleven more obstinate men in his life than the jurors who disagreed with him.'[10]

Expenses – including personal expenses – had been an issue from the start of the partnership. In a lengthy letter to his partner in March 1893 Wellcome complained about expenditure on advertising, excessive printing of price lists and show cards, hiring four travellers for the continent, bonus payments, and Burroughs's trip to Chicago. He found Burroughs guilty of 'unnecessary and unremunerative … extravagance and needless' expenditure and spoke of his need to protect the firm's interests from Burroughs's 'hostile and erratic course'.[11] Another objection was to Burroughs sending private letters via office staff. Burroughs in turn considered Wellcome stingy, and not infrequently, when thwarted by Wellcome, he would use his own money to pay for advertising or other things he considered would benefit the firm. In expectation of criticism from his partner, he sarcastically ended one letter from Chicago: 'Awaiting your account of any needless expenses made by me at the Paris Exhibition, I remain, Yours truly.'[12]

Another bone of contention was Wellcome's tardiness in implementing decisions: this greatly annoyed Burroughs, who instinctively adopted swift and decisive action necessary to pre-empt rivals. His cautious partner, on the other hand, always wanted facts and evidence before making any decisions.[13] Issues could become deeply personal, as when Burroughs raised with Wellcome his contribution towards the cost of a testimonial for the explorer Stanley – to take the form of a shield. When, two to three years later, he discovered that it was not yet in Stanley's possession, he challenged Wellcome: 'Is it possible that you have fancied that the shield was intended for yourself? If so I do not think it was the general impression of those who have contributed to it.'[14] As things turned out, Wellcome had told Stanley that he would present the shield to him in May 1890 on the occasion of the dinner to celebrate his return from the Emin Pasha expedition, but the shield was actually sent to Stanley only ten years later.

More tensions arose from their conflicting political and social principles. Burroughs's increasingly radical beliefs and the way he promoted them greatly irritated his partner, who inclined to conservativism. Burroughs missed no opportunity to push his liberal views, his Christian conscience leading him to seek more radical change and paternalism in the firm's management. In Chicago the partners had rowed over political pamphlets left on the firm's stand at the fair, and later Wellcome again complained of political meetings held in the factory grounds.[15] Quite rightly, he felt that Burroughs had no right to make him a party to the dissemination of political views. Linking the name of the firm to the single tax issue jeopardised its reputation and risked losing clients; religion and politics should be kept out of commerce; liberalism was well and good, but too much of it and business would be lost.

Burroughs thought Wellcome's approach to the staff was patronising and mean.

And then there remained the old issue of Burroughs's business loans to Wellcome, which still waited for a resolution:

> He ought to write a book as a guide to enterprising young men who wish to become possessed of partnership shares in business without putting up any capital by merely promising to do so sometime or who wish to become part owners of factories &c by means of something very like forced loans ... A long and mournful experience has satisfied me that generous treatment is thrown away on Mr Wellcome, for the more money I have loaned him & the lower the interest when he appeared to think further favours were uncertain the more unkind has been his treatment toward me till I am utterly nauseated.[16]

He expounded his anger to Olive: 'HSW is acting as meanly as usual and I certainly think deserves the title of the meanest man in the world ... I was a fool to continue to lend him money to enable him to draw profits from the business to which he was not entitled by services or capital.'[17]

The hostility centred on three issues: firstly, the repayment of the large amount of money that Burroughs had loaned to Wellcome and the firm from its beginning; secondly, the purchase by Burroughs, expansion and later resale to the firm of the Dartford works; and, thirdly, the renewal of partnership agreements and possible conversion of the firm into a joint stock company. At the root of their quarrels were their complex financial arrangements, stemming from the basic problem that Burroughs had provided by far the larger amount of the partnership capital – 75% – but had to share decision-making equally with Wellcome and take most of the risk; Wellcome, while providing relatively little capital, had equal power in determining how this capital should be used and how the business should be managed. By choosing at the outset to have no more than one partner and then being unable to amend the terms of this partnership without Wellcome's agreement, Burroughs had placed himself in a straight-jacket. He had only himself to blame, which made his frustration all the more keenly felt.

Disagreement turned on the firm's internal accounting procedures, about which there is incomplete information. One point of contention involved their individual 'drawing accounts' and how profits were divided. It was the practice of the firm to transfer three-quarters of the annual profits to which the partners were entitled to the credit of their respective drawing accounts and to transfer the remaining quarter of their profits to their respective capital accounts. Interest at 5% was added annually to the balance of these accounts.[18] The partners were under no obligation to draw down their funds from these accounts, so very high balances could accumulate. This was especially the case with Burroughs's account: in August 1885, for example, it carried a balance of almost £5,500 (which came close to exceeding his partnership capital of £6,500), yet on the same date the cash-strapped Wellcome maintained only a small balance of just under £100. The problem for Wellcome, if not for the firm, was that these balances, attracting 5% interest, proved a drain on the firm's resources. This was inevitably another source of dispute between the partners. Gaps in the financial records and a lack of good auditing mean that it is not possible to know for sure which partner was being unreasonable in these disputes, but without question their financial disagreements were crucial.[19]

The articles of partnership were clear about the decision-making process and authorisation of expenditure: for this both partners had to give their approval. Frustrated by not being able to have his way over Wellcome in long-term investment decisions that he considered essential, Burroughs used his own private capital to buy Dartford and to fund other investments in the plant and buildings required by the firm for its manufacturing. As it happened, this funding proved critical to the firm's expansion and success: delay could well have placed it at a disadvantage vis-à-vis its rivals. However, the subsequent transfer of Dartford into the ownership of the firm now became an issue of serious contention between the partners.

Burroughs had ended up buying Phoenix Mills in 1888 on his own at the huge cost of £5,000, then leased the property to the firm for 49 years at an annual rent of £250, with the option that Wellcome could require him to sell to the firm within seven years at the sum he had paid for it. In effect, the £5,000 investment was treated as a loan from Burroughs at 5%. Even the cost of the conveyance became an issue between them. 'We think Mr Wellcome's conduct with regard to the costs of conveyance is unreasonable & mean,' Burroughs' solicitors wrote, 'but we fear he has a technical advantage in holding you to the terms of the agreement for a lease & in taking up the position that he will pay nothing he has not expressly agreed to do. Probably you will have an opportunity before long of refusing to comply with some requirements of his & so be even with him.'[20] This unsatisfactory financial arrangement later created massive difficulties.

Within a few months of the Dartford opening, Burroughs gave orders for a new building to be erected there to accommodate additional manufacturing. Wellcome was livid – he considered the building unnecessary, had previously protested about the proposal and refused to sanction the expenditure. So Burroughs funded the investment himself. 'I will say no more about the matter', Wellcome wrote to him, 'if you will confirm in writing the promise which you made to me verbally this morning which was that you would pay out of your own pocket any excess over 100 pounds in expense of erecting the building. Furthermore, the building must of course be regarded as one of the original structures on the premises and must be included in the lease without any extra payment in any way on the part of the firm.' Clearly Wellcome believed that he would face insurmountable repayment obligations.[21] The timing was opportune, however, as within two years Dartford was working to full capacity with 200 employees.

The partners next disagreed over the inclusion of Dartford's depreciation value in the firm's accounts. Although a standard accounting practice, it would reduce the large profit of the firm for the year to a moderate loss and leave Wellcome without any profit share that year. Burroughs was further irritated that his annual rental income of £250 for Dartford was 'not even that', since Wellcome had refused to pay him his share of the costs of acquiring the property. The matter was still unresolved some nine months later, in April 1890, when Wellcome made some 'unusual unreasonable' provisions to the draft lease which

Burroughs's solicitors advised he should not submit to. Subsequently, when Wellcome wanted the firm to buy the mills, Burroughs did not make it easy for him.

At the end of 1891, Burroughs, in addition to his capital holding, had loaned the firm just over £13,000 at 5% interest (had he deposited this money in a bank he would have received a lower rate of interest). Wellcome, not unreasonably, requested that the amount of this loan be reduced as rapidly as possible without cramping the firm's finances.[22]

The following May, Wellcome sent Burroughs a cheque for £10,000 in part payment of this loan, which Burroughs returned, saying he was entitled to reasonable notice before being paid off and gave formal notice for the repayment of the whole amount. This Wellcome arranged soon afterwards. Eventually, after prolonged negotiation on valuation and reimbursement of legal expenses, an independent value of £18,500 was agreed.[23] In the end matters had worked to Burroughs's advantage; he had received interest on the loan and the company then had to repay the amount in full. The deeds to the mill were placed in a safe deposit, each partner holding a separate key – a sobering insight into the degree of mistrust between them.[24] Their financial wrangling continued, however. In 1893 Wellcome again drew Burroughs's attention to the disadvantages to the firm of the unnecessarily large amount outstanding to Burroughs's credit with the firm: 'The interest which the firm receives on this sum is trifling, while the liability of the interest to you is very heavy,' and he called on Burroughs to fulfil a promise made the previous summer and withdraw it.[25]

In 1891, Burroughs's solicitors informed Wellcome that matters had now reached such a point that a dissolution of the partnership was extremely desirable, and to achieve it Burroughs was willing to offer 'very liberal terms'. This communication took place just before Burroughs's trip to Palestine, and on his return he was still desperate to dissolve the partnership, but negotiations persistently foundered over the terms. Significantly, an entry in his diary in October 1891 reveals that he hoped to be rid of his partner within four months; it was wishful thinking on his part. Civilities continued to be exchanged, but correspondence between the men became franker and angrier. Wellcome reminded Burroughs that, after the court case the previous year, they had both shaken hands in the presence of Mr Kirby and that Burroughs had asked Kirby to 'bear witness that the hatchet was at that moment buried and that all differences past should be mutually forgotten.' He claimed he alone had strictly observed the pledge but that Burroughs had not. Burroughs retorted: 'I will first refer to the fact that you are constantly in the habit of assuming an aggressive attitude towards me ... I have never entertained any malice toward you and never shall, I feel that you have treated me shamefully but it is not my business to punish you. For your own good I would like you to see you reform your ways.' It was a reply which Wellcome found 'offensive in tone'.[26]

At this time many businesses were being converted from private partnerships to joint stock companies with limited liability, although some mistrust and hostility to this new form of ownership was still held throughout society, by liberals and conservatives alike.[27] Burroughs had registered Kepler as a joint stock company in 1879 and had suggested this as a way forward for the firm in 1884; among the advantages, it would allow employees to have an ownership stake in the business. The reasons for Wellcome's opposition to this proposal are not recorded but can probably be explained by a fear of losing joint control of management; he was a man who always sought strict control in every aspect of his life.

Interestingly, the possibility of the firm amalgamating with Wyeths through the formation of a joint stock company was also raised by Burroughs. Wyeth replied that, although he could see advantages, he would want tighter controls over the finances in management ('I am largely influenced in this feeling by my experience with you') and noted: 'possibly there would be one advantage to you in the fact that it would settle Mr Wellcome's status definitely.'[28] Nothing came of the overture, and by 1893 the on/off relationship between the two firms had deteriorated again, with Burroughs believing Wyeths wished to take over the trade and goodwill BW&Co. had built up. Services he had rendered their firm for the past 24 years came to an end, and he considered legal action, significantly revealing his views by writing: 'I am very sorry for this as I do not like legal complications or lawsuits.'[29]

Wellcome used a key clause in the partnership negotiations which ensured that termination would need to be in writing, and *the partner wishing to terminate* had to issue notice. When Burroughs's solicitors wrote to Wellcome in 1891 asking him how much money he would require for retiring from the business and, alternatively, how much money he would offer Burroughs to retire, they were reminded that it was *Burroughs* who was seeking to secure to himself the business; Wellcome had no desire to sell his interest in the partnership unless sufficient inducements were offered, nor was he anxious to purchase, and he would make no offer. Wellcome then suggested that the business be divided between them to create two independent businesses, one led by Burroughs, the other by himself; it appears that Burroughs did not deign to reply to this.[30]

Profit-sharing, bonus schemes and salary increases were fought over annually. Neither Burroughs nor Wellcome drew a salary from the business, their remuneration consisting of the profit share alone. The firm had introduced a radical and generous staff profit-sharing scheme back in 1884 which was relaunched in 1886 and fixed at 5% of the company's profits, divided according to employees' wages and salaries. Such schemes were being introduced more widely at this time. Burroughs was always keener on the whole idea of a bonus scheme than Wellcome, who preferred to award fixed and secure increases in salaries where they were merited; it was another example of Wellcome's desire for control.[31]

In 1892 Burroughs wrote to Wellcome urging him to agree to a more generous allocation of profits to employees: 'No money is spent by me with greater pleasure than the payment of this percentage of the profits of the business as a gift to all who are engaged in it.'[32] The following year, when in Chicago, he asked the office about the bonus and whether Wellcome had agreed to join him in giving employees a double percentage of profits in future. Wellcome responded firmly that no business sense existed in doing so when the firm's net profits were in decline, whereon Burroughs commented:

> It seems as if Mr Wellcome hinted in his letter at legal action in case I should persist in the intention of doubling the employee's percentage of the profits of the business. I am very much surprised that Mr Wellcome should object to this as he got a very large percentage of the profits without having to put up any capital at all other than what I loaned him. He now tries to use as a weapon against me my desire to increase the employees share of the [profits], a principle which he opposed for some time.

To Wellcome he wrote: 'You did not object to receiving 40% of the profits of the business without having to put up any capital and I cannot therefore now understand why you should object to my proposal to give the employees a [larger] share of the profits than this esp[ecially] since many of them [the workers] have families to support and [you are] a single man.'

Their disagreements affected staff caught up in the crossfire. Both partners frequently complained to each other about staff instructions being issued without due consultation; they were unable to hear each other's concerns impartially, each believing the other was unreasonable and had ulterior motives. In one instance, for example, Burroughs supposedly encouraged secret manoeuvres by Dartford's general manager to disregard Wellcome's wishes and authority. Burroughs also criticised him for making salary payment arrangements contrary to his wishes and ignoring his rights. At the end of 1893 Wellcome instructed Kirby not to change the bonuses without the permission of both partners, and the following year he prevented Burroughs from introducing a bonus payment to travellers calculated on the number of medical practitioners or chemists they visited.

Each man suspected the other of failing to pull his weight. Burroughs believed that his partner had not done any real work for the firm when he was in America between August 1886 and June 1887. Meanwhile Wellcome dismissed Burroughs's travel to America in August 1893 as 'unnecessary'. Burroughs's constant travels led Wellcome to complain that they were unable to meet to discuss business matters, although, as their communication was usually now by letter, and the post was very good, this cannot entirely explain their inability to work together.

When the legal dissolution of the partnership was first raised, in 1888, Burroughs's counsel advised him 'to use the utmost care in his dealings with Mr Wellcome.' In turn, Wellcome told his solicitors that he did not accept anything that Burroughs or his solicitors put forward supposedly in good faith; he regarded any negotiations as uncertain and could not rely on the usual honour between solicitor and solicitor. Extraordinarily, a discussion between their solicitors indicates that Humphreys – Burroughs's solicitor – had not fully understood the terms of the partnership agreement and the situation that would arise when the current agreement terminated in 1895. In conversation with Charles Stewart of Markby, Stewart & Co. – Wellcome's solicitor – he had 'dropped the remark' that 'at the end of the expiry of the partnership the business would belong to his client [Burroughs] as being the owner of the larger interest in it.' Stewart pointed out that such an idea 'was of course quite incorrect', and that the partnership would have to be divided on an equitable basis in accordance with the respective shares. This statement was underlined by Wellcome, who well appreciated its vital significance.[33]

A joint stock company solution was raised yet again in May 1893, but, before it could be acted on, Burroughs was informed by Wellcome's solicitors that their client proposed going to America and might find it desirable to remain there for several months. Burroughs's solicitors retorted: 'Our client instructs us to state that Mr Wellcome must take the responsibility of adopting what course he chooses, but Mr Burroughs as his Senior Partner, distinctly objects to his neglecting his duties with reference to the business of the Firm.'[34] The day before his departure, Wellcome instructed his solicitors that, if Burroughs's solicitors raised any further questions about a joint stock company, they could say they knew he was 'favourably disposed towards a <u>proper</u> plan of this kind, but that any proposition from Mr Burroughs must be full, clear, explicit and definite.' At this critical moment Wellcome left the country, stating that he needed to see his mother, who was 'near her end', and that he would return 'in a few weeks'. Before sailing, he put into storage his belongings and those of Mrs Sheldon; in the event, he did not return until December, some five months later.[35] With the firm's work increasingly jeopardised by disagreements between the partners, and with the renewal date of their agreement coming up in 1895, pressure was mounting on both men to find a solution. In the circumstances, Wellcome's extended visit to America at this vital time smacked of disregard, if not arrogance. It might even be seen as a deliberate action on his part to postpone a decision, since procrastination concerning a settlement could perhaps work in his favour.

Acrimonious disputes between the partners intensified throughout 1894 with the reopening of old wounds such as expenses and the hiring of overseas agents. The possibility of a further court case loomed when they repeatedly failed to reach agreement through arbitration on the dissolution of their partnership. The year was to end with Burroughs exhausted, low in spirits, and suffering from influenza.

Burroughs, not unreasonably, considered that the hiring of overseas agents was something that fell more into his area of responsibility, since he was the partner who travelled abroad and knew the local situation. But Wellcome disagreed with his choice of people and insisted on being consulted at all stages. Neither come out well from their exchanges on the subject.

Arrangements over newly appointed agents abroad led to Wellcome protesting about Burroughs's lack of consultation, despite both men being in the office; he now refused to deal with any contract agreed without his written consent. Burroughs countered by declaring he was unaware of Wellcome's presence in the office at the time and that Sudlow had considered the arrangement good and fair. 'It seems to me mostly unreasonable that you should try to hinder & harass me in my efforts to serve the firm's best interests … in distant countries as Morocco where I am informed of the situation & you are ignorant of it.'

Expenses caused irate exchanges between them. 'You have never, that I am aware of, taken any trouble to attend to the interests of the business when you have been in Italy,' Burroughs snapped. 'I have done a great deal of work there which I have not yet charged anything to the firm ... As you show a total lack of appreciation for this and for all other favours done to you by me I shall when convenient to myself make out my account and collect it from the firm for my expenses ... in Italy and elsewhere.' When Wellcome criticised unagreed expenses in France, it added to Burroughs's fury. These comments ignored the large and unagreed expenses incurred there by Wellcome, leading Burroughs to add more fat to the fire: 'I understand however that you made some interesting antiquarian studies there but do not know that the firm have drawn any benefit from them.' When the firm produced its celebrated 'Tea Tabloids', the partners disagreed over the need to advertise them. Burroughs dug into his own pocket at times to ensure adequate publicity, which helped to make the tabloids a great success.[36]

Wellcome's ceaseless procrastinations infuriated Burroughs. Issues over printing and distributing a medical circular meant that it appeared two or three months late, causing a great loss and making the firm 'the laughing stock of the trade and medical profession'. Wellcome's tardiness in settling bills for Burroughs's purchases was also irksome. He vigorously denied that he had 'repeatedly threatened' to override Wellcome's rights in any and all business matters at their firm; 'I defy you to show any evidence in support of your statement.' Wellcome in turn wrote to his mother of Burroughs's 'new tricks or old ones repeated'. When Burroughs wanted to extend the bonus scheme and increase pay, it led to further ructions. The firm's large profits meant Burroughs wished to share them 'liberally', whereas Wellcome still preferred fixed increases where merited. To rub salt into wounds, Burroughs offered a prize to the worker who produced the best essay on profit-sharing.[37]

It is hard to imagine how, in spite of the seemingly endless skirmishes and arguments, the partners still managed to function and plan for the future. Yet the firm thrived and major changes were in hand. Burroughs realised that superior and cheaper dialysed iron could be made by them compared with Wyeths, and this they did. But the biggest breakthrough came at the end of 1894, with their development of an anti-toxin serum. Experimental research in France and Germany in the 1890s had shown that animals could be immunised against diphtheria and tetanus, and so the race was on to develop a bacterial toxin and serum for humans. Following the publication of results by the Pasteur Institute in Paris and trials by the British Institute for Preventive Medicine (BIPM), BW&Co. tried to become agents of the BIPM for their sera but were pipped to the post by Allen & Hanbury's.[38] Undeterred, they pushed ahead with developing an anti-diphtheria serum, and in November the *Chemist &*

Druggist announced its imminent distribution by BW&Co. Their first advertisement for the serum appeared in *The Lancet* on 5 January 1895, that for the BIPM a week later.

This was a huge coup, and Burroughs must have been party to such a crucial decision, although sole credit for this development has been given to Wellcome. Experimental laboratories had existed at Snow Hill from 1891, and now there were nearby stables where anti-toxin research was conducted on horses. In May 1894 Burroughs's private diary contains a simple note, 'Anti-toxin', and on 12 December he gave an interview to publicise the breakthrough and his plans to popularise and cheapen the anti-toxin remedies.[39] Interestingly, as far back as 1884 Burroughs had noted research into a vaccine on the continent, but his proposal to initiate research by the firm at that time was rejected by Wellcome.

By the end of 1894 Burroughs increasingly addressed his correspondence impersonally to the firm, though its content was obviously meant for Wellcome, who in turn felt that his opinions and rights were being ignored and so deployed delaying tactics and issued legalistic threatening letters. In his eagerness to get things done, and infuriated by delays and problem-finding, Burroughs had a strategy of ignoring or working around his partner, financing some changes out of his own pocket. Since they were unable now to discuss matters face to face, their correspondence seethes with anger and resentment. Working together had become an unbearable nightmare.

A solution was essential to avoid a return to court, and in July that year Burroughs suggested management of the business by a committee, which would include themselves along with Searl, Sudlow, Kirby, one or two of the travellers, and a few from the office with long experience of the management of the business. Discussions were suspended during his absence abroad in August but renewed with vigour in September, when additional proposals were made, including, yet again, the formation of a joint stock company.[40] This move would enable employees – including committee members – to become shareholders and be more prominent in managing the business.

Burroughs's friend Gavin Clark MP, a doctor and Liberal land reformer, had several interviews with Wellcome on his behalf and gathered that Wellcome preferred to divide their business, Wellcome taking the tabloid portion. At this juncture Burroughs made the startling suggestion: 'I have no objection to this course if it means that you are to take the copyrighted word 'Tabloid' and all trademarks connected with the compressed drug business. But as in my opinion the compressed drug business has a great future before it I would not wish to be debarred from entering into it in future if I thought fit.' If these proposals were not agreeable he would be glad to hear what Wellcome proposed should be done to settle matters. Burroughs's previous letter had been typewritten by one of Wellcome's clerks, and Wellcome declined to discuss it, so this time Burroughs made sure to write in his own hand, 'desirous to meet your wishes as far as I can.'[41] This suggestion by Burroughs to gift access to trademarks appears unduly generous, and indeed he subsequently had second thoughts about it.

Wellcome's delayed response led to a further letter eleven days later: 'I do not think it is businesslike on your part to wish to delay so long a time giving any definite reply to my proposals re- termination of our partnership. Your remark regarding your preparations for litigation are entirely uncalled for and do not terrify me in the least.' Unless he had some definite reply regarding his proposals within two days, Wellcome could consider them all withdrawn. 'I regret for your sake as well as mine that you should still maintain such an unfair & offensive attitude toward me to the detriment of this business.'[42] Long after this deadline, a reply arrived on a Sunday morning in an envelope marked 'Personal Immediate', to which Burroughs responded angrily that his Sunday would not be spent on such matters. Moreover, Wellcome's reason for the delay was his need for figures on which to base his proposal, but he failed to attach them, apparently expecting a reply drafted in ignorance of the figures. Was Wellcome willing to give him copies? As for the division of the business, should Wellcome not have waited to see if Burroughs agreed in principle before announcing what portion he proposed to take? Would he be willing to take the factory and leave Burroughs the office, or to take the Beef and Iron Wine, Hazeline and other lines which aggregate a quarter of the net profits and leave him the tabloids?[43]

Further negotiation about which partner took what from a dissolution made no progress. Burroughs could not accept several of Wellcome's proposals, especially the one that, for five or seven years after termination, he could not enter into the compressed drug trade either directly or indirectly: he would not have his hands tied in this way, especially as he made no such requirement of Wellcome and did not care what Wellcome did. The more Burroughs considered Wellcome's proposal to take the 'tabloid' department, the more insurmountable were the difficulties. He had previously asked if Wellcome would agree to a dissolution based on Burroughs taking the tabloids and office and leaving him the factory and enough of their other 'articles' (i.e. their products) to make up his one-fourth interest, but Wellcome replied evasively, referring only to taking the factory. Would Wellcome agree to a deal whereby Burroughs kept the tabloid business and Wellcome acquired the rest – namely the office or factory, or neither of them but only products? Or would he be willing to accept as his share the products he had brought into the business and leave Burroughs with those that he had brought into the business? There were multiple options but no decisions.

Burroughs complained that, instead of replying in a businesslike and straightforward way, Wellcome merely repeated questions asked of him. 'Such a policy if followed by both of us would of necessity bring our business to a standstill,' he noted.[44] Wellcome meanwhile referred to Burroughs as a 'fiendish spirit', writing to his mother of

> much time wasted in the battle for my rights … [Burroughs] has been tricky through it all like a fela [*sic*] he will not stick to anything and has not yet shown any disposition to settle in a straightforward and equitable manner but rather seems to be trying to draw me into some trap so that he can secure the whole business without paying me value … I have good legal and business advisers and am quietly standing by my guns.[45]

With 1894 drawing to a close, and no solution in sight, the partners agreed to appoint friends to arbitrate on their behalf and be bound by their recommendations. Wellcome chose Dr Alfred Chune Fletcher, who was also his medical adviser; Burroughs chose Dr Clark. A conference of all four men took place on 13 December, although two days earlier Burroughs had stayed indoors to try to shift a very severe cold. That evening Burroughs thought the whole affair was settled when he handed Clark a letter agreeing to the terms arranged between Clark and Fletcher covering formation of a joint stock company and the division of the firm's assets and goodwill.[46] Yet the following day Wellcome reportedly would not abide by the arbitration and 'held out for certain essentials'.[47] He now wished to change the size of the share-owning qualification for a directorship; did not approve of the directors proposed; and was not now willing to part with any of his interest in the business, wanting Burroughs to supply all that was to be sold. This effectively meant that, were there to be any directors other than Burroughs and Wellcome, Burroughs would have to allocate them shares from his own shareholding.

This was the final straw for Burroughs, who wrote in despair to Clark that Wellcome had failed to abide by the findings of his own nominated arbitrator; negotiations had closed, and they were no nearer a settlement than when they had started, yet closer to the deadline of 1895 when the articles of partnership would expire. Under no circumstances whatever would he consent to renew the present partnership agreement or make a new one with Wellcome on any terms. 'After his conduct in this matter I have come to the conclusion that it will be best not to include him in the formation of any Company, and that we will be better off without his presence or name. I think that Burroughs & Company or The Burroughs Company Ltd will go just as well as if Mr Wellcome's name was associated with it.'

On reflection he wrote a second letter to Clark the same day and came up with new proposals. The first was that each would draw lots to determine which of them should fix a price at which he would buy or sell, the other partner being obliged to accept one or the other. The second proposal was that Clark and Fletcher would value the business and the partners would draw lots to see which of them would have the choice of buying or selling at the price fixed, the other partner being bound to accept one offer or the other. It is not at all surprising that Wellcome would not be keen on either of these bizarre proposals; he was not a gambling man and anyway he did not have the same amount of money as his partner to invest in the business. They do, however, demonstrate Burroughs's desperation and frantic state of mind at this time.

Fletcher, needless to say, confirmed Wellcome's refusal to draw lots or adopt any similar indefinite solutions and requested that Burroughs made clear definite offers to purchase Wellcome's share of the business with full and explicit details as to price, terms of payment and general conditions, such as a right to use the firm's name or not and with right to compete or not. As to any failure to abide by the arbitrators' recommendations, Wellcome claimed that no final decision had been reached: proposals had been made only for consideration and discussion, and it was Burroughs who had failed to comply with the counsel that identical letters, agreeing to the decision of any arbitrators, should have been submitted and signed.[48]

What is one to make of all this? It appears that, following the meeting on 13 December, Burroughs and Clark – who was by no means a novice in business matters – were both under the impression that an agreement between the arbitrators had been reached. To claim five days after this meeting that procedural issues had not been observed and that Burroughs had failed to organise two identical signed letters of submission would appear to be a deliberate delaying tactic on Wellcome's part. Yet Wellcome and Fletcher now claimed that this meeting was merely a further step in the discussions. Wellcome wanted everything in black and white, but the regular delays in his responses, often on the basis of requiring firm proposals and definite figures, meant a never-ending cycle of answers being responded to with further questions.

Over the previous months Burroughs had proposed a whole range of solutions as the basis for more detailed discussion. The terms of dissolution were always going to be complex, but one issue dominated: Wellcome had much to lose and little to gain from conversion to a joint stock company with multiple directors. If, as would be likely, this was based on his one-quarter ownership as opposed to Burroughs's three-quarters, then his room for manoeuvre would be much curtailed and his profits reduced. In addition, the partners' approach to competition in the event of a decision of the business between them differed. Wellcome did not relish the prospect of business rivalry with Burroughs, whereas Burroughs was confident in such a prospect.[49] Nevertheless, after six months of negotiation, this latest setback to a resolution he had thought was close to fruition must have devastated Burroughs, and he was exhausted. With the onset of a hard winter, he developed a bad cold verging on influenza. Partnership negotiations yet again were put on hold, but they were soon to be resolved in the most unexpected and tragic way.

Chapter 15

'Service to the Cause of People': Philanthropy and the Livingstone Hospital

It pleases you greatly to find that a keen man of business like Mr Burroughs … is not too deeply immersed in money-making to be impervious to the demands of humanity.[1]

The establishment of a cottage hospital in Dartford in 1894 was Burroughs's major philanthropic achievement. This was the golden age of Victorian philanthropy, and he would have been aware of the munificent donations to charitable causes by American and English philanthropists, including Burdett Coutts, Thomas Holloway and Andrew Carnegie. His own philanthropy was driven by his staunch religious beliefs, his desire to assist the townspeople of Dartford, and his determination to help the needy by means of political change. The year was one in which, as always, his travels in Europe consumed much of his time and energy. It started, as it was to end, with poor health, but during the year he enjoyed holiday breaks, worked as hard as ever in promoting the firm, and increasingly spent time supporting charitable and radical causes.

January 1894 was bitterly cold, and the firm provided every member of staff with a daily quinine tabloid and used eucalyptus in the ventilating system to keep influenza at bay. Olive came down with the same flu as her husband. Early in January she travelled to Montreux, staying at her favourite Hôtel du Cygne, then moved on to Rome with her friend Alice Miller. Burroughs managed to get briefly to Dieppe and Newhaven with Frank and Marie Louise Mattox, Frank having agreed to introduce the firm's goods to French doctors.[2] But Burroughs had been over-sanguine in thinking that his health was restored, and at the end of the month he wrote to Wellcome that his doctor had advised a change and he would leave London for a while. He expected to sail for Gibraltar and then to Tangier, so would be away for three weeks or more. While there he planned to promote the firm's interests, taking samples and goods with him. Gibraltar was an important trading centre called at by many steamers; high tariffs virtually priced Spanish goods out of the market, so it was a good place to push BW&Co.'s products. In response to his invitation to the Stanleys to accompany him, Dorothy Stanley wrote: 'Bon voyage Dear Mr Burroughs. There is, alas, no holiday in prospect for us just now. It would have been delightful for Stanley could he have accompanied you to Tangier, but he has much to do here.'[3] Instead, he was accompanied by his friend Dr Ernest Hart, who also sought warm climes for his health, along with Hart's secretary.

Tangier was fine and sunny, and hotel bills record the hiring of mules for excursions, as well as lavish spending on sherry, claret, wines, champagne, liqueurs and Bass Ale. Since Burroughs had in theory renounced alcohol, this begs the question of how well he had kept to his undertaking. He was still not well, however, and was forced to consult a doctor and spend a day in bed with 'slight pleurodymia' and mild deafness.[4] He wrote to BW&Co. that, probably owing to the good weather and use of the firm's Vereker Inhaler, his deafness had disappeared. At the same time he believed that Vitalite socks had helped his health, and the firm should order a gross or more so that every employee who wished them could have two pairs.[5] A Frena camera and films were sent to him, as he wished to take pictures of many curious things and people. And he seized every opportunity for global publicity. On reading a report in *The Lancet* in which Stanley praised the firm's elegant tabloids used by travellers, Burroughs immediately suggested an electro

26: Burroughs in Moorish costume at the Alhambra, 1894.

text (an electro-etched metal plate) be made in order to have cheap copies sent as a cutting to Thomas Cook & Co. and to every newspaper in Britain, Europe, Asia, Africa, Australasia and South America.[6]

Dr Hart wished to see Ronda and Granada, so they travelled together, visiting an olive oil factory; at Ronda station restaurant they enjoyed 'the best of everything edible and drinkable' that grew along the line of the 75-mile railway. The weather was glorious, the air exhilarating and the views magnificent. On his return to England in mid-March, Burroughs found his energy levels evidently much improved, which was just as well, as his European travels in the next few months would have taxed most people.

Hardly had he returned than Burroughs set off again, dividing the next week between Genoa and Rome, then on to Naples and Florence. In Rome he hosted a ball for 200 Anglo-American visitors, where he served 109 bottles of Grand Vin Brut. The firm had obtained a prominent position for their stand at the exhibition of the 11th International Medical Congress at Rome's Palace of Fine Arts and gave free coloured photographs of the city's sights to the doctors attending. Burroughs was present daily until coming down with a four-day bout of fever, possibly a return of his malaria, thereby missing a visit by the king and queen of Italy. Nevertheless he was able to report that the couple spent a long time at the firm's stand and had accepted a Congo medical chest and some Tea Tabloids.[7] Following his return to England in mid-April, Burroughs was present at the laying of the foundation stone of the Livingstone Hospital in Dartford. At this juncture Olive had rented Durrington Lodge in Surbiton, Surrey, close to the River Thames, where the family could go boating and play tennis in their ample garden.

In early May, Burroughs left for the Universal Exhibition in Antwerp, where BW&Co. had the largest stand in their section, the central feature of which was the now somewhat dilapidated and discoloured Stanley medicine chest and 'Travellers Medical Guide'. The firm had the only stand 'of a strictly pharmaceutical character' and gained attention in part for its comfortable 'Rendezvous for Physicians and Pharmacists', where Tea Tabloids were available. While there Burroughs discovered the importance of the forthcoming Vienna Exhibition and decided to go there unless he was needed in London. This turned out to be 'a splendid affair, quite eclipsing the Indian Colonial Health exhibition in London, the buildings finer than in Antwerp.' He organised improved deliveries of goods, appointed a local agent, and BW&Co. received the exhibition's highest award, the Grand Diploma of Honour.

That month, business took Burroughs to Budapest, Vienna, Munich, Heidelberg, Koblenz, Frankfurt, Hamburg, Brussels and Antwerp. Only one letter to Olive survives from this period, and this he wrote in a cab on his way to Budapest after writing business letters all the morning. 'My hands and head are full of work', he wrote, 'or [I] would be very lonesome with not a friend in town that I have any time to call on.' His apartment in Budapest was basic, but not as bad or expensive as one he had had in New York, and he hoped to finish business there in day or so, then hurry back to London.[8] One of the many postcards he sent to his children notes how glad he would be to see them all: 'Am very tired of this long journey. The train left Antwerp this morning and is now going down the shore of a wide river where the country like the people is very flat. They are so slow.'[9]

In June and July, Burroughs stayed in England, then in August he enjoyed a demanding cycling holiday in Germany. There is no evidence that Olive took up cycling with him (and it is likely that Wellcome would have regarded cycling as below his dignity), but Burroughs did persuade Lina and Jai Riggs to join him and, with other friends, they delighted in cycling excursions abroad. A cycle ride from Baden-Baden to Dieppe in 1892 evidently whetted his appetite further, and now he explored the Rhine and the Black Forest, but this time at greater leisure. Typically, his message to the firm on this occasion simply said: 'Gone to the continent perhaps for 2 weeks.' The Riggs family had come to England that year and stayed with the Burroughs family in Surbiton. Their local New York press reported their intention of spending the winter with Burroughs 'at his country seat on the Thames', a description he would have found amusing, given his dislike of the aristocracy and pretension. Now Lina, Jai and nephew Harold, as well as Frank Mattox, Dr Gubb, the Hirschlers, Miss Steel and her family, accompanied or joined him at different stages of the cycle trip. They followed the Rhine from Cologne to Heidelberg, then crossed the Black Forest via Baden-Baden to Schaffhausen. One day Burroughs boasted to Olive that he had cycled 110 kilometres in the Tyrol, and he told Kirby how 'much benefitted in health and strength [he was] by the cycling trip', implying that his health on leaving London had, yet again, not been robust.[10]

This trip was just one of many – the family briefly joining him in Switzerland during the summer. When they were not together – which was often – he wrote almost daily to Olive and sent postcards regularly to each of his children in turn, recounting his adventures: the electric lights over Lucerne; his boat excursion on the Immensee and the odd dip in a river on a hot day. 'Dear Daisy, my darling child', Burroughs would address his youngest, strongly implying that she was a favourite child. Stanley (rarely called 'Junie' now he was older) was sometimes 'My dear Boy'. Anna was more frequently 'My Dear'; references to her temper and bad behaviour towards her brother and sister suggest a prima donna and difficult child.

A souvenir booklet advertising the firm's tabloids and goods was published for those attending the British Medical Association Conference in Bristol that August. It carried an advertisement for 'Photographic "Tabloids"', illustrated with a photograph of Burroughs's four-year-old daughter, Daisy, looking pretty in a white smock, wearing a nervous smile, and carrying a placard pronouncing: 'My PA always uses the PHOTOGRAPHIC TABLOIDS.' Burroughs proudly boasted of this to his friends.[11]

Burroughs demonstrated in many ways his consideration for his staff, to whom he regularly gave small gifts, photographs and souvenirs from his travels. Sometimes the gifts had a religious or political connotation: a copy of Walter Crane's celebrated picture *The Triumph of Labour*, for example, was sent to any employee who wanted one.[12] The highlight of the year for employees was their summer excursion, which took place again at Southsea; it was the eighth such event and the most splendid to date. Nearly 500 employees travelled on a special train, and Burroughs, 'with his customary thoughtful courtesy', took a large quantity of roses and flowers to distribute to the ladies. A festive atmosphere prevailed. It was a gloriously hot June day, but this did not stop everyone from tucking into a generous lunch of roast meats, veal and ham pie, plum pudding, blancmange, fruit tarts and cheeses. A photographer recorded the event, showing an orchestra that played in the gallery and Burroughs and Wellcome both seated at the high table. In response to the first toast to the firm by John Moss, a manufacturing chemist, Burroughs, after 'loud and protracted cheers', seized the opportunity to push his personal vision of the firm converting into a joint stock company, in which the employees would hold 10% of the capital (citing the newspaper *Tit Bits*, where employees nearly all had a share in the business). Wellcome, who then rose to be 'enthusiastically received', avoided any reference to profits, joint stock companies or business-sharing and reiterated that the phenomenal success of the firm was due to the earnest endeavours of the *principals* and the hearty co-operation and intelligent devotion of their employees, who should prosper 'in proportion to its prosperity'.[13] At the end of the day, after promenades on the pier admiring steamers and pleasure boats, a concert and a strawberry tea, a happy crowd headed home. The train did not arrive back in Dartford until after midnight.

Burroughs and Wellcome were not the only businessman in Dartford with philanthropic ideals: Everard Hesketh, manager of J. & E. Hall's engineering works, was active in local politics and interested in improving the housing and working conditions of his employees. Hesketh shared with Burroughs an ability to see possibilities in new technology. They met in 1889 when BW&Co. moved into Dartford, and, although never close friends, both agreed on the need to improve the town's amenities. Together they had been chiefly responsible for the establishment of the Dartford Free Lecture Society, and, as president, Burroughs inaugurated its winter session. He invited friends and the committee to a 'tea' – which was more of a banquet – in his 'beautifully furnished' room at Phoenix Mills, 'a bright cheerful office being rendered additionally attractive by the display of pretty hot house plants and ferns'. The local press noted that all was done with that 'unstinted generosity' for which he was so well known; 'indeed no person has been so genuinely respected in Dartford or the neighbourhood, everything having for its object the welfare and well-being of the people of the town.'[14]

In the late 1880s Hesketh started collecting information about cottage hospitals. He communicated his ideas to Burroughs, who had previously proposed a scheme for public baths in Dartford and was immediately enthusiastic about the idea. In December 1892 the *West Kent Advertiser*, under the heading 'Proposed Cottage Hospital for the Dartford District: A Munificent Offer', printed Burroughs's offer to contribute £1,000 to such a hospital. To Hesketh he wrote: 'when you consider that the thousand pounds which I am giving is the entire fortune given me by my mother to start in life with, which I have not spent on personal comforts or luxuries, but have saved, and brought to England, and now desire to use it for the benefit of the sick and unfortunate … you will realize that I am very anxious that it should do the full amount of good that it is capable of.'[15] He clarified that the donation should not be taken as an indication of his wealth but, rather, of his 'earnest desire to be of service if possible to any and all of the working classes of Dartford and vicinity who might be so unfortunate as to be ill and to require medical attention in a hospital.'[16] The people of Dartford were delighted, but thorny questions needed resolving. Where would a hospital be located? How could Burroughs be sure that the rest of the money would be forthcoming? During 1893 these problems seemed insurmountable, and it appeared that the project would founder or that a much smaller scheme would emerge. Burroughs fought on: a sum of £3,000 was required to cover all the costs, and he considered that the local community should be able to raise the remaining £2,000.

Initially, Burroughs hoped that land would be donated by a local landowner, possibly Viscount Tredegar. Tredegar, however, did not have a convenient centrally located site and rejected Burroughs's suggestion that he give land – worth about £300 – which could be sold to fund the purchase of a suitable site.[17] When a subsequent approach failed, Burroughs proposed that, if a site in the Phoenix Mills grounds would answer the purpose, he would be glad to give his interest in it, 'which is 3/4ths and

[I] suppose that Mr Wellcome will be willing to give the other fourth … The position is near the large works, is adjacent to the railway station and experience shows that it is very healthy … The hospital patients could have the use of the lawn & boat on pond and convalescents & staff could have use of tennis court when not required by our employees.'[18] But Wellcome refused to agree. In the end a site on East Hill, about half a mile from the town centre, was purchased for £350.[19]

Burroughs set out a number of other conditions: the hospital was to be under popular control and non-sectarian; admission was to be free to those too poor to pay; patients who could afford to pay were to be charged the cost of

27: Henry Morton Stanley, the explorer, c. 1890

board and attendance only; the site was to be a healthy open space; and alcoholic medicines or beverages were to be avoided as much as possible or altogether. The Hospital Committee had no problem in complying with these requests.[20] The name of the hospital was more problematic. Burroughs suggested the 'Stanley Hospital' or the 'Livingstone and Stanley Hospital', after the great explorers, but by this date Stanley's reputation was tarnished by reports of his cruelty to Africans in the Congo. Burroughs's friendship and admiration of Stanley evidently blinkered him to these reports, as indeed they did to Wellcome. Many liberal and radical contemporaries were by now aware of colonialism's failures and wrongs and were trying to bring them to the public's attention, yet there is no indication that Burroughs contemplated or was concerned by them. Hesketh meanwhile alerted Burroughs that the name 'Stanley Hospital' was unacceptable:

> There was some difference of opinion about [the name]: as you are aware Mr Stanley's name is not a charm in every household; on the contrary many people hold very strongly antagonistic opinions about him, hence the name would doubtless stir up some animosity which would be I am sure

the very last thing you would wish in a scheme like this which should bind everyone together with enthusiasm. The meeting thought that the name should be the Dartford Cottage Hospital and that any large donor like yourself shall be at liberty to perpetuate any name ... by attaching it to a wing or ward of the hospital.[21]

Burroughs replied: 'I think that Mr Stanley would not be desirous of having the Hospital named after himself but that he would be glad to have it named the Livingstone Hospital of Dartford. This would tend to keep alive in the memory of all who saw it the good work & example of one of the noblest Christian missionary physicians.' 'The Livingstone Cottage Hospital for Dartford and District' was finally agreed on, shortened in 1910 to 'Livingstone Hospital'.

In spite of much support, the biggest stumbling block was raising the outstanding funds required (indeed, an earlier scheme for a dispensary in Dartford had failed for this reason). A hospital fund was established and received contributions from J. & E. Hall workmen, who agreed a deduction of 1d per week from their wages to raise £40 in a year; donations from a City Temple collection; subscriptions from local employers of £150 yearly; and proceeds from a sale – to which Burroughs offered a 'free' St Bernard dog (hardly a cheap pet to keep) and a hospital football match. Although the majority of patients were expected to pay for their bed and board, the cost of actually running the hospital does not seem to have been addressed, and charitable income was unlikely to be sufficient. Burroughs remained adamant that, although his £1,000 was sitting in the local bank, he would not release it until he was certain that sufficient funding had been committed by others. Not unreasonably, he wrote: 'I simply wish to avoid the danger of loss of money subscribed by others and myself, which appears imminent, unless it is put up in sufficient amount to pay for the building before the work is started.'[22] The *Dartford Chronicle* reported the taunts and malicious sneers of a Conservative-backed paper on the problems faced by Burroughs.[23] A chicken and egg situation arose: Hesketh argued that, once the building was started and people knew it was actually going to happen, the money would come in, whereas Burroughs, often accused of being hasty and impulsive, was very wary about this proposed arrangement. His solicitors adopted an even more cautious attitude, and by July 1893, with Burroughs abroad, negotiations appeared to be at a stalemate. The intervention of Mr Searl, the works manager, broke through the deadlock with a compromise agreement whereby further money was promised on the surety of 200 guarantors.[24]

But, even with guarantors, raising funds was hard going, and tempers became decidedly frayed. Hesketh wrote to Burroughs's solicitors: 'I have expended far more time in trying to meet Mr Burroughs' conditions than I can, consistently with my other engagements, fairly afford, & I cannot continue to do so.'[25] The scheme seemed ill-fated.[26] Eventually guarantees obtained by Hesketh permitted progress, but to the bitter end Burroughs held back his contribution until the maximum amount of money and commitment could be obtained from others. On Saturday 21 April 1894, the date of the laying of the foundation stone by Stanley, Burroughs scrawled a hasty note: 'The [Hospital] Committee have signed the contract to make themselves responsible for the cost ... I think that will be sufficient', and he authorised the release of his £1,000.

The event received huge coverage in the local press – although Stanley was given a muted reception; his 'civilizing influence' was praised, but his methods were criticised. Townspeople turned out in full: tradesmen decorated their shops with flags and banners, and two saloon trains chartered by Burroughs transported the Stanley family and members of the medical profession and press to Dartford. Bands played as a huge procession of various trade unions, the National Deposit Friendly Society, boys from the St Vincent Industrial School, Druids, Buffaloes, Oddfellows, Phoenixes, Sons of the Temperance, Rechabites, Hearts of Oak 'and others of that ilk' marched with the 4,000-strong crowd. Burroughs spoke of the hospital's purpose in alleviating suffering and disease among poor people who were unable to obtain treatment at home and thanked Stanley for the brave work he had done in Africa and for the sympathy he had shown to humanity throughout the world. Ernest Hart spoke of Livingstone's achievements, then Stanley spoke for over half an hour about Livingstone's career. Further speeches, votes of thanks and repeated cheers followed at the Victoria Assembly Rooms, where Burroughs and Olive entertained supporters and guests to a tea.

On 4 July even greater Dartford festivities marked the formal opening. In fact the two-storey building, with two principal wards, surgery, dispensary and administration areas, was still far from finished, but work was sufficiently advanced for people to see what it would be like. All the main shops in town closed at 1pm; the vicar of Dartford, Hesketh and Earl Stanhope (lord-lieutenant of Kent) gave speeches; Countess Stanhope was presented with a bouquet by 'little Miss Burroughs' (Daisy); and the crowds enjoyed a bazaar, a floral parade, mounted military sports, bands, refreshment stalls and a café chantant. Telegraphic communication was made with several London theatres, which caused great interest and admiration: orchestral and dramatic

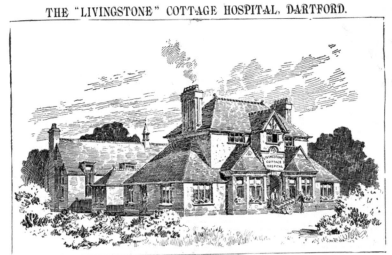

THE "LIVINGSTONE" COTTAGE HOSPITAL, DARTFORD.

MEMORIAL STONE LAID BY MR. H. M. STANLEY, ACCOMPANIED BY MRS. STANLEY, ON SATURDAY, APRIL 21st, 1894.

28: Livingstone Hospital c. 1906. The hospital, opened in 1894, was Burroughs's greatest legacy to Dartford. Its memorial stone was laid by H.M. Stanley.

performances interspersed with audience applause could be distinctly heard from 20 miles away.[27] Oddly, one person absent was Wellcome, whose name does not appear in the press coverage, although he had attended at the annual firm outing the previous week. Could he have been embarrassed that he had not been involved by his modest financial contribution? What was certain, however, was that employees and Dartfordians were leading a better life since Burroughs and Wellcome had come to town, with rising employment, paternalistic employers, and now a new hospital.

That autumn Burroughs visited Switzerland, Austria and Belgium, mixing business and pleasure as usual. He attended the 8th International Congress of Hygiene and Demography in Budapest and made several visits to Cham on the Immensee, where he stayed some time with David Page, manager of the Anglo-Swiss Condensed Milk Co. – later Nestlé – in his luxurious home with views over Lake Zug and Lucerne. Business visits and new contacts were made, one to the head of a Photochrome firm in Zurich, presumably to discuss Photographic Tabloids.[28] In both Budapest at the congress and then at the 6th Universal Peace Congress in Antwerp, Burroughs spoke on international peace, managing to introduce important social issues and raise the cause of free trade as a peace promoter. On his return to England there was much to attend to. In addition to the negotiations with Wellcome over their partnership, there was involvement with the Livingstone Hospital; the presentation of a paper at the Sanitary Institute's autumn congress in Liverpool; a tour of the Dartford works; publicity for the new Tabloid Tea; preparation for the firm's forthcoming announcement on a diphtheria anti-toxin serum; and his inaugural lecture as president of the Bexleyheath Liberal and Radical Club.[29] The pace of his life was seemingly unrelenting.

Burroughs's desire for social reform and his increasing radicalism were reflected in his subscriptions and donations to a wide range of charities, individuals and political bodies. His generosity and open-handedness were such that he was sometimes seen as a soft touch. Among countless donations were contributions to hospitals in America and Britain; the welfare of refugees; the temperance movement; the mission to the Congo; the Italian Evangelical Church in Genoa; the Ceylon mission; a memorial to Lincoln; expenses for the Hyde Park demonstration in support of the Liquor Traffic (Control) Bill 1893; the Mariners' Friend Society; and the Pharmaceutical Society of Great Britain. The City Temple, which Burroughs attended, regularly received money, along with a bust of Livingstone. He also supported the Council of British and Foreign Arbitration Association, the International Peace and Arbitration Society, and the City Liberal and United Democratic clubs.

When Burroughs was elected president of the Bexleyheath Liberal and Radical Club in November 1894, a large gathering gave him a warm welcome for his inaugural address, on 'The Outbreak of Liberalism'. The room was suitably decorated with rousing mottoes: 'Down with the Lords', 'Constitutional Reform', 'Tax the Land and Relieve the Industries' and 'Health and Long Life to our President'. In his speech Burroughs emphasised the key aims of the Newcastle Programme – drawn up in 1891 by the National Liberal Federation. It set out a radical agenda: Irish Home Rule was a key element, but other proposed reforms included Scottish and Welsh disestablishment, reform of district and parish councils, a veto on drink sales, employers' liability for workers' accidents, land reform, abolition of the 'monstrosity' of the House of Lords; payment for MPs; and free trade. 'Being a manufacturer himself', Burroughs supposed he should be a protectionist, but 'he would be sorry to think that he supported taxation to ensure bigger profits for his goods. People like that were anything but good citizens and patriots,' and he was surprised that 'his own fellow country-men of the Stars and Stripes and supporters of liberty should tax other traders.' Property ownership and taxation should be changed: iron and coal mines should be regarded as public property, and royalties should go to the public benefit. Cottages were heavily taxed whereas mansions surrounded by acres of land were under-taxed in comparison: changes to land taxation would change the labour market and help abolish poverty, since building more houses would mean more work and higher wages. Burroughs concluded his address by presenting the club with a portrait of his hero, Gladstone.

Political and economic reform, especially support of the single tax movement and Liberal Party, now occupied yet more of Burroughs's time. He was a member of the National Liberal Club, City Liberal Club, United Democratic Club, and Dartford Liberal and Radical Association and an executive member of the London Reform Union, English Land Restoration League and Tenant Tradesmen's National Union. Added to this, he had dealings with many other bodies, such as the National Reform Union Manchester, the Financial Reform Association, the Electoral Committee for the Taxation of Ground Values, the Highlands Land Reform movement and the Scottish Land Restoration League.[30] A consummate networker, Burroughs knew many eminent thinkers and activists, among them Ignatius Singer and Lewis Henry Berens, both esteemed friends. He corresponded with and probably met the radical activists Tom Mann (trade unionist and founder of the Eight Hour League) and Ben Tillett (socialist and trade union leader) and knew T.P. O'Connor (Irish nationalist, MP, journalist and newspaper editor), who praised the firm's products in his paper. Unfortunately, his letter book containing correspondence with some of these major figures in trade unionism is now virtually illegible. Many contacts came from his travels, such as W.H. Towsey, the British Consul in Palermo, with whom he corresponded about free trade, taxation and poverty, and his Liberal MP friends William Saunders and Gavin D. Clark.

Burroughs's interest in temperance remained, and in June 1894, when he suffered from influenza and was recommended various tonics, he found his health improved under a regime of total abstinence. He determined yet again to give up drink, with the caveat: 'I daresay however there is a virtue in alcoholic stimulant when it is required as a medicine.' He joined the National Temperance League and Central Association for Stopping the Sale of Intoxicating Liquors on Sunday and sometimes even sported a blue ribbon in his buttonhole, indicating his support for the movement. When invited at this time to join the British Medical Temperance Association, he accepted, though he carefully enquired if it was pledged to total abstinence or if members were permitted to take alcohol in any form under medical advice. His lavish hospitality in serving drinks to friends continued.[31]

Burroughs pressed on with support for the single tax movement. He tried to get Henry George to return to the UK, telling him of the importance of strengthening the Liberal Party. More importantly, he purchased 60,000 copies of George's *Protection or Free Trade: An Examination of the Tariff Question with Especial Regard to the Interests of Labor* for distribution in the UK. At this time he was also publishing in the UK, at his own cost, a single tax newspaper, 'a thoroughgoing Liberal paper', and another paper 'published for me in America'. Heartened to know that the single tax cause was making good headway in America, but aware that it had not been taken up as rapidly in Britain, he wrote to George: 'Unjust taxation robs the many and enriches the few – which has its foundation in selfishness and flourishes upon monopoly fostered by ignorance and prejudice ... To my mind socialism would be the worst form of despotism.'[32] Burroughs did not mince his words about his disgust when a bill relating to land tax was thrown out by the House of Lords ('foxes who have disguised themselves in the skins of sheep ... self-styled patriots'). To another friend he declared: 'the ending of the House of Lords will soon be the Liberal programme to the credit of Englishmen.'[33]

During 1894, Burroughs's involvement in the radical movement led people to suggest he enter Parliament as a member for the constituency of East Islington.[34] He wrote of being deeply conscious of the honour of being invited but that he was 'much engrossed in business affairs.'[35] To another acquaintance he said: 'It is not my wish to stand for Parliament. I have no ambition whatever, but merely a desire to see legislation carried on which will be to the benefit of all classes.'[36] A further suggestion that he offer himself for election as a member for Banbury provoked a similar response:

> While I desire to be of the greatest possible service to every good cause and to the useful reforms enunciated in the Liberal program I must not in any way neglect attention to our business upon which probably a thousand people in all depend for a living either directly or indirectly. The business now takes nearly all my time excepting that necessary for sleep & health recreation. Therefore I would rather be of service to the cause of the people outside Parliament than inside.[37]

It was later said of him that he seemed to live half a dozen lives,[38] and clearly he was pulled in so many directions that his mental and physical exertions put him under huge strain, exacerbated by his never-ending battles with Wellcome over the future of the partnership.

Chapter 16

From London to Monte Carlo

His sun indeed went down when it was yet night.[1]

Christmas 1894 found Burroughs in Antibes on the Riviera, having been advised by his doctor that he needed warmth and to recuperate from influenza. He was also mentally and physically exhausted from the months of negotiation with Wellcome over dissolution of their partnership. The Riviera would surely improve his health and renew his energy, as it had done in previous years. Every winter bar one, from 1888, Burroughs had headed south to warmer climes to escape the smog and cold of England, which exacerbated the cough, colds, bronchitis and influenza to which he was prone. His medical report of 1894 noted pleurodymia in San Francisco in 1876, and he had pleurisy in Paris in 1884 and slight pleurodymia again in 1894. His life was insured with four companies, and in November 1894 he insured his life yet again, perhaps concerned by the increasing frequency of his bouts of illness.

The Mediterranean was recommended by physicians as a region where those suffering from tuberculosis and other lung conditions should visit to improve their condition. By the end of the century numerous British physicians had settled on the Riviera, creating an increasing need for English-speaking pharmacists and for drugs prescribed by doctors for their English patients. In Nice, Messrs Nicholls and Passeron's grand frontage of the *pharmacie anglaise* on the place Massera was granted a royal warrant; Menton had four pharmacies and four English doctors; along the coast, just into Italy, a Mr Squires ran the San Remo pharmacy. In Monte Carlo there was only one pharmacy, for many years run by M. Cruzel, whose right-hand man was Burroughs's good friend M. Naftel.

The winter of 1894–5 saw some of the worst weather on record, with a cold easterly wind moving across the UK; it affected most of Europe in February. Although rare, snow does fall in the Riviera, and Burroughs had experienced it in Cannes four years previously.[2] But in southern France in December 1894 and early January 1895 it was still fine: the climate was, as usual, mild and bright, the atmosphere dry, but it was still chilly at night, and 'decidedly winter'.

Burroughs had cycled in this part of France several times. This time he went with Lina, who had bronchitis. She had been in London since September with her husband and son; Jai returned to America, and Harold remained in London with Olive. Lina and Burroughs were joined for some of the time by friends, including Dr and Mrs Clark and William Saunders and his wife – Saunders was wonderfully cheerful notwithstanding his serious illness from dropsy. Burroughs continued to work hard and play hard and used bicycle, bus and train to zigzag along the Côte d'Azur and the Italian coast between Antibes and San Remo, mainly keeping to a schedule known to Sudlow so that business mail could reach him. Although this break was intended to improve his and Lina's health, Burroughs never stopped working, planning sales, visiting pharmacists and discussing the market with acquaintances. The two stayed in good but not always top of the range hotels, the

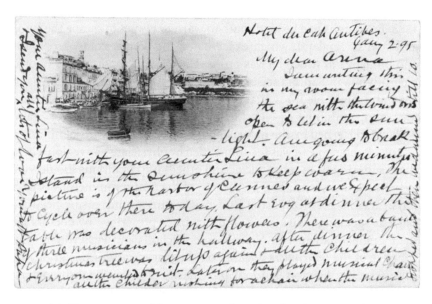

29: Picture postcard from Burroughs to his daughter Anna from
Antibes, 2 January 1895. Burroughs sent cards nearly every day
to his family when he was away.

longest stay being two weeks in Antibes at the beginning of the trip, after which they frequently stopped for only a couple of nights at any one place.

As usual, Burroughs wrote virtually daily to Olive and sent postcards in turn to each of the children. Christmas Day in Antibes was spent cycling with Lina and the Clarks and taking a small boat trip to view the ironclad warship at Toulon. At breakfast on New Year's Eve he was able to sit by an open window bathed in sunshine at the Hôtel du Cap Antibes and wrote – to a no doubt envious Sudlow – that he had no need for a fire. 'The air has a pleasant crispness and is very dry & clear, quite an absence of those mists & fogs which give me oh such awful colds & catarrh in London.' He enjoyed the evening in the hotel when the Christmas tree was relit, a band of musicians performed, and children played musical chairs, but missed his family. His very unpleasant cough had quite left him, he reported.

However, a few days later he was asking Sudlow about a powder or spray which he could take for chronic catarrh and thickening of the inner membrane of the nasal passages. Could Sudlow enquire of Dr Illingworth or ask Dr Ball what he thought of Dermatol? Before leaving England he had evidently visited his doctor, Henry McNaughton Jones, to have the thickening burnt out with an electric cautery but, faced with a long wait, had gone off to the office. He was administering himself Naso-Pharyngeal Tabloids dissolved in hot water and snuffed up the nose, after which he used Boroline with menthol and cocaine and also sometimes a spray of menthol solution. 'Think I am getting much better & my cough is mainly gone but I would like to get clear cured of the catarrh which remains after the influenza, perhaps as a reminder or bequest so it shouldn't be forgotten.' Lina was 'greatly improved' and could now cycle 5 or 8 miles at a stretch without difficulty. In mid-January Burroughs was well enough to telegraph Olive, asking her to send cycling gear, socks, tennis rackets and photos of the family and one of herself, c/o the Cruzel Pharmacie Monte Carlo.[3] Olive's cough concerned him, and he suggested she use Extract of Malt and go to Bournemouth for a few days. He planned to return home by 13 February and attend a charity ball and signed off: 'Kiss the kids for their pops.'[4]

On one particular cycle ride with Lina, from Nice to Monte Carlo, they were accompanied part of the way by Burroughs's pharmaceutical friends Mr Jaffe and Mr Nicholls; all delighted in the orange trees, heliotrope hedges, roses and narcissus. The next day saw the first rain since they had started cycling, but there were more friends at the hotel to spend time with, including T.P. O'Connor and his wife, who planned to visit the Burroughs family in the spring. The Stanleys were also there, Stanley's health being 'much improved' by his visit. Burroughs told his son: 'I saw your noble namesake at Monte Carlo. He did not gamble and I hope you never will.' When questioned by Stanley if he ever visited the tables, he responded that he did, but added that he didn't bet at them. Stanley's reasons for not betting were apparently the same as his – that 'he didn't wish to lose any of his money or win any of theirs.'

On 21 January the roads were heavy with the morning's rain, so Lina took a carriage while Burroughs cycled from Menton to Bordighera.[5] The next day saw heavy rain storms, and a scattering of snow fell in Cannes; it was a foot deep on trains arriving from Genoa. The light was poor for a Riviera morning when Burroughs wrote to Olive by candlelight before breakfast, saying that he had lots of business letters to attend to. He had proposed that the firm establish a branch or depot in Italy[6] and mentioned that he had been asked for a loan but would not be able to agree to it until he knew the magnitude of financial demands on him should he buy Wellcome out of the business. 'Wellcome is getting himself in a hole & corner by refusing all sorts of fair offers ... I will make Wellcome no more offers whatever having done everything in that line that could possibly be expected of me.' The London division of the County Council had again requested that he stand for office, 'but of course [I] shall decline having my hands full & quite as much as I can attend to.' As was his habit, he had sent flowers to family friends and colleagues, and his letter ended with compliments to a long list of mutual friends and kisses for the children.[7]

On 28 January Burroughs wrote to his son from San Remo that snow had fallen the previous night and that everyone was surprised to see the beaches white. He expected to cycle to Bordighera and maybe Menton that day; 'Auntie Lina' was getting stronger but still a long way from being fully recovered. On 29th they returned to Monte Carlo and stayed at the Hôtel Windsor, where Dr Naftel found Burroughs in apparently perfect health on 1 February.

Then on Sunday 3 February Burroughs went cycling; some reports said he had been wearing a thin jacket and the weather was bad; another report stated that he insisted on taking a cold-water bath when in a high perspiration.[8] What is sure is that he developed pleurisy which rapidly developed into pneumonia. His body, weakened by flu, meant that his immune system left him vulnerable to developing pneumonia. It is hard to tell when flu develops into pneumonia, but the symptoms would have been a worsening cough, sharp chest pains, then coughing up phlegm, a more rapid heartbeat, a rising temperature, and sweating and shivering from a fever. Increasingly he would have struggled for breath as his lungs filled with fluid.

Lina and two nurses from the Holland Institution of English Hospital Trained Nurses attended him, and he was seen by Drs Fagge, Hutchinson and Fitzgerald.[9] But in spite of the care he received Burroughs did not improve. Perhaps he was attended by too many doctors, as later Olive was to write that 'it was professional etiquette that hurried her husband out if this world.' Presumably by this she was suggesting that the doctors who saw him did not wish openly to contradict one another's judgements as to the best course of action. It was, however, the case that, in this pre-antibiotic age, pneumonia could, and did, strike suddenly, and there was no effective drug or cure. Initially Burroughs may well have assumed that he would recover from his flu and bronchitis, as he had done so many times previously. But his state worsened and his fever rose. These days must have been terrible ones for him, with his wife and children far away and being horribly conscious that he had left unresolved the future of the firm and his partnership.

On Tuesday Lina sent Olive a telegram that her brother was ill but that he was not in immediate danger. Nevertheless Olive hastily packed and set out immediately from London to make the journey by boat and train in the bitter cold. When she arrived at Marseille station the following day, Wednesday 6th, she was met by Mrs Naftel. There she was given the devastating news that her husband had died a few hours earlier.[10] His illness had lasted just three days.

Two days later, after a short service at the Anglican Church in Monte Carlo, Burroughs was buried in the cemetery on the edge of the town. His funeral was attended by Olive, Lina, Dr Clark, many local pharmacists and all the English doctors of Monte Carlo. No expense was spared on the large and impressive funeral cortege; his oak coffin was covered

30: Burroughs's grave in Monte Carlo. Silas and Olive are buried together in the Cimetière de Monaco. The grave inscription reads 'Remembering without ceasing your work of faith and labour of love and patience of hope in our Lord Jesus Christ'.

with flowers and palm leaves, and the flowers he loved were strewn all around the grave. Burroughs was 49 when he died, the same age at which his father had died.

News of his death spread swiftly. Many found it impossible to believe, thinking that his constitution was sound and that he 'always looked & seemed the embodiment of health.' How could this man, 'the impersonation of tireless energy', working all hours, restless in his pursuit of endless goals, die so suddenly? Some considered that with his 'health and spirits he might have overcome any illness that might have overtaken him.'[11] Hutton recalled meeting him the previous August, when he was 'as full of his well-known energy as ever'.[12] Peter van Schaak in Chicago told Olive: 'Your husband seemed so well when last at my house I felt he had a long lease of life.' But another friend reckoned that Burroughs did not look well to her when she saw him in London: 'I spoke of it but he turned it off.' Another noted after seeing him in December that 'he seemed then to be completely broken down with work and care, and his friends in town all shared in his belief that a few months of rest would restore his health and strength.'[13] Yet another wrote: 'we fear the weather in its severity overcame the loved one who was never weighted with strength so far as his chest was concerned and whose natural fearlessness sometimes led him to lack care of himself.'

Burroughs had made an impact on everyone he encountered, his forceful personality reaching out to a huge network of family, friends and acquaintances wherever he went. As one mourner put it: 'It seems a strange providence that a man like Mr Burroughs, so generous, kind-hearted so helpful to the poor so needed in the world should be called home in the midst of his life's work.' The irony of his death may well have crossed people's minds. Here was a man who had spent his life promoting the effectiveness of pills and medicines, offering advice on health, and who took regular exercise, yet no tabloid drugs or medical equipment, even those from the huge range offered by his firm, could help. His life had stopped at a point when he had the will, ability and money to do far more good in the world; 'to be taken away just as he is reaching the top of the ladder of success & prosperity at his early age is altogether too sad.'[14]

Newspapers worldwide, from Dartford to America, from India to Australia, reported his death; obituaries in pharmaceutical and other journals followed, and there were countless letters of condolence. Burroughs had been an exceptional networker who had been universally respected: his generosity, his unselfish desire to help people and his many lovely traits of character were repeatedly mentioned, as well as his stirring enthusiasm, warmth and charm. All who knew him claimed some part of his kindly nature, and it was noted by many that he was a friend to all who came into contact with him. 'Very few people have the gift of making and keeping friends as he had – what will the factory people and the missionaries do without the friend who was always planning for their happiness and best welfare? How can I write our respect for his talents, his honesty, sincerity and goodness? How genial he was, and so hospitable in his own house, "a prince of good fellows" and yet so simple in his tastes.' A school friend wrote: 'he always brought the sunshine with him … his great happiness was to make others happy. His unfailing kindness covered all our school days with rosy light.' His Christian beliefs and philanthropy were also noted.[15] Sunshine was a recurrent theme: 'What could he do to throw a little sunshine into the lives of others.' 'I cannot realize that I am not to see his cheerful countenance and hear his merry laugh again.' Another said he was a true, faithful, unselfish friend, 'generous to a fault if that be possible, kind and courteous to young and old, rich and poor alike; honest and just in his dealings with all men; taking a personal interest in the affairs of all with whom he had to do. … Many a kind deed was his of which the world never knew.' His political beliefs and endless promotion of the single tax movement in his conversations did not interfere with close friendship of stalwart Conservatives. At the same time he was intolerant of all conventions which were not based upon moral or ethical premises.[16]

Dr Gubb wrote that he had 'never lost anyone whose disappearance has left such a blank in my existence.' Henrietta Parke, mother of Surgeon Major Parke, wrote that her late son spoke frequently in the highest terms of Burroughs and was very grateful to him for his gift when they met at Stanley's before his departure for Africa. Dorothy Stanley commented on his exceptional kindness, and Stanley sent Olive a long, warm letter:

> I am grieved to the heart to hear of this very sudden termination to a life so useful, so good, & so full of heartfelt projects as that of your husband. I regard it as quite a calamity the weight of which will be felt within a very wide circle. To my wife and myself it is especially sad. It is only two weeks ago that we parted from him bearing away with us additional proofs of his kindness of heart & a full sense of his invariable friendship.[17]

Colleagues and acquaintances commented on Burroughs's business acumen and invaluable contribution to the world of pharmacy. The *Chemist and Druggist* noted that 'His absolute want of affectation, the equality of his demeanour towards all, and his utter contempt of

31: Studio photograph, late 1880s. The image shows Burroughs as a stereotypical businessman and was widely used from the late 1880s.

snobbishness, struck one the more because of the rarity of these virtues among men of his social position.'[18] There was widespread belief that commercial England has lost both one of its most notable and distinguished personalities and the premier pharmacist of the country. Joseph Remington, his old lecturer at the Philadelphia School of Pharmacy, wrote to Wellcome: 'the whole trade today have but one opinion which is freely expressed & that is that we have lost an honest big hearted man ... it was a terrible shock to us all, not only to me personally, for I feel as if I had lost a very dear friend.'[19] Mr Stratton at Fellows Medical Manufacturing, New York, said his 'dear friend' was 'one of the few men who commanded my perfect confidence and esteem. I wept when the message came and felt as if a brother had been called away.' Another pharmacist said: 'I need scarcely say that I formed a very high estimate of his character as a man of high principles and exceptional business genius.'

His eccentricities were referred to, one being that it was reportedly impossible to talk with him for five consecutive minutes without referring to the 'Single Tax'.[20] Alfred Tindall, medical and scientific publisher, told Wellcome that, 'notwithstanding his little peculiarities, no one entertained a higher regard for Mr Burroughs than I, no friend has grieved me more at his untimely death than I.' Van Schaak wrote: 'with all his faults, and we are all human, he had many good traits of character and his energy was unbounded.' According to the obituary in the *Pharmaceutical Era*: 'On occasions impulsive moods seemed to take control of his better qualities, and at such times he would develop a vexatious, cantankerous manner that was almost childish.'[21]

Many of the firm's staff felt that they would never see another employer as kind and considerate.[22] Sudlow and Searl reported to Olive: 'All employees of the firm extend to you their most sincere sympathy in your bereavement; they have lost a true friend therefore share your great sorrow in this irreparable loss.' Kirby wrote: 'The blow falls very heavily, & we do not yet realise the blank that will be keenly felt now that our kind friend & generous employer has passed away.' One employee recalled: 'One always felt brighter, and more braced up as it were – at every interview one had & reckoned of such and felt quite lost, and to regret extremely, when such interview had terminated.' 'We all miss dear Mr Burroughs more every day,' wrote another; 'he was indeed a friend to us all, we all miss his cheerful face and kind words, which he had for all whenever he came down to the works and passed through the different rooms.'

Communities in which Burroughs lived and places he visited regretted the loss of such a public-spirited man. Dartford Council sent Olive their formal commiserations and mentioned 'the deep sense of loss which has

32: Relief of Burroughs in Livingstone Hospital, c. 1896, commissioned for the hospital after his death and still there. The plaque underneath reads 'This ward is dedicated to Silas Mainville Burroughs / Through whose initiative the hospital was founded / The employees of Burroughs, Wellcome & Co, / Have erected this tablet to place on record the esteem and affection / In which they hold his memory: their grateful recognition of his constant / Desire to promote their happiness and welfare and their deep sorrow / At his death, which occurred after a very short illness in the / Riviera on 6 February 1895 / In the 49th year of his age.'

occurred to the town'. Hesketh commented that, in the comparatively short time during which Burroughs had been connected with Dartford, 'he had, by his never-failing kindliness & by his earnest interest in all things pertaining to the public welfare, made a large circle of friends by whom his loss will be severely felt. I hear on all sides his name mentioned with sincerest regrets, and he will for long be remembered in Dartford for his philanthropy as well as for those personal qualities which endeared him to so many.' The Dartford Liberal and Radical Association described his loss as an international one, for in every place he visited he increased the number of his friends and enlarged his benevolence. The numerous causes and organisations Burroughs supported all sent messages of sympathy.[23]

In Medina, the news cast a sad gloom over the whole community. In New York, Henry George spoke of him warmly and wrote: 'I have lost one of my best friends, a man who seemed to have before him a long career of usefulness.'[24] In Chicago, news of his untimely death brought sorrow to many who had encountered him during the World's Fair.

Many attempted to console Olive that the world was better for his having lived and that his memory would be an influence for good, 'and his good deeds must always remain as an ideal of all that is noble & generous.' But the reality was that the impact of his death on Olive and Lina was devastating: Lina broke down under the strain and was unable to return to England with Olive. Sudlow advised Olive to be careful of her own health. Offers of help came from many sides. Emmie Gardner, wife of Charles F. Gardner, one of Burroughs's oldest friends, left immediately for Monte Carlo, and the Naftels, De Giovannis and other friends and acquaintances there gave what practical support and comfort they could. And Wellcome? He must have had very mixed reactions to the loss of what had once been a very close friend, the man who had helped make his career and fortune, but who had become a thorn in his flesh. He sent telegrams and letters to both Olive and Lina, conveying his 'whole heart's sympathy' in their sad bereavement – 'I feel shocked and grieved beyond expression ... it is a sorrow in which many hearts will claim a share' – and offered his services if he could help in any way – to go to Monte Carlo or send a representative or make any arrangements Olive might desire.[25]

After a few days Olive left the Hôtel Windsor for the Hôtel St Petersburg in Nice and then moved on to Hôtel du Cap Antibes. By 3 March she was back at Durrington Lodge, Surbiton, with her children: Anna, who was nine, Stanley, six, and Daisy, just turned five. It now fell to her to deal with Burroughs's business affairs and with Wellcome. Burroughs had died at a critical moment and had left no instructions. Everything was in disarray and the challenge Olive faced was massive.

Chapter 17

Olive versus Wellcome

A woman of great determination ...[1]

Olive's handling of affairs after Burroughs's death demonstrated an indomitable character. Her immediate concerns were to locate her husband's last will, clarify its implications and find out what was to happen to the firm. What rights did she have in it and would she play any part in its future? Who should she turn to for legal advice? Her husband's death had been so unexpected that no consideration had been given to what were now vital matters. She had the unenviable task, working with her joint executor Theodore Barrett (a lawyer friend of Burroughs based in Philadelphia and unknown to her), of sorting out a huge estate, difficult to value and administer, and negotiating with Wellcome, whom she mistrusted. Business agreements, assets, life insurance claims, and numerous loans on both sides of the Atlantic had to be tackled. This at a time when she and her three children were coming to terms with the huge chasm left in their lives. At home in Durrington Lodge, Alice Chamberlin and the nanny helped look after her children, along with Lina's son Harold, and did their best to deal with enquiries.

The challenge was enormous, and Olive rose to it with an energy and a competence that would have made her husband proud. In accounts published to date, she is portrayed as the furious wife who 'created maximum difficulty', whose lawyers urged her on by challenging Wellcome 'vehemently and insultingly'; that she 'unwisely' took legal action against Wellcome, and that her solicitors deliberately delayed actions. Wellcome claimed that, initially, he made 'the most liberal proposals possible'.[2] Yet the records show a rather different

33: Olive Burroughs – photograph taken after her husband's death.

story. Long delays, friction and mistrust certainly occurred, but to some extent this was inevitable given the complex legal and financial situation and the need for skilled accountants to value the business and establish rights in it. However, significant delays were also caused by the behaviour of Wellcome and by their firms of leading lawyers – Markby, Stewart & Co. acting for Wellcome, Humphreys, Son & Kershaw for Olive.

Charles Humphreys had previously advised Burroughs, and Olive thought it best to continue to use his firm. Theodore Barrett agreed that Humphreys should also act for him. Throughout the negotiations Olive was greatly supported by a number of people, chief among them James Foley, a New York attorney who had known Burroughs for more than 30 years and counted him as one of his oldest and truest associates. He handled Burroughs's American assets, gave invaluable advice on other financial issues, and proved loyal and dependable, in due course becoming a friend, although it was to be four years before they met. Other support came from two old friends of her husband: Charles

F. Gardner, who managed her accounts and financial affairs in England, and Henry A. Lyman, who lived in New Haven and who had holidayed with them.[3]

Finding the latest will was the first step. Radford and Frankland located one dated 7 February 1884, and a search was initiated at BW&Co., where another dated 23 November 1889 turned up. But Olive reckoned her husband had made a third will about three years earlier; indeed, he had done so in January 1893, before departing for America. His solicitors had forwarded the copy to him in America, where he undoubtedly discussed it with his friend and lawyer Barrett. Jai Riggs hurriedly sent Olive a certified copy of it before joining Lina in London.[4] It contained detailed burial instructions, not known about at the time of his death: that he be cremated or buried, enclosed only in a basket. Ever open to new ideas, Burroughs had taken on board the recent interest in cremation and the use of wicker baskets instead of coffins.[5]

It is characteristic of Burroughs that he distributed his estate widely and generously and did not seek to establish a business dynasty by leaving the bulk of his wealth to his son, as most successful businessmen would have done. He left his desk to Mrs Ferguson (wife of John Ferguson, whose family were old friends from Medina) and his copy of Stanley's *Darkest Africa* to his son Stanley. His personal estate was divided into

34: The three children, Anna, Daisy and Stanley, photographed in Surbiton, c. 1894.

24ths. In Medina he left 1/24th to John Parsons, the father of his old schoolfriend; 1/24th went to the Cemetery Fund in Medina, where his family was buried; and 1/24th and '[his] pictures at that place' to the First Presbyterian Church. 1/24th each was bequeathed to the Edinburgh Medical Mission, the Presbyterian Mission Society and the North African Mission of Hope House in Tangier. Henry George received 1/24th and so did Theodore Barrett. Lina was given 1/12th (2/24ths), his children 3/24ths each, and Olive 1/6th. Finally, he gave 1/24th to be divided among all of his employees, a recognition of their contribution to the success of the firm.

Burroughs directed his executors that, as soon after his decease as they could, they should close his interest in the business and add the money to his residual estate. He could not have imagined how long that process would take. The partnership agreement specified that Wellcome, as surviving partner, was entitled to purchase Burroughs's interest, detailing the way in which this was to happen. Crucially for Wellcome, this was his legal right. He was required to pay on demand Burroughs's share in the profits calculated on the average profits of the last three years and to pay Burroughs's share of the goodwill in the business, also calculated on the basis of the annual profits for the last three years.[6]

Immediately an issue arose over access to Burroughs's papers. Wellcome told Olive that he could not hand them over to anyone without authority from Burroughs's executors, and, as there were several wills, it was uncertain who the executors were. As if that were not enough, on 18 February Lina received a private letter from J. Collett Smith, Burroughs's assistant at the firm, recounting interesting events during the previous week. Collett Smith explained how he had hoped to be 'serviceable' to Mrs Burroughs and Lina but unfortunately could do very little. He had expected, 'as he knew more of Mr Burroughs' personal matters than anyone else', that he should have been allowed to put Burroughs's papers in order. Evidently Sudlow thought so too, as he had instructed both Collett Smith and Kirby to take this matter in hand. On the morning of Monday 11th, however, Wellcome declared that nothing in Burroughs's office must be touched, as he personally was responsible to the executors and he wished to give special instructions regarding scheduling the effects. Collett Smith therefore waited, and on Friday was informed that Kirby alone was to do the work. On 18th he found Burroughs's office stripped of all his papers and correspondence and was told they had been moved to Wellcome's office, where, he reported to Olive, Kirby and another clerk were drawing up a schedule.

Collett Smith commented that, while Kirby was better acquainted with monetary transactions than he, 'I have a good memory & a fair knowledge of what Mr Burroughs had in his room, & I place myself at the disposal of Mrs Burroughs, yourself [Lina] & the executors at any time. I have managed to keep Mr Burroughs' letter book locked up in my desk, as I may want it for some addresses.' This letter displayed a courageous loyalty and reflected Collett Smith's suspicions about Wellcome's motives.

Any private papers would have formed part of Burroughs's estate, and retention of them, or at least denial of access to them, would, on the face of it, seem utterly unreasonable. Although the partners had private and business letter books, business and private correspondence was to some extent intermingled, which probably gave Wellcome room to retain all, read much that would have been private, and manoeuvre for time.

Olive was increasingly concerned about the integrity of Burroughs's papers and other documents at Snow Hill and Dartford. When she learnt of Collett Smith's story she wrote to her solicitor Humphreys that she had good reason for believing that he should at once demand possession of all her husband's letters, deeds, securities books and other documents. She informed Wellcome of her instruction to Humphreys, to which Wellcome replied:

> Dear Madam [no longer 'Dear Mrs Burroughs'!],
>
> Your favour of March 4 is duly received. As I informed you in my letter of February 12 … I have placed all matters connected with Mr Burroughs' affairs in the hands of my solicitors, Messrs Markby Stewart & Co., who, as I then informed you, will deliver over the papers etc to any properly authorised person, and they have my instructions to render every facility to the Executors which they can do consistently. Yrs truly.

The next day Wellcome wrote a more measured letter: he had prepared a very complete and comprehensive schedule of Burroughs's important papers in order to facilitate matters for the executors. This schedule was with Markby, Stewart & Co., who would hand it to her solicitors upon request. In case there should be any delay in the probate of the will, and should she need funds for her immediate requirements, he would be very pleased to make advances as a personal loan. 'As you will understand', he added, 'it will be impossible for me to make any payment [relating to

the business] until the Court has duly approved the will and empowered
the Executors to act.' Olive replied that she was glad that his position was
not entirely antagonistic as she had been led to suppose, commenting:

> In this letter you express your willingness to do all you can to
> facilitate the work of the executors and you also speak of your
> deep regret and your desire to show your respect for the memory
> of your late partner. This desire can best be expressed if you will
> allow me to the opinion, by following out his ideas of a stock
> company – with of course such modifications as we can mutually
> agree upon. Will you let me have your opinions upon the subject.

She signed off: 'Thank you – I am not in need of friends. Believe me,
Yours very truly, O.C. Burroughs.' With customary sharpness, Olive had
spelt out the crux of the issue facing the firm, writing clearly and politely
about the crucial matter that had concerned her husband in his final
years. Wellcome immediately responded that he was unable to adopt or
discuss the question of a stock company or do other than comply with
the terms of the partnership agreement made between Burroughs and
himself – 'the contingency of the death of either of the partners was
fully foreseen and therein amply provided for. The terms of the deed are
definite and will be carried out in every detail.'

Changing tack, Wellcome subsequently declared that the will had to
be *proved* before any papers could be handed over. When Olive learnt of
these further delays, and his refusal to allow any employees well known
to Burroughs to assist in the investigation of the papers excepting
through Markby & Co., her attitude hardened.

In mid-March Wellcome informed Olive that he had sent her a sealed
package of Burroughs's personal private letters which had been sorted
from the firm's papers and from personal papers which had a business
or monetary character. 'These I think ought to go to you direct and not
pass through the hands of any outside parties.' On receipt of this Olive
replied frostily:

> Dear Sir, I am in receipt of yours of 14th [March] in regard
> to Mr Burroughs private letters – I beg to say that had this
> delicacy been shown on 6th February last I should indeed
> have appreciated it and been able to thank you – Letters that
> have passed through your hands and those of your solicitors
> would have been perfectly safe with the gentlemen who are
> authorized to receive my husband's papers. I am sir, Yours
> truly, Mrs S.M. Burroughs.

Olive's dislike of Wellcome now was such that, on the same day she wrote this letter, and on receiving a picture of Burroughs from the firm, she wrote to Sudlow that she did not know whom to thank for it, but would he kindly pass on her thanks, 'that is supposing it is not your chief' – for she 'could not keep it' if this was the case. Growing friction was reflected in Wellcome's insistence that communication be conducted only through solicitors, distancing himself from both Olive and Dr Clark, who had also tried to intervene. While he was naturally cautious, it was also the case that this strategy gave Wellcome more time to sort out his own affairs and arrange finances for his purchase of Burroughs's interest in the firm.

Humphreys had sent Olive the partnership agreement very soon after Burroughs's death, and on reading it she probably assumed that Wellcome had insufficient finance to purchase outright her husband's three-quarters share in the firm. She may well have reasoned that his only option in raising finances would be to convert it into a joint stock company and thereby share ownership with others; in this she was to be sorely mistaken. Wellcome later complained that, from the moment of Burroughs's death, the executors had persistently endeavoured to get the business turned into a joint stock company but that he had no intention of doing so. He wanted sole control and had received abundant offers of loans from friends and sound financial houses and had sufficient collateral to enable him to achieve this. 'These particulars', he wrote to a business friend, 'I cannot make public as I do not deem it necessary to take the public into my confidence ... our progressive policy and executive direction which was always in my hands will remain the same ... I regard our business as in its infancy.'[7]

As the year moved on, delays in getting access to information continued. Strongly worded solicitors' letters were exchanged, while at Snow Hill and Dartford Burroughs's accountants (Sears, Hasluck & Co.), in their attempts to value the business, were met with hostility and were treated like spies. Wellcome meanwhile was enjoying the freedom offered by the death of his partner. In a letter to Frank Wellcome he expressed his sadness at Burroughs's death but made it clear that now he felt much better in himself and saw a rosy future:

> Notwithstanding the serious friction and strained relations which continued up to the date of Mr Burroughs' death – this tragic ending of a 15 years partnership in a business without parallel in the business history of London – came as a terrible shock to me and my heart went back to the happy times when he and I were bosom friends – the intervening time of strife

I desire to forget and it only adds the more pain and sorrow when I contemplate the sad events. My health and strength will improve and life and work will be easier for me for the future – I feel that a great load has been lifted but alas in what a sad and unforeseen way.[8]

Charles Humphreys sought counsel's opinion on a number of issues relating to the partnership agreement and executors' rights. When he tried to arrange an additional advance payment to Olive from the firm's account at City Bank, Wellcome reiterated that any request would have to be channelled through their solicitors. Wellcome told the bank manager that, although he had the right to advance monies to Mrs Burroughs, she could not reasonably expect any undertaking or assurance from himself: privately he commented that the manager had no right to expect one.[9] And so a convoluted arrangement meant that Humphreys had to ask Markby to get Wellcome to instruct the bank to make payments due under the terms of the will once probate was obtained. 'We forbear making any comment upon Mr Wellcome's conduct,' Humphreys said to Olive.[10]

Probate was granted two months after Burroughs's death.[11] Only now was Olive able to receive some belongings from Snow Hill and Dartford, not even having been notified of the existence of some of them until early April. One of the things that had worried her was the whereabouts of her husband's gold watch. Kirby now sent it, along with Burroughs's copy letter book. Olive, wary of being treated badly and denied access, asked Humphreys to write to Markby about her husband's effects at Dartford and for a date when she could itemise them and have them valued there, as this would save her unnecessary time and delay. 'I wish to get from [Markby] a distinct refusal to allow me to do this – for future use.'[12]

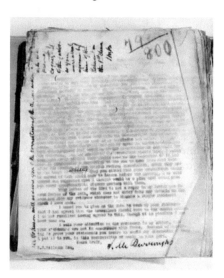

35: Burroughs's personal letter book, sadly so badly water damaged it is virtually illegible.

By mid-April Humphreys had occasion to write to Markby complaining of the manner in which

Olive was treated, presumably when collecting some items. They responded that her complaints were unreasonable and unfounded, and in turn requested her key to the safe deposit box in Chancery Lane which contained the deeds of Phoenix Mills (the other key to the box being held by Wellcome). This, Humphreys advised her, should not be done; possession of the deeds was seen as fundamental in forcing Wellcome to come to a settlement. In acquiring the freehold to the Dartford Mills in 1888, Burroughs had quite rightly anticipated that expansion of manufacturing was essential for the firm's prosperity: with the adaptations and additional changes, the mill site was now not only extremely valuable but essential to the business.

Wellcome, aware that finalising the accounts would not be swift, sent Olive a cheque for £6,000 in part payment on account, and he then made quarterly payments on interest from the firm's profits.[13] After her accountants had checked the books, they remarked on the 'considerable lack of harmony and want of confidence between the partners' evinced before and after the execution of the deed of partnership, not only about the business in general but particularly with reference to accounts. They also uncovered the extraordinary fact that the firm's accounts had never been audited by an independent chartered accountant, even though this was a requirement under the partnership agreement, a fact which Humphreys found 'very startling'.[14] They commented on obstructions to their work, such as Wellcome's insistence that all enquiries should be made in writing through his solicitors. They reckoned that Olive was due £124,136, whereas Wellcome's accountants, Messrs Kemp, thought that the sum was £113,099. As if this were not enough, Humphreys considered that Burroughs's loans to the firm would be withdrawn and a claim made for payment of the amount with interest. Having obtained counsel's opinion, they thought that it would be prudent to get the directions of a judge for a ruling by the court.

Olive, angry at the time her solicitors were taking to achieve anything, and infuriated by the firm's Mr Thompson, 'whose slow laboured ways drive an American to the point of distraction', asked Humphreys:

> If you have anyone who can show energy and life – can compete with Mr Stewart [Wellcome's solicitor] – I should like you to produce the man and put him in charge of these affairs ... Now the time has come for action. I am a woman – without business or legal training – I feel strongly my limitations but at the same time I am not content to take any less consideration than a man in the same position and with the same knowledge

would have. I am trying to understand and I know I am not
very dull of comprehension ... What I wish to say is this – if I
am being put off because I am a woman – I should like at once
to have Mr Barrett over here and hand to him some of the
responsibility which I am no longer willing or able to assume
under the present conditions.[15]

One distraction of Charles Humphreys at this time was Oscar Wilde,
for whom he was acting in his celebrated court case against the marquess
of Queensberry: Olive was understandably worried that this case had
taken his attention away from her own affairs. She expressed a commonly
held view: 'I hope your client Wilde will win for your sake – but a few
years imprisonment were it for no greater crime than the matter and
irresponsible silliness which he has exhibited should do him no harm.'[16]

In one letter to her solicitors Olive used a strong analogy, declaring
that, where medical etiquette had been the cause of her husband's
'hurried' death, she now considered 'legal professional etiquette will
complete the ruin of what he left behind.' She had wired Humphreys
from Monte Carlo and always felt they had had plenty of time to secure
the private papers against intrusion – had they done so, all the delays in
proving of the will could have been avoided.

By August, Olive's frustration was greater than ever; Humphreys was
doing all he could to take matters forward, but 'everything seems to be
waiting for Mr Wellcome's attention.' While Wellcome always played
his hand cautiously, certain of his actions are hard to view as anything
other than obstructive and unnecessarily harsh. Olive formed the
opinion that he was 'a deeply crafty man and has left no annoying thing
undone, while on the surface & for all the world a pattern of all that
is noble & he has some very clever lawyers – not scrupulously honest
ones – but noted for their sharp practice.'[17] Disputes over the dates at
which Wellcome should make further payments to Olive, and the
amount of such payments, led to Humphreys, confident now of his own
figures, serving notice on Wellcome for a portion of the money due.[18] If
there was no reply by a specified date they would not hesitate to take out
a writ, and indeed this they did in September. Wellcome responded with
a counter-claim for an order to give him sole ownership possession and
control of the mills and all other assets of the partnership.[19]

Humphreys's writ was issued before the tragic news emerged in
late September that Kirby, the firm's assistant general manager, had
been killed in a gas explosion at his home. Along with Sudlow, Kirby
had been appointed by Burroughs in 1879 before Wellcome came to
England. The news upset Wellcome deeply. Yet two years later, when

Kirby's widow found herself in financial difficulties, it was Olive, not Wellcome, to whom she turned for financial assistance, reminding her of her husband's service in dealing with Burroughs's papers after his death. Charles Humphreys noted that, although Kirby did not appear to have treated Olive very courteously at that time, Wellcome might have compelled Kirby to act as he did, and there could be no doubt that Kirby had helped in winding up Burroughs's affairs. He added: 'Mr Wellcome acted towards you in a most reprehensible manner which does not engender sympathy or kindness towards those who had to carry out his instructions.'[20]

It was now November, and matters were indeed far from settled. That month Charles Humphreys advised Olive that his firm had recently had some very 'controversial correspondence' with Markby & Co. as to the investigation of the partnership books, which would be copied and sent to her. He noted that Wellcome evidently did not feel disposed to abide by the views of his solicitors or of his accountants, but he thought things were going 'a bit more smoothly now that Wellcome has been given to understand that he must either submit to the solicitors' first requirements or have an application made against him in Court.'[21]

On 21 January, nearly a year after Burroughs's death, Humphreys filed a further affidavit over Wellcome's failure to disclose some key correspondence between him and his partner.[22] The affidavit led to the uncovering of a document from Wellcome to Burroughs, dated 18 December 1891, which revealed that a larger sum was due from the firm to Burroughs in respect of a loan.[23] Humphreys also reported that Wellcome was having difficulty in obtaining business finance, as Olive had declined to allow him possession of the mill deeds, which he could have used as security for a loan.[24] By now Olive was fast losing confidence in her lawyers and felt that most of the estate business was being delegated to subordinates in whose hands the case would fail. Echoing a sentiment about lawyers familiar to us today, she complained that they sent her lots of superfluous letters saying nothing: Foley commented that 'nothing short of a discharge of dynamite' would get things going. Perhaps, Olive wondered, she should have changed her solicitors when Burroughs died? But she had been abroad, too far from England to have the advice of friends when having to make her decision. She noted that, had her actions not been based on the judgement of a sound businessman (undoubtedly Foley), some of her investments would have been lost through the ineptitude of Humphreys.[25]

After months of wrangling by both parties, a memorandum of agreement and a court order in May 1896 set out settlement terms. Wellcome was to pay £40,000 for the mills on receipt of the title deeds.

Foley thought this settlement 'very favourable' to Olive – 'I am sure your firmness has been the one thing that has finally brought Mr Wellcome to his senses' – and Gardner also considered Wellcome's offer a good one.[26] Yet Humphreys now inadvisedly told Olive to retain the title deeds until all questions had been settled by an arbitrator, on the basis that they had a very strong suspicion that 'Mr Wellcome's anxiety to obtain possession of the Phoenix Mills deeds is to make use of the same in connection with some latent project or scheme which he has in mind and does not care to divulge and so long as the deeds are kept back it will force him to have the Arbitration closed as soon as possible.'[27] With some justification, it was Wellcome's turn to say that Olive's solicitors were stalling, albeit for reasons of strategy.

The arbitrator, F. Whinney, reported in October 1896, and an award in Olive's favour was made in the High Court of Justice.[28] Yet, following this, counsel endorsed an application to the court to rectify the Whinney award, and for some reason Olive's accountant fully approved of this.[29] When Foley subsequently looked over the points filed by the accountant before the arbitrator, he was very surprised that her solicitors had permitted the *whole* of the amount due to Mr Burroughs to become a matter of arbitration, when only about a couple of thousand pounds was in dispute. 'This conduct I call extraordinary … nothing less. It was probably too late to remedy this step.'[30] Henceforth, Olive decided to be more personally involved in directing the work of her lawyers.

Many issues were still to be resolved. In March 1897 Olive learnt that the award was to be set aside, as Whinney had exceeded his powers, and a new order dated 29 June 1897 was agreed based on a revised payment by Wellcome on or before 6 December 1897.[31] Lina received news of the legal battles and commented to Olive: 'You wrote that Wellcome was trying to avoid payment of £6,000 interest. How did that come out? I cannot think of him without the most intense feeling for all he did to make dear Mainville's life unhappy.'[32]

In July 1897, when definitive figures had been settled, Burroughs's will was finally proved at over £125,000; regarded as a fortune then, it would be worth several million pounds today.[33] Some of the legatees were impatient about the delay in receiving their bequest. To complicate matters, a few of these were unclear, in particular that to the Presbyterian Mission Society.[34] When counsel's opinion was again sought, the advice was that Burroughs's intentions could not be challenged. Foley, believing that an English court could delay things for a very long time, and critical of Humphreys for not getting court advice earlier, recommended a partial distribution of £3,000 to the larger legatees whose bequest was not in question.[35] So Olive gave partial payment to some and started identifying employees of the firm at the time of Burroughs's death, placing adverts in major newspapers. It was August 1898 when counsel finally clarified the legatees' position, and only in November 1901 was final payment made to them. Each employee received 6 guineas.[36]

Many people wrote grateful letters to Olive, describing Burroughs as the best and kindest of employers: some told of their unhappiness with the new regime, and a number no longer worked at the firm. One employee had been informed that his services were no longer required, as Wellcome 'would not participate in any more Exhibitions ... It is Mr Wellcome's only object to get rid of all men who worked with Mr Burroughs.' He added that he had been at the 1883 World's Fair in Chicago and informed Burroughs about Wellcome's removal of papers from the stand (presumably those deemed political). 'This, with other things, go to show that it is nothing but spite and I happen to know the whole business about him ... I thought I would like to tell you how Mr Wellcome treats a man after ten years.'[37] Another said that he was pleased to be out of the firm, as 'when Mr Burroughs went the place was not worth being in.'[38]

Olive had hoped that the estate would be completely settled by the end of 1898, but the legal process ground on, with the Inland Revenue adding to the complications. 'Can't you dig a pit for that Wellcome in the houses of Surbiton and lure him into it?' one of her friends commented.[39] It was not until April 1899 that the conveyance of Phoenix Mills to Wellcome took place.[40] Nearly six years after Burroughs's death, Olive was still dealing with 'no end of red tape', and Foley noted that, if he referred matters relating to the American side of the executorship to Humphreys, he was merely asked more questions. He got far more satisfactory answers from Olive than from her solicitors.[41]

Numerous people had owed Burroughs money, and their bonds, bills and promissory notes, with interest, totalled £7,320.[42] Some shares were held as security for debts owed to him, notably in America by Carl Jackson, his old schoolfriend from Medina. 'My husband was a man of large charity,' Olive wrote; 'he gave constantly and generously to every good cause – not only did he give whenever he could but I think no friend requiring a loan was ever sent away unsatisfied.' She found the business of collecting the loans a painful one.[43] In some cases she had to take legal action against her husband's old friends, explaining that it was her legal duty as an executor to do so. 'I am not acting for myself but for the over four hundred people who are entitled to share in this money.'[44] De Giovanni, whose employment had been a cause of disagreement between

Burroughs and Wellcome, owed c.$500.[45] Ernest Hart, Burroughs's friend, also owed a very great deal, and Olive ultimately resorted to arbitration to recover the money from him.[46] Burroughs's cousin Silas Hood was especially difficult: he was not a beneficiary and requested that Olive ask the legatees to give him some of their share. Burroughs had assumed that he was a wealthy farmer, not in need of any money, and Olive pointed out to him that her husband had other relatives on his mother's side who might as justly claim a share of his money. At the same time she received begging letters and was asked for loans from former employees, acquaintances and old friends who had fallen on hard times. Even her solicitor, Edwin Woodhead, and Theodore Barrett applied to her for loans. It must have been a seemingly endless and disheartening task, but she was judicious and firm and certainly not a soft touch.

Olive had come under pressure from Lina to move Burroughs's body to America, and the Boxwood Cemetery in Medina urged his reburial there alongside his family. She considered the matter and obtained a quotation from the undertakers in Monte Carlo. Foley noted that it had not been practicable to carry out Burroughs's wishes regarding his funeral when he died and advised that, if Olive decided to move his remains, she should do so before the estate was settled, otherwise the cost of removal would be payable from her own pocket. He picked up on her resentment of Lina, suggesting that possibly, as Olive had intimated, Lina had looked upon herself as the person most affected by Burroughs's death. This might be explained, if not excused, since brother and sister were particularly close, having grown up together without the individual care of their father and mother. 'They were in a peculiar way, drawn together. I think Mrs Riggs is a perfectly kind-hearted woman, and I know you think so – indeed you admitted in every way all her good qualities – but still I think it is quite possible that in speaking of the loss of Mainville she has too much emphasized her own loss.'[47] Uncertain now where she would live, but still regularly going abroad to Switzerland every August, Olive postponed a decision on whether to move Burroughs's body. John Parsons may well have influenced her by pointing out that Burroughs had not wished to be in a vault, that the family vault at Medina was full, and that perhaps if Olive remained in Europe she would feel nearer his grave.[48] Olive hated the long sea voyage to America and, indeed, never returned there after her husband's death, although initially she had expected to visit again. Lina came round to Olive's wish that her brother's body should remain where it was, 'particularly in view of the beautiful spot where he now lies.' His grave is still to be found in Monte Carlo.[49]

On the third anniversary of her husband's death Olive had laid aside her veil. Friends were worried the toll her responsibilities had taken. 'Is this not the year of your release from Law, Lawyers and Lepers (a fine firm they are) or have you still another year of conflict with those evil powers?', one had written, noting that, in spite of all the problems, Olive had retained her 'sweetness ... You are a most wonderful woman.'[50] Another trusted that Olive's bitter disappointments 'would not take the sunshine from her soul'.[51] The worry of finalising affairs undoubtedly affected her health, and she admitted that she hoped to bounce back when the burden of anxiety and trouble lifted a little. Her eyes gave her trouble, and she suffered from painful rheumatism.

All this time Olive was sorting out a further range of financial and legal issues, many of which needed legal advice. She moved out of Durrington Lodge in the autumn of 1895 and sold at auction Burroughs's furniture, books and items such as wine.[52] After staying in Bournemouth, she purchased a house of her own, 'Dunrobin', in Lovelace Road, Surbiton, in 1898. This was the first house she had owned, as the family had always rented, and she filled it with the spoils of her travels. Other property to be dealt with included land Burroughs had rented near Dartford so that his employees could play football. More problematic were his shares in a number of companies overseas, many of which were run by his friends.[53]

Although she was a wealthy widow, Olive's last years were far from easy. Increasingly crippled by rheumatism and gout, she moved to Switzerland for the sake of her health: there are touching drawings by her daughter Daisy depicting her bent double using crutches. She died at Territet, Montreux, on 21 October 1905 at the comparatively young age of 54 and is buried with Burroughs in Monte Carlo. Following her marriage she sacrificed her own career, and her life had been consumed in supporting Burroughs as a much loved and respected wife and mother. After his death she did all in her power to bring about what she knew he would have wanted for the firm and its employees. Burroughs would have been immensely proud of her. She stands out as a woman battling against the deeply entrenched masculine professional world of Victorian Britain. As is so often the case with the wives of successful driven men, her own role has been overlooked.

Postscript

All three children inherited a great deal of money from Olive, but their fortunes were soon spent. Stanley went to live in America and became a successful lawyer; he married Elise Gleason, with whom he had three children – Stuart, Olive and Elise. Anna married Sidney Stillwell and had three children – Richard, Suzanne and Stanley – and it was through Richard that the Burroughs papers, which have been used in writing this biography, came to the Wellcome Library in 1998. Frances Margaret (Daisy) married Leslie Williams and had one son, Stanley David, who changed his name to Burroughs.

Money raised by the Dartford 'Burroughs' Memorial Fund paid off the outstanding amount needed to clear the Livingstone Cottage Hospital of any financial obligations, and the men's ward was renamed the Burroughs Ward. The relief marble bust of Burroughs, which was presented to the hospital by Olive, is now located in the Wellcome Ward rather than the Burroughs Ward. The hospital was the only one in Dartford until 1913; it was extended in 1910 and a maternity wing opened in 1938. Mick Jagger and Keith Richards of the Rolling Stones were born there in 1943. Attempts to close what is locally viewed as the 'people's hospital' have been strongly resisted; it remains open as the Livingstone Community Hospital, providing care for the elderly.

The Burroughs Memorial Fund also raised £840 for a Burroughs Scholarship. Administered by the Royal Pharmaceutical Society, this established an annual grant for a suitably qualified pharmacist to work for 12 months in a research laboratory. In 1993 the scholarship was renamed the Wellcome Foundation Ltd/RPSGB Research Awards and continued with additional funding.

In April 1941 the BW&Co. building on Snow Hill was razed by bombing, which also severely damaged the City Temple, thereby destroying the stained-glass window, 'David Livingstone, the Apostle of

Africa', which Burroughs presented to the church in 1893, as well as the marble tablet in memory of Burroughs which had been installed near the pulpit by the employees of the firm.

In Medina, Burroughs had supported a number of religious and charitable institutions. The Boxwood Cemetery spent a large part of his bequest in setting out lawns and paths, and a chapel was erected to his memory which contains a fine Tiffany-style stained-glass window. It is still maintained to a high standard. The Presbyterian Church in Medina was able to install an extra floor. The family home, the gothic Burroughs mansion, was destroyed by a fire in 1916, and its site is now State Street Park.

Henry George received £4,000. He died before this sum could be given to him personally, but it enabled his widow to purchase the first house she had ever owned. George's son described Burroughs as his father's 'ardent single tax friend', but later biographies of George largely overlook Burroughs's role.

In 1901 Wellcome married Gwendoline Maud Syrie, daughter of the philanthropist Dr Thomas Barnardo, who was 26 years his junior. After a quarrel, and in spite of attempted mediation by mutual friends, including Dorothy Stanley, he utterly refused to have any contact with Syrie, and they divorced acrimoniously in 1916. In an echo of Wellcome's treatment of Olive, he refused to allow Syrie to discuss their situation with his friend Chune Fletcher (who had represented him in negotiations with Burroughs) and neglected to return many of her personal possessions to her. Their son Henry Mounteney (named after the explorer), born in 1903, had minor learning difficulties and was unsuited to running the firm. Syrie went on to another unhappy marriage with Somerset Maugham and became a successful interior designer. In his later years Wellcome became a withdrawn and lonely figure.

Following Burroughs's death, Wellcome's collecting mania became more obsessive and gradually dominated his life: he financed important archaeological excavations in Palestine and Sudan and spent lavishly on acquiring objects, creating one of the largest private collections of artefacts, pictures, books and manuscripts in the world. Plans for a Museum of Medical History commenced around 1903, although it did not open until 1913. Wellcome's inability to collaborate and trust others, taking on too much and wanting to reserve honours for himself, ultimately meant that his museum plans failed. His collection was eventually housed in the Wellcome Research Institution, constructed in 1931–2 at 183–93 Euston Road, now the Wellcome Building. The library and parts of the collection remain there, and much else can be found in the Science Museum, London; other items – duplicates or not deemed to be of historical medical importance – were distributed worldwide by his trustees. He founded many other institutions: the Wellcome Chemical Research Laboratories (1896), with F.B. Power as director; the Wellcome Physiological Research Laboratories (1899); the Wellcome Tropical Research Laboratories, at Khartoum (1903); and the Wellcome Bureau of Scientific Research (1913).

Wellcome wisely retained the firm's name of Burroughs, Wellcome & Co. after his partner's death, appreciating its value as a very well-known brand name. The name Burroughs was dropped only in 1924. Never keen on profit-sharing or a joint stock company, Wellcome retained sole ownership. Profit-sharing was abandoned four years after Burroughs's death. In the late 1890s there was a rapid deterioration in relations between the firm and the pharmaceutical trade which resulted in bad feeling between Wellcome and the local chemists over pricing of the firm's goods. In 1905 he delegated responsibility of the firm to his general manager, George Pearson (who was renowned for his 'parsimony'), and spent much of his time travelling and collecting, being less concerned about the company's progressiveness. In 1924 he finally incorporated his business as the Wellcome Foundation Ltd.

Wellcome became a British citizen in 1910, was knighted in 1932 and died in 1936. Under the terms of his will he created a charity to advance medical research and history. His trustees (who were advised to avoid appointing 'persons of rash and speculative tendencies') held all the shares in the Wellcome Foundation, and after his death they spent much time defining their responsibilities. The Wellcome Trust, the charitable arm, expanded, while the Wellcome Foundation continued with its commercial role: until the 1980s, the Wellcome Trust remained the only shareholder of the Wellcome Foundation. However, in 1986 the Wellcome Foundation was floated on the stock market as a public company under a new name, Wellcome plc, and the trust sold a quarter of its holdings in the company. This was followed by a second share sale in 1992. Then, in 1995, the Wellcome Trust sold its remaining interest in Wellcome plc to Glaxo plc. This led to the creation of Glaxo Wellcome plc, which merged with SmithKlineBeecham in 2000 to create GlaxoSmithKline. The name Wellcome therefore no longer exists in the pharmaceutical industry.

The Wellcome Trust is now one of the wealthiest medical charities in the world, funding biomedical research to improve human and animal research and supporting the public understanding of science. Its investment portfolio in 2020 was worth £29.1 billion.

Burroughs's name is now remembered through the Burroughs Room in the Wellcome Building, so named in 1998, and by the Burroughs Wellcome Fund in America, founded in 1955; it received a grant from the Wellcome Trust in 1993. A non-profit medical research organisation, it grants more than $40 million each year to research, focusing on infectious disease, biomedical science and other health-related fields. A dwindling number of people remember the name of the firm Burroughs, Wellcome & Co. or know of his contribution to Dartford and the pharmaceutical industry. It is hoped that this book will help bring him back into the public's consciousness.

Appendix: Pharmacy and Change

Traditional folk medicine relied on the administration of herbal remedies, and in the mid-19th century countless powders, mixtures, elixirs, tinctures and pills were sold with claims for miraculous cures. But few of the plant-based drugs in use in the early 19th century helped aid recovery, the most therapeutically effective being digoxin (from foxglove), quinine (from cinchona bark) and morphine (from the opium poppy). However, by that time chemists were able to extract and concentrate traditional plant-based remedies – beginning to isolate the active constituents and discovering how they worked; by 1840 practically all the important active plant principles were isolated.

While minor symptoms such as headaches, coughs and constipation might be relieved, serious illnesses such as gout, syphilis and heart disease, and many others, including tuberculosis, typhoid, cholera and pneumonia, were not treatable despite claims to the contrary. Although most medicines were harmless or totally useless, some contained dangerous ingredients – for instance, cocaine or morphine. One common ingredient was alcohol: it could make up 40% of the content of some drugs, especially remedies called 'bitters', and many temperance followers were unaware of their alcohol consumption. Many wrongly attributed cures to their medicines when in fact relief, if it came, was simply from the passage of time, nature and its healing power, and the placebo effect.

In 19th-century America, as in Britain, most so-called patent medicines were not in fact patented, and manufacturers tried to protect their products by using trademarks and copyrighting literature and labels. 'Letters patent' were granted to many compound medicines – where individual ingredients are mixed together (for instance, Hooper's Female Pills) – but many other well-established proprietary medicines (for example, Godfrey's Cordial and Daffy's Elixir) were not patented. Gradually the term 'patent medicines' came to be applied to all proprietary or trademarked remedies intended for self-medication. Some preparations were claimed to be based on ancient discoveries by 'native tribes', hence the success of the Kickapoo Indian Medicine Company. Travelling quacks attracted enormous crowds to watch their tricks, and 'quack' or 'patent medicines' became very popular in the absence of effective cures and remedies from the medical profession.

With the spread of literacy and a newspaper-reading public, advertising created huge sale opportunities. Indeed, manufacturers of patent medicine were trailblazers of new methods of advertising in America, not only using advertisements backed up with testimonials but producing literature that could be kept, including almanacs, calendars and medical guides for the home. The annual budget of the manufacturers who pioneered the celebrated Lydia Pinkham's Vegetable Compound at the end of the century was around $1 million. So important was patent medicine advertising to the finances of newspapers that it made many reluctant to expose or criticise the malpractices of manufacturers. There were many critics of the patent medicine trade in America and the UK, but it was hard to challenge the system in a laissez-faire economy. Moreover, pharmacists and doctors were swayed in their turn by self-interest, making money from selling useless patent medicines yet blaming each other for facilitating the trade. The pharmacists argued that, if they did not sell the remedies, the public would buy from other sources, such as the grocer, fancy-dealer or confectionery store.

Until the 1860s most common medicines had been made from basic remedies such as quinine sulphate, opium powders or calomel and using simple processes (crushing, drying, extracting and distilling). Modest equipment – an open furnace, boiler, jacketed copper pan, filter press and drying room – was employed: dried, crushed and powdered cloves produced an anaesthetic; juice from belladonna, extracted and distilled to concentrate, was used as a heart stimulant. Drugs and medicines were supplied to dispensing physicians and the public by apothecary shops and wholesale druggists, and very small firms might prepare bulk drugs based largely on botanicals, doing little or no research or development. During the century many of these expanded into manufacturing, some on quite a small scale, and by the 1850s the number of such firms was growing.

In America the Civil War created a demand for drugs when supplies from the British were cut off, and new remedies spread from the colonies. The pharmaceutical industry developed rapidly as a result. There was a need for chemicals that had previously been imported from England

and a necessity to manufacture domestically using new techniques to replace the chemicals. Large quantities of quality medicines were produced, many by newly established companies, although substandard drugs also found a market in the rush to supply the military. Patent medicines sold very well after the war, and an enormous number of new products came on the market. However, changes in therapy created demand for more specific drugs with smaller measured doses and standardised preparations. These were composed mainly from natural products derived from plants and salts made into pills, powders or syrups. New technology was used in the drying, grinding, mixing and distilling processes, and stronger extracts of more uniform strength could be produced.

From the 1870s a growing number of American firms introduced large-scale pharmaceutical manufacturing. At the same time they gradually distanced themselves from pharmacists, moving away from popular patent medicines, creating a new 'ethical' brand or category of reputable medicines. Often larger companies were not undertaking systematic research as we would understand it today so much as recombining accepted recipes into new products. Most of their profits still came from patent preparations and proprietary medicines, but at the same time the firms sought to be perceived as trusted producers of high-standard and reliable quality drugs.

Innovations in mechanisation, standardisation and reliable 'ethical medicines' in the production of drugs were essential elements in the establishment of several US firms, including Wyeths, Smith, Parke-Davis, E.R. Squibb, and Eli Lilly. Important among these innovations was the introduction of the compressed pill. In England in 1843, William Brockedon took out a patent for 'shaping pills, lozenges and black lead by pressure in dies': a small hand punch shaped the pill into a compressed tablet. Although the English failed to recognise its potential, the Americans did not, and advances by Jacob Dunton and Henry Bower led to the Wyeths' development of one of the first rotary machines to be used in the US: 'compressed powders and pills' largely replaced the powder or liquid form of medicines. Philadelphia dominated the pharmaceutical trade and training in pharmacy.

One of the salesmen employed by Wyeths in Philadelphia was Silas Burroughs, who stepped onto this rapidly changing pharmaceutical scene early in his life. His achievements were to make him a leader in the modern pharmaceutical industry.

Notes

Chapter 1: Father and Son

1. President of Senate, House of Representatives, on the death of SMB's father, 1860.
2. Although Medina is still called a village in the US, in the UK it would be considered a small town. In 1870 its population was 2,821.
3. A handwritten document in PP/SMB shows a family line of descent from a Jeremiah Burroughs (b. 1580) in Barnstaple, Devon, to a John Burroughs and on to a Benjamin (b. 1731) in Long Island, New York.
4. The name Mainville (sometimes spelt Maineville) can be traced in the family for two generations; its origins are obscure.
5. 1850 Federal Census for Orleans County: property valued at $36,540. This figure possibly includes the real estate owned by his wife Laura. When she died in 1854, he inherited more money.
6. *The Bucktail* was started by him and appeared weekly from 1839; it folded after two or three years.
7. In 1837, 1850, 1851 and 1853; he also represented New York's 31st district in the House of Representatives. Burroughs changed to the Republican Party following disagreement over the Erie Canal issue, covered below.
8. A transcript from the Burroughs family Bible – from Cayuga County – states that he was born on 31 December; however all obituaries use the date 24 December. WA/Ref 82/1, box 38.
9. There is a mystery concerning another child of Burroughs snr. In 1894 SMB completed a medical report for insurance purposes, and in this he mentioned the existence of a half-brother (same father) who died, aged 15, from inflammation of the stomach. It is possible, despite the age difference, that this was the Tullius already mentioned.
10. There is a copy of an 1870s lithograph of the house in PP/SMB. The building was sold to S.A. Cook for $5,500 in 1889 (*Medina Tribune*, 17 Oct 1889) and was last owned by Ella H. Chamberlain. It was used as a smallpox quarantine home in 1903 when already in a poor state and demolished following a fire c.1915.

11. Variously estimated at from $2,000 to $4,000. Fires in Medina were very common, especially with the wooden buildings. The house was insured for $4,000: the damage to furniture and library, on which there was no insurance, amounted to some $1,000.

12. In the event of her husband's death, Laura's brother, Jacob, and sister were named as guardians of the children. As well as clothes and jewellery, her sister Emily inherited considerable stocks, bonds and mortgages to be held in trust for the three children, the income from which was to be used for their education until they were 21. Will dated 17 March 1854, witnessed by Isaac K. and Anna Burroughs.

13. SNB snr made a deal with the village – giving the land in return for the old school building that had previously been the arsenal. The academy was incorporated in 1850 by special act of legislature, therefore combining features of district and high school. Medina was the first village to make this advance and provide free secondary education in Orleans County; in 1851 it had 603 scholars.

14. Private tuition was more frequent in America than in England, especially for girls: it is not known if SMB's sisters attended the Free Academy.

15. Caroline lived in Canandaigua, Orleans County, and was the sister of John Richards, later to be SMB's friend in London.

16. *Medina Register*, 1 April 1897.

17. From 300 in 1823, and 700 in 1840, it tripled in the following 15 years. By 1888 a village census recorded 4,550.

18. When SMB snr was 40, the 1850 Census figures show his real estate estimated as $36,540.

19. Forest was cleared for the site, and bodies, including those of the Burroughs family, were moved from the old cemetery. The new cemetery was opened in 1850.

20. There used to be a marble slab on the building, commemorating Col. Silas M. Burroughs and Robert L. Hill, officers of the militia.

21. Obituary notice, *Lockport Advertiser and Democrat*, 1860.

22. Bloomer, *Life and Writings*.

23. The Committee of Indian Affairs, of which he was a member, dealt with around 800 white settlers on the Miami reserve in Kansas who petitioned that they had settled in 'good faith'. In rejecting the settlers' petition, it was noted that the rights of Native Americans and treaty obligations had been wholly disregarded in the western territories – indeed, that there was scarcely a reservation anywhere exempt from the trespasses of the whites.

24. Speech on the Kansas question, House of Representatives, 23 Feb 1858. See also *Remarks of Hon. Silas M. Burroughs, of Orleans, in Assembly, Jan. 25 and Feb. 13, 1850, on the Resolutions relating to the Subject of Slavery*.

25. The 1850 and 1900 Census for Washington, DC, gives Charlotte's age as 19 and 68, respectively, meaning that she was born in 1831/2. The couple married at the Church of the Epiphany, Washington, DC, on 11 May.

26. SMB jnr's medical examination report of 1894 curiously records his father's death as due to 'Blood poisoning. Nat[l] Hotel Disease'. PP/SMB.

27. Mr Hamlin's resolution and others in *Proceedings of Both Houses of Congress ... 1860*.

28. Newspapers and publications of his speeches reveal a man of great energy and eloquence, a forcible speaker, who 'always [secured] the attention of the Assembly whenever he rose to speak.' *New York Tribune*, 6 June 1860.

29. *Proceedings of Both Houses of Congress ... 1860*.

30. It was his father who acquired the first buggy or carriage, made for him in Medina. The horse and buggy period is noted as being from 1865, so SMB snr was in advance of his times in having one at this date.

31. *Medina Register*, 5 July 1883.

32. Hopkins was one of Medina's pioneers, a staunch Presbyterian and a merchant tailor.

33. SMB and his sisters are listed as living with Isaac in the 1860 Census, taken on 29 August, six weeks after their father's death. The house was purchased by Horatio N. Hewes for $2,805 and passed to one of his daughters in 1862.

34. In 1861 Isaac went to court to demand Jacob supply an inventory of Laura's estate, and there was even the threat of Jacob's imprisonment for non-compliance with the orders of the court. The documents suggest that Jacob Bennett was nothing like as well organised and businesslike as Isaac. The next year a surrogate was appointed, Jacob was ordered to hand over $140.15 for the children, and Isaac was named as their guardian (Jacob and his wife had, in theory, been named by Laura as guardians in the event of Silas Burroughs's death, but under the terms of Burroughs's will Isaac was named as guardian).

35. Report submitted by Isaac to Hon. E.R. Reynolds, Surrogate of the County of Orleans, 12 March 1866, that total liabilities of the estate were $12,232 and the whole amount of assets received from all sources $5,318. Funeral expenses were $121; the expense of settling the estate was $136. The costs were detailed by Isaac down to the last bushel of corn and sack of potatoes.

36. Samuel was the son of his aunt Elizabeth Burroughs. She was the eldest child of his grandparents David Burroughs and Louisa Kinne.

37. However, see Russell, *Hitching Post Days*, which notes that, soon after the death of SMB snr, Isaac left the mercantile business and looked after his deceased brother's estate; he never re-entered the retail business.

38. By the late 1860s Medina had developed into a town of substance with 3,500 inhabitants.

39. Healy was SMB's preceptor (that is, the practising physician/apothecary who had given him training) in his applications to the Pharmaceutical College in Philadelphia.
40. Coann also supported SMB's application to the Philadelphia College, certifying his two-year employ in his Albion drug store.
41. SMB's speech at firm outing, Southsea, *Dartford Chronicle*, 17 July 1891, PCB.
42. SMB kept in touch with the Coanns and the Barretts (who had been partners the last year he was with Coann). Coann tried to persuade him and Olive to move manufacturing to Albion. See SMB letter to OB, 6 May 1886, PP/SMB.
43. The 1870 Census (18 July) shows SMB at Isaac's home with Lina. The siblings are each listed as owning $300 in real estate and $8,000 of personal estate.
44. The Lockport Census of 1875 notes daily earnings of a printer at $2.25, monthly earnings of a teacher $100.

Chapter 2: On the Road

1. John Wyeth to SMB, 13 April 1881, PP/SMB.
2. The economic disorder of the 1812 war and its aftermath made it easier and cheaper to manufacture many products than import them. Several successful fine chemical manufacturers were established between 1818 and 1822.
3. Miller, *Timebends*. Other playwrights, including Eugene O'Neill, employed the salesman in their plays, representing, as he did, a nostalgic figure in American culture.
4. The census listed 7,262 in 1870 and 90,000 in 1900. However, the Society of Commercial Travellers estimated that there were 50,000 salesmen in the US in 1869. See Spears, *100 Years on the Road*.
5. Allen, *The Ambassadors of Commerce*.
6. Extract from 'Talk', 21 July 1893, on 'Medicine Making up to Date', WF/L/006.
7. In 1860 there were over 30,600 miles of track: by 1870 this had increased to 53,000 miles, and in the following ten years the figure nearly doubled, to reach 93,000 miles.
8. The *Guide Book* included information about the best hotels, populations, specific stores, money orders and express offices, listed towns on railroads or those easily accessible from them, and tabulated tariffs and stamp duties.
9. Eardley-Wilmot, *Our Journey in the Pacific*.
10. Pacific Coast Architecture Database, cited in 'Bella Union Hotel', https://en.wikipedia.org/wiki/Bella_Union_Hotel.
11. SMB to HSW, 21 March 1882, Allahabad, PP/SMB.

12. Photo held by the University of Sciences, Philadelphia. It was possibly taken in 1874, but the studio may have used the 1873 Vienna award design on this photo until 1876, so it cannot be assumed to have been taken that year. A letter to Olive Chase in 1882 mentions that he wrote to her when on horseback in Yosemite. PP/SMB.

13. Medical report, 1894, PP/SMB.

14. Over 1,200 indigenous drugs were exhibited by one company alone. The Committee on the Centennial Exhibition drew attention to the pharmaceutical exhibits by sending out a circular to all exhibitors from home and abroad.

15. John Wyeth & Brother Product list 1878. WF/M/PB/33/04/01.

16. Minutes of the 24th meeting of the APhA, which took place 12–20 Sept 1876.

17. It is likely that SMB met HSW around this time. HSW had graduated from the College of Pharmacy in 1874 and undoubtedly would have attended the APhA meetings in Philadelphia.

18. England, *The First Century of the Philadelphia College of Pharmacy*. HSW complained of his employer's treatment when he was apprenticed.

19. Anon, *57th Annual Announcement* states that, by 1877, 5,262 students had attended lectures and the degree of Graduate in Pharmacy had been conferred on 1,319 gentlemen, representing nearly every state in the Union, and a number from Canada, Cuba, and various parts of Europe.

20. HSW's thesis was on urethral suppositories.

21. 4 March 1872, John Wyeth to HSW, Chicago, WF/E/02/01/02/01.

22. Worthen, 'Joseph Price Remington', notes that the course normally took two years to complete, and C&T, p. 5, suggest that SMB attended part time for a longer period. However, I believe that SMB and HSW both attended for one year, given how the college operated by the 1870s and SMB's lengthy trips to California. The recording of their attendance was for one year only (HSW registered 1873 and qualified class of 1874; SMB qualified class of 1877).

23. Wyeth to Prof Bridges, 24 Feb 1877, quoted in C&T, p. 497, n. 14 (Archives of the University of the Sciences in Philadelphia). SMB's thesis title page gives that the duration of his studies was 'about 7 years'. In fact he had worked with Wyeths about this length of time, but far longer in pharmaceutical employment if one calculates his previous work in upstate New York.

24. Lectures covered the non-metallic elements and the classification of metals with their compounds, as well as organic chemistry, which considered all compounds of general or pharmaceutical interest, commercial impurities, and toxicological relations.

25. 1871 questions.

26. WF/E/02/02/01.

27. William Brockedon, FRS (1787–1854), who in 1843 patented 'a mode of manufacturing pills and medicated lozenges by causing the materials, when in a state of powder, granulation, or dust, by pressure in dies, so as to solidify the same.' This was the first major breakthrough in the history of tablet-making. See Wilkinson, 'William Brockedon, FRS'.
28. *C&D*, 21 Dec 1895, p. 897. SMB may possibly have received commission as well. When HSW had been offered a post by the firm in 1872, Wyeths had told him that they would not engage him unless he stayed for two years; they would pay $200 the first year and $300 the second, and $250–$350 and $450 if he stayed for three years.
29. SMB to HSW, 21 March 1882, boasting: 'When I first went to San Francisco I took or had sent out to me $2500 worth of goods which I had no difficulty in selling right off and the Drs began prescribing them the day they were distributed.'
30. Wyeths to SMB, 13 April 1881, WF/E/02/01/02/05.
31. See obituary of SMB by John Wyeth, PP/SMB.
32. SMB to Robert Page, Cham, Switzerland, 17 Sept 1894. This letter goes into more details of SMB's and the firm's dealings with Frank and John Wyeth.

Chapter 3: London and S.M. Burroughs & Co.

1. SMB to John Wyeth, June 1878.
2. Church, 'Trust, Burroughs Wellcome & Co.'.
3. Richards, *With John Bull and Jonathan*, p. 175.
4. HSW's letter to editor on 'British Injustice', *C&D*, 11 Jan 1896, p. 63.
5. Richards, *With John Bull and Jonathan*, pp. 76–7. Richards was president of the American Society in London, 1901–01.
6. 1 April 1878. SMB covenanted to pay Wyeths the full amount on receipt of their goods and supply statements every 30 days. The expenses for the agency were to be decided equally between the parties, but SMB agreed not to charge for his own time, office rent or any personal expenses except when travelling in the interest of the agency. Every 90 days he would calculate sales expenses, profits and losses and deduct money for reimbursement, plus half of net profits, and remit the balance to Wyeths. He also promised to 'unite with him one person as partner or assistant in the Agency who would give his time and services without charge to Wyeth, personal expenses excepted, when travelling in the interest of the Agency.' Any partner of SMB's was to have the right to engage in business and accept other agencies, and the agreement was to continue in force so long as Wyeths continued to conduct their business and so long as SMB continued to act as their agent. SMB deposited with Wyeths a sum of money to cover the cost of the first invoice and agreed that he would deposit from time to time additional sums to meet future

orders or would accompany orders with cash. They in return would give 6% on half the monies deposited or advanced on the goods until SMB had received this said amount from receipts of sales of goods at the quarterly settlements. WF/E/02/01/02/5.

7. SMB to Wyeths, 6 June 1878 and July 1878, WF/E/02/01/02/05.
8. J.W. Joplis reminiscences, WF/02/02/33, Box 76.
9. The first price list, issued May 1878, WF, Box 112.
10. Small London notebook, PP/SMB.
11. Sometimes Kelley was spelt without an e. He registered as owner of Nubian spelling with an e.
12. C&T, p. 10. In 1896 there was an estimated profit margin of five times the manufacturing cost; C&T, p. 165. According to Church, 'The British Market for Medicine', pp. 291–2, it was one of the strongest international brands until the 1930s. Church considered that SMB was extremely manipulative and was hugely resented by the inventor of Kepler (email to author, 6 Jan 2004).
13. SMB to Wyeth, 13 & 19 June 1878, WA LB35.
14. Sudlow, Kirby and Collett Smith all became masons (which was a bond shared with HSW, a keen mason).
15. J.M. Richards to 'Bro Sudlow', reminiscences, 15 Aug 1907, WF/02/02/33.
16. He had been advised to contact American medical gentlemen of Paris as soon as possible, but had been too busy to get there earlier. SMB asked his fellow PCP student Edward Lindewald (who was based at the American Bureau at the fair) to act on his behalf and exhibit and take orders for Wyeths' products. For whatever reason, Lindewald failed to do so, thus SMB wanted to get there quickly. SMB's letter book, PP/SMB LB35, covering 13 May – 26 Oct 1878.
17. SMB to Kelley, 18 Sept 1878, WF/E/02/01/02/02.
18. SMB to Wyeths, 22 Oct 1878.
19. This was quite cheeky, given that space in the store didn't only house Wyeths goods and under their contract SMB paid for the office rent.
20. SMB to Wyeths, 13 July 1878.
21. SMB to Wyeths, 22 Oct 1878.
22. Obituary of Laura Richards, *New York Tribune*, 18 Aug 1914.
23. PP/SMB, London notebook, p. 48.
24. Pearl Mary Teresa Craigie (1867–1906). Her first book, *Some Emotions and a Moral* (1891), was a sensation.
25. SMB to Frank Mattox (employee of firm and engaged to marry Miss Hart), Melbourne, 7 Sept 1882.
26. These arc lights had been placed along a section of the Embankment only two years earlier, and in fact they were to prove too expensive and too brilliant for more general use elsewhere.
27. He was at the Lillie Bridge Gymnasium with Samson Lemaire, 'a remarkably well-developed gymnast & swings a 44th Club with the greatest of ease.' The Lemaires were a famous family of gymnasts.

Chapter 4: Brotherly Love and Henry Wellcome

1. SMB to HSW, 6 Jan 1879, WF/E/02/01/02/31.
2. Mayo's sons later founded the celebrated Mayo Clinic in Rochester.
3. Albert T. Williams, 17 Aug 1870, in RRJ, p. 33.
4. RRJ, p. 52.
5. SMB did not actually join the American Pharmaceutical Association until 1877. HSW was working for McKesson & Robbins when he went on a sales visit to Buffalo in October 1876. This could have provided a meeting place for them, as suggested by Haggis, who also says that SMB had 'recently joined' the APhA. However, his dates are a year out.
6. Cited by Haggis, pp. 80–99. However, this letter has not been found in the Wellcome Archives and must now be considered lost.
7. HSW to Fred Wellcome, March 1895, LB3 pp. 7–11.
8. SMB to HSW, 6 Jan 1879, WF/E/02/01/02/31.
9. SMB agreed with HSW on Kepler's value; sales had exceeded expectations, being four or five times as large as Wyeths'; ibid.
10. SMB to HSW, Aug and Oct 1879 and Feb 1880.
11. The malt extract offer was significant as about $6,500 worth of malt and oil goods had been sold between March and August 1878, and new malt lines were about to come out. SMB to HSW, 6 Jan 1879. Elixirs (tonics) were almost unknown in Britain (no drug house was pushing them, few doctors knew anything about them and there was a 50% import duty on all goods containing alcohol).
12. SMB to HSW, 30 Aug 1879.
13. SMB to HSW, 20 Oct 1879; see also WF/E/02/01/02/31.
14. SMB to HSW, Nov 1879.
15. London notebook 1880, PP/SMB, p. 19. In SMB's will of 1887, which he subsequently changed, he left 1/12 of his estate to Maggie Steers.
16. SMB to HSW, 7 Feb 1880.
17. HSW to McKesson & Robbins, 18 Aug 1880, cited in RRJ, p. 85.
18. Sudlow was appointed 3 Feb 1879, Kirby 10 March 1879.
19. Draft letter, HSW to Wyeths, Vienna, 19 June 1880, WF/E/02/01/02/05.
20. John Wyeth to HSW, 10 July 1880, WF/E/02/01/02/05.
21. The news was announced to the trade on 30 Sept 1880.
22. Extract from 'Talk', 21 July 1893: 'Medicine making up to date', WFA, 172 82/1, Box 13, re 'Tabloid'.
23. Letter dated May 1881, RRJ, p. 92.
24. RRJ, p. 97.
25. WA, Records of Travellers: Book 1, Medicos 1881–1885; Book 2, Chemists and Druggists at Home and Abroad 1881–87; WF, Guard-books. Described as a significant introduction of market analysis and research into the business, it is not known if this was SMB's or HSW's idea, but in the event it produced some fascinating insights into the way

the firm viewed those with whom it dealt and gave valuable information to future salesmen.

26. HSW to SMB, 13 Aug 1881.

Chapter 5: 'A Little Excursion'

1. SMB, Bombay, to Mr and Mrs Wilson, San Francisco, 4 Feb 1882.
2. A wealthier middle class also heralded the new 'tourist industry'. Thomas Cook, who created the internationally famous company for travellers, saw the opportunities presented by tourism back in the 1840s, and many people (SMB included) used Cook's company to book transport, hotels and guides, transfer of money, and effectively have a packaged holiday (though this expression is a later one). Business was made easier with the formation of the General Postal Union in 1874 and an International Postal Treaty in 1875 which facilitated a worldwide system of cheap post.
3. The *Ceylon*'s route was Bordeaux, Lisbon, Gibraltar, Malaga, Marseille, Malta, Port Said, Suez, the Suez Canal, the Red Sea, Bombay, Japan, the Sandwich Islands, Honolulu, San Francisco, Central and South America, the Falklands, Rio de Janeiro, St Vincent and the Canaries. She arrived back on 22 Aug 1882 after completing about 36,500 miles. The voyage was not repeated and almost certainly was not a commercial success.
4. *Northern Territory Times and Gazette*, 26 November 1881.
5. Built in 1858 for P&O as a mail and passenger steamer for its India service, the *Ceylon* was 'stately', 'a splendid sea boat, strongly built, with high bulwarks like an old frigate, and barque rigged', her attractive light dove-colour and graceful figurehead distinguishing her from other vessels. P&O had recently sold the boat to the Inter-Oceanic Steam Yachting Co., which had converted her into a 'cruising yacht'. She had a reputation for speed and was very comfortable, with a wide upper deck and roomy accommodation, most of cabins being single. Due to leave Southampton on 20th, the *Ceylon* was delayed loading stores, livestock and pianos. SMB complained that some of the directors of the business were 'duffers ... very tardy in supplying the ship with many necessary things'.
6. Letters to be sent to medical journals, copies of recent reports to be sent to chemists in Scotland followed up by visits by a traveller, and his spare ball ticket to be given to Mr van Schaak, a prospective employee whose visit from America was imminent. John van Schaak joined the firm and stayed with it until the end of 1884.
7. The principal role of consuls was in promoting trade, assisting companies to invest and to import and export goods and services both inwardly and to their home country. The consul recommended Mr Christie of Christie & Bernal as being energetic and reliable, and Christie proved a valuable

8

agent who later worked elsewhere for the firm, although Spain was not as profitable as SMB hoped. Again the wholesale and retail druggists and doctors were visited and reported on to HSW. Via his American friends the Fergusons, SMB received a letter from Gen. Wesley Merritt (1836–1910), who had distinguished service in the American Civil War, introducing him to consuls at several places he intended visiting.

8. SMB's letter to HSW was also published in the *Christian Commonwealth*.
9. From 23 November, when in Naples, he started jotting in the margin the date and place at which he had read the text.
10. The *Ceylon* was not a freighter and so was excused from paying port duties. However, SMB could not get through the custom house without a Spanish consul's certificate in London, which he did not have.
11. SMB to HSW, Marseille, 17 Nov 1881, WF/E/02/01/01/03.
12. By now SMB had received only two communications from the firm since he had left, nearly a month previously, from which he learnt that HSW had been in Paris. WF/E/02/01/01/03.
13. Dr Frederick Power joined the firm after SMB's death.
14. SMB to HSW and Sudlow, Constantinople, 7 or 9 Dec 1881, WF/E/02/01/01/03.
15. SMB, Cairo, to Mr and Mrs Wilstead, Cairo, 19 Dec 1881.
16. 6 Dec 1881, WF/E/03/01/01.
17. SMB's travel journal, 19 Dec 1881.
18. There are accounts by other passengers who sailed on her on this and other occasions. Wilkinson, author of *Sunny Lands and Seas*, joined the ship at the port of Suez and then re-joined her in Calcutta at the end of January for the rest of her voyage to Manila, Hong Kong, Nagasaki, the Sandwich Islands, Hawaii and California.
19. SMB to Pearl Richards, later Craigie, 'My dear friend Pearl', 2 Jan 1881, notebook.
20. SMB's first article appeared on 24 Nov 1881. He also wrote for other journals, including *The Fountain*.
21. SMB to Mr and Mrs Ferguson [in Medina], 22 Dec 1881, and following letters from his notebook.
22. SMB to HSW, 30 Dec 1881, notebook. SMB had expressed concern for HSW's health, writing that he hoped he was getting regular meals and plenty of sleep, 12 Nov 1881. WF/E/02/01/01/03.

Chapter 6: 'A Superficial Jaunt'? India and Ceylon

1. SMB to HSW, 18 March 1882.
2. See his *Following the Equator*, pp. 215–16.
3. SMB letter, 11 Jan 1882, published in *Christian Commonwealth*, 9 March 1882, pp. 11–12.

4. SMB letter, probably written for *Christian Commonwealth*, 20 Jan 1882, PP/SMB.
5. Cook's Monday lectures in Boston, where he spoke on numerous topics, attracted thousands. He was now half-way through a world tour of English-speaking countries.
6. SMB to 'D.L.A.', Bombay, 19 Jan 1882, travel journal, p. 25.
7. After hearing him lecture in Poona SMB wrote a letter to *The Times of India*, published 28 Jan 1882, small jottings notebook 3.
8. Lytton was blamed for the huge death rate of 10 million people during the famine as a result of the severity with which he implemented Britain's trading policy.
9. Poona, 22 Jan 1882, letter book.
10. Bombay, 29 Jan 1882, letter book.
11. Pharmacopoeias were produced by the British for their use and for those trained in Western medicine. At the same time British colonisers started to recognise the importance of Indian herbal knowledge and indigenous remedies.
12. Cholera had been a major killer in Bombay, but cholera deaths decreased from c.1,400 to c.200 between 1878 and 1882. India had also recently experienced severe famines in Bengal, Madras and Bombay.
13. SMB to Bishop, Bangalore, 16 May 1882.
14. Travellers' forms, Chemists and Druggists Book 2, Calcutta, from April 1882, WF/M/GB.
15. Travellers' forms, Medicos Jeypore, March 1882, ibid.
16. SMB noted that *The Practitioner* had a fair circulation, while few subscribed to the *British Medical Journal* or *Press Circular* or *Journal & Gazette*. Travel journal, 10 May 1882.
17. SMB to Valentine, 20 Feb 1882.
18. SMB to HSW, 2 Feb 1882, PP/SMB.
19. He had been told a story by Dr H.M. Scudder, of the famous missionary family in India, that it could be used to make hair grow. SMB visited him in the Nilgiri Hills.
20. A letter from SMB describing Delhi, written on 21 Feb 1882, was sent to the *Christian Commonwealth* and published on 23 May.
21. This and quotes in the previous paragraph, SMB to HSW, Coonoor, Madras, 10 May 1882.
22. HSW to SMB, n.d. [between 23 Jan and 16 Feb 1882], LB10, pp. 32–44.
23. SMB to HSW, c.21 March 1882; letter commenced Allahabad and finished Benares.
24. SMB, Calcutta, 28 March 1882, letter book, p. 502.
25. On 6 April he set off for Rangoon on the steamer, expecting to get to Madras on 24 April, and then on to Colombo by 1 June. At this stage he said he had enough samples for India and for use in Australia and in part for China and Japan.

26. SMB to Frank Mattox, 10 May 1882, journal.
27. SMB, Bangalore, to Sudlow, 19 May 1882, journal.
28. SMB, Bangalore, 20 May 1882, journal (possibly published in *Christian Commonwealth*, 4 October).
29. Arnold, 'Medical Priorities and Practice'.
30. SMB notebook 2, April–May 1882.
31. The firm's most popular sellers there were quinine, morphia, rhubarb and other capsules; Burroughs's Beef and Iron Wine; Fellow's Syrup of Hypophosphites (a nerve tonic); Wyeths' Compressed Chlorate of Potash (a throat lozenge); Hazeline (for inflammation, etc.); Com. Cathartic ISP (a purgative); Ergotin and Soda Mint (for dyspepsia). Tonics were popular and contained dietary nutrients (although SMB himself would not have been aware, since vitamins were not known, that malt is rich in vitamin B and cod liver oil in vitamins A and D).
32. BW&Co. to HSW, 11 Jan 1901.
33. SMB letter, 10 June 1882.
34. 'Queen Victoria evidently thinks more of truth and righteousness than of policy. That one decision opened India to the free entrance of the missionaries of the Gospel by which the conversion of this great country to truth and salvation is progressing slowly but surely.' Letter, 10 Jan 1882, published in *Christian Commonwealth*, 9 March 1882, letter book.
35. Letter, 6 Jan 1882, ibid.

Chapter 7: The Antipodes

1. SMB to HSW, 19 Oct 1882.
2. Letter, 10 July 1882. He stayed until 2 August.
3. 20 Sept and 30 Aug 1882 [for *Christian Commonwealth*?], journal.
4. SMB to Mattox, Melbourne, 7 Sept 1882.
5. Aug 30 1882, journal. Adelaide was the only freely settled British province in Australia; it had liberal aims of treating all equally, regardless of race or colour, and was the only province which had not treated the native Aborigines badly.
6. 31 July 1882, journal.
7. SMB to HSW, 21 July 1882, journal.
8. Forbes was a war correspondent and military historian whose lectures were very popular. By 1882 he had reported on the Franco-Prussian War, the Bengal Famine (1874), the British occupation of Cyprus (1878), the Russian–Turkish War (1877–8) and the British campaigns in Afghanistan (1878–80), South Africa (1879) and Burma (1885–7).
9. 21 Aug 1882, journal.
10. Mid-Sept 1882. According to SMB's notes, Cook sought to give medical weight to the argument against drink on the basis that it poisoned the body.

11. Dr W.B. Richardson of Hinde Street, London, had made this suggestion in *The Lancet*. SMB, Melbourne, 14 Sept 1882.
12. SMB to HSW, 22 Aug 1882, journal.
13. HSW was also concerned by the prevalence of drinking, especially in large cities, and disliked the sale of alcohol in pharmacies. By March the next year, however (when SMB was once more in Australia), the issue came up again when SMB wrote to HSW that there was some resistance by doctors to prescribing the Beef and Iron and he thought that the use of 'Elixoid' might be a more professionally appealing name. HSW may for a time have been teetotal, although his concern later was for complete sobriety at work. RRJ, pp. 67–8.
14. Melbourne, 30 March 1883. The article is unfinished and there is no evidence that it was published. Top copy in travel notebook.
15. Sir William Fox (1812–1893), author and statesman, helped shape the Constitution Act of 1852, which established home rule for New Zealand.
16. On the night of 10 June 1886, when, without warning, the town was also buried and over 150 people (mostly Maoris) were killed. See photos of the terraces in PP/SMB. At least one of these photos is dated on the reverse by SMB, Jan 1883.
17. See correspondence, WF/E/02/01/01. Steamer journey times between Auckland on the North Island and Dunedin on the South took about five days.
18. SMB mentioned that a new drug house setting up in Colombo was extracting crude alkaloids from bark, and that if HSW could purchase crude stuff at a fair price 'it would be less risky than buying the bark and less trouble to make up.' Squibb retired in 1895 and passed most of the responsibility for managing the firm to his sons, Charles and Edward, who then sold out.
19. SMB noted – presumably based on a report he received – that there were 'no educated Drs in China, there being no medical schools – there are however plenty of Quacks who are much prejudiced against foreign medicines of all kinds.' WFA, Records of Travellers, 1881–85, 'Medical Men', pp. 187–8.
20. HSW to SMB, 27 June 1883, LB10, p. 279.
21. Ibid. He sent a copy of the letter c/o Reddington & Co. in San Francisco, LB10, p. 282.
22. At this time the celebrated Father Damien was still working at the leper colony at Molokai but no record exists whether SMB visited the colony. However, among the photographs SMB kept, with his annotation on the reverse, is an image showing the colony set in a lush mountainous area of the island.
23. Isaac died 26 June 1883, aged 82. HSW wrote to Mr Buck, 28 July 1883, that SMB would learn of his uncle's death only once he got to San Francisco. LB1, p. 145.

24. HSW to SMB, 28 July 1883, LB1, p. 147.
25. There had been a serious fire at the Saracen's Head Buildings next door to the new Wellcome building on Snow Hill.

Chapter 8: 'This Lovely Opposite Sex'

1. SMB journal, Easter 1883.
2. HSW to SMB, 15 March 1883.
3. SMB to Frank Mattox, 7 Sept 1882.
4. See obituary by Gubb, letter sent to OB after his death, and note by Harris of BW&Co. staff. Also 'Progress in Pharmacy' reprint from *C&D*, 28 Jan 1888.
5. SMB to Frank Mattox, 7 Sept 1882.
6. HSW to SMB, 26 May 1882, LB19, p. 129.
7. SMB to Carrie Davis, Mount Abu, Gujarat, 14 Feb 1882, letter book pp. 288–.
8. SMB to Carrie Davis, Waiwera, New Zealand, 24 Dec 1882, in which he mentions that he had wanted to marry her.
9. SMB had written when sailing to Bombay, where an earlier letter from Olive awaited his arrival. His proposal letter, 27 July 1882, was sent from Adelaide.
10. Letters from New Zealand to London, for example, took 38 to 43 days via the States, or 48 to 60 days via Suez. By the 1880s the country's telegraph networks were extensive.
11. SMB, Adelaide, 4 Aug 1882. This would have been for the *Christian Commonwealth*, copies of which he often sent to friends. In Greek mythology, Phineus was the tormented king of Thrace, and Atalanta the swift-footed huntress whom Melanion/Hippomenes wanted to marry.
12. SMB mentioned 'good old times in Kansas City', drives at Gloversville and Broadalbin, as well as a lovely starlit evening at Burlington, Iowa, where he first saw Olive on the deck of a boat. See his letter to her from Melbourne, 20 Sept 1882.
13. See *Amsterdam Evening Recorder*, 13 Jan 1919. Benjamin Chase owned more than most Broadalbin citizens: in the 1870 Census his personal estate was $1,000 and real estate $7,500. By comparison, the 1850 Census shows that Silas Burroughs snr's real/personal estate was worth nine times Benjamin's, and in 1870 Isaac Burroughs was two and a half times wealthier than Benjamin.
14. Both graduated from Boston University medical department in 1877 and were the first women to be elected to the Minneapolis Homeopathic Society the following year. Swain probably met Olive in Hennepin, Minnesota, when she was living there (listed in the 1880 Census as single, a physician, and head of household with three other women). She worked at Massachusetts Women's Dispensary in Boston.

15. HSW to SMB, Sept 1882.
16. SMB to Olive, c.1 Sept 1882.
17. The original letter was tucked into his journal, and thus we can see where Olive was living and how long the letter took to arrive: 'Miss Olive A. Chase, 32, 7 St S, Minneapolis, Minn OR Broadalbin NY'. Posted Melbourne, 6 Sept; San Francisco postmark, 3 Oct; Minneapolis postmark, 9 Oct.
18. Ranimanzo probably derived from the Italian *romanzo* for romance.
19. Certainly both men were interested in publishing and saw the advantages of literature underlying their sales and products, but I have not found the idea of them starting a medical journal mentioned elsewhere. SMB did mention to HSW in October 1882 the possibility of taking a medical degree.
20. SMB to Olive, 20 Sept 1882.
21. SMB to HSW, 23 Sept 1882, journal.
22. 13 and 14 Nov 1882, journal.
23. SMB, 23 Dec 1882, travel diaries.
24. SMB to HSW, Waiwera, 23 Dec 1882.
25. Emma Dean died 19 April 1882. Her son, Burdett, died aged 13, after a long and painful illness, on 13 Feb 1882. Her obituary in the *McKean County Miner* newspaper stated that she was 'highly educated' and that 'her mind had been impaired since the death of her son in January last.'
26. SMB to Carrie Davis, Waiwera, 24 Dec 1882.
27. He visited Medina in January 1879 and again in January 1882 but was unable to see Lina on that occasion as she was confined. She had married Riggs in October 1880, and Harold was born 24 Jan 1882.
28. HSW to SMB, 15 March 1883. Cited in full in RRJ, pp. 126–7.
29. SMB to Carrie Davis, Waiwera, 24 Dec 1882.
30. SMB to HSW, Medina, 9 Oct 1883, WF/E/02/01/01/88.
31. 'In one of your letters rec'd lately you seem to think if I got over by December it will be soon enough but matters may have taken such turn since that you require [me] sooner … If you have urgent business for me to attend to or if you are ill just telegraph the time you would like me to sail and I shall have no difficulty in engaging passage at this season of the year.' SMB to HSW, Ithaca, NY, 20 Oct 1883, WF/E/01/03/02.
32. SMB to HSW, 5 Oct 1883.
33. HSW to SMB, 17 Nov 1883, LB1, pp. 202–3.
34. HSW to SMB, 19 Oct 1883, LB1, p. 17; 26 Oct 1883, LB1 pp. 177–82.
35. SMB to HSW, 20 Oct 1883, WF/E/01/03/02.
36. HSW to SMB, 5 Nov 1883, LB1, pp. 193–201.

Chapter 9: 'Bones of Contention' and Brotherly Strains

1. SMB to HSW, 18 June 1882.
2. HSW to SMB, 26 May 1882.

3. 20,000 copies bound in leatherette, 5,000 with cloth and interleaved for memos, and 500 interleaved, bound in beautiful blue leather. HSW to SMB, 25 May 1882.

4. SMB to HSW, 30 Sept 1882.

5. Both HSW and SMB had worked on this plan from 1881. SMB to Frank ?Mattox, Melbourne, 7 Sept 1882. Wellcome had 'got quite sick and tired of dealing with Mr Lockwood, who is altogether too sharp for us and has got a good price out of us for which he gave us nothing.' See C&T, pp. 23–6, for details of the complex negotiations and questionable actions taken by the partners in their dealing over this.

6. Both also built on the foundation of SMB's visit to India for the Calcutta International Exhibition of 1883, which was supervised by William Shepperson, an American who had worked for the firm for two years.

7. The 1812 Act was intended to stop the import of quack medicines, but from the early 1880s officials began to use it to place a heavy stamp duty on imported drugs, although 'pure drugs' were exempt. HSW to SMB, 6 Dec 1883. The firm in fact started importing pure drugs in 1882. One reason for settling duties on compressed tablets was that BW&Co. were on the point of marketing them in the UK rather than importing them.

8. Wyeths had not obtained patent protection in Europe, and their goods were being imitated there, as BW&Co. had warned them would happen.

9. SMB to HSW, n.d. [1882], WFA Acc 87/33, and HSW to SMB, 15 March 1883, LB1, pp. 1–3.

10. Located at the mouth of the River Wandle, which was fast flowing and had a long tradition of industry and manufacturing, and well sited for moving goods along the Thames.

11. SMB to HSW, Sydney, 24 Nov 1883, WF/E/01/03/02.

12. The original asking price was £1,800 p.a.; HSW managed to beat this down to £900 for the first year and £1,245 each year thereafter. The lease started 1 June 1883. See also HSW to SMB, 27 Jan 1883, LB1, pp. 84–107.

13. HSW to SMB, 6 Dec 1881, LB1, pp. 1–8.

14. HSW to Isaac and Anna Burroughs, 22 April 1882.

15. HSW to Mr Buck, 26 Oct 1882, LB1, pp. 51–8.

16. Wyeths to SMB, 13 April 1881, WFA Acc 82/1, Box 15.

17. SMB to 'Brother Sudlow', Bangalore, 19 May 1882, notebook.

18. This happened several times, most seriously when SMB failed to receive samples until he got to Colombo, June 1882.

19. HSW to SMB, 5 May 1883, LB10, pp. 254–9.

20. HSW to SMB, 23 Jan – 16 Feb 1882, LB10, pp. 32–44, and 27 June 1883, LB10, p. 270.

21. SMB to HSW, Allahabad, 21 March 1882, notebook. SMB to HSW, Benares, 22 March 1882, notebook.

22. SMB to HSW, 10 May 1882, journal.
23. HSW to SMB, 24-page letter, 26 May 1882, LB10, pp. 107–30.
24. SMB to HSW, 18 June 1882; cited by Haggis, pp. 188–9. Details of the Kepler arrangements are covered in C&T, pp. 110–11.
25. SMB to HSW, 10 May 1882. Also quoted by HSW in his reply, 26 May 1882, LB10.
26. HSW to SMB, 25 Aug 1882, LB1, pp. 1–15. According to Haggis, p. 198, by 30 Nov 1883 HSW's capital holding was equal to that of SMB.
27. SMB to HSW, Adelaide [9] Aug 1882.
28. SMB to HSW, 22 Aug 1882, journal.
29. The fire was probably caused by spontaneous combustion and the damage, covered by insurance, was not very great, although only through luck did it not destroy the premises totally. HSW to SMB, 27 Aug 1883, LB1, pp. 157–8.
30. SMB mentioned that he had taken exception at HSW apparently ignoring his proposal to pay Lakeman a salary of £20, although this had since been declined by Lakeman and a percentage cut agreed in lieu, but on a second reading of HSW's letter the settlement 'appeared to be about the right thing.' HSW to SMB, 9 Aug 1883, LB10, pp. 284–91, WF/E/02/01/01/85. SMB to HSW, Medina, 10 Sept 1883.
31. HSW to SMB, 5 Nov 1883, LB1, pp. 185–201.
32. HSW to SMB, 24 Nov 1883.
33. SMB to HSW, 27 or 29 Nov 1883, WF/E/01/03/02.
34. SMB to HSW, Medina, 4 Dec 1883, WF/E/01/03/02.
35. HSW to SMB, 6 Dec 1883, LB1, pp. 213–30.
36. There is no information as to where they lived initially, although they possibly lodged with the Lymans at Wyoming, Beulah Hill, Norwood, until they obtained rented accommodation.

Chapter 10: Atlantic Crossings and Divided Lives

1. Obituary, *Christian Commonwealth*, 14 Feb 1895.
2. SMB to HSW, Auckland, 16 Dec 1882.
3. See 'Progress in Pharmacy', 25 Feb 1888. *C&D* had commented favourably on the building earlier.
4. In 1878 the only compressed goods known in London were Brockedons, Coopers and Wyeths.
5. HSW had written to SMB on 10 Oct 1883.
6. SMB to HSW, Melbourne, Sept 1882. See also SMB to HSW, March 1883, WFA Acc 87/33/35e and Acc 85/16.
7. He also noted that, if McKesson & Robbins were unwilling to set up a factory in England, the firm had better cancel its contract with them and begin to manufacture on its own account. SMB to HSW, 7 Aug 1884, LB10, p. 371, and 24 July 1884, WF/E/01/03/02.

8. Corning Weld from Medina had caused offence in some way, evidently as a result of alcohol and an affair. SMB did his best to help him and keep secret whatever misdemeanours he had committed, while advising him to renounce the bottle. He kept Weld on in the firm on a weekly basis until able to talk with HSW. SMB wrote to Weld (April 1884) that he was glad he was trying to retrieve his reputation, etc. If he didn't make a success of his life, he would be 'one of the greatest fools that ever lived for you have had opportunities for success and those whose confidence you have tried whose friendship you have treated so lightly etc.' SMB's private letter book, pp. 5–7.

9. SMB to HSW, Kiel, 9 Aug 1884, WF/E/01/02/03.

10. SMB to HSW, 17 Sept 1884, WF/E/01/02/03.

11. Sudlow to HSW, 16 Oct 1884, WF/E/01/03/02. HSW was in America for three months.

12. Telegram, SMB to HSW, Liverpool, 26 Nov 1884.

13. George Radford, of Radford & Frankland, to SMB, 14 Jan 1885, WF/E/01/02/03; R&F to HSW and his reply, WF/E/02/01/30. The gross returns of the business increased from £17,811 in 1880–81 to £33,158 in 1881–2 and £57,156 in 1882–3. SMB requested that a sufficient sum be transferred from his drawing account into the capital account to make it £10,000, and HSW should pay him £750 plus interest due.

14. SMB to OB, 18 April 1885.

15. SMB to OB, 5 May 1885.

16. SMB to OB, 14 and 23 May 1885. It is not known if Sudlow was ever informed of SMB's wish for him to become a partner.

17. In May 1885 SMB and HSW respectively transferred £3,985 and £253 from their drawing accounts.

18. At this time both partners secured written permission re further business interests outside the firm: SMB became director of a tobacco company, Terry & Co., and HSW bought an interest in Saxon & Co., a small publishing house. In 1886 the Sheldons bought an interest in Saxon & Co. RRJ, pp. 138 and 143.

19. SMB to OB, April or May 1885.

20. Another reading is 'Hansie', but it is unclear. OB to SMB, from 35 Union Park, 23 May 1885.

21. Mrs Perry was one of the good London friends with whom he had stayed; and she had gained his gratitude by accompanying OB to America. SMB to OB, 23 May 1885.

22. SMB to HSW, Boston, 9 June 1885, WF/02/01/01/94. The nurse was Mrs Ellis.

23. The 'Baby Book', in possession of the Stillwell family in 2020, notes the birth at 35 Union Park, Boston.

24. SMB to Sudlow: 'I sent you a hurried post-card informing you of the increase of family by two daughters. You will be pleased to hear further that they & the mother are well the latter especially very happy.'

25. SMB to Sudlow, Boston, 27 June 1885, WF/02/01/01/94.

26. Twins can develop different types of malnutrition, and marasmus is an inadequate intake of all forms of food, including protein. OB and SMB had concerns over correct baby foods after her death.
27. SMB to BW&Co., 1 Sept 1885, WF/02/01/01/94, and Baby Book.
28. SMB to OB, undated incomplete letter c.Oct 1885. Jeal, in *Stanley*, p. 300, notes that HSW advised Stanley, when searching for a wife, to take some ladies boating.
29. HSW to SMB, 10 Sept and 28 Oct 1885, LB1, pp. 398–401 and 409.
30. SMB to OB, undated letter [28 Sept 1885]. He returned on 25 September.
31. SMB to OB, 3 Oct 1885.
32. This was a recent innovation in America, bringing adult education, culture and Christian instruction to rural areas.
33. Mrs Ellis also lived with Aunt Anna and OB travelled with nurse Maggie.
34. SMB to OB, 2 Oct 1885.
35. SMB to OB, 7 Nov 1885. SMB thought that money was the problem and sent a telegram to the firm: 'Coming with thousand pounds', but HSW disabused him. SMB to BW&Co., telegram, Rochester, received London, 9 Nov 1885, WF/02/01/01/94; HSW to SMB, 12 Nov 1885, LB1, pp. 411–14.
36. HSW to SMB, 12 Nov 1885, LB1, p. 411.
37. The christening took place on 16 November at 133 North Street, Auburn, presumably the home of Jai and Lina. Baby Book.
38. SMB to OB, 20 Nov 1885. He sailed from New York on 21 November and arrived on 29 November.
39. SMB to OB, 3 Dec 1885.
40. SMB wrote to OB on 26 Jan 1886 that Wellcome was getting into the office only once or twice a week. On 16 July 1886 HSW wrote to his friend John P. Lee in Chicago that he had been confined to bed almost constantly for six months with neuralgia of the bowels. LB1, p. 487.
41. SMB to OB, 9 Feb 1886.
42. SMB to OB, 26 Jan 1886.
43. Syrie married HSW in 1901 and they had one son. She subsequently married Somerset Maugham in 1917.
44. SMB to OB, 25 March 1886.
45. SMB to OB, 10 April 1886.
46. Charles Hutton, a wealthy wool merchant, lived at Belair house from 1859 to 1891. SMB to OB, 10 April 1886. SMB to Sudlow, Medina, 12 May 1886, WF/02/01/01/96.
47. SMB to BW&Co., London postcard, 17 April 1886, WF/02/01/01/96.
48. SMB generously ascribed her lying as not from malice so much as 'to while away the time, she being of an active disposition.'
49. 'At my suggestion Dr Witte has mixed some milk with extract of malt & condensed both together. The malt milk is delicious when mixed with water it dissolves readily.' SMB to OB, 6 March 1886.
50. SMB to OB, 14 May 1886.

51. SMB to OB, 13 May 1886.
52. SMB to OB, Lafayette Hotel, Philadelphia, 30 May 1886.
53. On 2 June President Cleveland married Frances Fulsom at the White House in Washington. SMB received formal notification of the wedding as he knew Frances from her Medina days and had spoken publicly in support of Cleveland. Frances had attended the Medina Academy as a teenager before 1879.

Chapter 11: Partnership in Crisis: The High Court

1. SMB to HSW, 27 July 1887.
2. HSW to SMB, 18 May 1886, letter book 1, p. 484. *C&D*, 26 June 1886, p. 630.
3. SMB to OB, December 1885.
4. Quoted in *Successful Pharmacy*, 1 Jan 1889, reprinting a section in *C&D*, 28 Jan 1888.
5. Bushell, in *Profit-Sharing and the Labour Question*, reported on evidence given at a recent royal commission on labour that, before 1884, there were only 28 instances of firms profit-sharing and, by 1892, a total of 75 British firms. It notes BW&Co. as starting to share profits in 1886, when the employees numbered 260. Only 11 other firms are mentioned as starting earlier than 1886, and of these only one other was a manufacturing chemist.
6. SMB to OB, 13 March 1886.
7. SMB to OB, 19 March 1886.
8. The Story of Metlakahtla appeared in 1887 was a great success; it went into several editions.
9. 'I consider that the perils of the deep require me, in ordinary prudence, to make a will before departing.' SMB left one-third of his estate to his wife, to hold in trust for their daughter Anna; one-third to the Presbyterian Missionary Society of the US; one-sixth to his sister, one-twelfth to Miss Steers of New York, and one-twelfth to Mr and Mrs John Parsons in Medina. Witnessed by Collett Smith at Snow Hill, 22 April 1887, WF/01/04/24.
10. SMB to Sudlow, SS *Alaska*, 24 and 30 April 1887, WF/E/02/01/01/97.
11. *The Standard*, New York, 4 June 1887. Henry George reported that SMB would have preferred to live in America and that the new materials he needed could be provided to advantage there.
12. Dr Witte informed SMB that he and HSW had argued in SMB's absence abroad, but after discussing his position in March 1886 the partners invited him to remain with the company on a salary of £3,000, with conditions laid down not to communicate any formulae or processes to others. Two months later, HSW had occasion to write concerning the continued complaints about the quality of the malt, which threatened

the reputation of the company. Witte was held responsible and told that he had to perfect the process and not to make any changes without informing HSW. SMB to OB, 6 Feb 1886.

13. HSW to SMB, 2 May 1887.

14. SMB to BW&Co., Grand Union Hotel, New York, then Philadelphia, 13 May 1887, WF/E/02/01/01/97. Haggis, p. 49, stated that HSW made every effort to get in touch with SMB without success. This does not tie in with the evidence from the correspondence in the archives, which shows that SMB met HSW in New York in mid-May and expected to see him there again on 4 June, on his own return from Philadelphia and on HSW's return that day 'from the west', while Dr Witte was 'up river prospecting'. Also statements made by both SMB & HSW in legal documents in 1889 that they met several times in America. WF/E/02/01/01/ 97 and 94.

15. SMB to OB, Fitchburg, 24 June 1887. Not to be confused with Cold Spring Harbor, now a centre for scientific research. When in Philadelphia, he met the Wyeths and discussed the issue of manufacturing tablets in the UK ('the "Tablet" matter', as he called it); he was 'relieved of much anxiety' to learn from HSW that their position with Wyeths was 'quite solid and satisfactory'. SMB to BW&Co., Grand Union Hotel, New York, 4 June 1887, WF/E/02/01/01/94.

16. HSW to SMB, 24 June 1887, WF/E/01/04/5. HSW travelled with the Sheldons. SMB thought that HSW had left and therefore went up the Hudson; HSW said he had promised to telegraph in the event of his deciding to sail and that he thought SMB would regard silence as evidence of postponement. SMB sailed on SS *Aurania* on 2 July (telegram sent to Burcome (BW&Co.), 2 July, WF/E/02/01/01/97) and was back in the office on 13 July.

17. SMB to Christie, Buenos Aires, 5 Jan 1888, LB10, pp. 517–18.

18. Haggis, pp. 49–50.

19. SMB had loaned this money to Kelley and had asked HSW to collect it from him while he was on his world tour; see Haggis, p. 180. On SMB's return from America at the end of 1885, HSW had asked his further indulgence on a loan, which SMB then extended for a further six months from September 1885. HSW to SMB, 26 Nov 1885, letter book 1, p. 422.

20. SMB to HSW, 28 July 1887.

21. HSW to Sam and Ben Fairchild, 10 Aug 1887, letter book 1, pp. 533–7.

22. J.J. Fellows to HSW, 18 Feb 1888; quoted by Haggis, p. 215. A similar letter was also sent to SMB.

23. HSW to S. and B. Fairchild, 11 April 1888. Haggis stated that it was SMB, not HSW, who spread the rumours and that HSW wrote only this one letter to the Fairchilds, whereas he certainly wrote others, including the one quoted above, August 1887. To others he wrote: 'Facts are more powerful than fiction and facts and justice are both on my side … I have

let my opponent do the talking and be aggressive and stand by my guns.'
HSW to Mr Young (of Young, Ladd & Coffin) 2 July 1888, letter book 2,
p. 17.

24. Office memo dated 8 March 1888 by unidentified employee of firm,
quoted in full in RRJ, pp. 157–9. HSW was worried enough about the
rumours that, before the court case with SMB in 1889, he made a
private statement about his friendship to his lawyers, presumably to
forestall any accusation from SMB. His account of events was that he
had been amazed to learn from May Sheldon that Dr Burrows had
made some improper remarks which she had 'indignantly resented'.
When confronted, Dr Burrows had retaliated that HSW had
'misconducted himself' with Mrs Sheldon, whereupon HSW threatened
to horsewhip Dr Burrows if he ever heard a word of such allusion from
him again, there being not the slightest foundation for any such charge.
After this incident, HSW had been confined to bed and had reason to
believe that Dr Burrows had made insinuations to the housekeeper,
who had afterwards made remarks to others. Serious doubts, HSW
said, had been cast on the character of the housekeeper and proprietors
of the house he shared with the Sheldons, and all three had left the
property as a result.

25. SMB sent a copy to OB, telling her that he had been so busy he had not
yet read it himself, though on 28 April 1886 he wrote to HSW that he
had read it on the steamer coming over and thought it a wonderful gift;
he purchased 50 copies as presents for friends. But the following year
he was to describe it as a 'lamentable and near-pornographical work'
(RRJ, p. 138). In England in the late 1880s, Flaubert's works were
increasingly considered to be immoral. See Rouxeville, 'The Reception
of Flaubert'.

26. See office memo cited note 25 above. SMB told the court that he had
spoken in self-defence, since HSW was telling employees that it was his
(HSW's) intention to take over the business and that he would promise
to assure the position of those employees who would stand by him in
the litigation now in hand.

27. HSW to SMB, 26 Nov 1887, letter book 10, p. 513.

28. 'I hope & pray that I may be delivered from … that serpentine Wellcome
whom I verily believe is a real "snake in the grass".' SMB to OB, 1 Jan
1889.

29. HSW noted this happened on 15 April 1886.

30. RRJ (p. 143) discussed HSW's medical records with Lord Butterfield,
who concluded that HSW suffered from ulcerative colitis.

31. Mr Justice Kekewich was called on to hear the evidence of the Plaintiff
(Mr Ralph Neville QC acting for SMB) vs. the Defendant (Mr Warrington
QC acting for HSW).

32. See *The Times*, 25 and 26 June 1889.

33. In comparison, HSW's need to control staff is clearly evidenced and analysed by Larson in *An Infinity of Things*.

34. Although SMB initially sent HSW a letter in which he praised *Salammbo* as a 'wonderful book' that 'would excite the curious interest of all literary people and especially those who delight in studying the customs and ways of the people of ancient times', he now contradicted this with a statement in court that he admired the book as a word picture, but as literature considered it obscene. He had not appreciated that HSW effectively *was* Saxon & Co., believing that he was assisting its publication and not that he was giving permission for HSW to run a general publishing business (the firm had also published other works such as an *Illustrated Book of American Humour* and *Everybody's Joke Book*).

35. According to Haggis, HSW learnt of SMB's wish to change the partnership arrangement earlier in the spring when both were in America.

36. No statement was taken from Leonard Oswald Johnson of Mitchell & Co., who, HSW was told, as an intimate personal friend of SMB might have been a hostile witness.

37. Yet SMB had said in a statement to his solicitors, dated 15 March 1888, that he had repeatedly raised the issue verbally with HSW after the latter's return from the US in May 1887.

38. St Bartholmew's Hospital Student Medical Registration Book, 9 May 1889.

39. Haggis, pp. 218–20.

Chapter 12: Henry George and the Phoenix Mills Philosopher

1. George, *Progress and Poverty*, chap. 1.

2. By 1888 the site had been unused for some years, the property was practically unmarketable, and a relatively nominal figure was required as rent. HSW had preferred the erection of a temporary building at Bell Lane Wharf in Wandsworth but, since its lease was soon due for renewal, this option failed.

3. See WF/E/02/01/02/18. The following year, when SMB gave instructions for the erection of an additional building at the mills, HSW insisted that SMB pay out of his own pocket any costs above £100 and that the new building should be considered part of the original structures and be included in the existing lease without any extra payment. Needless to say, when the firm eventually purchased the mills from SMB in 1893, more disagreements arose over valuation. An independent value of £18,500 was eventually decided, reflecting the additions and improvements to the works in the interim. In the end matters had

worked to SMB's advantage. The acquisition also doubled the company's fixed assets, from £7,952 in 1888 to £16,658 in 1889. The mills were eventually transferred in 1893.

4. WA, PCB.

5. The 'girls' would work from 8am to 6pm, 'the hours thus being unusually short', and would earn between 8s. and £1 per week according to their tasks. *Dartford and West Kent Advertiser*, 3 Nov 1888.

6. HSW to SMB, 22 March 1890, LB2, pp. 216–.

7. 'I am paying in rent and taxes ten thousand dollars per year for doing business in a building which cost hardly double the annual rental and have had to make improvements upon the premises to make them fit for occupation said improvements having cost me $25,000. May God speed your good work.' SMB to HG, 4 April 1884. HG papers at New York Public Library.

8. *The Democrat*, 1 Aug 1889, p. 855.

9. In 1879 Davitt formed the Irish National Land League, and the following year he went to America to organise the American Land League.

10. *Pharmaceutical Era*, 14 Jan 1895.

11. Presumably the home was that of Valentine Augustus Browne, 4th earl of Kenmare (1825–1902).

12. These, he pointed out, were 'the very chaps detailed to arrest anyone counselling not to pay rent & I had just been saying no one had anything more than a legal right to charge others for the earth air or sea.' SMB, Kenmare, to OB at Lowestoft, 8 Aug 1887.

13. SMB proposed a vote and Davitt also spoke. *The Times*, 12 April 1887, p. 9.

14. PCB. SMB spoke in Hyde Park at the right to protest rally, 5 July 1890, with William Saunders MP. *Lloyds Weekly Newspaper*, 13 July 1890.

15. *Dartford Express*, 22 Jan 1891.

16. SMB was re-elected in spring 1891.

17. It aimed to spread knowledge of the truth that God had made ample provision for the needs of all men during their residence on earth, and that poverty was the result of human laws that allowed individuals to claim as private property that which God had provided for the use of all.

18. Reported in *Pharmaceutical Era*, 14 Feb 1895. Cleveland was defeated, and George considered this was partly owing to his lack of radical aggressive tactics. George, *A Life of Henry George*, p. 512.

19. HG was also entertained to a banquet in London. Among those there was Dr Gavin Brown Clark (1846–1930), MP for Caithness, president of the London Highland Land Law Reform Association and a radical supporter of crofters. He became a close friend of Burroughs.

20. See *Dartford and West Kent Advertiser*, 30 Nov 1889, report on his talk on 25 Nov 1889 in Dartford on 'How to Advance Wages', PCB.

21. While the first three verses are from *The Good Pirate*, the final one here is from a letter by SMB to the *West Kent Advertiser* in 1889 (PP/SMB PCB).
22. Reviewed in *Dartford Chronicle*, 23 Oct 1891; see PCB.
23. *The Standard*, 10 Aug 1889, WA 82/1, Box 38.
24. Sent out from the offices of *The Standard*, the note stated: 'An American merchant now doing business in London, a son of Gen. Silas M. Burroughs, who was twice elected to the House of Representatives from the Twenty-eight New York District, and was a member of that body at the time of his death in June 1860. Mr Burroughs, at whose cost this book is sent to you, is a man of large and liberal views and a writer of no mean ability. He considers *Protection or Free Trade* the best exposition of the tariff question yet made.' *Pharmaceutical Era*, 14 Jan 1895. See also note in SMB's papers dated April 1887. The US President's Office, acknowledging receipt, specifically noted that the president understood that it was 'one of several distributed at the instance and cost of Mr Burroughs of London'.
25. *Dartford and West Kent Advertiser*, c.11 Feb 1889.
26. PCB.
27. See *San Francisco Newsletter*, n.d. [1889], PCB.
28. PCB, p. 29.
29. Editor's diary, Dartford press, 21 Dec 1889.
30. SMB to Esme Howard, 8 July 1893, in connection with Charles Booth's survey. See London School of Economics, NB93, Booth survey notebook.
31. The cemetery was actually higher than St Mary's church, hence the ditty. SMB letter to *Dartford and West Kent Advertiser* and also his letter to editor of local press [?1890] re a public park for the town; PCB.
32. SMB offered to be one of the local ratepayers lobbying the local board on this issue. PCB.
33. PCB.
34. The first musical and social gathering of the firm for employees and their friends was November 1890. At the December meeting HSW delivered a talk on American Indian tribes and Searl gave a rendition of Hiawatha; about 100 people kept warm by dancing and stamping in the hall. Employees who wished to attend classes also had their fees paid by BW&Co. and Hesketh's firm: evidently it was mostly ladies who attended these classes. PCB, 21 Nov 1890.
35. PCB.
36. 25 June 1890. Subscriptions from the fete raised £70. The opportunity was taken to show the public the patent automatic fire extinguishing apparatus used by the firm. PCB. See also *The Times*, 26 June 1890, with the government's response, by Edward Stanhope, to heroes' needs.
37. The third photograph was taken at the BW&Co. stand at the Chicago World's Fair in 1893.

Chapter 13: Citizen of the World

1. *Pharmaceutical Era*, 6 June 1895.
2. Obituary, *Druggists' Circular and Chemical Gazette*, March 1895.
3. In his application (1 May 1890) he stated as qualifications that he had 'lived so long in the country, was so completely identified with its interests, and took so deep a concern in its social welfare.' He also cited his growing business, his many friends in England, that he regarded Englishmen and Americans as 'really of one nation', and that he aimed and hoped for free trade and federation between them.
4. HSW to SMB, 22 March 1890, in response to SMB's letter from Salzburg of 19 March. 15-page letter, LB2, pp. 216–. SMB's certificate of nationality (no. 197629), 10 May 1891.
5. Amanda Lougee (b. 1842) became head of a large business in Boston for the manufacture and sale of rubber clothing and patented the pinback button.
6. Quoted by Gabin, *American Women in Gilded Age London*, p. 17.
7. Interestingly, from this date he more commonly, though not exclusively, signs off as 'Silas' in letters to OB. To his American friends he was always 'Mainville'. SMB to OB, from Nice and Menton, 27 Jan 1891.
8. SMB's description of this tour, 'In the saddle: Jerusalem to Hebron', written 30–31 March and 10 April, *Dartford Chronicle*, 22 May 1891. See also Burroughs, 'Pharmacy in Palestine'.
9. SMB to OB, Ismailia, 20 March 1891.
10. SMB to OB, Beirut, 21 April 1891.
11. SMB to OB, Constantinople, 16 May 1891.
12. SMB to *C&D*, 8 Nov 1890, p. 664.
13. SMB to *C&D*, 24 May 1890, p. 720.
14. 'The Central London Railway' letter from BW&Co. supporting the Bill, n.d., and SMB to the editor of an unidentified newspaper on 'Free Travel', 14 Aug 1890, WA, PCB.
15. Other speakers included Mrs Sheldon, Max Müller and Sidney Webb.
16. *Dartford and West Kent Advertiser*, October 1891, WA, PCB.
17. Letter to the editor of the *Star*, Dartford, 4 July 1890. WA, PCB.
18. SMB's travels in Morocco, published in *C&D* in 1891 and 1893, were subsequently republished. See Burroughs, *An Enlightened Policy in Morocco*.
19. The incident took place on 24 May. SMB to OB, National Liberal Club, 3 June 1892.
20. SMB proposed to take up an agency for them for England. While there he purchased a share at £500 to join a syndicate of 20 in the Rosbach Water of Hamburg, hoping to make a lot of money out of it. SMB to OB, Hotel zum Kronprinzen, 29 Oct 1892.

Chapter 14: Partnership in Peril

1. SMB to HSW, 8 June 1891.
2. The fair's organizers were awkwardly placed as they had already given a monopoly to another water company. One of the best sellers at the fair was to be carbonated soda, and BW&Co. were sole agents for Franz Josef Water. See advertisement in *C&D*, February 1893.
3. SMB apologised to OB for not getting to Boston, 18 March 1893.
4. SMB to OB, and HSW's letter to SMB, 14 March 1893.
5. Samuel Heitshu was a wholesale druggist in Portland, Oregon.
6. SMB to OB, 10 Aug 1893.
7. SMB's printed proposition at the congress is mistakenly entitled 'The International Peace Congress and the International Peace and Arbitration Association'.
8. An action bought by Benno Jaffe & Darmstaedter against John Richardson & Co. for infringement of the Lanolin patent. SMB gave evidence in the High Court of Justice on the properties of lanoline from wool fat. Judgement was given against Richardson. BW&Co.'s popular product Hazeline used lanoline, and from 1886 they had been agents for the plaintiff's lanoline, so judgement against the defendant ensured their continued use of the product.
9. Correspondence between SMB and HSW, 26 Jan and 2 Feb 1891, WF/E/02/01/02/33.
10. SMB to HSW, 15 Oct 1891, LB10, p. 607.
11. HSW to SMB, 14 March 1893; cited in Haggis, pp. 281–3.
12. SMB to HSW, Bournemouth, 21 Dec 1893, WF/E/02/01/01/117. SMB frequently gave presents and souvenirs of his travels to employees, and at the end of 1893, in addition to the bonus, proposed giving each employee either a Chicago souvenir spoon or a BW&Co. product such as a perpetual motion calendar or pocket diary.
13. An example is SMB to BW&Co. from Paris, 3 May 1893, concerning delay in an agreement with French chemists: 'Mr Wellcome should no longer delay stating what he will agree to, as a policy of obstruction is very bad for our business & reputation.' WF/E/02/01/01/115.
14. SMB to HSW, July 1892, personal letter book, p. 312.
15. HSW to SMB, 22 March 1890, and from Chicago, where he removed pamphlets on the tariff question from the firm's exhibit, 29 Sept 1893, LB37, p. 59.
16. SMB to Sudlow, Nice, 30 Dec 1891 and 2 Jan 1892; quoted in RRJ, pp. 183–4.
17. SMB to OB, 17 April 1893. HSW's parsimoniousness was also commented on by his future brother-in-law, who said that Wellcome kept Syrie 'on a frightfully tight rein in spite of his wealth … he was terribly mean.'

18. Statement re finance of company, February 1895. See WF/E/1/4, Box 14. Profits distributed to partners were paid into drawing accounts each quarter (from 1892, each half year).

19. The New Companies Act of 1900 addressed some accounting issues, but calls for the government to audit company accounts were firmly rejected by the Victorians.

20. Radford & Frankland to SMB, 9 April 1889, WF/E/02/01/33. Sir George Heynes Radford (1851–1917) evidently shared Burroughs's political outlook.

21. HSW to SMB, 22 Oct 1889, WF/E/01/03/02.

22. The interest on this loan was a heavy expense, and expenditure (out of their modest capital of about £36,000) of the enormous sum of more than £20,000 on and in the Phoenix Mills – not including the £5,000 purchase money – had forced the firm into SMB's debt.

23. The agreement in July 1892 reflected the additions and improvements to the works. The acquisition also doubled the company's fixed assets, from £7,952 in 1888 to £16,658 in 1889.

24. HSW's solicitors, Markby, Stewart & Co., a leading firm in the City, advised that the company deeds should be housed with the company bankers: SMB's solicitors, on the other hand, suggested that HSW might try to use the deeds to get an overdraft on behalf of the firm. Oscar Wilde joked of Markby, Stewart & Co. in *The Importance of Being Earnest*, referring to Markby & Markby.

25. Markby, Stewart & Co. to SMB, 9 Jan 1893, WF/1/4/24.

26. SMB to HSW, 8 June 1891, and reply June 1891, WF/E/02/01/02/31. Some of these letters quoted more fully in RRJ, p. 176.

27. Between 1884 and 1889 the official number of limited companies increased from 7,950 to 11,200.

28. Wyeth to SMB, 7 Sept 1891, WF/E/02/01/13. Haggis, p. 266, implies that HSW knew nothing of this approach, but this seems unlikely.

29. Wyeths intended to ignore the firm's legal rights and sell compressed goods in areas outside those agreed. SMB wrote to HSW: 'I now observe that however friendly they are in correspondence and personal relations, their intention is to appropriate as much as possible the trade and goodwill which we have established here in this country.' SMB to Wyeths, 1 Feb 1893, WF/E/02/01/02/14; 25 April 1893, LB10 pp. 632–4; SMB to HSW, 13 April 1893, private letter book, pp. 361–2.

30. HSW would take stock, plant, machinery and trademarks in compressed drugs, Fairchild preparations, and 25% of the remaining assets, and his name would disappear from the company within a year. SMB would keep premises in London and Dartford, retain Kepler and Fellows goods, representing 75% of the assets, and HSW would pay SMB

£40,000 from his own resources, on the basis that the partners could manufacture or sell only the products assigned to them and that neither could use the other partner's name in advertising.

31. Profit-sharing had been introduced in 1886. C&T, pp. 122–3, state that the bonus system was introduced by SMB in 1891. It was terminated by HSW in 1899.
32. SMB to HSW, 18 April 1892, WF/E/02/03/01.
33. Stewart to HSW, 8 May 1893, WF/E/1/25.
34. Humphreys to Markby, Stewart & Co., 13 June 1893, WF/E/01/4/25.
35. RRJ, p. 224, notes HSW visited his mother only once after 1886, 'even when it was obvious after 1891 that she was seriously ill with a breast carcinoma.' His mother died on 19 Sept 1897.
36. HSW told *C&D*: 'They will advertise themselves.' SMB lent agents £25 to ensure space for the tabloids at the Antwerp Exhibition.
37. The winners were announced on 22 Dec 1894; Collett Smith, SMB's close colleague, was one of them.
38. Allen & Hanbury's were initially also turned down. By the time the BIPM changed its mind about appointing agents, BW&Co. had made other arrangements and were no longer interested, so it entered into an arrangement with Allen & Hanbury's.
39. SMB's diary, 20 May 1894. 'Commercial Conversations', in *Christian Commonwealth*, which appeared after SMB's death, WF/E/02/02/19. Since SMB died within a few weeks of the firm's new drug being announced, development of the bacteriological research in the laboratories was being claimed as HSW's initiative. See C&T, p. 204.
40. Capital would be about £120,000, management by five directors, two of the five appointed by HSW, whose interest could remain as at present, or he could sell any portion as he pleased.
41. SMB to HSW, 27 Sept 1895, private letter book, pp. 827–8.
42. SMB to HSW, 8 Oct 1894, private letter book, p. 839.
43. SMB to HSW, 1 Nov 1894, private letter book, pp. 864–5.
44. SMB to HSW, 12 Nov 1895, private letter book, pp. 876–80.
45. HSW to his mother, 17 Nov 1894; cited in RRJ, p. 192.
46. These were (1) that the business should be put into a stock company for £120,000; (2) that SMB should sell a third of his 75% holding and HSW a third of his 25% holding; and (3) the qualification for director should be £1,000, the directors to be SMB, HSW, Sudlow, Kirby, Searl, Ball and Clark. Clark and SMB were of the opinion that Stanley would make a good director, but he was unwell and they were unable to ask him.
47. Haggis, p. 274.
48. 'Before we meet it is well that essentials should be arranged. If you and I are to act Mr Burroughs must sign a letter as that we drew up here, and I hereby give you my personal undertaking that Mr Wellcome will sign it also.' A. Chune Fletcher to Dr Clark, 18 Dec 1894, WF/E/1/4/25.

49. For example, SMB to L.W. Cress, Trommer Extract of Malt Co., Fremont, Ohio, June 1894: 'Like yourself, I am enthusiastic about the subject of extract of malt and the great benefit which ensues upon its administration in the large majority of cases of ills to which human flesh is heir to. I believe with yourself also in friendly competition.' Cress purchased the company in 1889.

Chapter 15: 'Service to the Cause of People': Philanthropy and the Livingstone Hospital

1. See WA, PCB, c.1889.
2. HSW complained of this arrangement. See chapter 13 and SMB's letter of 14 Feb 1894, private letter book, p. 647.
3. Mrs Stanley to SMB, 23 Jan 1894. When in Tangier, SMB ordered what he described as a three-seater 'Democratic Waggon' to be made in America and shipped over to Stanley; it would carry 12 people and when the seats were removed would carry goods (it was in fact used by the firm's employees to carry light goods to and from Dartford station until the election the next year). He also loaned money, probably to an agent in the Liberal Unionist Association, to assist Stanley's election. 'He [Stanley] is thoroughly honest and conscientious and therefore when well informed will be sure to vote right,' wrote SMB from Tangier to Kirby, 24 Feb 1894, WF/E/02/01/01/ 118.
4. Pleurodymia is a general term for pain from the lining around the lungs and in the chest or upper abdomen when breathing. Noted in SMB's Medical Report, 27 June 1894, WF/E/02/02/11.
5. SMB to BW&Co., Tangier, 14 Feb 1894, WF/E/02/01/01.
6. SMB to BW&Co., Tangier, 15 Feb 1894, ibid.
7. SMB to BW&Co., Naples, 10 April 1894, ibid.
8. SMB to OB, 14 May 1894.
9. Postcard to Daisy, May, 1894, written when SMB was travelling with Mr Molloy and had been in Koblenz, picture card album.
10. SMB, Innsbruck, to Kirby, 29 Aug 1894, WF/E/02/01/02/33.
11. See BMA, souvenir booklet issued by BW&Co. for the BMA meeting Bristol.
12. SMB corresponded with Walter Crane and discussed profit-sharing; see his private letter book, 28 April and Sept 1894, pp. 674 and 818.
13. *Dartford and West Kent Advertiser*, 7 July 1894, WA, PCB.
14. *Dartford Express*, 26 Oct 1894, ibid.
15. SMB to Hesketh, 5 June 1892. See also SMB's postcard to Searl from Turin, November 1892, with cheque, WF, 86/98, 8–9. 'I have more pleasure in doing this than I would in spending the money on a house for myself because the sick poor need a home & care more than I do.'

16. SMB to Digby Turner, Hon. Sec. of the Hospital Committee, 6 April 1892.
17. Tredegar subscribed £50 to the hospital on 15 Nov 1894.
18. SMB to Turner, 4 June 1893.
19. See HSW reply to SMB from US, July 1893.
20. On payment of board and attendance it was proposed that there would be a charge of 10/6 a week, proportionate according to the capability of the patient to pay. Alcohol was to be given only upon a doctor's orders. SMB suggested that the building should not be subject to rates and taxes and 'an understanding should be arrived at with the local authorities', but this suggestion, not surprisingly, was not accepted. Hesketh to SMB, 20 Feb 1893.
21. Hesketh to SMB, 28 Dec 1892.
22. SMB, 5 June 1893.
23. *Dartford Chronicle*, 30 June 1893, referring to a recent edition of *Dartford and West Kent Advertiser*.
24. Searl to Hesketh, 18 July 1893.
25. Hesketh to Humphreys, 5 Aug 1893.
26. C.O. Humphreys to Digby Turner, 14 Nov 1893.
27. Stalls were open the next day too. About 4,000 people attended and about £500 was raised. The hospital opened fully in December 1894.
28. SMB to Kirby, Cham, 20 Aug 1894, saying that he had invested £100 from his private account in Anglo-Swiss, WF/E/02/01/01/119.
29. SMB to BW&Co., 17 Sept 1894, WF/E/02/01/01/119.
30. According to the *Dartford Express*, 5 May 1893, he was also a generous subscriber to the England Land Restoration League. SMB queried his membership of the Democratic Club in June 1894, as he did not have the time to visit it, and resigned from the City Liberal Club for the same reason. Private letter book, p. 717.
31. SMB to [name illegible: ? Dr A. in Wimbourne, Dorset], c.17 June 1894, private letter book, p. 736; also SMB to Dr J.J. Ridge, Enfield, June 1894, ibid., p. 743. See also Haggis, p. 294. One obituarist commented that SMB was a total abstainer only for periods.
32. SMB to HG, 24 Nov 1893, 28 April 1894 and ?24 Oct 1894, private letter book, pp. 578–9, 676 and 850.
33. SMB to Rev. Stopford Brook, Bedford Chapel, and Arthur Sam Dixon in Dartford, November 1893, ibid., pp. 575 and 584.
34. C.W.C. Sutton (City Liberal Club) to Sudlow, 18 May 1894. Cited by Haggis, p. 293.
35. SMB to James Laughland, of Laughland, Mackay & Baker, 50 Lime Street, London, 31 May 1894, private letter book, p. 705. See also SMB's comments in interview 'Profit Sharing in Practice: A Chat with Mr Silas Mainville Burroughs', in *The Merry Go Round*, March 1894, pp. 188–97, WF/E/02/01/02/26.

36. SMB to Dr Mead, Newmarket, Suffolk, 5 July 1894, private letter book, p. 755.
37. SMB to Dr George Bird of 49 Welbeck St., London, 12 Sept 1894, WF/E/02/01/01.
38. *C&D*, 9 Feb 1895.

Chapter 16: From London to Monte Carlo

1. Letter of condolence from Hennessay to OB, words used by her on SMB's memorial card.
2. SMB to OB, writing from Menton, 27 Jan 1891, reported that there had been two inches of snow at Cannes which had quickly disappeared.
3. Postcards, SMB to Stanley and Anna, from Cannes and Menton, January 1895.
4. SMB to OB, Antibes, 10 Jan 1895.
5. January and February 1895 experienced some of the coldest temperatures on record in the UK; indeed, it was noted as being the most severe frost since 1814. Many people died from hypothermia and respiratory conditions. Pneumonia was a major cause of death, and by the end of Feb the weekly death rate from this and related illnesses was 950 per week, far higher than the average for the period. BW&Co. advertised approved therapies for influenza, including inhalers of chloride of ammonium, menthol and hot air, Naso-Pharyngeal Tabloids and other medicines, but these were of no real help.
6. A suggestion which HSW rejected on 28 Jan 1895.
7. SMB to OB, Bordighera, 22 Jan 1895.
8. Reminiscences of chief purchasing officer, Euston, who was given the information by Mr Warden. Collected by M. Falder c.1973–9, WF/M/H/07/03.
9. Dr T.H. Fagge, MD Brux 1883, wrote 'Monte Carlo considered as a health resort'; Dr W. Alex Fitzgerald, MD 1879 FRCSI 1883, specialized in ophthalmology; no information on Dr Hutchinson; *Medical Directory 1895*. OB was unhappy that the doctors had not treated SMB well.
10. Lina and Dr Naftel's American wife were at his bedside when he died. Dr Clark arrived, presumably from Antibes, the following morning. *C&D*, 16 Feb 1895.
11. Samuel Heitshu to OB, Portland, Oregon, 21 March 1895. See also Libbie Field to OB, 12 Feb 1895.
12. Percy Hutton to OB, 10 Feb 1895; Hutton recalled seeing SMB at the BMA meeting in Bristol.
13. Annette L. Noble, Grand New Hotel, Jerusalem, to OB, 19 March 1895. The obituary in the *Druggists' Circular and Chemical Gazette* in March 1895 noted that SMB's health had not been of the best for some months past.

14. Letter of condolence from Hennessay to OB.
15. The Varleys wrote of their last meeting with him at the Holborn Viaduct Hotel, when he 'seemed so serious & expressed himself so clearly and satisfyingly as to his being a Christian.'
16. *Medical Press & Circular*, February 1895.
17. Stanley to OB: 'We lived in constant expectation of hearing that he had returned to London & being assured that in the imminent General Election we should find him labouring by our side to save our constituency from the control of the Radicals. From our point of view, he was one that could scarcely be spared. His public sympathies were so large his projects for benefiting his employees his friends & adopted countrymen so many, his spirit so brave & cheery that one instinctively wished him long life, and abundant success, because his days & means were sure to be consecrated to the general good. I cannot help being reminded of the warmth of his affection for his children for he was never tired of praising them, and of letting them share in his hopes of their growing beauty and intelligence, showing in these human traits that if his mind was lofty and ample he was no less lovingly paternal.'
18. *C&D*, 16 Feb 1895, pp. 254–8.
19. Remington to HSW, February 1895, HSW papers.
20. *C&D*, 16 Feb 1895.
21. *Pharmaceutical Era*, 6 June 1895.
22. For example, when SMB learnt from HSW of an accident in which several members of staff were injured, he at once wrote asking that all their doctors' bills should be charged to his personal account. Haggis, p. 279.
23. Including the British and Foreign Arbitration Association, the Article Club, the Pharmaceutical Society of Great Britain, the Dartford Liberal and Radical Association, the Dartford Working Men's Club and Institute and the single tax movement. The International Arbitration and Peace Association passed a resolution: Burroughs was 'a warm supporter of the peace movement and a liberal contributor to the funds of this Association which he represented on various occasions at Peace Congresses. ... a model employer of labour, and a generous friend of many progressive movements by which his loss will be severely felt.'
24. HG to OB, 8 Feb 1895.
25. HSW to Lina and OB, 6 Feb 1895, HSW 82/1, Box 34.

Chapter 17: Olive versus Wellcome

1. James Foley to OB, 17 Sept 1901.
2. HSW to his mother, July 1895, cited in RRJ, p. 198.

3. Gardner was legally appointed 'Next Friend' to the Burroughs children, 30 March 1897. He was friendly with Lyman, who also came to England around 1870 and was appointed one of OB's executors. Barrett was the only one to have a pecuniary interest in the estate (although OB insisted that Foley send a bill for all his work, which he did).

4. The copy will is dated February 1893 (no day) and was witnessed by P. Collingwood (of his business associates Hertz and Collingwood), of 101 Leadenhall Street, London, and George St John Leavens, an American active in the single tax movement.

5. It was also recognised that a body outside a coffin would decompose faster and speed up the circulation of animal and vegetable material. It is likely that SMB discussed the matter with Ernest Hart, who wrote to *The Times*, 20 Aug 1884, that burial grounds could be healthy places.

6. This would be done in six half-yearly instalments for SMB's three-quarters share in capital and property in the partnership on the basis of the last general annual accounts (taken 1 Sept 1894).

7. HSW to J.C. Stratton at Fellows Manufacturing Co., 29 April 1895, LB3, pp. 59–61.

8. HSW to Frank Wellcome, 1 or 13 March 1895, LB3, pp. 7–11. He wrote in the same vein to several other people, saying how much his health had improved.

9. HSW to Nicholls, City Bank, 5 April 1895, LB3, p. 24.

10. Humphreys to OB, 27 March 1895.

11. Probate granted 10 April 1895 in UK and shortly afterwards in the US. A second probate was granted in July 1897 when the full value of the estate had been finalised. Dr Clark meanwhile helped negotiate with the City Bank to release money to Olive on a promissory note. It is interesting to note that HSW behaved in similar fashion when he separated from his wife, withholding her possessions for a long period.

12. OB noted also that she was sorry that any advances had been made by her solicitors to Messrs Markby, Stewart & Co. in regard to a probable purchase for the interest of the estate in the business and urged delay in the matter until the accountant had reported. OB to Humphreys, 28 April 1895.

13. Humphreys to OB, 30 April 1895, noting also HSW's comments on this.

14. Humphreys to OB, 1 May 1895, following the report by Sears, Hasluck & Co. of 30 April.

15. OB to Humphreys, undated letter.

16. See incomplete draft letter, OB to Humphreys, c.1 May 1895, and his letter to her of 3 May 1895. Humphreys replied that the firm was congratulated far and wide with the present result, but that Wilde now had other charges to face.

17. OB to Foley, 7 Aug 1895, carbon letter book, 1895–6, p. 27.

18. They claimed £33,135/6/7, plus interest.

19. 14 Sept 1895, *Burroughs* v. *Wellcome*, and 30 Nov 1895, defence and counter-claim, *Wellcome* v. *Olive Burroughs and Stanley Burroughs*. Figures stated that, at death, SMB had to his credit in respect of capital in business £45,503/11/11 and HSW £15,167/17/4 (75/25 proportion). HSW declared he was entitled to sole ownership possession and control of the Phoenix Mills and of any patents, patent rights, trademarks cases or other assets of the partnership.

20. Humphreys to OB, 18 Oct 1897. RRJ, p. 200, claims that HSW ensured that Kirby's family was well provided for, which rather begs the question why Mrs Kirby approached OB.

21. Humphreys to OB, 26 and 27 Nov 1895.

22. OB to Foley, 21 Jan 1896. She questioned HSW's motives, and Foley responded that he did not think they needed to be too concerned with them, 'provided one course or another has moved him to do what is just.' Foley to OB 3 March 1896.

23. Humphreys to OB, 5 March 1896.

24. Humphreys to OB, sending extract, 12 March 1896.

25. OB to Barrett, 24 Jan 1897. She probably refers to Foley. In this letter she also wrote that she thought there would not be a final settlement until February or March 1898. Delays in getting a final settlement and bill from Humphreys prompted Barrett to threaten to come to England to discuss matters with them, at which point Foley sent OB (30 March 1900) his comment about the need for dynamite. He also considered that Humphreys's charges (1895–1900, of £10,491) were 'outrageous'.

26. Foley to OB, 6 May 1896.

27. Humphreys to OB, 30 June 1896.

28. Whinney's report dated 12 Oct 1896 and award 4 November. Whinney was a reputable accountant (Jones, *Accountancy and the British Economy*). This determined on the amount of money HSW owed the estate, after the payment of £40,000 for Phoenix Mills, as £63,563/5/9 plus interest from 2 Nov 1896, interest to be decided by Judge Kekwitch.

29. Humphreys commented with surprise at the accountant's behaviour to OB, 19 Jan 1897.

30. Foley to OB, 11 Dec 1896.

31. The amount was £23,706/7/6, with £1,199/6/2 interest (from 16 Nov 1896 to 6 Dec 1897), making a total of £24,905/13/8, less tax.

32. Lina to OB [24 July 1897].

33. Will proved 28 July 1897. £125,926, of which $15,000 was in the US. Of the 97 businessmen noted in the *Dictionary of Business Biography* who died between 1890 and 1900, in terms of wealth SMB would have stood in the middle range (55th). The average estate was just under £323,000, but this includes some very large bequests. Wills are not entirely reliable as a method of measuring philanthropy, but in 1889 only one in seven wills normally contained a charitable bequest.

34. In the end this 24th was divided between the Board of Foreign Missions of the Presbyterian Church of the USA and the Board of Home Missions of the Presbyterian Church of the USA.
35. The first distribution to legatees was made in July 1897.
36. The amount distributed to legatees amounted to £129,783. Final executorship accounts, 6 Nov 1901. The cost of administration was £3,803 – over 3% of the estate's value – and £7,580 was paid in duty. Before inheritance tax OB received £21,630; the children £16,233 each; Lina £10,815; John Parsons, Theodore Barrett, Henry George and the societies £5,407 each (the Board of Home Missions and the Board of Foreign Missions shared this figure). The employees as at the time of SMB's death (including those in Melbourne) shared £5,407; the 6 guineas each received (a great deal, bearing in mind that a year's salary for a factory worker in 1885 was c.£100) was reduced to £4/13/0 after duty was paid. In view of his age, Foley had sent Parsons some interest already; he was very grateful to OB, and when he died (c.December 1899) his daughter received the money. HG died 29 Oct 1897, the money going to his family.
37. Thomas Luigi to OB, c.Feb 1896, Walter Mears to OB, 20 Feb 1896, Mr Yewbury to OB, 4 March 1896.
38. J.G. Prevost to OB, c.Nov/Dec 1901. A.W. Ball to OB, 18 Oct 1895, noted that HSW was not appreciated by the trade generally and that their policy at Snow Hill had changed, he feared to their detriment.
39. Lyman to OB, 27 Nov 1898.
40. By an order of 25 July 1898 and under an indenture dated 27 April 1899, in consideration of the sum of £21,784/15/6 paid by HSW to OB, she finally handed over the deeds. HSW was able to pay SMB's interest in the firm by withdrawing £38,512 from the partnership between 1895 and 1897 (when cumulative profits amounted to £47,629) and by borrowing £40,000 as a loan advanced on security from the City Bank. See also C&T, p. 125, who note that in 1897 this was roughly equivalent to 33% of the equity capital in the business. By 1913 the loan was £39,059, or c.5%, such was the growth in the firm's asset value by then. The final accounts presented to OB indicate that HSW paid her around £143,500 for capital and goodwill, profits in the business and Phoenix Mills.
41. Foley to OB, 17 Dec 1901. By February 1899 Foley had ensured that all SMB's assets of any value in the US had been turned into cash.
42. It is estimated that in 1894, the year before he died, SMB gave away c.£5,000 (Haggis's notes extracted from 'Schedule of papers referring to monetary transactions of Mr Burroughs', WF/E/02/02/33). See also final executorship accounts, 6 Nov 1901. OB questioned the amount charged by Sears, Hasluck & Co. SMB's life insurance policies alone had yielded £2,012.

43. 'A task I would gladly forego in many cases where possible. I would not in any instance do otherwise than as my late husband would have me do were he here to direct.' Draft letter, OB to Alice Hart, c.Sept or Nov 1895.
44. OB to Mr Hayward, n.d., draft copy.
45. James J. Fellows owed £2,016 (paid half July 1895), J. Moss £5,400, F.J. Rebman more than £768, Corning Weld more than £320, Martinez £160, and so on. In America money was owed by Carl Jackson (c.$17,000, according to Foley), Elijah Molloy, Van Heusen and Jacob Hertz (of Hertz & Collingwood).
46. Humphreys to OB, 19 June 1895. OB was awarded £1,217. Hart in fact claimed that SMB had borrowed money from him.
47. Foley to OB, 9 March 1900.
48. Parsons to OB, 23 Sept 1899. Foley subsequently reported (16 Jan 1900) that there was room in the vault, but Olive was unlikely to return to the US.
49. This was nearly not the case. The author visited the grave in 2002 to find a notice that it was to be destroyed in spite of the 'à perpétuité' agreement when SMB was buried. The Wellcome Trust, alerted to this, negotiated its renovation and retention.
50. Lyman to OB, 8 Feb and 28 July 1897.
51. Elijah Molloy to OB, 30 Sept 1895.
52. Sales details, William Waterman, auctioneer; £54 was raised. Legal papers, 12 and 13 June 1895.
53. They included the Otis Elevator Co., Hertz & Collingwood, Anglo-Swiss Milk Co., Chamberlin Investment Co., Denver, Berners Bay Co., Niagara White Grape Co., Rosbach & Franz Joseph Co., Colorado Fuel & Iron Co., and Lockport Hydraulic Co. American assets, shares or debentures of public companies brought £2,875.

References and Bibliography

Allen, A.P., *The Ambassadors of Commerce* (London: T. Fisher Unwin, 1885)

Anderson, Stuart, 'The Edwardian Finishing School for Dispensers on the French Riviera', *Wellcome History*, 13 (2000), 2

—— (ed.), *Making Medicines: A Brief History of Pharmacy and Pharmaceuticals* (London: Chicago Pharmaceutical Press, 2005)

Anon, *57th Annual Announcement of the Philadelphia College of Pharmacy*, 1877

—— 'The Wellcome Research Laboratories', *British and Colonial Druggist*, 24 July 1896, 100–2

Arnold, David, 'Medical Priorities and Practice in Nineteenth-Century British India', *South Asia Research*, 5/2 (1985), 167–83

—— 'Cholera and Colonialism in British India', *Past and Present*, 113 (1986), 118–51

—— *Colonizing the Body: State Medicine & Epidemic Disease in Nineteenth-Century India* (Berkeley: University of California Press, 1993)

—— 'The Rise of Western Medicine in India', *The Lancet*, 348 (19 Oct 1996), 1075–8

—— *Science, Technology and Medicine in Colonial India* (Cambridge: CUP, 2000)

—— 'The Medicalization of Poverty in Colonial India', *Historical Research*, 85/229 (2012), 488–504

Arnold, K., and Olsen, G. (eds), *Medicine Man: The Forgotten Museum of Henry Wellcome* (London: British Museum Press, 2003)

Aron, Cindy Sondik, *Ladies and Gentlemen of the Civil Service: Middle-Class Workers in Victorian America* (Oxford: OUP, 1987)

Bailey, P., 'A Grave Affair', *Trustlink* (June 2002)

Barker, C.A., *Henry George* (Oxford: OUP, 1955)

Bartrip, Peter, *Mirror of Medicine: A History of the British Medical Journal/ BMJ* (Oxford: Clarendon Press, 1990)

Bax, Ernest Belfort, *Reminiscences and Reflections of a Mid and Late Victorian* (New York: Augustus M. Kelley, 1967)

Beckett, Chris, 'Attitudes to Political and Commercial Endorsement in the Business Papers of Silas Mainville Burroughs, with Particular Reference to Henry Morton Stanley', *Medical History*, 52 (2008), 107–28

Bennet, J. Henry, *Winter in the South of Europe* (London: John Churchill, 1865)

Bloomer, D.C., *Life and Writings of Amelia Bloomer* (Boston: Arena, 1895)

Boniface, Priscilla, *Hotels & Restaurants, 1830 to the Present Day* (London: Royal Commission on Historical Monuments (England), 1981)

Booker, John, *Travellers' Money* (Stroud: Alan Sutton, 1994)

Brassey, Mrs, *Sunshine and Storm in the East, or, Cruises to Egypt and Constantinople* (London: Longmans, Green, 1880)

Bremer, Robert H., *American Philanthropy* (2nd edn, Chicago: University of Chicago Press, 1988)

Briggs, Edward P., *Fifty Years on the Road: The Autobiography of a Travelling Salesman* (Philadelphia: Lyon & Armor, 1911)

British Medical Association, *Secret Remedies, What They Cost and What They Contain* (London: BMA, 1909)

Brockett, Linus P., *The Commercial Traveller's Guide Book* (New York: H. Dayton, 1871)

Buckham, George, *Notes from the Journal of a Tourist*, vol. 1 (London: Forgotten Books, [1890] 2015)

[Burroughs], Mainville, *'The Good Pirates': A Semi-historical Comic Opera* (London: Simpkin, Marshall, 1888) [in verse]

Burroughs, Silas, *An Enlightened Policy in Morocco and Other Notes of Travel* ([London: Spottiswoode, 189?])

———— *A Strange Dream* (London: Green, McAllan & Fielden, 1891)

———— *Free Trade & Free Travel* (International Peace Congress, 1891)

———— 'Pharmacy in Palestine', *Pharmaceutical Record and Weekly Market Review*, XII/22 (1891), 356

———— 'Free Travel', *Report of the British Association for the Advancement of Science*, 1891 (London: John Murray, 1892), 740–2

———— 'Pharmacy at Gibraltar', *Chemist and Druggist* (28 July 1894), 156–7

Burroughs, Silas M., snr, *Remarks of Hon. Silas M. Burroughs, of Orleans, in Assembly, Jan. 25 and Feb. 13, 1850, on the Resolutions relating to the Subject of Slavery* (Washington, DC: Library of Congress, 1850)

———— *Speech on the Kansas Question delivered in the House of Representatives February 28, 1858* (Washington, DC: Congressional Office, 1858)

Busa, Joseph, *Wellcome to Hell: Was Sir Henry Wellcome Jack the Ripper?* (CreateSpace, 2015)

Bushell, T.W., *Profit-Sharing and the Labour Question* (London: Methuen, 1893)

Cannadine, David, *Ornamentalism: How the British Saw Their Empire* (London: Penguin, 2002)

———— *The Victorious Century* (London: Allen Lane, 2017)

Carpenter, Charles, *Co-Partnership in Industry* (London: Co-Partnership, 1912)

Chapman, S.D., *Jesse Boots of Boots the Chemists: A Study in Business History* (London: Hodder & Stoughton, 1974)

Church, Roy, 'New Perspectives on the History of Products, Firms, Marketing, and Consumers in Britain and the United States since the Mid-Nineteenth Century', *Economic History Review*, 52/3 (1999), 405–35

—— 'Advertising Consumer Goods in Nineteenth-Century Britain: Reinterpretations', *Economic History Review*, 53/4 (2000), 62–145

—— 'The British Market for Medicine in the Late Nineteenth Century: The Innovative Impact of S.M. Burroughs & Co.', *Medical History*, 49/3 (2005), 281–98

—— 'Trust, Burroughs Wellcome & Co., and the Foundation of a Modern Pharmaceutical Industry in Britain, 1880–1914', *Business History*, 48/3 (2006), 376–98

—— 'Creative Use of Archives and the Widening Scope of Recent Research into the History of Marketing and Trading in Britain', *Business Archives: Reflections and Speculations*, 97 (Nov 2008), 27–38

—— 'Salesmen and the Transformation of Selling in Britain and the US in the Nineteenth and Early Twentieth Centuries', *Economic History Review*, 61/3 (2008), 695–725

—— *Burroughs Wellcome in the USA and the Wellcome Trust* (Lancaster: Crucible Books, 2015)

Church, Roy, and Tansey, E.M., *Burroughs Wellcome & Co., Knowledge, Trust, Profit and the Transformation of the British Pharmaceutical Industry, 1880–1940* (Lancaster: Crucible Books, 2007) [C&T]

Claremont Manufacturing Co., *The Commercial Traveller's Pocket Companion, for a Business Trip through Vermont and New Hampshire, containing the Names of all Business Men* (Claremont, NH, 1871)

Cook, Joseph, *Boston Monday Lectures* (London: Ward Lock, 1891)

Corley, T.A.B., 'Interaction between the British and American Patent Medicine Industries, 1708–1914', *Business and Economic History*, 16 (1987), 111–29

—— 'American Patent Medicines', paper given at a symposium held at the Wellcome Centre, 20 June 2003

—— *Beecham's, 1848–2000: From Pills to Pharmaceuticals* (Lancaster: Crucible Books, 2011)

Crick, T., *Sketches for the Diary of a Commercial Traveller* (London: Joseph Masters, 1847)

Cripps, Ernest C. (comp.), *Plough Court: The Story of a Notable Pharmacy, 1715–1927* (London: Allen & Hanbury's, 1927)

Cross, Whitney R., *The Burned-Over District: The Social and Intellectual History of Enthusiastic Religion in Western New York, 1800–1850* (Ithaca, NY: Cornell University Press, 1950)

Daunton, Martin, *Trusting Leviathan: The Politics of Taxation in Britain, 1799–1914* (Cambridge: CUP, 2001)

Davenport-Hines, R.P.T., and Slinn, J., *Glaxo: A History to 1962* (Cambridge: CUP, 1992)

Davies, John, 'Silas M. Burroughs, Early Years from Medina to Medicines', *Wellcome Journal* (Feb 1991), 10–13

De Mille, Anna George, *Henry George, Citizen of the World* (Chapel Hill: University of North Carolina Press, 1950)

Dexter, Edwin Grant, *History of Education in the United States* (New York: Macmillan, 1904)

Doherty, Teresa, and Steel, Adrian, 'Wellcome Home to the Wellcome Foundation Archives', *Medical History*, 48 (2004), 95–111

Eardley-Wilmot, S. (ed.), *Our Journey in the Pacific by Officers of HMS Zealous* (London: Longmans, Green, 1873)

——— (ed.), *Voyages and Travels of Lord Brassey, 1862–1894*, 2 vols (New York: Longmans, Green, 1895)

Eaton, Somers, 'How Mainville Burroughs and Henry Wellcome, Super Salesmen, Built a Famous House', *Drug Jobbers Salesman* (April 1923)

Engineer, Amanda, 'Illustrations from the Wellcome Library: Wellcome and "The Great Past"', *Medical History*, 44 (2000), 389–404

England, Joseph W. (ed.), *The First Century of the Philadelphia College of Pharmacy, 1821–1921* (Philadelphia: College of Pharmacy and Science, 1922)

Feinstein, Charles, 'A New Look at the Cost of Living 1870–1914', in James G. Forman-Peck (ed.), *New Perspectives on the Late Victorian Economy* (Cambridge: CUP, 1991), 151–79

Flannery, J.A., and Smith, K.M., *Sir Henry Wellcome, Backwood to Knighthood* (Leeds: Boston Spa Media, 2011)

Francis, F., *War Waves & Wanderings: A Cruise in the 'Lancashire Witch'*, 2 vols (London: Sampson Low, Marston, Searle & Rivington, 1881)

Gabin, Jane S., *American Women in Gilded Age London: Expatriates Rediscovered* (Gainesville: University Press of Florida, 2006)

Gattey, Charles Neilson, *Bloomer Girls* (London: Femina Books, 1967)

George, Henry, *Protection or Free Trade: An Examination of the Tariff Question with Especial Regard to the Interests of Labor* (New York: privately pubd, 1887)

——— *Progress and Poverty* (New York: Doubleday & McLure, 1898)

George, Henry, jnr, *A Life of Henry George* (New York: Doubleday, 1900)

Go, Sun, and Lindert, Peter, 'The Uneven Rise of American Public Schools to 1850', *Journal of Economic History*, 70/1 (2010), 1–26

Goldsmith, Barbara, *Other Powers: The Age of Suffrage, Spiritualism, and the Scandalous Victoria Woodhull* (London: Granta, 1999)

Goodman, Jordan, 'Pharmaceutical Industry', in R. Cooter and J. Pickstone (eds), *Medicine in the Twentieth Century* (Amsterdam: Harwood Academic, 2000), 141–54

Goodwin, L.G., and Goodwin, M.E., 'Letters from S.M. Burroughs: The Birth of a Worldwide Pharmaceutical Enterprise', *Clinical Medicine*, 1/4 (2001), 320–2

Goodwin, L.G., Beveridge, E., and Gorvin, J., *Wellcome's Legacies* (London: Wellcome Trust, 1998)

Griffith, Elizabeth, *In Her Own Right: The Life of Elizabeth Cady Stanton* (New York: OUP, 1984)

Grinnell, E.W., *Medina, Here's to Our Heritage: A Partial Community History*, ed. Catherine Cooper for Medina Area Historical Society (Albion, NY: Lake Country Pennysaver, 1996)

Haggis, A.W.J., 'The Life and Work of Sir Henry Wellcome', unpublished typescript, London, 1942, Wellcome Library, WA/Wellcome PE/C.12 [Haggis]

Hardiman, David, 'Christian Therapy: Medical Missionaries and the Adivasis of Western India, 1880–1930', in Hardiman (ed.), *Healing Bodies, Saving Souls: Medical Missions in Asia and Africa* (Amsterdam: Rodopi, 2006), 137–67

Harper, Jim, *American Railroads of the Nineteenth Century: A Pictorial History in Victorian Wood Engravings* (Lubbock: Texas Tech University Press, 1998)

Harrison, B., 'Philanthropy and the Victorians', *Victorian Studies*, 9/4 (1966), 353–74

Harrison, Mark, *Public Health in British India: Anglo-Indian Preventive Medicine, 1859–1914* (Cambridge: CUP, 1994)

Helmstädter, Axel, 'Controlling the Quality of Tablets: From Their Invention to the Dissolution Test', *Pharmaceutical Historian*, 50/2 (2020), 53–8

Higby, G.J., 'American Pharmacy's First Great Transformation: Practice, 1852–1902', *Journal of the American Pharmaceutical Association*, 40/1 (2000), 9–10

—— 'Chemistry and the 19th-Century American Pharmacist', *Bulletin for the History of Chemistry*, 28/1 (2003), 9–17

Higby, G.J., and Stroud, E.C., *The History of Pharmacy: A Selected Annotated Bibliography* (New York: Garland, 1995)

Hobsbawm, Eric, *The Age of Empire: 1875–1914* (rev. edn, London: Abacus, 2001)

—— *The Age of Capital: 1848–1875* (rev. edn, London: Abacus, 2003)

Holloway, S.W.F., *Royal Pharmaceutical Society of Great Britain, 1841–1991: A Political and Social History* (London: Pharmaceutical Press, 1991)

Holmes, R., *Eleanor Marx* (London: Bloomsbury, 2014)

Homan, Lynn M., and Reilly, Thomas, *Visiting Turn-of-the-Century Philadelphia* (Charleston, SC: Arcadia, 1999)

Honeywell, R.J., *Broadalbin in History*, 1907, www.fulton.nygenweb.net/history/Broadhist1907.html

Hosgood, C., 'The "Knights of the Road": Commercial Travellers and the Culture of the Commercial Room in Victorian and Edwardian England', *Victorian Studies*, 37 (1994), 519–47

Hudnut-Beumler, James, *In Pursuit of the Almighty's Dollar: A History of Money and American Protestantism* (Chapel Hill: University of North Carolina Press, 2007)

Inwood, S., *City of Cities: The Birth of Modern London* (Basingstoke: Pan Macmillan, 2016)

Jeal, Tim, *Stanley: The Impossible Life of Africa's Greatest Explorer* (London: Faber & Faber, 2008)

Jeremy, D. (ed.), *Business and Religion in Britain* (Aldershot: Gower, 1988)
—— *Capitalists and Christians: Business Leaders and the Churches in Britain, 1900–1960* (Oxford: Clarendon Press, 1990)

Jeremy, D., and Shaw, C. (eds), *Dictionary of Business Biography* (London: Butterworths, 1996)

Jex Blake, S., *A Visit to Some American Schools and Colleges* (London: Macmillan, 1867)

Jones, Edgar, *Accountancy and the British Economy, 1840–1980: The Evolution of Ernst & Whinney* (London: Batsford, 1981)

Jones-Parry, S.H., *My Journey Round the World*, 2 vols (London: Hurst & Blackett, 1881)

Kahn, E.J., *All in a Century: The First 100 Years of Eli Lilly and Company* ([Indianapolis: Eli Lilly & Co.], 1976)

Kark, Ruth, 'From Pilgrimage to Budding Tourism: The Role of Thomas Cook in the Rediscovery of the Holy Land in the Nineteenth Century', in Sarah Searight and Malcolm Wagstaff (eds),*Travellers in the Levant: Voyagers and Visionaries* (Durham: Astene, 2001), 155–74

Kellogg, Clara Louise, *Memoirs of an American Prima Donna* (New York: Knickerbocker Press, 1913); www.gutenberg.org/ebooks/38023

Larson, Frances, *An Infinity of Things: How Sir Henry Wellcome Collected the World* (Oxford: OUP, 2009)

Lattin, C.W., *Architecture Destroyed: In Orleans County, New York* (Albion, NY: Cobblestone Society, 1984)

Lawrence, Elwood P., *Henry George in the British Isles* (East Lansing: Michigan State University Press, 1957)

Liebenau, Jonathan, 'Marketing High Technology: Educating Physicians to use Innovative Medicines', in R.P.T. Davenport-Hines (ed.), *Markets and Bagmen: Studies in the History of Marketing and British Industrial Performance, 1830–1939* (Aldershot: Gower, 1986), 82–101
—— *Medical Science and the Medical Industry: The Formation of the American Pharmaceutical Industry* (Basingstoke: Macmillan, 1987)
—— 'Ethical Business: The Formation of the Pharmaceutical Industry in Britain, Germany, and the United States before 1914', *Business History*, 30/1 (1988), 116–29
—— 'Evolution of the Pharmaceutical Industry', in C. Hansch et al. (eds), *Comprehensive Medicinal Chemistry* (Oxford: Pergamon Press, 1990), 81–98

Liebenau, Jonathan, Higby, Gregory J., and Stroud, Elaine C. (eds), *Pill Peddlers: Essays on the History of the Pharmaceutical Industry* (Madison, WI: American Institute for the History of Pharmacy, 1990)

Lloyd Williams, W., 'English Pharmacy in the Riviera', *Chemist and Druggist* (27 July 1895), 160–3

Loftie, W.J., *Orient Line Guide: Chapters for Travellers by Sea and by Land* (4th edn, London: Sampson Low, Marston, Searle & Rivington, 1890)

Long, Ossian, *History of Freemasonry in the State of New York* (Albany, NY: Hamilton, 1922)

Macdonald, G., *One Hundred Years 1880-1980: In Pursuit of Excellence* (London: Wellcome Foundation, 1980)

McKie, David, *Jabez: The Rise and Fall of a Victorian Rogue* (London: Atlantic Books, 2004)

McKnight, Gerald, *The Scandal of Syrie Maugham* (London: W.H. Allen, 1980)

Mahoney, Tom, *The Merchants of Life: An Account of the American Pharmaceutical Industry* (New York: Harper, 1959)

Marion, John Francis, *The Fine Old House: SmithKline Corporation's First 150 Years* (Philadelphia: SmithKline Corporation, 1980)

Mather, William H., *On the Road to Riches* (Chicago: J. Fred Waggoner, 1878)

Matthews, L.G., *History of Pharmacy in Britain* (Edinburgh: E. & S. Livingstone, 1962)

—— 'Mr Burroughs Reports: Glimpses of a Man of Many Parts', *Wellcome Foundation News* (Feb 1963), 3–4

Merrill, Arch, *The Towpath* (New York: Garnett, 1947)

Miller, Arthur, *Timebends: A Life* (New York: Grove, 1987)

Moore, Harry T., *Henry James* (London: Thames & Hudson, 1974)

Moss, Laurence S. (ed.), *Henry George: Political Ideologue, Social Philosopher and Economic Theorist* (Malden, MA: Blackwell, 2008)

Munro, William, *A Two Months' Cruise in the Mediterranean in the Steam-Yacht 'Ceylon'* (London: Hurst & Blackett, 1884)

Murphy, Dan, *The Erie Canal: The Ditch that Opened a Nation* (Buffalo, NY: Brian Meyer, 2001)

Nevett, T.R., *Advertising in Britain: A History* (London: Heinemann, 1982)

Newsome, David, *The Victorian World Picture: Perceptions and Introspections in an Age of Change* (London: John Murray, 1997)

Norman, Bruce, *The Inventing of America* (London: BBC, 1976)

O'Day, Alan, *Irish Home Rule, 1867–1921* (Manchester: Manchester University Press, 1998)

Owen, David, *English Philanthropy, 1660–1960* (Cambridge, MA: Harvard University Press, 1965)

Palmowski, Jan, 'Travels with Baedeker: The Guidebook and the Middle Classes in Victorian and Edwardian England', in Rudy Koshar (ed.), *Histories of Leisure* (Oxford: Berg, 2002), 105–30

Parascandola, J., 'Patent Medicines in Nineteenth-Century America', *Caduceus*, 1 (spring 1985), 1–41

—— 'The Emergence of Pharmaceutical Science', *Pharmacy in History*, 37/2 (1995), 68–75

Parry, Benita, *Delusions and Discoveries: India in the British Imagination* (London: Verso, 1998)

Parsons, Brian, *Committed to the Cleansing Flame: The Development of Cremation in Nineteenth-Century England* (Reading: Spire Books, 2005)

Poore, B.P., *A Descriptive Catalogue of the Government Publications of the United States* (Washington, DC: Government Printing Office, 1885)

Poynter, F.N.L. (ed.), *The Evolution of Pharmacy in Britain* (London: Pitman, 1965)

Presbrey, Frank, *The History and Development of Advertising* (New York: Doubleday, Doran: 1929)

Proceedings of Both Houses of Congress upon the Announcement of the Death of Hon Silas M. Burroughs of New York, June 10th, 1860 (Washington, DC: Thomas McGill, 1860)

Prochaska, Frank, *The Voluntary Impulse: Philanthropy in Modern Britain* (London: Faber & Faber, 1988)

Quain, Richard, *A Dictionary of Medicine* (London: Longmans, Green, 1890)

Ramanna, Mridula, *Western Medicine and Public Health in Colonial Bombay, 1845–1895* (London: Sanyam Books, 2002)

Repplier, Agnes, *Philadelphia: the Place and the People* (London: Macmillan, 1898)

Rhodes James, Robert, *Henry Wellcome* (London: Hodder & Stoughton, 1994) [RRJ]

Richard, Henry, *Memoirs of Henry Richard, the Apostle of Peace* (London: Forgotten Books, [1889] 2012)

Richards, Caroline Cowes, *Village Life in America, 1852–1872, including the Period of the American Civil Wars Told in the Diary of a School Girl* (New York: Henry Holt, 1913)

Richards, John Morgan, *With John Bull and Jonathan: Reminiscences of Sixty Years of an American's Life in England and in the United States* (London: T. Werner Laurie, 1905)

Richmond, L., Stevenson, J., and Turton, A. (eds), *The Pharmaceutical Industry: A Guide to Historical Records* (Aldershot: Ashgate, 2003)

Rouxeville, Annie, 'The Reception of Flaubert in Victorian England', *Comparative Literature Studies*, 14/3 (1977), 274–84

Russell, Colin A. (ed.), *Chemistry, Society and Environment: A New History of the British Chemical Industry* (Cambridge: Royal Society of Chemistry, 2000)

Sammarco, Anthony Mitchell, *Images of America: Boston's Back Bay in the Victorian Era* (Charleston, SC: Arcadia, 2003)

Schlereth, Thomas J., *Victorian America: Transformations in Everyday Life, 1876–1915* (New York: HarperCollins, 1991)

Schupbach, W., 'Sequah: An English "American Medicine"-Man in 1890',
  Medical History, 29 (1985), 272–317

Seaver, James Everett, *Narrative of the Life of Mary Jemison: The White
  Woman of Genesee* (3rd edn, Batavia, NY: W. Seaver & Son, 1844)

Sheppard, Julia, 'Silas Burroughs, the Unknown Partner', *Wellcome News*,
  no. 16, Q3 (1998), 36

—— 'Death in Monte Carlo', *Wellcome News*, Q2 (2002), 28

—— 'A Forgotten Life: Silas Mainville Burroughs (1846–95)', paper given at
  the Wellcome Centre (UCL) Work in Progress Seminar, 6 Nov 2002

—— 'Mainville and Monte Carlo', *Friends of the Wellcome Library and
  Centre Newsletter*, 27 (summer 2002)

—— 'The Charity and Philanthropy of Henry Wellcome and Silas
  Burroughs', paper given at the American Association for the History of
  Medicine meeting, Wellcome Trust, 21 March 2003

—— 'Silas Mainville Burroughs', *Oxford Dictionary of National Biography*,
  vol. 8 (Oxford: OUP, 2004), 1013–14

Signor, Isaac S. (ed.), *Landmarks of Orleans County New York* (Syracuse, NY:
  D. Mason, 1894)

Singh, Harkishan, *History of Pharmacy in India and Related Aspects* (Delhi:
  Vallabh Prakashan, 1994)

Slinn, Judy, *A History of May & Baker, 1834–1984* (Cambridge: Hobsons,
  1984)

—— 'Research and Development in the UK Pharmaceutical Industry
  from the Nineteenth Century to the 1960s', in Roy Porter and Mikulas
  Teich (eds), *Drugs and Narcotics in History* (Cambridge: CUP, 1995),
  168–86

Sonnedecker, G., Cowen, D.L., and Higby, G.J. (eds), *Drugstore Memories:
  American Pharmacists Recall Life behind the Counter, 1842–1933* (Madison,
  WI: American Institute of the History of Pharmacy, 2002)

Soskice, Janet, *Sisters of Sinai* (London: Vintage Books, 2010)

Spears, Timothy B., *100 Years on the Road: The Travelling Salesman in
  American Culture* (New Haven, CT: Yale University Press, 1995)

Spier, Peter, *The Erie Canal* (London: Angus Hudson, 1998)

Stanley, H.M., *In Darkest Africa, or, The Quest, Rescue and Retreat of Emin,
  Governor of Equatoria,* 2 vols (London: Sampson Low, 1890)

State University College of Education, *Historical Sketches relating to the First
  Quarter Century of the State Normal and Training School at Oswego, N.Y.*
  (Oswego: R.J. Oliphant, 1888)

Steel, Adrian, and Hall, Lesley A., 'Sir Henry Wellcome's Archival Legacy and
  the Contemporary Historian', *Contemporary British History*, 17/3 (2003),
  95–111

Suttner, Bertha von, *Memoirs of Berthe von Suttner*, vol. 1 (Boston: Ginn,
  1910)

Symons, J., *Wellcome Institute for the History of Medicine: A Short History*
  (London: Wellcome Trust, 1993)

Taft, Pauline Dakin, *The Happy Valley: The Elegant Eighties in Upstate New York* (Syracuse, NY: Syracuse University Press, 1965)

Tansey, E.M., 'The Wellcome Physiological Research Laboratories, 1894–1904: The Home Office, Pharmaceutical Firms, and Animal Experiments', *Medical History,* 33 (1989), 1–41

—— 'Medicines and Men: Burroughs, Wellcome & Co., and the British Drug Industry before the Second World War', *Journal of the Royal Society of Medicine*, 95 (2002), 411–16

Taylor, David, and Bush, David, *The Golden Age of British Hotels* (London: Northwood, 1974)

Taylor, James, *Creating Capitalism: Joint Stock Enterprises in British Politics and Culture, 1800–1870* (London: Royal Historical Society, 2006)

Thomas, Arad, *Pioneer History of Orleans County* (Albion, NY: H.A. Bruner, 1871)

Thompson, Peter, *Cassell's Dictionary of American History* (London: Cassell, 2002)

Thomson, David, *England in the Nineteenth Century: 1814–1914* (London: Penguin, 2002)

Thorsheim, Peter, 'The Corpse in the Garden: Burial, Health, and the Environment in Nineteenth-Century London', *Environmental History*, 16/1 (2011), 38–68

Todd, G., 'Some Aspects of Joint Stock Companies, 1844–1900', *Economic History Review*, 4/1 (1932), 46–71

Townsend, Avis A., *Images of America: Medina* (Charleston, SC: Arcadia, 2005)

Turner, E.S., *The Shocking History of Advertising* (London: Michael Joseph, 1952)

Turner, Helen, *Henry Wellcome: The Man, His Collection and Legacy* (London: Wellcome Trust and Heinemann, 1980)

Twain, Mark, *Innocents Abroad* (New York: Penguin, [1869] 1966)

—— *Following the Equator* (Washington, DC: National Geographic, [1897] 2005)

Tweedale, Geoffrey, *At the Sign of the Plough: 275 years of Allen & Hanburys and the British Pharmaceutical Industry, 1715–1990* (London: Murray, 1990)

Vann, J. Don, and VanArsdel, Rosemary T. (eds), *Victorian Periodicals and Victorian Society* (Toronto: University of Toronto Press, 1995)

Waddington, Keir, '"Grasping Gratitude": Charity and Hospital Finance in Late-Victorian London', in M. Daunton (ed.), *Self-Interest and Welfare in the English Past* (London: Routledge, 1996)

—— *Medical Education at St Bartholomew's Hospital, 1123–1995* (Woodbridge: Boydell Press, 2003)

Waller, David, *The Magnificent Mrs Tennant* (New Haven, CT: Yale University Press, 2009)

Waters, Robert E., *Medina Historic Photo Album* (Medina, NY: Pediment, 2000)

Watton, E.B., *Holborn Viaduct to Calder Hall* (London: Babcock & Wilcox, 1956)

Weatherall, Miles, *In Search of a Cure: A History of Pharmaceutical Discovery* (Oxford: OUP, 1990)

Wellcome, H.S., *The Story of Metlakahtla* (London: Saxon, 1887)

White, Cecila A., *Medina Past and Present: Compiled on the Occasion of the 150th Anniversary of the Incorporation of the Village* (Medina, NY: Medina Historical Society, 1982)

Wilkinson, Hugh, *Sunny Lands and Seas: A Voyage in the SS Ceylon* (London: John Murray, 1882)

Wilkinson, Lise, 'William Brockedon, FRS (1787–1854)', *Notes and Records of the Royal Society of London*, 26/1 (1971), 65–72

Williams, David M., 'The Extent of Transport Services' Integration: SS *Ceylon* and the First "Round the World" Cruise, 1881–1882', *International Journal of Maritime History*, 15/2 (2003), 135–46

Williams, Keith John, 'British Pharmaceutical Industry, Synthetic Drug Manufacture and the Clinical Testing of Novel Drugs, 1895–1939', PhD thesis, University of Manchester, 2005

Williams, Peter, *The Story of the Wellcome Trust* (Hindringham, Norfolk: JJG, 2010)

Williams-Ellis, Amabel, *Darwin's Moon: A Biography of Alfred Russel Wallace* (London: Blackie, 1966)

Williamson, Andrew, *The Golden Age of Travel: The Romantic Years of Tourism in Images from the Thomas Cook Archives* (Peterborough: Thomas Cook, 1998)

Woloshyn, Tania, 'Vers la lumière: Painters and Patients on the Côte d'Azur', *Wellcome History*, 41 (2007), 19

Woodhead, Lindy, *Shopping, Seduction & Mr Selfridge* (London: Profile, 2012)

Worthen, Dennis B., 'Joseph Price Remington (1847–1918)', *Journal of the American Pharmaceutical Association*, 42/4 (2002), 664–6

Index

References in *italics* are to illustrations. References including 'n' are to endnotes. 'SMB' refers to Silas Mainville Burroughs. 'HSW' refers to Henry Solomon Wellcome. Most relatives of SMB are identified in brackets, e.g. 'aunt'.

BV - #0012 - 120522 - C0 - 234/156/20 - PB - 9780718895990 - Gloss Lamination